A WORLD BANK COUNTRY STUDY

Angola

An Introductory Economic Review

The World Bank
Washington, D.C.

First printing January 1991

World Bank Country Studies are among the many reports originally prepared for internal use as part of the continuing analysis by the Bank of the economic and related conditions of its developing member countries and of its dialogues with the governments. Some of the reports are published in this series with the least possible delay for the use of governments and the academic, business and financial, and development communities. The typescript of this paper therefore has not been prepared in accordance with the procedures appropriate to formal printed texts, and the World Bank accepts no responsibility for errors.

The World Bank does not guarantee the accuracy of the data included in this publication and accepts no responsibility whatsoever for any consequence of their use. Any maps that accompany the text have been prepared solely for the convenience of readers; the designations and presentation of material in them do not imply the expression of any opinion whatsoever on the part of the World Bank, its affiliates, or its Board or member countries concerning the legal status of any country, territory, city, or area or of the authorities thereof or concerning the delimitation of its boundaries or its national affiliation.

The complete backlist of publications from the World Bank is shown in the annual *Index of Publications*, which contains an alphabetical title list (with full ordering information) and indexes of subjects, authors, and countries and regions. The latest edition is available free of charge from the Publications Sales Unit, Department F, The World Bank, 1818 H Street, N.W., Washington, D.C. 20433, U.S.A., or from Publications, The World Bank, 66, avenue d'Iéna, 75116 Paris, France.

ISSN: 0253-2123

Library of Congress Cataloging-in-Publication Data

Angola, an introductory economic review.
p. cm. -- (A World Bank country study)
ISBN 0-8213-1748-2
1. Angola--Economic conditions--1975- 2. Angola--Economic policy.
I. International Bank for Reconstruction and Development.
II. Series.
HC950.A64 1991
330.9673'04--dc20 90-25901
CIP

PREFACE

This report is based on a UNDP-financed economic mission to the People's Republic of Angola in Noviiember/December 1987, for which the World Bank served as Executing Agency. The mission comprised the following consultants: Jose Silva Lopes (Mission Leader and Principal Author), Hendrik Koppen (Deputy Mission Leader), Milton P. de Assis (Macroeconomist), John Caskey (Macroeconomist), Jorge Braga de Macedo (Macroeconomist), Ana Neto (Research Assistant), Jorge Moita (Institutional Specialist), Witold Teplitz Sembitzky (Energy), Rob Harrison (Transport), Martyn Marriott (Mining), Alberto Mello e Souza (Human Resources), Richard Lacroix (Industry), Richard Callahan (State Enterprises), David Goodman (Regional and Urban Development), Stahis Panagides, Cesar Aguiar, and Alberto Castanheira Diniz (Agriculture). Jaime Biderman (Southern Africa Department), coordinated mission planning and report-writing. Dora Hollister assisted in the preparation of the mission and the report. The report was discussed and updated with Angolan Government authorities in February 1989, and was issued on June 26, 1989. It has since been updated further based on additional or corrected information obtained in November/December 1989, when further dissemination of the report's findings and recommendations also took place.

As indicated in the UNDP Project Document (ANG/87/001), dated September 1987, the major objectives of this introductory economic review were to examine the structure and evolution of the Angolan economy and key sectors, and to provide recommendations on an economic rehabilitation strategy. Due to the fact that this is a first report, it includes more background information than is common for a typical Country Economic Memorandum.

ABSTRACT

Despite abundant natural resources, and the rapid development of an enclave oil sector (which provided nearly US$2 billion in exports in 1985), the Angolan economy has been characterized by enormous distortions and poor output performance since Independence in 1975. These problems may be attributed to three main factors: (a) the continuing war against UNITA and South Africa, which has made much of the countryside too insecure for agricultural production and transport, requires heavy military expenditures (contributing to chronically large fiscal deficits), and has destroyed a substantial part of the economic and social infrastructure and production capacity; (b) unusually severe human resource constraints, due to the massive exodus of Portuguese settlers at Independence and the resulting skill shortages; and (c) deficiencies in economic management and inadequate policies (i.e., ineffective central planning and pervasive administrative controls, including administrative allocation of foreign exchange in the face of a fixed, overvalued exchange rate, price controls for most goods and services with differences of 40:1 between official and parallel market prices, inadequate control over government finances, inefficient public enterprices, and a generally distorted incentive framework for producers and consumers). The decline in oil prices which began in late 1985 aggravated the situation by worsening the budget deficit while reducing the Government's ability to import essential inputs and consumer goods (especially food for the urban population).

Recognizing that organizational and policy shortcomings have contributed significantly to the country's economic difficulties, the Angolan authorities announced a program of "Economic and Financial Restructuring" (known as SEF) in 1987. Although the formulation and implementation of SEF are still at an early stage, the program envisages a more important role for market prices and the private sector and the reduction of the multiple distortions created by bureaucratic controls. In this context, this report recommends economic policy measures oriented towards three main objectives: (a) control of domestic demand (reduction of the budget deficit and more effective control over the expansion of domestic credit); (b) stimulation of domestic supply (more attractive prices for agricultural products; incentives to the establishment of small private enterprises); and (c) improvements in the allocation of resources (reduction of bureaucratic controls, including in particular price controls and the administrative allocation of foreign exchange; depreciation of the exchange rate; review of public expenditure priorities; stimulation of more competition in the productive sectors; reform of public enterprises; and reduction of the difference between official and parallel market prices.

Although the Government's limited implementation capacity makes it unlikely that all of these major transformations can be fully undertaken in a short period, the distortions in the Angolan economy are so large that it will be imperative for the Government to introduce, already in the initial stages, very strong measures in the areas of price, wage and exchange rate policy and public resource management. The resulting improvement in the incentive framework is essential in order to elicit a supply response from the productive sectors and will enable the Government to undertake other actions outlined in this report to promote sectoral development and accelerate rehabilitation activities when the war-related constraints are eased.

ABBREVIATIONS AND ACRONYMS

ANGONAVE	National Shipping Company
AUP	Agrupamentos de Unidades de Produçao (state farms)
Auto-consumo	Internal Consumption in Enterprises
BNA	National Bank of Angola
BPA	Popular Bank of Angola
CABOTANG	Coastal Shipping Company
Cafangol	National Coffee Company
CDA	Angolan Mail Service
CFB	Benguela Railway Company
CFL	Luanda Railway Company
CFM	Mocamedes Railway Company
CIMCAE	Angolan Interministerial Commission for Coordination of Emergency Assistance
CPL	Provincial Commissariat of Luanda
Deslocados	Refugees/Displaced Population
Diamang	Diamond Company of Angola
DINAMA	National Distribution Company for Agricultural Direcçao Nacional
de Precos	National Price Office
DNCT	National Council for Mail and Telecommunications
DNMMP	National Directorate for Merchant Marine and Ports
DSCT	Mail and Telecommunications Directorate
ENATEL	National Telecommunication Company
ETP	State Transport Company
IMPORTANG	Angolan Importing Agency
EDA	Agricultural Development Stations
EDINBA	National Wholesale Food Distribution Company
EDINBI	National Wholesale Distribution Company for Industrial Goods
ENAMA	National Agricultural Mechanization Company
ENANA	Airport and Navigation Company
ENAS	National Water and Sanitation Company
ENCIB	Basic Infrastructure Construction Company
ENCODIPA	National Distribution Company for Agricultural Products
ENDIAMA	National Diamond Company
EPAL	Luanda Provincial Water Company
GARM	Office for Musseque Renewal and Rehabilitation
GRP	Regional Planning Office
INE	National Statistical Institute
MANAUTO	Vehicle Maintenance and Workshop Organization
MED	Ministry of Education
MIC	Ministry of Internal Trade
MINTEC	Ministry of Transport and Telecommunications
MPLA-PT	Popular Movement for the Liberation of Angola - Workers' Party
Musseques	Human Settlements on the Fringes of Urban Areas
OGE	General State Budget
Roque Santeiro	Major Parallel Market in Luanda
RPA	People's Republic of Angola
SEF	Program of Economic and Financial Restructuring
SONANGOL	State Oil Company
TAAG	Angolan National Airline
UEE	State-owned Enterprise
UNTA	National Labor Union

CURRENCY EQUIVALENT

Since 1975	US$ 1.00 = Kz 29.92

FISCAL YEAR

January 1 - December 31

TABLE OF CONTENTS

MAIN REPORT

Page No.

Annexes and Statistical Appendix

LIST OF TEXT TABLES

Chapter 2

Chapter 3

Chapter 4

COUNTRY DATA ANGOLA

AREA (Thousand Sq. Km.)	POPULATION (1986)	DENSITY (1986)
1,276.7	9.0 million	7.0 per square km.
	Rate of Growth: 2.5% (since 1980)	

POPULATION CHARACTERISTICS (1980/85)		HEALTH (1985)	
Crude Birth Rate (per 1,000)	47	Population per physician	15,521
Crude Death Rate (per 1,000)	22	Population per hospital bed	634
		Infant mortality (per 1000 live births)	160

INCOME DISTRIBUTION		ENERGY CONSUMPTION PER CAPITA (1986)	
% of national income, highest quintile	..	(Kilograms of oil equivalent)	229
lowest quintile	..		

ACCESS TO SAFE WATER (1985)		ACCESS TO SEWERAGE (1985)	
% of population - urban:	80	% of population - urban	26
- rural:	15	- rural	16

NUTRITION (1980)		EDUCATION (1985)	
Calorie intake as % of requirements	87	Adult literacy rate (%)	28
Per capita protein intake (grams/day)	..	Primary school enrollment	44

GDP PER CAPITA IN 1987: US $564 a/

Gross Domestic Product in 1987

	US$ Mln	&
GDP at Market Prices	5,197.0	100
Investment	903.8	17
Gross Domestic Savings	1,515.4	29
Resource Balance	-611.6	-12
Exports of Goods & NFS	2,354.6	45
Imports of Goods & NFS	1,743.0	34

Annual Rate of Growth of GDP at Constant Prices (%)

1960-1973	1974-1981	1982-1986
6.5	..	b/

Government Finance / **General Government**

	Kwanza Billion 1987	% of GDP 1987	% of GDP 1982-87
Current Revenue	64.4	28.9	
Current Expenditure	76.4	34.4	
Current Surplus	-12.0	-5.4	
Capital Expenditure	11.30	4.9	

Money and Credit [b/]

	1984	1985	1986	1987	1988
	---------Kz billion, end of period---------				
Money and Quasi-Money	172	204	220	257	313
Bank Credit to Central Government	118	130	187	247	297
Other Bank Credit [c/]	97	113	78	54	53
	(Percentages)				
Money as % of GDP	89.0	101.0	112.5	113.6	..
Annual Percentage Changes in:					
Bank Credit to Central Government	48.7	10.1	43.6	32.2	20.0
Other Bank Credit [c/]	-10.9	15.2	-30.7	-30.4	-2.9

Balance of Payments	1984	1985	1986	1987	1988
			(US$ million)		
Exports (g & nfs)	2,129	2,344	1,406	2,354	2,579
Imports (g & nfs)	2,058	1,928	1,543	1,657	2,294
Resource Balance	71	416	(137)	698	285
Net Factor Income	(314)	(329)	(370)	(382)	(845)
Official Transfers (net)	26	20	139	51	32
Current Account Balance	(217)	107	(368)	368	(528)
Public M< Borrowing (net)	173	171	7	(73)	(344)
Other [d/]	101	(260)	(283)	232	843
Change in Reserves (- = increase)	(57)	(18)	78	(63)	(29)
Gross Official Reserves [e/] (end of Period)	240	257	179	242	272

Major Merchandise Exports (Average 1984-88)

	US$ Million	%
Crude Oil	1,801	87.4
Refined Oil	73	3.5
LPG	27	1.3
Diamonds	85	4.1
Coffee	52	2.5
Other	23	1.1
	2,062	100.0

External Debt, December 31, 1989

	US$ Billions
Total Outstanding & Disbursed	6.3

Debt Service Ratio for 1987

	%
Total Outstanding & Disbursed	21.9

IBRD/IDA Lending

Not applicable

EXECUTIVE SUMMARY

Country Background

i. Angola is the third largest country south of the Sahara, with a population of about 9 million, and a low population density of 7.2 inhabitants per Km2. The population is growing at an average rate of around 2.5% per year and the proportion of the urban population is increasing rapidly. The country is very rich in natural resources. The abundance of arable land and the diversified climatic conditions provide favorable conditions for extensive development of a wide variety of agricultural crops of tropical and temperate regions (cotton, coffee, sugar, tropical fruits, maize) as well as livestock. There are also abundant fishing and mineral resources (especially diamonds). Petroleum reserves are extensive and the production and export of oil is the mainstay of the economy. The energy and irrigation potential of the rivers is considerable. Infrastructure in the energy, transportation, and communication sectors was fairly well developed by African standards, but its state of conservation has deteriorated substantially in recent years when it has been seriously affected by the war and deferred maintenance.

ii. The development of the Angolan economy under the Portuguese colonial regime accelerated considerably in the post-war period. It was stimulated initially by a coffee boom, reflected in an increase of the production of that crop from 14,000 tons in 1940 to 210,000 tons in 1974. During the sixties and up to the end of the colonial period in 1974, the rapid development of a wide variety of agricultural, fishing, mining, and industrial activities led to an annual average growth rate of GDP of nearly 7% in real terms. However, the most spectacular development was that of oil production, which started in the late 1950s and had reached 144,000 barrels per day in 1973. The favorable economic opportunities attracted thousands of Portuguese settlers, whose number increased from 40,000 in 1940 to 340,000 in 1974. A significant proportion of the rural population was employed in the growing plantations, mines and factories, either on a voluntary basis (at very low wages), or under a system of forced labor, which was abolished only in 1961. However, the vast majority of the Angolan population continued to live in poverty and social indicators remained extremely low.

iii. The transition to Independence in Angola was painful. The struggle against the colonial regime started in 1961. The armed struggle for independence was conducted by three rival movements (the MPLA, the UNITA and the FNLA) which in 1975 became involved in a civil war with each other, with the military support of foreign powers. The MPLA assumed control of the government in 1975 after defeating the FNLA and UNITA. In 1976, the Government forced the retreat of the invaders from South Africa with the assistance of Cuban troops and Soviet material assistance. However, UNITA has continued the war and related economic disruption since then, mainly with the support of South Africa which has invaded parts of Angola repeatedly.

The Economic Crisis Since Independence

iv. The exodus of the Portuguese settlers at the time of Independence and the armed struggle after 1975 led to drastic reductions in productive activities. From 1973 to 1978, the decline in output reached 68% in coffee, from 80% to 98% in several other agricultural crops, 72% in gross manufacturing production, 85% in diamonds, etc. The oil industry, which plays a key role in the economy, was also severely affected.

v. After these sharp economic contractions, there was some recovery of total production in subsequent years, although with fluctuations. It is estimated however that during the first post-Independence decade (1975-85) average real growth probably did not exceed 1% per year. GDP per capita is thus certainly much lower now than at the end of the colonial period.

vi. In most sectors, particularly in agriculture and manufacturing industry, output has remained far below levels reached during the colonial period. Angola, which before Independence was an important net exporter of agricultural products, has in recent years been increasingly dependent on food imports (and food aid) to supply its urban population. There are severe shortages of essential consumer goods and services both in rural areas and in the cities. The capacity utilization of manufacturing industries has been badly affected by the lack of inputs, of spare parts and of maintenance services. The oil industry, an economic enclave, has been the only important exception to the general decline of economic activity. In 1977 the output of oil had already exceeded the pre-Independence level of 144,000 barrels per day and by early 1989 it had reached about 450,000 barrels per day.

vii. The serious difficulties and decline experienced in productive activities are explained largely by three factors. First, the war, in which the Government has been involved during the entire post-Independence period against UNITA guerillas and against repeated South African invasions, has created insecurity in many areas of the country (probably 80% to 90% of the territory). The war has forced the exodus of more than 600,000 people into the cities, and has destroyed important economic and social infrastructure as well as productive units (power plants, electric transmission lines, mines, manufacturing plants, coffee plantations, bridges, railways, health and education facilities, etc.). It has disrupted internal transportation, imposed a heavy burden on the budget (with defence accounting for more than 40% of government expenditure), absorbed a large proportion of the limited supply of technicians and skilled manpower, and created enormous suffering and deprivation among the population.

viii. The second factor is the massive exodus during the period of transition to independence of about 300,000 Portuguese settlers (90% of the total) who held practically all administrative, managerial and skilled jobs. This exodus created a situation of chaos in the economy. Few Angolans had the professional qualifications to run the enterprises which were abandoned or to fill the jobs which had been left. In spite of the progress made by Angola in education, the scarcity of trained human resources continues to be one of the major constraints on economic development.

ix. The third factor is the inefficient economic management and inadequate economic policies which have prevailed, as described below. These organizational and policy shortcomings have contributed significantly to the decline in aggregate production, scarcities in the supply of consumer goods and inputs for industry, and distortions in the distribution of income. Without the contribution of expanding oil production, the economic crisis in Angola would have been far more serious. During the period 1980-87 the oil industry accounted for about 30% of GDP and for 40% to 65% of government revenues. Oil exports, comprising about 93% of total exports, provide the foreign currency resources for imports of war material, inputs for industry, food for the urban population, and other consumer goods. In view of such dependence on oil exports, the decline of international oil prices in 1985 has had a strongly negative impact on the Angolan economy. It is estimated that in 1986, GDP expressed in current US dollars may have fallen about 11%. The reduced availability of imports was reflected in lower levels of industrial production and in more severe scarcities of consumer goods.

x. Exports of goods and nonfactor services increased from US$1.8 billion in 1982 to US$2.3 billion in 1985. The subsequent decline to US$1.4 billion in 1986 is entirely explained by the fall in international oil prices. In 1987, however, due to the recovery of oil prices and a 27% increase in oil production, exports of goods and non-factor services went back to US$2.4 billion. Exports of diamonds and coffee, which were very important before Independence, have fallen drastically in the post-colonial era and in 1986 accounted for less than 7% of total export earnings. Import restrictions have ensured consistent trade surpluses, but these have been exceeded by deficits on the service account. Current account deficits have been financed by capital inflows, mainly medium and long term loans. The external debt reached US$3.9 billion in June 1988, corresponding to about 150% of exports of goods and services. Beginning in 1986, capital inflows were insufficient to finance the current account deficit and Angola began to accumulate arrears in its external payments (US$378 million at the end of 1986 and US$648 million at the end of 1988). Angola has been engaged in negotiations to reschedule its official debt. Even with success in these negotiations, the balance of payments situation will continue to be extremely difficult in the years ahead, unless there is a substantial increase in international oil prices. Severe scarcities of consumer goods and of inputs for domestic industries are likely to persist in the medium term.

The Administrative and Productive Structures

xi. The Angolan economy consists not only of a formal sector, but also of parallel markets and a substantial subsistence sector. The subsistence sector, which covers most of the activities in rural areas, has grown in recent years, mainly because of disruptions in trade and transportation between the countryside and urban areas due to the war. The formal sector is organized in accordance with the official socialist ideology, on the basis of central planning, State ownership of a large proportion of productive enterprises, and rigorous administrative control of economic activities.

xii. The MPLA-PT is the party in power and is installed at all levels of administrative and economic activity (public administration, regional and local authorities, residential areas, trade unions, etc.). The party provides basic orientation for the economic policies implemented by the Government and intervenes at different levels of the country's economic activity. The Government extensively regulates all economic activities using a complex system based on authorizations and controls which affect a large proportion of decisions concerning prices, foreign exchange allocations, financing of enterprises, investments, composition of output, sources of inputs, distribution of consumer goods, etc. Since the capacity of the public administration is affected by severe shortages of trained personnel, the bureaucratic interventions involve serious problems of inefficiency, lack of coordination, and generalized lack of discipline at all levels.

xiii. The modern sector of the Angolan economy is dominated by State enterprises which resulted from the nationalizations and confiscations in the early years of the post-independence period. The only significant exception is the oil industry, in which foreign private companies play a key role. In 1984 there were almost 400 public enterprises, accounting for three quarters of employment in modern productive activities. The public enterprises are subject to tight controls and authorizations from the government, especially from the sectoral ministry to which they report. Rates of return for public enterprises are substantially influenced by administrative decisions concerning the allocation of foreign exchange, prices, financing, wages, labor relations, etc. With such widespread administrative interference, it is impossible to evaluate the performance of the managers of public enterprises and to make them accountable for the results achieved. It is recognized that the efficiency of public enterprises has been highly unsatisfactory. Only about half report a profit. Losses of public enterprises have been partly financed by transfers from the budget. Over the period 1980-85, profit transfers from public enterprises to the Government budget, and payments from the budget to cover losses of public enterprises (including price subsidies), were roughly of the same order of magnitude.

xiv. In 1984, there were 267 private enterprises and 19 mixed enterprises but their average size tended to be significantly smaller than that of public enterprises. The activities of private enterprises strictly depend on government decisions as regards import licences, allocations of foreign exchange, supplies of raw materials and other inputs, prices, operating margins, purchases by the public sector, etc. The influence of administrative decisions on the operation of private enterprises implies that the autonomy of those enterprises is very limited. They are not subject to the stimulus of market forces or the constraints of competition. It is noteworthy, however, that Angola has maintained a relatively open policy on cooperation with foreign companies. These companies, operating as enclaves, are particularly important in the oil industry. They have been established under special regimes or on the basis of joint ventures and production sharing agreements with the national oil company.

xv. Severe shortages of goods and services at official prices have led to the rapid development of parallel markets in which prices are freely determined by demand and supply. Technically, these markets are illegal but in fact are tolerated by the Government. The parallel markets play an important role in the Angolan economy especially in the area of Luanda. They provide most consumers the only possibility of finding goods and services that are not available in the official market. They stimulate production of goods and services that would not take place at official prices. Competition in the parallel markets is fairly active. Available evidence on parallel market prices shows that differences between those prices and controlled prices in the official market are enormous and have increased continuously in recent years. While the official price of the US dollar has been maintained at 29.92 Kz without any change since 1975, parallel market prices for that currency have increased from about 600 Kz in October 1984, to 2,500-3,000 Kz at the beginning of 1989. The average ratio between prices for most common goods in the parallel markets and in the official market in Luanda seems to have risen from around 20:1 at the beginning of 1985 to about 50:1 in November 1987.

Economic Policies in Angola

xvi. As mentioned above, the crisis in the Angolan economy is due not only to the war and the scarcity of skilled managers and workers, but also to inadequate economic policies. The economy has been run essentially by administrative decisions. The market has not been allowed to play a significant role. Prices have been maintained at artificially low levels. The exchange rate has been grossly overvalued. The budget deficit has fuelled inflation. Distortions in relative prices have made economic calculations almost impossible. Serious problems of lack of discipline are found at different levels of public administration and enterprises.

xvii. Central planning plays, in principle, a key role in the system. In view of shortages of qualified personnel, of widespread lack of discipline, and vulnerability to external shocks (especially fluctuations in international oil prices),the experience of Angola with the planning system has been far from satisfactory. Medium term plans which should provide a basis for annual plans have not been prepared and annual plans have been incomplete and unrealistic in their targets and in their assumptions concerning implementation capacity. Control of the execution of annual plans has in general been inadequate and the degree of fulfilment of planned targets has usually been very low (often less than 50%). Because of these deficiencies, administrative or bureaucratic controls on an ad-hoc basis have certainly been more important than planning. The efficiency losses resulting from the insignificant role of market mechanisms have been very substantial.

xviii. Given the significant dependence of the Angolan economy on imports, foreign exchange policy has had a far stronger influence on levels of consumption and production than any other component of the plan. The exchange rate has been pegged to the dollar and maintained at 29.92 Kz per US$ without any changes since 1975. Foreign exchange is allocated administratively on the basis of an annual foreign exchange budget. However, foreign oil companies and other enclave companies operate outside of the foreign exchange allocation process.

xix. Price policy is based on government controls which affect practically all prices of goods and services. This policy has been a major cause of the persistent difficulties in the Angolan economy since independence. There has been an excessive rigidity and stability in the levels of controlled prices. In many cases, prices have not been changed since Independence. The price adjustments which have taken place were extremely modest when compared with increases in the nominal puchasing power of the population. As a consequence of the price policies, the production of many goods has been discouraged, relative prices have been severely distorted, wastage in the consumption of some goods has been stimulated, and very wide gaps have appeared between the demand and the supply of practically all goods and services in official markets. Thus, severe rationing of the most essential goods was introduced. In 1987, an average worker in Luanda was unable to spend more than 5% to 10% of his salary in purchases of goods and services sold at official prices. Widespread scarcities of practically all goods and services led to the rapid development of parallel markets which at present are quite important. The authorities were forced to create special shops for senior personnel in the public sector in which there are far more possibilities of obtaining consumer goods at official prices than in the shops which serve the rest of the population. Likewise, the foreign enclave companies created special shops of imported products for their employees. Manufacturing enterprises sell part of their production to their own employees, who in turn trade these goods in the parallel market for consumption goods which they need. The system of controlled prices and of administered distribution of goods implies that there is no competition among enterprises operating in the official market.

xx. Both foreign trade and domestic trade activities are constrained by rigid and pervasive government regulations and restrictions and by the predominance of inefficient public enterprises in imports and exports, in distribution, in wholesaling and in the retail network. There are also some 60 private trading enterprises, but their role in providing competition to the public sector is very weak because of the administrative allocation of imports, fixed margins of commercialization imposed by the Government, and constraints in getting more merchandise or diversifying the range of products sold. The level of agricultural production has been particularly affected by shortcomings of the trade system. During the colonial period, bush traders, by providing consumer goods in exchange for agricultural products, played an important role in stimulating peasant farmers to produce more. The problems created by the disappearance of the bush traders have not been solved by recent attempts of the Government to place a high priority on the distribution of essential goods in rural areas. Implementation of a special program of commercialization in the countryside has been far from satisfactory.

xxi. An indication of the role of budgetary policy in the economy is that, since independence, a large and growing part of the official economy -- nearly two thirds in 1986 - has been financed through the Government budget. This situation is explained by the growth in government oil revenues, which in recent years have provided between 40% and 60% of total govenment income. Another factor accounting for the relative size of the budget has been the integration of the financial results and investments of public enteprises in government revenues and expenditures. The availability of oil resources was a major factor explaining the rapid rise (although with fluctuations) of public spending. Together with rising non-oil taxes, those resources have supported growing military expenditures, which doubled between 1980 and 1986 and which accounted in 1987 for about 48% of total recurrent expenditures. They also contributed to finance large current expenditures, mostly on wages and salaries (two thirds of the total) and subsidies (7%), as well as public investments (especially in public enterprises) which often have been unprofitable.

xxii. In spite of the rapid growth of revenues, the overall budget has consistently been in deficit. In 1987, total budgetary expenditure exceeded revenue by 36% and the budget deficit corresponded to about 7% of GDP. Since the deficit has been mainly financed through borrowing from the Central Bank, it has contributed to the rapid growth of the money supply. It has therefore been the major source of inflationary pressures.

xxiii. Monetary policy has been largely determined by the borrowing needs of the Government and by the flucutations in the net foreign assets of the National Bank of Angola. Because of the expansion of credit to finance government deficits, the money stock has risen rapidly, although with large year to year fluctuations. In recent years, currency in circulation and individual deposits have grown at about 20% a year. This growth in the money supply has aggravated scarcities of goods in official markets and has fuelled inflation in parallel markets. The apparent steady decline in the velocity of circulation since Independence essentially reflects increasing prices in parallel markets, which are not included in measures of GDP. It does not indicate rising money demand or forced savings.

The Reform of Economic Policies

xxiv. Recognizing that existing economic difficulties are due in large part to inadequate economic policies, the Angolan authorities announced in 1987 an ambitious Program of Economic and Financial Restructuring, usually designated as SEF. In 1988, they prepared a Program of Economic Recovery (PRE) covering the years 1989-90. At the beginning of 1989, the authorities had not yet taken the key decisions which are foreseen in the SEF and the PRE in such areas as the liberalization or adjustment of controlled prices, the depreciation of the exchange rate, the more effective control of public finances, etc. The decisions already taken and the policy guidelines which were defined suggest, however, that the general thrust of the SEF reforms and of the PRE measures are well adapted to the needs of the Angolan economy. If adequately implemented, the SEF and the PRE may bring substantial improvements in the economic situation and in prospects for future growth.

xxv. A program of economic reform in Angola must be oriented toward three main objectives: the control of domestic demand, the stimulation of domestic supply, and the improvement in the allocation of resources. The control of domestic demand will have to rely primarily on: (i) efforts to reduce the budget deficit, which has been the main source of inflationary pressures; and (ii) effective control of the expansion of domestic credit to the productive sector in order to avoid excessive growth of the money stock.

xxvi. The stimulation of domestic supply should be based mainly on agriculture, which is expected to respond quickly to adequate incentives. Policies to promote agricultural output should include: (i) more attractive producer prices; (ii) development of a network of private bush traders; (iii) greater availability of industrial goods for purchase by peasant farmers for consumption or use as inputs in agricultural production; (iv) better transportation and storage facilities for agricultural crops; and (v) improved support services and technical assistance. Other areas in which a supply response is much needed and could be rapid and significant include repair services, private truck transportation, and small-scale consumer goods industries. Efforts aimed at stimulating the production of manufacturing industries and of large scale agricultural activities should be more selective.

xxvii. Improvements in the allocation of resources will require, among other measures: (i) a reduction of administrative interference in the economy and more reliance on market forces; (ii) stimulation of more competition in the productive sector; (iii) substantial changes in price policy and the exchange rate; (iv) progressive unification of official and parallel markets; (v) a review of priorities for government public expenditures; (vi) reform of public enterprises; and (vii) an improvement of mechanisms for the evaluation and selection of public investments.

xxviii. The success of efforts aimed at economic reform will depend on progress in decentralizing economic decisions, reducing the generalized lack of discipline which at present is found at different levels of economic life, and improving the availability, allocation, and utilization of skilled personnel and foreign technical assistance. Not all of the very drastic transformations required in the reform of the economic system and of the economic policies of Angola can take place suddenly or in a short period. The full process of reform will have to be extended for several years and will have to involve a gradual approach. However, the existing economic distortions are so serious that it will be necessary to introduce, in the initial stages, radical changes in price and wage policies, the exchange rate, the system of allocation of foreign exchange, taxation, public expenditure, and incentives and regulations affecting private enterprises. A gradual approach risks failure if it is founded on weak measures. Moreover, since its results will not always be immediate, a gradual approach requires a strong political commitment from the authorities to be maintained for several years.

xxix. In considering economic reform measures, it should be recognized that the development of a network of competitive enterprises is indispensable to achieve more efficiency through the reduction of bureaucratic interference, a more important role for the market, and a greater decentralization of economic decisions. In order to attain these objectives, deep structural changes are necessary. The most important changes involve giving more autonomy to public enterprises, stimulating competition, and creating incentives to establish private enterprises. All these changes have been mentioned in the SEF guidelines. However many key issues have yet to be addressed, such as the extent to which greater autonomy for public and private enterprises is hindered by central planning, by price controls, or by the administrative allocation of foreign exchange. It is also unclear to what extent managers of public enterprises will have the professional capacity to run those enterprises without constant government support. The SEF reforms will also undoubtedly encounter political resistance to the liquidation of unprofitable public enterprises which provide jobs for large numbers of workers. In spite of the difficulties which will have to be faced, the authorities should give high priority to efforts aimed at legalizing enterprises which operate in parallel markets, easing conditions for the installation of new enterprises, and establishing a program of incentives for small and medium sized private enterprises (mainly in rural commercialization, transport, and repair services). Reducing administrative requirements which hinder competition and improving the legal environment for private enterprises (to provide better protection against unwarranted State interference) are necessary acompanying steps.

xxx. The reduction of the budgetary deficit, mentioned in the SEF as one of its major objectives, will require both the mobilization of non-oil revenues and improved control over the growth of public expenditures. Changes in the tax system should include: (1) simplification of the import tariff and elimination of most existing tariff exemptions; (2) an increase of tariff duties on less essential consumption goods; (3) an increase of internal indirect taxes on petroleum products, tobacco, beer, alcoholic beverages, and other consumer goods; and (4) the introduction of a unified profit tax on all (including public) enterprises. An improvement in tax administration should also be a priority, but it is unlikely to yield the expected benefits until some of the major distortions in the economy have been removed.

xxxi. Apparently, in addressing the budget deficit problem, the SEF puts more emphasis on tax reform than on the reduction of expenditures. The possibilities for reducing budgetary expenditures are constrained by the financial requirements of the war effort. However, measures aimed at controlling spending are likely to contribute more quickly to a reduction in the budgetary deficit than efforts to increase non-oil revenues. Such expenditure measures should include: (1) strengthening mechanisms of evaluation and selection of public investments and of monitoring their implementation; (2) reducing subsidies to public enterprises by allowing them more freedom in their price and labor policies and by increasing the accountability of their managers; (3) improving discipline over the admission of new staff into public administration and over the control of wages and salaries; and (4) reinforcing the mechanisms of budgetary control. In addition, a depreciation of the exchange rate and necessary increases in official prices could also contribute to a reduction in the budget deficit. After the devaluation, the value in Kwanzas of oil revenues and of indirect taxes would increase substantially. Government expenditures would also rise, but in principle there should be a net reduction of the budgetary disequilibrium, depending mainly on the international price of oil and the extent of wage adjustments.

xxxii. The SEF envisages important adjustments in price and wage policies. Although the authorities intend to maintain a system of generalized price controls during the first stage of implementation of the SEF, it is expected that significant changes will be introduced in the levels of many controlled prices and in the control process, which will become more flexible and more decentralized. The prices of a certain number of agricultural products were already liberalized in 1988. The authorities announced the intention of increasing the average level of controlled prices by 44% in 1989. While it must be recognized that conditions in Angola are not ripe for the introduction of full price liberalization (because of insufficient competition, and dangers of speculation and overshooting), there is a risk that the maintenance of generalized price controls will continue to create serious economic distortions. These distortions can be reduced, however, if the initial price reform measures meet three criteria: (a) the average level of prices which remain subject to controls should be raised very substantially and should reflect the large gaps existing at present between supply and demand; (b) in order to stimulate production, the authorities should liberalize specific prices already in the first stage of implementation of the SEF as they have done already for sine agricultural goods; and (c) the adjustments of controlled prices should take into account the need to correct the most glaring distortions in relative prices.

xxxiii. The increase in official prices must be accompanied by adjustments in wage levels. However, the average percentage increases in wages should be substantially lower than the average increase in prices. Workers would not necessarily lose with the change because for most of them the proportion of their wages spent in the official market is very low (less than 10%). For some categories of workers, including in particular the technical and managerial staff who benefit from access to special "baskets" of goods at official prices, adjustment in wages may have to be more substantial.

xxxiv. Regarding exchange rate policy, the SEF envisages a devaluation of the kwanza. However, on the basis of the preliminary indications, it seems that the devaluation being considered by the authorities, although substantial when expressed in percentage terms, would be far from sufficient to modify significantly the existing system of administrative allocation of foreign exchange. Although the price of the dollar in the black market (2,500-3 000 Kz at the beginning of 1989) is not a precise indicator, it suggests that a very large devaluation is in fact required. However, even if the necessarily large initial adjustment is undertaken, a policy of successive steps will probably be necessary in order to arrive at an adequate exchange rate policy. In order to avoid an inflation-devaluation spiral, it is indispensable to combine a policy of gradual devaluation with substantial cuts in the budget deficit. In the initial stages of a gradual devaluation process, foreign exchange would certainly continue to be rationed. In order to reduce the negative consequences of an administrative system of allocation of foreign exchange, the authorities should analyse the possibility of introducing on a temporary basis, partial solutions which might include: import surcharges, export subsidies to agricultural products, export retention schemes, auctioning of import licenses, or a system of dual exchange rates.

xxxv. The changes in monetary and credit policies embarked upon and envisaged in the SEF should bring better control of the money supply and improve the allocation of financial resources. In implementing these policies, the following points require special attention: (a) while better control over the growth rate of the money supply depends primarily on a reduction in the budget deficit, SEF reforms aimed at avoiding the full monetarization of that deficit and developing alternative instruments for financing it (such as public debt securities to be sold to households and non-financial enterprises) are also important; (b) the authorities have already published legislation creating Treasury bonds to be sold to the public; (c) SEF reforms aimed at separating the central bank and commercial bank functions of the National Bank of Angola should be continued; (d) the Central Bank should have adequate instruments (such as the power to set cash reserve requirements, rediscount quotas and credit ceilings) and political support to control the money supply; (e) interest rates on bank deposits and loans should be increased and in time they should become positive in real terms; (6) the financing of public enterprises must be shifted from the budget to the banking system, and the banks should be able to make their credit decisions exclusively on the basis of sound financial considerations; (7) priority should be given to improving the accounting system, the internal controls, operational capacity and training of staff of the National Bank of Angola; and (8) at a later stage it would be advantageous to promote competition in the area of commercial banking through the establishment of two or three independent banks.

xxxvi. The authorities must pay particular attention to the social impact of the policies of economic adjustment and reform envisaged in the SEF and the PRE. The benefits expected from such policies will be reaped to a large extent by some of the poorest strata of the population, especially the peasant farmers. However, significant difficulties are likely to arise as regards the changes in the real incomes of some of the employees of the public administration and of public enterprises, the unemployment which may be created by the restructuring or liquidation of unprofitable enterprises and the scarcity of budgetary resources to finance social programs. Special emphasis must therefore be attached to the policy measures aimed at reducing such difficulties, including, in particular, higher than average increases in the nominal wages of some categories of workers (especially technical and management staff), the introduction of unemployment subsidies or temporary employment schemes for workers who lose their jobs (especially in public works and housing construction) and the protection of priority expenditures on health and education in the preparation of the Government budget.

Sectoral Development

Agriculture

xxxvii. About three quarters of the population earns a living from agriculture. Given an abundance of arable land and a diversified ecological setting, Angola has potential for significant production of a broad range of tropical and semi-tropical agriculture, livestock and fishery products. Present output of most products is far below the level achieved before independence. Previously self-sufficient in food, Angola now depends on large amounts of food imports. Similarly, whereas Angola was previously a major coffee exporter, agricultural exports have now virtually dried up. The factors responsible for this transformation include the abrupt and massive exodus of the Portuguese and the resulting abandonment of most commercial farms, the impact of the war which limits access to the countryside, destroys infrastructure and disrupts rural life, and also the agricultural policies adopted by the Government, which ignore market forces and have led to the neglect of peasant farming even though such farming dominates agricultural production, especially food crops.

xxxviii. Most of the abandoned commercial farms were taken over by the State. State farms have not been effective, and have contributed to a further decline of agricultural sector performance. Agricultural policy has been highly centralized. The supply of inputs as well as the marketing and distribution of agricultural products and consumer goods, previously undertaken by numerous private traders, is the responsibility of various government departments. With unattractive producer prices and inadequate agricultural support services and investment, these agencies have failed to satisfy the needs of smallholders and to create the incentives and conditions necessary to encourage production for the market. Despite the lack of security, a significant increase in agricultural production could be achieved in the 15% to 20% of the territory that is relatively secure, if appropriate agricultural policies and incentives are introduced. Policy adjustment, aimed at greater reliance on market forces, should include measures that establish adequate price incentives and ensure the supply of inputs and consumer goods in the countryside, institutional reform in the area of marketing and distribution, investment for rehabilitation of storage and transport, and technical assistance focussed on strengthening selective agricultural support services. The authorities have liberalized the prices of a certain number of agricultural products. As a consequence of the liberalization, increases in output were already achieved, in the areas around Luanda and the province of Huila. Agricultural policy, however, remains inadequate and tied to overall macro-policy.

Fisheries

xxxix. Angola has rich potential fishing resources. The 1972 fish harvest reached 600,000 tons but the Portuguese exodus in 1975 depleted Angola of its fishing fleet and expertise and the catch declined to as low as 76,000 tons in 1983. Inadequate policies and management contributed to the sector's decline. Domestic fish supplies are supplemented by foreign fishing fleets operating under license in Angolan waters. In 1987, these fleets landed 123,000 tons (42% of their catch) in Angolan ports in payment of fishing fees. The program of SEF and of PRE attaches a high priority to the rehabilitation and development of the fisheries sector. The authorities are preparing a Master Plan for the sector which envisages an increase of financial autonomy to state enterprises, a greater role for the private sector, more assistance in the development of artisanal fishing (particularly in the Southwest region), retention of larger shares of foreign exchange earnings by exporting enterprises and increased efforts aimed at training staff for the fishing fleet. Support to small and medium privately owned fishing posts and selective private investment in larger projects, offer opportunities for rapid rehabilitation of this sector, which could make a significant contribution to the local diet and to exports.

Mining

xl. While there are a variety of mineral deposits in Angola, including iron ore, phosphates, copper, gold, mica, Kaolin, rare earths, uranium, granite, marble and quartz, the only significant mining activity at present is that for diamonds. Until independence the prospecting for and development of diamond deposits was largely in the hands of Diamang, a joint venture between the Portuguese Government and various foreign shareholders. Currently these activities are the responsibility of the state owned company Endiama, which has assumed Diamang's obligations and continued its operations. However, prospecting and development of the deposits is expected to be opened to private, including foreign, interests. Diamond production reached a high of 2m. carats in the early 1970s and diamonds were Angola's principal export until 1971. Following a sharp decline in output after independence, Endiama has recently entered into a number of contract mining operations, which are expected to ensure production of around 1m. carats in 1988, with steady expansion thereafter. The value of diamond production is projected to grow from US$125 million in 1988 to around US$230 million in 1992 and U$360 million in 1995. Mining operations are severely handicapped by the security situation which limits mining and prospecting activity and greatly increases operating costs. Following an increase in output in 1987, the company's net foreign exchange earnings reached US$16 million in that year and more than US$40 million in 1988. An estimated US$50 million worth of diamonds has been smuggled out of Angola every year, the major part from direct theft in the mines. Strong efforts have been made to tighten security in the mines.

xli. The longer term future of the diamond mining industry lies with the successful development of the Kimberlite pipes, of which there are 638. In size alone they are among the largest in the world. In view of the high investment cost and long gestation period involved, development of these pipes is not expected to start until peace has been restored. The iron ore mine at Cassinga was closed after independence. A re-opening of the mine is not economically viable at current international prices and with the best of the high grade deposits depleted. The possibility of exploiting other mineral deposits, including phosphate, kaolin, granite, marble and quartz have been constrained by the impact of the war, the distorted prices and exchange rate as well as the lack of management expertise and capable artisans.

Industry

xlii. At independence Angola had, for a country of its size and level of income, a relatively large and broadly based manufacturing sector. By 1974, there were almost 4000 registered manufacturing enterprises in the country employing 200,000 workers. The influx of settlers from Portugal during the few decades before independence had helped create a market for a range of consumer goods, and was a source of entrepreneurial, technical and administrative skills. The imposition of exchange controls in 1962 led many large Portuguese trading and agricultural enterprises to invest in manufacturing activities. The situation changed radically at independence when the massive departure of the settlers deprived the sector of many of its human resources as well as a major part of its market. Within a few years, industrial output had dropped to less than 30% of its pre-independence level. The partial recovery since then has been constrained by the progressive deterioration of industrial facilities as well as by a growing scarcity of foreign exchange to purchase inputs. The manufacturing sector as a whole has been turning in a net loss at least since 1978. In 1987, this loss was estimated to be the equivalent of 17% of gross output, or 31% if the mining sector was included. The distorted price structure, low rates of capacity utilization and the inability to lay off workers when they are not needed, contribute to these losses. These losses could only be sustained over such a period because they were covered by government subsidies.

xliii. The Government's industrial development efforts have been marked by an absence of clear objectives. The fundamental question of the economic viability of industrial activity has not been addressed. A principal long term aim of the Government should be to restructure the industrial base so that it better reflects relative scarcities of resources. This would require a major adjustment of the system of incentives as determined by policies affecting external trade, prices, interest rates and labor. As these policy reforms will take time, the Government should at an early stage undertake a review of the major public industrial enterprises with a view to phasing out those that will clearly not be viable. The remaining industries should be given greater operational autonomy.

Construction

xliv. Output in the construction sector has fallen throughout the 80's and has been unable to keep pace with the demand. In recent years the sector has been operating at less than half of capacity and output has been on the order of 50% of planned targets. Expenses of the large firms of the enginnering and building subsectors exceeded revenues by more than 40%. A large proportion of the need for new housing is met by small units working in the parallel or informal market. Contracting with international construction companies has played an important role in the sector.

xlv. The main problems in the major construction enterprises include poor and irregular supply of materials, both from local and imported sources; poor training and motivation of personnel and increasing absenteeism; poor accounting and inventory controls, leading to waste, losses and theft of costly items; frequent breakdowns of equipment due to insuficient maintenance and lack of spare parts and low availability of transport services. The improvement of macro-economic management will create more favorable conditions for the development of the construction sector. The financing and recovery of the sector should include a reduction in the number of government entities by focussing on the key production centers and cutting those that are absorbing resources without prospect for improvement; strengthening the role of mixed and private enterprises; the implementating of control and accounting systems; and the introducing measures to motivate and train personnel. Investment programs must be carefully prepared and should take into account the existing constraints regarding financial resources and the capacity of the sector.

Energy

xlvi. By African standards, Angola is well endowed with energy resources, which include a large hydro potential, ample biomass stocks and substantial oil and gas reserves. While primary energy supply per capita (2.2 toe in 1986) is exceptionally high, final energy consumption is moderate (229 kgoe). The petroleum sector is of crucial importance to Angola's economy, and has been developed in a fairly efficient way. Large investments undertaken in the 1980s (by foreign private capital) laid the basis for a continuous increase in oil production since 1982. A non-distortionary tax regime, favorable geological conditions and relatively low production costs have attracted the foreign capital required to keep the sector prospering. Between 1980 and 1986 annual investment in oil exploration and development averaged US$390 million. Expenditure in upstream activities during the period 1987-90 is scheduled to exceed US$500 million a year. Financial and management constraints of Sonangol, the state-owned oil company, may make it difficult to maintain such a high level of investment. For the next three to four years the crude oil production rate is by and large determined by the level of past and current investment in field development. Petroleum output, is expected to increase to 450,000b/d in 1989, but the reserves to production ratio has now dropped to below 10 years. Apart from the investment in oil exploration and development required to prevent reductions of the reserves-to-production ratio, there is no need for heavy investment in up or downstream operations. In particular, the Government should not attempt to integrate the oil enclave into the economy through large downstream projects such as fertilizer production or refinery modernization/expansion.

xlvii. In the power sector the main task will be the rehabilitation of the existing infrastructure rather than the provision of additional capacity which will not be required until the mid 1990s. The 4 x 130 MW hydroplant at Capanda, whose cost could reach US$2 billion, will not contribute to solving the power sector's most pressing problems. The additional generating capacity will not be needed, and the project will add greatly to the country's external debt as well as to the sector's financial difficulties. Angola's vast biomass resources can under normal conditions easily meet rural and urban woodfuel demand. With a return to peace, measures will be required to improve the efficiency and competitiveness of woodfuel (charcoal) production and trade, and to ensure the adoption of environmentally sound practices. The key to a more rational use of energy resources are major improvements in the sector's incentive framework, combined with efforts to upgrade the organizational and managerial capability of the institutions involved in the supply and distribution of energy products. Measures should include the establishment of a domestic price structure in line with import and export parities, privatization of part of the petroleum products distribution, upward adjustment of electricity tariffs and improved collections, and the development of policy instruments to help increase the competitiveness of woodfuel markets.

Transport

xlviii. The present configuration, though not the condition, of Angola's basic transport infrastructure is essentially unchanged since independence. The system is based on a modal mix-- of rail, highway, air, cabotage and shipping - which has excellent potential for supporting economic development. It has three lateral railport corridors, supported by feeder roads. Additional highways provide very basic north-south provincial links and access to national borders. The air mode, which links all key provincial cities, has become the only dependable means of passenger and light freight transit over much of the country, due to the security situation. Between 1980 and 1985 the value of government controlled transport and communication services showed significant decline in the road sector, with rail and maritime services holding steady, port output rising slightly, and communications and air travel showing strong growth. Overall, the total value of services in 1985 was less than half of that achieved in 1974.

xlix. The security problem has disrupted all transport modes. Services have been cut, investment programs cancelled, infrastructure destroyed, and domestic transit efficiency lowered. The sector is in urgent need of restructuring at all modal levels. It is characterized by the following constraints: inadequate fleet sizes of vehicles, trains, ships and aircraft; short service lives of vehicles, railway engines and mechanical handling equipment; distorted tariffs; unsatisfactory service schedules; failure of urban passenger transit systems to meet rapid growth in demand; a chronic lack of all modal spare parts; weak trans-shipment facilities, especially at ports; inadequate maintenance facilities and insufficient technical staff; poor management, remuneration and control of staff; and inconsistent road vehicle licensing arrangements.

l. The sector has limited capacity to absorb investment. A sector program focussed on short term high impact projects with modest financing requirements seems appropriate, supported by policy reforms. The program prepared by MINTEC proposes to reduce the demand for air services, both for cargo and passengers, by raising service levels in other modes, notably highways and cabotage. This needs to be accompanied by a review of the tariff structure. In the road sector, the emphasis should be on maintenance and rehabilitation of vehicles and highway infrastructure, the latter through the creation of an effective road maintenance organization. Also the private sector should be allowed to play a bigger role in road transport. Cabotage has an excellent potential for providing part of the regional transport link betwen producer and consumer. The program proposes investment in the ship fleet for both cargo and passenger cabotage. Investment requirements for the railway system are considerable, and include the need to rehabilitate the permanent way, replace damaged bridges, renew rolling stock, purchase new engines, renovate signalling and communications, improve transshipment facilities, develop an adequate technical staff, and ensure a regular supply of spare parts. The Benguela corridor requires a separate, in-depth analysis using standard evaluation criteria and taking into account demand and security considerations, as well as the ongoing rehabilitation of other corridors. In the air transport sector, the underutilized fleet needs to be rationalized, the number of personnel should be cut and management improved. An adjustment of the tariff structure is urgently needed to allow TAAG to operate on a sound financial basis. Finally, all transport modes could benefit from assistance to develop and retain good management and technical staff.

Education and Human Resources

li. Limited data on the labor force indicate that in 1985, 44% of the total population of about 9 million was of working age, with the participation rate being 53% and official unemployment 3%. The vast majority of the labor force - in some provinces more than 95% - is functionally illiterate, despite the high priority given to education since Independence. This is due primarily to the almost complete lack of education for Angolans during the colonial period, the exodus of the Portuguese at Independence, and the inefficiencies and constraints of the present education system, which have been exacerbated by the continuing war. Enrollment in primary education almost tripled in the first years after Independence, then dropped by nearly 50% to a gross enrollment ratio of 44% in 1984. This decline shows the effect of the war as well as the attempt to increase access to education without a major investment in educational facilities and teacher training. Internal efficiency is low, indicating serious wastage. Secondary education, which has grown rapidly, has faced serious difficulties due to a lack of equipment, inadequate and inappropriate teaching materials, and a high proportion of part-time teachers and "cooperantes" among the staff.

lii. Enrollment in higher education is now nearly twice as high as before Independence. Despite limited resources, the university offers a wide range of specializations. The quality is affected by a shortage of qualified staff and of teaching materials and equipment. The regular education cycle is complemented by opportunities for adult education, including literacy classes and vocational training.

liii. The Government should focus on generally raising the quality of education, especially through an increase in the supply of qualified teachers. Expenditures on buildings, equipment and teaching materials are also needed. The government has recently increased its efforts to improve the performance of the sector by revising curricula, building new schools and increasing the wages of teachers. International technical assistance should play an important role in dealing with the difficulties faced by the sector, especially as regards the training of teachers. Finally, since education, including board and lodging is free, some cost recovery could help reduce resource constraints.

liv. Available information on child malnutrition, as well as on infant and maternal mortality point to extremely low levels of health status. Causes include the disruption and destruction due to the war, precarious water supply and sanitation facilities, malnutrition due to inadequate food supplies, and the foreign exchange shortage which limits the availability of medical supplies and equipment. The provision of health services is based on a primary health care strategy, which is directed mainly towards children in the 0-5 years age group and pregnant mothers as well as reductions in the incidence of communicable disease. However, health services have deteriorated significantly, as indicated by increases since Independence in the ratio of inhabitants per health post, hospital and physician.

Regional Development and Basic Urban Services

lv. Spatial development patterns since independence have been shaped largely by the volatile security situation rather than economic forces. The continuing internal conflict since the 1960s has provoked significant movements of displaced people, currently estimated to number 10% of the rural population, who are seeking security and reliable supplies of food. These movements have been an important source of urban population growth. The security situation effectively precludes the application of regional economic analysis. Only the South-Southwest provinces of Huila, Namibe and Cunene have constituted what meaningfully can be described as a region in economic and institutional terms. Only here has the situation been sufficiently stable to contemplate the implementation of a regional development program to meet emergency relief needs and to promote immediate economic reconstruction. A program currently is being formulated which will comprise specific projects and policy recommendations in the areas of pricing, institutional development, and regional planning. A positive response from the international donor community is absolutely vital to its successful implementation.

lvi. The issue of institutional decentralization is a central one in regional development. In the absence of guidelines defining relationships, routine coordination between institutions operating in a regional context and the regional branches of central government ministries is effectively non-existent. The degree of autonomy at present found in the South Southwest region is an exception and is not institutionalized. A related problem is that given the highly centralized structure of public administration in Angola and the acute shortage of administrative personnel, there are no local institutions capable of taking over decentralized activities. While decentralization must be preceded by national administrative reforms, the weakness of local institutions presents a major obstacle to its realization.

lvii. Patterns of urban development since independence have been determined mainly by the disruptive effects of the war. Though the data on urbanization trends is very limited, there is little doubt that urban population growth has been very rapid. This has overburdened the capacity of urban infrastructure and public utility systems. Lack of managerial and technical cadres, limited equipment, and the precarious financial condition of public utility companies have led to a marked declined in both service standards and service coverage. With only limited investment since independence and grossly inadequate maintenance, the basic urban services of water supply, sewage and sanitation, and refuse collection are now in a critical state. The housing stock has also deteriorated due to lack of maintenance and no provision has been made for sites and services or upgrading of the areas which have absorbed the bulk of the new migrants. The situation is exacerbated by the virtual absence of any urban planning. Moreover, the operational capacity of urban institutions is in most cases extremely weak, in part reflecting the loss of local financial autonomy and the decision to replace municipal utility agencies with national companies.

CHAPTER 1

COUNTRY BACKGROUND

A. Geographical Charcteristics

Physical Setting

1.01 The People's Republic of Angola is, after Zaire and Sudan, the third largest nation south of the Sahara. It has an area of 1,276,700 sq. km. (including the 7,270 sq. km of the oil-rich Cabinda enclave) and is the largest Portuguese speaking African country. Angola is located on the West Coast of Africa and is bordered to the north by the People's Republic of Congo, to the northeast by Zaire, to the east by Zambia, and to the south by Namibia. Without considering Cabinda province (a separate enclave in the northwest separated from the rest of the national territory), Angola has a roughly square shape (see Map I), measuring 1,277 km from north to south and 1,236 km from west to east (from the mouth of the Cunene river to the Zambia border). Plateaus, averaging altitudes between 1,050 and 1,350 meters, account for about two thirds of the Angolan territory (see Map II). The Angolan coast, with an extension of 1,650 km, is mountainous to the north of the mouth of the Kwanza river, and quite flat with occasional cliffs to the south. The coastal plains are separated from the inland plateau by a score of irregular "terraces" that form a subplateau. The most important rivers in the country originate in the plateau regions and flow in three directions: east-west to the Atlantic, south-southeast, and northeast. Most rivers, however, do not provide easy access to the interior regions as they are not navigable. Nevertheless, they offer energy and irrigation potential. The main rivers of Angola include the Kwanza (with an extension of 960 km, 200 of which are navigable by small watercraft), and the Cunene (945 km long and bordering Namibia to the south). Though the Kasai and other rivers are better known for their importance to Zaire, the Kasai's tributaries in the Lunda region contain important diamond reserves.

Climate

1.02 Angola's location in the intertropical and subtropical zones of the southern hemisphere, its proximity to the sea and the cold Benguela stream, and its topographical characteristics are the factors which create two distinct climatic regions with two seasons: the dry and cool season (from June to September) and the hot and humid season (from October to May). The northern region from Cabinda to Ambriz has a humid tropical climate with heavy rainfall, while the region from Luanda to Namibe (Moçamedes) has a moderate tropical climate, with the rainfall reduced on the coast by the Benguela wind stream. The southern strip between the plateau and Namibia has a desert climate, given the proximity to the Kalahari, with irregular rainfall between 600 and 1000 mm. annually. Temperatures average 23 degrees C in the north and the coastal areas, and 19 degrees C in the interior, including the central plateau.

Natural Resources

1.03 The country's flora is quite diversified given Angola's size, the variety of climates, and the diversity of soils. In the Cabinda region, very dense forests predominate (Maiombe forests) with economically important timbers such as black wood, ebony, African sandalwood, and ironwood. The abundance of land and the diversified climatic conditions provide favorable conditions for the development of a wide variety of agricultural crops of tropical and temperate regions, including coffee, cotton, sugar, sisal, palm oil, tropical fruits, maize, and horticultural, as well as livestock. With a coastline of 1650 km, Angola's waters are rich in fish, mollusks, and crustaceans. The cold water species predominate in the Namibe coast and the tropical species along the Benguela coast. Angola also has large mineral resources. The most economically important are oil, diamonds, iron, manganese, copper, asphalt and marble. The main petroleum basins under exploration are located near the coast of Cabinda and Zaire provinces. The main diamond producing area is located in Lunda Norte province. Finally, as noted in para. 1.01 above, the energy and irrigation potential of Angolan rivers is considerable.

Transportation and Communications

1.04 Angola's road network is estimated at around 72,323 km, 8,317 of which are asphalted. The main roads link Quimbele (Uige) in the north to Namibe (down to the Namibia border), and the capital city of Luanda to other major cities and to Lumbala (Moxico), near the Zambia border. Traffic on many of the most important roads has been interrupted because of the destruction of bridges, bad road conditions, and problems of security. The railway network was built with two objectives in mind: making access from the interior to the coast easier, and allowing the export of Zambia's copper and Zaire's zinc through the port of Lobito. Thus, railways cross the country only in east-west directions, without connecting with each other. The railway network, with 3,069 km, is composed of three main railway lines: Luanda-Malange, Benguela (connecting Zambia to Lobito) and Namibe-Menongue. A large proportion of the railway network is not used at present because of war-related destruction and insecurity. All internal air transportation is provided by the national airline TAAG. Given the insecurity of ground travel, air transportation has been increasing. Angola has a significant airport network, the main ones being in Benguela, Cabinda, Huambo, Lobito and Namibe. Luanda has the only international airport. As for shipping, the major ports in Angola are Lobito, Luanda, and Namibe, while Cabinda is almost exclusively used to handle the country's petroleum production.

B. POPULATION

1.05 Recent population figures are difficult to obtain due to the lack of a full national census. A limited census was carried out in the province of Luanda in 1983, which was extended to the provinces of Cabinda, Namibe and Zaire in 1984. War-related problems make it impossible to carry out a national census. Appendix Table K.1 presents the available population data. It took 70 years for the population to double from 2.7 million in 1900 to 5.6 million in 1970, with the rate of growth accelerating in the 1940-1970 period, due to significant Portuguese immigration. In 1980, according to official estimates, the population reached 7.7 million, implying an average annual growth rate of 3.2% for the previous decade. This rate is incredibly high considering the mass exodus of Portuguese settlers at Independence in the mid-1970s and the war. Though data is scanty, the population was projected to grow at an annual rate of 2.5% during the 1980s, reaching about 9 million in 1986. Population density (7.2 inhabitants per Km2) is quite low, with the most populous provinces being Huambo, Luanda, Bie, Malange, and Huila, which together account for 56% of the total population (see Map III). About three-quarters of the population comes from three ethno-linguistic groups: the Makongo in the Northwest, the Ovimbundu in the Central plateau region, and the Mbundu living in a belt extending from Luanda to the east.

1.06 The rate of growth of the urban population, estimated at 7.6% per annum for the 1980s, compares with 0.8% for the rural population. This may be largely attributed to the massive dislocation, rural insecurity, and rural-urban migration related to the war. As a result, the urban population increased from 1.8 million in 1980 to 2.8 million in 1986, increasing its proportion of total population during this period from 23% to 31% (see Appendix Table K.2). The capital city of Luanda and its satellite city of Viana had a combined population of 1.2 million in 1986, representing 44% of the urban population. In the period 1940-70, the population of Luanda grew at an average annual rate of 7%, i.e., it nearly doubled every decade. In the 1980s, the pace of Luanda's growth has declined slightly to 6.2% per annum, but remains quite high. Other important cities, such as Malanje, Huambo, Benguela, Lobito and Lubango have populations in the 100-250,000 range.

1.07 The crude birth rate of 47 per thousand for the 1980-85 period reflects a high total fertility rate (6.4) combined with a large proportion of women of fertile age. The crude mortality rate of 22 per thousand for the period 1980-85 is influenced by widespread malnutrition, precarious sanitary conditions, a large proportion of illiterate mothers, and inadequate health facilities. The main causes of death are tetanus, measles, diarrheal diseases and malaria. Infant mortality is very high, although precise estimates are very difficult to obtain, ranging from 200 per thousand according to United Nations figures to 325-375 per thousand according to a recent UNICEF study, both for children under five in 1985. For infants under one, UNICEF estimates mortality at 200 per thousand, while U.N. figures show a decline from 193 per thousand for 1960-70 to 166 per thousand for 1980-85. For Luanda, another source reveals an increase in the infant mortality rate, from about 107 per thousand in the years before Independence to 130 per thousand in 1980. UNICEF has found rates in the 240-300 per thousand range in emergency areas directly affected by the war. Life expectancy has increased from 35 years in 1960-70 to 42 years in 1980-85 but remains quite low. The rapid growth of the population, together with a relatively low life expectancy, are clear indicators of a young population. Indeed, the proportion of the population under 15 years of age is 45%, whereas those 65 years or older represent only 3%. As a result, the dependency ratio is extremely high.

C. ECONOMIC DEVELOPMENT DURING THE COLONIAL PERIOD 1/

1.08 In the early decades of the 20th century, there had been some development of the modern sector of the Angolan economy based on railway building, diamond mining, plantation agriculture and trade. However, rapid economic growth began only after the Second World War. The initial stimulus came from the coffee boom. Coffee production rose from 14,000 tons in 1940 to around 100,000 tons in the early 1960s. In 1950, coffee was already the most important of Angolan exports, accounting for 30 percent of total foreign currency earnings. Widening economic opportunities contributed to an increase in the population of Portuguese settlers, from 44,000 in 1940 to 172,000 in 1960. However, most Angolans continued to live in extremely difficult conditions. Subsistence peasants, having little contact with the market economy, made up the great majority of the population. However, many of them became employed in the plantations and mines, either on a voluntary basis (at very low wage levels), or under the so-called system of contract labor, which imposed forced labor on about 350,000 workers by the mid-1950s and was only abolished in 1961.

1.09 The pace of economic growth accelerated considerably in the period 1960-74, despite the anti-colonial war of independence which began in 1961. In fact, it was in response to popular unrest that the Portuguese colonial administration initiated policies in the early 1960s to promote further economic growth. Public investment in economic infrastructure increased significantly, restrictive investment laws were liberalized in 1965 to encourage foreign investment and the Portuguese authorities also encouraged the immigration of Portuguese settlers. During the period 1960--74, GDP rose at an annual rate of almost 7% in real terms, representing one of the highest real growth rates in Africa. The Portuguese population continued to increase rapidly and reached 340,000 in the last year of the colonial period (representing about 5% of the total population). The volume of annual coffee production doubled to 210,000 tons between 1960 and 1974 and, by the early 1970s, Angola ranked fourth among the world's coffee producers. Besides coffee, several other cash crops (such as sisal, sugar, tobacco, and cotton) contributed to foreign exchange earnings or supplied local industries. Angola was almost self-sufficient in basic foodstuffs and exported maize, while the rich fishing waters off the Southern coast provided the basis for an export-oriented processing industry. In the early 1970s, Angola was also the fourth largest producer of diamonds (over 2 million carats a year), and the production of iron ore, which was negligible in 1960, exceeded 6 million tons per year in 1970-73. The most spectacular development, however, was that of oil production. The first commercial discovery of oil resources was made in 1955 and production rose rapidly in subsequent years, particularly after 1969. In 1973, output was already on the order of 144,000 barrels per day and, following the price increases in that year, oil overtook coffee as the leading export commodity, accounting for more than 30 percent of total export revenues.

1/ Annex I provides a detailed description and analysis of the colonial economy.

1.10 The growth of the domestic market, resulting from the rapidly increasing Portuguese population, opened up profitable opportunities for the development of the manufacturing sector. Consequently, manufacturing increased at an average annual rate of more than 20% between 1964 and 1971 and, on the eve of Independence, Angola had one of the most developed manufacturing sectors in Sub-Saharan Africa. The range of manufactured products was quite diversified, including not only the transformation of agricultural products, and the production of beer, tobacco and cement, but also textiles, paper, glass, paints, steel rods, electric cables, cellulose, agricultural implements, etc. However, most industries depended to a large extent on imported inputs.

1.11 Overall, although per capita income increased significantly, the growth patterns which characterized the colonial economy did not necessarily benefit the bulk of the Angolan population. In some areas the best land was taken away from the Angolans and given to Portuguese settlers, and the compulsory relocation of large numbers of African peasants into protected villages (as a counter-insurgency measure) was also very disruptive of traditional African agriculture. Educational standards were very low and Africans were denied access to education. As a result, native Angolans were not only absent in managerial, professional, and technical employment, but due to the influx of poorly educated Portuguese settlers (on a scale unparalleled in the British and French colonies), almost all semi-skilled jobs and a high proportion of low skilled jobs were reserved for European immigrants.

D. THE TRANSITION TO INDEPENDENCE

1.12 The armed struggle for the independence of Angola from Portuguese colonial rule began in 1961 and was conducted by three rival movements: the MPLA (Movimento Popular para a Libertaçao de Angola), the FNLA (Frente Nacional de Libertaçao de Angola) and UNITA (Uniao Nacional para a Independência Total de Angola). A separatist movement appeared also in the Cabinda region (Frente para a Libertaçao do Enclave de Cabinda - FLEC). In 1974, after a coup d'etat against the Portuguese regime that had maintained colonial rule, Portuguese authorities opened negotiations with the independence movements. Those negotiations culminated in the Alvor agreement of January 1975, which provided for the establishment of a transitional coalition government, with the participation of ministers from Portugal and from the three liberation movements.

1.13 However, the coalition government was short-lived. Its activities were disrupted by intense rivalries between the three liberation movements, which degenerated rapidly into open civil war. The FNLA, which received extensive support from Zaire and other sources, occupied the Bakongo provinces of the North. The MPLA, assisted by Cuban advisers and anti-Zairean rebels from Katanga, reinforced its position in Luanda and in the major inland cities, while UNITA had its bases in the Ovimbundu regions. With the evolution of the civil war, there was increased intervention of foreign powers. In the summer of 1975, the FNLA was being supported by Zairean troops. South African forces invaded Angola, occupying the Southern provinces and coming within about 200 km of Luanda. The intervention of Cuban troops in November 1975 and the supply of Soviet material assistance enabled the MPLA to force the retreat of the South African invaders in the South and of the Zairean and FNLA forces in the North. The independence of Angola was officially proclaimed on November 11, 1975, with the MPLA in control of the Government. Although large-scale warfare against the forces of South Africa, Zaire, FNLA and UNITA ceased in 1976, UNITA maintained a guerrilla war in the South, with the military support of South Africa and others. This war was enlarged in subsequent years to the central and northern provinces, creating extremely severe disruptions to the economy.

1.14 Angola's war-torn transition to Independence inflicted very heavy damage to the economy. In the face of the chaos, insecurity, and uncertainties created by the civil war, most of the Portuguese settlers who were running the economy left Angola in the second half of 1975. That departure, together with the disruptions of the economy caused by the war, led to drastic reductions in productive activities. In the immediate aftermath of the 1975-76 conflict, the economy was devastated. Economic infrastructure was destroyed. Thousands of commercial farms and enterprises were abandoned by the departing settlers, who took with them every asset that could be transported. Some sectors of the economy, such as the coffee and diamond industries, lost most of their African labor force as well, since people returned to their tribal homelands or migrated to urban areas for security. Between 1974 and 1976, every sector of the economy experienced sharp output declines (ranging up to nearly 100%). Moreover, the mass exodus of the bush traders destroyed the traditional rural marketing system, forcing the peasants to revert to subsistence agriculture, while the Government resorted to imports to feed the urban population.

1.15 Since the economic dislocations of 1975-76, the Government has aimed at restoring production to the levels achieved before Independence. However, with the notable exception of oil production (which returned to its 1973 output levels by 1977 due to its relatively insulated enclave nature and good protection after 1976) this has remained an elusive goal and in some key sectors (e.g., agriculture), there have been further declines even from the depressed levels of 1975-76. This negative economic performance (outside of the enclave oil industry) is particularly striking in view of the steady growth in oil earnings (until the sharp fall in oil prices in 1985-86), which under more normal circumstances could have facilitated rehabilitation of the rest of the economy.

1.16 The legacy of the colonial period and the disruptions of the Independence process have left an indelible mark on the Angolan economy. These factors, together with the prolonged war, the rapid development of the oil sector and the policies pursued after Independence, have left the Angolan economy in a unique situation, characterized by very uneven indicators of development. For example, Angola's substantial oil production leads to a per capita GDP (approximately US$554 in 1987) that would place it among lower middle income countries. 2/ On the other hand, the war has

---

2/ See Annex II for a more extensive discussion of Angolan social and economic conditions in comparison to those found in other Sub-Saharan African countries.

required the country to devote a disproportionate share of its limited resources to military expenditures at the expense of desperately needed investments in economic and social development. Due to the war, large segments of the population have little or no access to educational institutions or health services. Moreover, the extreme shortage of human resources resulting from colonial policies and subsequent upheavals have compounded the need for social as well as economic development measures. For these reasons, on the basis of such social indicators as life expectancy, infant mortality rates, educational levels, and health status, Angola is very disadvantaged, even compared to low income countries and other Sub-Saharan African countries. Thus, a modern enclave oil sector, the war, and Angola's historical background, together with the economic organization and policies followed since Independence, leave the country with unique problems, as will be described in detail in subsequent chapters. The authorities are actively engaged in contributing to the solution of those problems by changing their economic policy and introducing reforms in the economic system. The results of their efforts will be determined to a decisive extent by the steadiness of their commitment to the process of reform, by the prospects for internal peace and for the end of external agressions and by the volume and quality of the technical and financial assistance which may be received from the international community in forthcoming years.

CHAPTER 2

THE ECONOMIC SYSTEM OF ANGOLA

A. THE DEVELOPMENT OF THE ECONOMIC SYSTEM SINCE INDEPENDENCE

2.01 After independence, the new People's Republic of Angola declared itself a socialist country. According to the Constitution, the organs of the State are subordinated to the ruling party, which was renamed the MPLA-PT (Movimento Popular para a Libertaçao de Angola - Partido do Trabalho) in 1977. The basic decisions concerning the organization of the economic system are taken by the MPLA, in its Congresses, in the Central Committee, and in the Political Bureau. The Party approves the strategies and main instruments of economic policy. The government is an executive body with responsibility for implementing the policies approved by the Party.1/

2.02 The establishment of a socialist economic system, based on central planning, nationalization of a large proportion of productive enterprises, and rigorous State control of economic activities, was determined not only by official ideology, but also to a large extent by the conditions prevailing after independence. Immediately after independence, the major objective of the Party was to revive production rather than to establish a fully socialist economy. Neither collectivization of farmers nor wholesale nationalization of enterprises was attempted. The large number of productive assets, both agricultural and industrial, that ended up in government hands arrived there for the most part as a result of abandonment by their previous owners. The law on State Intervention (3/76), which formally nationalized these private enterprises and the subsequent law on Foreign Investment (10/79) allowed for a significant role for the private sector. The initial resolution on economic policy approved by the Central Committee in October 1976, the year after independence, stated that a centrally planned socialist economy ("with agriculture as its base and industry as the decisive factor") was a strategic goal rather than an immediate objective. However, central planning and administrative controls quickly became entrenched ideas in both the Party and the Government.

2.03 A National Planning Commission was established in 1976 as an organ of the Council of Ministers. That Commission was given the task of coordinating planning at all levels and directing activities in almost all sectors of the economy. From 1976 to 1978, state monopolies were established in foreign trade, banking, and insurance. The nationalization and confiscation of enterprises after independence meant that the State quickly assumed major responsibilities not only in managing the economy but also in operating a wide range of specific productive activities.

1/ For more information concerning the institutional structures of economic management in Angola see Annex III.

2.04 A problem that arose in the early days of independence was the role of workers in company management. Neighborhood and workers' commissions increasingly took an active part in company management, particularly of those industries that had been abandoned by their owners and kept in operation by the workers. This led to growing conflicts within enterprises between the workers and management, which caused many strikes and disruptions of production. Thus, an important decision taken at the 1976 Central Committee was to end the system of collective management and replace it with more conventional forms of company operation. It was re-emphasized, though, that enterprise directors should be picked from party ranks and should be approved by the Political Bureau. The workers' commissions, organized by the Union Federation, were abolished and the Union Federation itself was brought under strict party control.

2.05 The First Party Congress, in December of 1977, reviewed economic performance since independence and concluded that the pace for building a socialist economy should be accelerated by improving centralized supervision and planning of the economy, by continuing the policy of nationalizations and confiscations, by establishing rural cooperatives, and by other policies related to the productive sector. The Special Party Congress of 1980 declared that progress had been made in implementing past guidelines and creating structures for building a socialist society, but noted continuing problems. A delay in drawing up the national plan had led, it was alleged, to a failure to achieve some important objectives. These included recreating a rural distribution system, re-establishing links between industry and agriculture, and reducing the exodus of rural populations to the towns. It was noted that the country had failed to institute a rational system of production and that the total amount of wages paid far outstripped the total volume of production. The existence of a black market caused by price controls was also acknowledged. Although specific achievements in agricultural production were hailed, it was also admitted that agricultural units under state control produced only 12% of the food needs of the population and only 15% of the raw material requirements of Angolan industries. With respect to industrial production, significant increases were noted in the output of several products, but it was recognized that aggregate production remained far below the levels achieved before independence.

2.06 At the Second Party Congress in December of 1985, the MPLA-PT reaffirmed that Angola had chosen the socialist path of development and that the national plan should be the main instrument of economic management. However, it was recognized that the economic results achieved (although due in large part to the war and to the scarcity of skilled managers and technicians) were far from satisfactory and that important changes were needed in the economic system and in economic policy. The strategic guidelines approved by the Congress called for an improvement in the methods of socialist planning and a more efficient utilization of prices in the management of the economy.

2.07 In the framework of the policy changes approved by the Second Congress, the Central Committee of the MPLA approved in 1987 a Program of Economic and Financial Restructuring (Programa de Saneamento Económico e Financeiro), known as SEF. That program reaffirms that the economy of

Angola will be organized along socialist lines, but it envisages the introduction of substantial changes in the system of economic management. In particular, the SEF calls for introducing a more important role for the private sector, more flexibility in the price system, less centralization in economic planning, and more autonomy for public enterprises. In addition, the SEF stresses the need for a reduction in the government budget deficit and a correction of other important financial disequilibria.

2.08 The present chapter discusses the most important features of the system of organization and management of the Angolan economy. It analyses the key roles played by central planning, the foreign exchange budget and administered prices in the management of the economy. It also presents a brief description of some of the main productive structures and units in the economy.

B. THE INSTITUTIONAL ORGANIZATION OF ECONOMIC MANAGEMENT

2.09 Three principles guided the design of institutions in Angola: (i) the principle of "unified management" aimed at ensuring a single direction for all the country's political, economic, and social life at the level of administrative central, sectoral, or regional units; (ii) the principle of "centralism" aimed at ensuring that decisions made by the nation's higher organs would be binding on lower units and that each unit would develop the necessary means to execute these decisions in its own area of competence; (iii) the principle of "planning" aimed at defining national priorities, ensuring inter-sectoral and inter-regional economic coordination, and selecting the most efficient alternative uses of factors of production.

2.10 These principles created a bureaucratic-administrative structure with a sophisticated legal basis, in which nearly all decisions are regulated. The principles of unified management and centralism imply the presence of the MPLA-PT, the party in power, at the various organizational levels of administrative and productive units. Indeed, party structures are installed at all levels of economic and administrative activity, including central, regional and local authorities, residential areas, enterprises, trade unions, etc. It is the generalized presence of the party which resolves conflicts. All the other authorities are subordinated to its political power.

2.11 The institutional principles of unified management, centralism, and planning have created a "culture of dependency" in the relations between lower administrative units and higher units or levels. In effect, little or nothing is decided without consulting and receiving approval from the overseeing government department, and sometimes from several departments with contradictory interests. This system has apparently led to very slow decision-making and implementation of policies and programs both at the level of public administrations and of state enterprises.

2.12 The organization, functions and responsibilities of all departments of public administration are specified by regulations, which often are very detailed. Many of such regulations also specify in great detail the interventions of the public administration in the main areas of economic policy (price controls, licensing of practically all economic activities, planning, investments, etc.). The bureaucratic structure which has thus been created introduces great rigidity, complexity, and distortions in economic management. The design of that structure does not reflect the lack of trained personnel in public administration and is not adapted to the realities of Angolan economic life. As a consequence, there are serious problems of inefficiency and lack of coordination in the system of bureaucratic controls on which the management of the economy is based. Not surprisingly, the motivation of civil servants, even at high levels in the hierarchy, is affected by the overlaps in responsibilities, interference in routine decisions of the government by party structures, and low levels of remuneration (in spite of the "baskets" of consumer goods sold to them at official prices in order to improve the purchasing power of their salaries).

2.13 Paradoxically, excessive regulations and centralization in public administration and economic policy have resulted in a generalized lack of discipline and fragmentation. Ministries and other important departments and public enterprises tend to become self-contained organizations, which often have overlapping jurisdictions with other units. In order to circumvent bottlenecks and regulations, both government departments and civil servants do not hesitate to adopt informal solutions (esquemas), in what may be called a "parallel institutional market". The following examples illustrate the operation of that "market". Some government offices or ministries, in the face of shortages of foodstuffs for their employees, have created farms operated and financed by themselves. This had led to fragmentation, duplication of effort and waste of resources. Some departments, which have been unable to obtain import licenses and foreign exchange through regular channels, have entered into agreements with enclave companies, which have revenues in foreign exchange but which need kwanzas for their domestic operations. In such agreements, the enclave company will for instance import a car, which is paid for in kwanzas by the government department. The foreign exchange spent on the operation thus does not pass through the central bank and regulations on import licencing and on foreign exchange allocation are circumvented.

C. THE SYSTEM OF ECONOMIC PLANNING

2.14 As mentioned in the preceding section, the system of economic management in Angola is based on central planning. There are four levels of planning: national; sectoral; provincial; and at the level of productive units and some government institutions (for example hospitals, schools, scientific institutions, etc.). No national medium-term plan has ever been prepared. All plans have been annual. In principle, annual plans at the national level must include indicators and programs in the following areas: (i) growth projections of the aggregate social product and disposable national income; (ii) budgets for foreign exchange receipts and expenditures (imports, exports, invisibles, foreign debt, etc.); (iii) an aggregate financial program, including the state budget, credit policy, and foreign debt; (iv) a program of material balances, specifying the supply and planned distribution of essential goods for consumption or use as inputs in productive activity; (v) a program for internal trade; (vi) a program for investments and building activities; (vii) a program for the transportation and communications sectors; (viii) a program for employment and wages; and

(ix) a program for the production of high priority goods and services. In practice, not all of these components of annual plans have been prepared every year.

2.15 In spite of extensive efforts and improvements in recent years, the experience of Angola with the planning system is far from satisfactory. As mentioned above, medium term plans, which should provide the basis for the annual plans, have never been prepared. Annual plans have been incomplete and unrealistic in their targets and in their assumptions concerning implementation capacity. Control of the execution of annual plans has in general been inadequate, and the degree of fulfillment of the planned targets has usually been very low. In many cases, the actual results have corresponded to less than 50 percent of the targets.

2.16 The shortcomings of the planning process in Angola can be attributed to several factors. One important factor is the strong influence of fluctuations in the world oil market on the Angolan economy. Budget revenues and imports of goods for consumption, investment, or for use as inputs or spare parts in productive units are strongly influenced by the level of international oil prices. For example, the annual plan of 1986 had to be completely revised after the drastic fall in the price of oil in 1985-86. In spite of the revision, foreign exchange constraints were far more serious than had been projected and the authorities were not able to avoid drastic reductions in planned targets for industrial production and supplies of consumer goods to the population.

2.17 A second cause of difficulties in the planning process is the shortage of qualified personnel at all levels required to deal with the complex tasks of preparing the plans, as well as implementing, monitoring, and evaluating results. The statistical data required for the preparation of projections and targets for the plans are completely inadequate. Many enterprises do not have appropriate systems of accounting and have no possibility of satisfying the requirements of the planning process. Lack of discipline in the implementation of the plans is an important additional reason for disappointment with the planning process. There are no rewards for the fulfillment of the targets and no penalties for their non-fulfillment. Many important decisions concerning imports, financing, investments, and the allocation of scarce goods made at the level of ministries and enterprises, do not take into account the targets, constraints, and guidelines established in the annual plans.

2.18 The system of planning in Angola has failed to achieve an adequate level of economic efficiency. The system is based on quantitative targets and does not recognize adequately the role of prices in ensuring greater efficiency in the allocation of resources and in assessing the performance of productive units. As a consequence, examples of inefficiency and waste in planned activities are widespread. Productive units have not been encouraged to reduce production costs, to improve the quality of their output, or to produce the mix of goods for which there is the most demand at current prices (except when these goods are diverted to parallel markets). The absence of competition has severely limited pressures for better performance. Importing new machines and vehicles has often been easier than repairing existing ones. The activities of many enterprises have often been interrupted by shortages of spare parts, while at the same time foreign exchange was spent on imports of goods and services which were not significantly contributing to production or the welfare of consumers.

2.19 Central planning has implied that the economy is managed by administrative or bureaucratic controls. The overloading of various parts of the institutional system, which results from extreme centralism in economic decision making, has hindered inter-sectoral coordination and, hence, planning activities. In fact, given the problems described above, bureaucratic controls have certainly been more important than planning. Bureaucratic decisions are often taken on an ad-hoc basis rather than being based on consistent objectives and clear plan guidelines and priorities. An inordinate amount of the time of managers of enterprises is occupied with efforts to negotiate with the ministries in their sectors and with other authorities. The success of an enterprise depends more on the ability of its managers to get favorable decisions from the government than on their efforts to raise operational efficiency through reductions in costs, improvements in the quality of products, expansion of the volume of output, etc. The inability of central authorities to supply foreign exchange, spare parts, raw materials or other inputs is used by many managers as an excuse to release themselves from what would otherwise be their responsibility.

D. THE ALLOCATION OF FOREIGN EXCHANGE

2.20 Given the heavy dependence of the Angolan economy on imports, the allocation of foreign exchange plays a central role in the planning process. The availability of foreign exchange and the methods for its allocation have had a far stronger influence on consumption and production than any other component of the plan. Foreign exchange is allocated administratively on the basis of economic and social priorities (and, reportedly, in some cases, on the basis of pressures from special interest groups). With the exception of some companies (notably the oil and mining sectors), which retain their foreign currency earnings and operate outside of the foreign exchange allocation process, firms that earn foreign currency through exports must turn all of their earnings over to the central bank at the official exchange rate. An enterprise that requires access to foreign exchange for imports must obtain a license from the Ministry of Foreign Trade. Such approval is contingent upon the proposed use of the foreign exchange being in accord with the priorities established in the annual and quaterly foreign exchange budgets. If the license is granted, the enterprise presents the license to the National Bank of Angola (Banco Nacional de Angola (BNA)), along with a draft for the kwanza equivalent of the foreign exchange, and asks that the foreign exchange be released. In periods of severe foreign exchange shortages, such as 1981-82 and 1986-88, enterprises with import licenses have, in many cases, been refused the right to purchase the foreign exchange from BNA, the central bank. Currently, efforts are under way to improve the coordination between the Ministry of Foreign Trade and BNA so as to more closely link the granting of import licenses to the availability of foreign exchange.

2.21 The foreign exchange budget, "Orçamento Cambial", is drawn up annually by the Ministry of Planning with the assistance of the National Bank of Angola, the Ministry of Foreign Trade and the Ministry of Energy and

Petroleum. The foreign exchange planning process has three main steps. The first step is to forecast export earnings, with most of the attention given to the petroleum sector. Forecasts are also made of capital inflows. In the second step, foreign exchange allocations are made for external debt service, costs of oil and diamond exploration, technical assistance, international transport, and embassy operations. In the planning process, these items are referred to as "fixed costs". In the third step, planned merchandise imports are divided into four categories: direct consumption (mainly food imports), intermediate consumption (industrial and agricultural inputs), social consumption (education, health and culture), and state administration. Priorities are established among the categories and import ceilings are set. Currently, high priority sectors are defense, agriculture, and rural commercialization. Within the categories, more specific ceilings are set for particular products which are inputs into strategic goods. While the Ministry of Planning plays the primary role in drawing up the foreign exchange budget, its implementation is the responsibility of the central bank. In fulfilling this role, the central bank establishes allocations of foreign exchange for each quarter and receives monthly reports from the ministries regarding foreign exchange expenditures.

2.22 As discussed throughout this report, Angola's system of foreign exchange allocation severely taxes its administrative capabilities, results in substantial inefficiencies, and creates significant income inequities. A centralized non-market allocation of foreign exchange requires a heavy commitment of skilled administrators at all levels to provide and analyze information necessary to prioritize foreign exchange demands. Angola, with its severe shortages of skilled personnel, does not have the capacity to carry out this task, and scarce foreign exchange is often allocated inefficiently. Consequently, examples abound of potentially highly productive projects that are incapacitated for lack of foreign exchange while, at the same time, apparently low priority activities receive substantial allocations. In addition, workers with similar skill levels receive vastly different incomes as a consequence of differences in their access to foreign exchange.

E. PRICE POLICIES

2.23 Practically all prices of goods and services in the official market have been controlled by the government. The policy of controlled prices is administered by the National Planning Office (Direcção Nacional de Preços), a department of the Ministry of Planning. The Ministry of Finance and the sectoral Ministries are also often involved in price control decisions. Prices of several products (the so-called regional products) have been fixed or controlled at the regional level by the Regional Commissariats. The responsibility for monitoring and supervising controlled prices belongs to the Office for Inspection of Economic Activities (Direcção Nacional de Inspecção e Investigação das Actividades Económicas), a department of the Ministry of the Interior.

2.24 Angolan price control policy has been divided into four regimes (following Decrees 17/84 and 18/84). The fixed price regime has been applied to the most essential goods and services, including a certain number of food products, soap, clothing, footwear, housing rents, water and electricity, oil products, cement, tobacco, sisal and cotton. These prices have been fixed at the national level and are uniform for all the regions. They have been approved by the Council of Ministers on the basis of proposals of the Ministry of Planning. In principle, the distribution of products with fixed prices has been based on the annual plan and on administrative decisions which specify the amounts, origins, and uses of such products.

2.25 The controlled price regime has covered a large number of agricultural products, raw materials, and services which are considered important but which are not subject to fixed prices. Most controlled prices specify either minimum or maximum prices. Prices in this regime have been set by decisions of the Ministers of Planning, Finance, and of the sectoral ministry involved. The two remaining regimes are a fixed commercial margin regime and a declared price regime. In the former, prices are set through specification of mark-up margins. The margins take into consideration the costs of transportation and commercial distribution. This regime has been applied to a wide variety of products. In the declared price regime, prices of goods and services must be announced in advance to the appropriate ministry and they must be approved by that ministry. This system has been applied to all products and services not included in the other regimes.

2.26 In principle, prices of individual goods and services should be influenced by a transaction tax (imposto de circulação) and by production subsidies. According to intentions originally announced by the authorities, transaction tax rates and subsidies should be highly differentiated, in order to ensure: (1) equilibrium between incomes and consumption expenditures of the population; (2) equilibrium between the demand and the supply of specific goods and services; (3) relatively higher prices for less essential goods and subsidized prices for "merit goods" considered of high social priority; and (4) adequate profitability for enterprises involved in production and distribution. However, a generalized and consistent system of transaction taxes in accordance with the basic guidelines of the projected price policy was never introduced. At the same time, the subsidies that have been granted tend to respond more to the financing needs of producing enterprises than to the objectives of a well-defined price policy.

2.27 Price policies have been a major cause of the persistent difficulties in the Angolan economy since independence. Because of generalized controls and rigidities and inefficiencies in their implementation, prices have not been allowed to play a significant role in the allocation of resources and in equating demand with supply. In 1988 the authorities initiated a reform of the price regime in the framework of the SEF, as described in Chapter 5. They announced the intention of increasing most controlled prices and of liberalizing many others. They have already liberalized the prices of a certain number of foodstuffs, a particularly important decision which has already had noticeable positive effects on the agricultural output around Luanda. However, at the beginning of 1989 the controlled prices of a significant number of goods were still the same as 12 years ago. The price adjustments which had taken place until then were very moderate when compared with increases in the nominal purchasing power of the population. A rough indication of the increase in purchasing power of the population is provided by monetary statistics, which show that in the period 1980-85 the amount of currency held by the population increased 160 percent and the stock of M2 rose 180 percent. In that same period, the real supply of goods and services did not increase significantly, and may even have fallen, as suggested by available data on output and imports. In addition, there are no apparent economic reasons (such as increasing interest rates or declining inflationary expectations) to suggest that the velocity of circulation of money would have decreased voluntarily to a significant extent. In such conditions, if prices had not been controlled, they would certainly have risen on average by more than 20 percent per year in the period 1980-85. Table 2.1 shows, however, that this did not happen. During that period, many prices remained unchanged and most of the adjustments which took place were comparatively modest.

Table 2.1: CONTROLLED RETAIL PRICES OF SELECTED GOODS AND SERVICES (kwanzas)

	1980	1985
Bread (Kg)	17.00	17.00
Maize (Kg)	13.50	13.50
Rice (Kg)	21.00	35.00
Potatoes (Kg)	27.50	27.50
Beans (Kg)	40.60	45.00
Pasta (Kg)	29.00	31.00
Cassava (Kg)	9.50	15.00
Fresh fish (Kg)	28.00	30.00
Dried fish (Kg)	34.50	50.00
Beef (Kg)	90.00	90.00
Chicken (Kg)	85.00	110.00
Edible oils (L)	42.00	65.00
Margarine (Kg)	100.00	116.00
Coffee (Kg)	115.00	295.00
Salt (Kg)	3.00	3.00
Sugar (Kg)	22.00	22.00
Biscuits (Kg)	370.00	425.00
Banana (Kg)	7.00	13.50
Beer (1)	40.00	50.00
Soft drinks (1)	27.00	40.00
Tobacco (Kg)	396.00	646.00
Soap (Kg)	28.00	37.00
Matches (box)	1.50	5.00
Textile cloth (m2)	200.00	250.00
Blankets (each)	616.00	1,130.00
Towels (each)	267.00	275.00
Leather shoes (pair)	1,000.00	1,050.00
Radios (each)	644.00	950.00
TV sets (each)	25,000.00	25,000.00
Cement (50Kg)	60.00	120.00
Hoes (each)	50.00	50.00
Bicycles (each)	5,000.00	5,000.00
Kerosene (1)	4.00	4.30
Butane gas (12Kg)	161.00	180.00
Gasoline (L)	12.50	25.00

2.28 Relative prices have also been severely distorted. The product mix of the supplies available in the retail shops does not correspond to the structure of consumer preferences at official prices. The price distortions artificially stimulate consumption of goods with lower relative prices. Thus, for instance, there has been an artificial stimulus to the consumption of gasoline and other oil products which are in ample supply and have prices that are negligible when compared with prices in parallel markets for goods like sugar, soap, etc. The welfare of consumers would improve if the price of gasoline were increased and if consequent reductions in gasoline consumption were used to increase exports of oil products. The resulting increase in foreign exchange earnings would permit an increase in imports of soap, sugar, etc. The production of goods with artificially low relative prices is also discouraged. For example, private producers have not been interested in selling coffee at official prices because these are too low. In addition, there is no significant possibility of selling coffee in the parallel market. Since parallel market prices for cassava are more attractive than the official prices for coffee, peasant farmers have uprooted coffee trees in order to plant cassava. This choice is rational, given the alternatives open to such farmers. However, both farmers and consumers would benefit substantially if the domestic relative price of coffee in relation to cassava (and other goods) were closer to the ratio of the international prices for those products.

2.29 The artificial stability imposed by price controls and the rapid increase in cash balances held by consumers led to large and increasing gaps between the supply and demand of practically all goods and services in the official market. Thus, severe rationing of most essential goods had to be introduced. Rationed goods are often sold only once a month to each worker. The amounts of rationed goods sold to the holders of rationing cards vary from month to month, depending on the availability of supplies. Those amounts are always very small in relation to demand. In some months there is no supply at all of specific rationed goods. Goods which are not rationed are available only sporadically in retail shops, or are not available at all, which is more often the case. In 1987, the average worker in Luanda, without access to special shops, was unable to spend more than 5 to 10% of his salary in purchases of goods and services sold at official prices.

2.30 The widespread scarcities of practically all goods and services have produced several types of responses. For example, the authorities have created special shops for senior personnel with responsibilities in the political structure, in public administration, and in enterprise management. There are far greater possibilities of obtaining consumer goods at official prices in those special shops than in the shops which serve the rest of the population (lojas do povo). There are, however, limits to the monthly expenditure of each beneficiary in the special shops, depending on his level in the hierarchy. Moreover, the product mix available in the special shops does not usually correspond to the structure of demand. Consumers with access to these shops tend to purchase whatever goods are in sufficient supply at official prices and later trade them in the parallel market for products which they need but which are scarce in the official market.

2.31 The foreign enclave companies (in the oil sector, in construction works, etc.) and other foreign institutions have also created special shops for their workers. In those shops, there is a comparatively diversified supply of imported consumer goods at official prices. There is also a special shop which sells exclusively imported goods against foreign exchange. No questions are asked about the origin of the foreign exchange used in these shops. A large proportion of the goods purchased in the foreign exchange shop is channelled to the parallel market (especially beer, which to a large extent plays the role of a parallel currency).

2.32 In productive enterprises, especially those in the manufacturing sector, each worker benefits from the opportunity to buy a certain quantity of the products of such enterprises at official prices. This practice, which is designated as self-consumption (auto-consumo), applies not only to consumer goods (beer, tobacco, food items, shoes, etc.) but also to construction materials and other intermediate goods (cement, paints, etc.). The enterprises producing goods which cannot be sold easily in the parallel market (for instance steel rods), have replaced the "self-consumption" of their own products by the creation of special shops of the type described above. A large proportion of the goods purchased as self-consumption are exchanged in barter transactions or sold in the parallel market, in order to purchase other types of scarce goods.

2.33 In response to goods shortages in official shops, some public enterprises have established barter agreements among themselves in order to improve and diversify the supply of consumer goods to their workers or, more rarely, to avoid production bottlenecks caused by difficulties in getting scarce inputs. Some Ministries, enterprises, and other organizations have established not only special retail shops, but also their own farms and special fleets of buses to serve their employees exclusively. They have created special repair shops for their cars and are often directly engaged in the importation of the spare parts and components which they need. Finally, the parallel markets, which are analyzed in a separate section of the present chapter, play an important role in supplying scarce goods, although at very high prices.

2.34 It should be noted that regional authorities and sectoral ministries have not always complied with legislation on controlled prices. In some provinces, the controlled prices actually in force for certain goods and services are different from the prices fixed by the Council of Ministers for the entire country. Thus for instance, in the Southern provinces, the prices in official retail shops are sometimes more than double official prices. Another example of a lack of compliance with price legislation is provided by a decision taken in 1987 by the Ministry of Transportation to increase road transportation charges for merchandise, in complete disregard of the provisions of decree 17/84.

2.35 Three final points should be made concerning official price controls. First, the agencies and ministries with responsibilities in the area of price controls are not equipped with the information and technical capabilities which they would need to play their role satisfactorily. Moreover, the coordination of the activities of the different ministries and agencies that oversee and establish price controls are far from adequate.

Secondly, agricultural prices are especially distorted. For example, prices of agricultural products are not adjusted for seasonal fluctuations in supply. In addition, in Lubango, the same price of 100 Kz per kg was in force in December 1987 for all agricultural products sold in municipal markets, despite the fact that such products have different production costs, face different levels of consumer demand, and are subject to different fixed prices in the State shops. Finally, the system of controlled prices and administered distribution of goods means that there is no competition among enterprises operating in the official market. The commercial margins fixed officially by the authorities are often very wide. Those margins, combined with the absence of competition, are a cause of inefficiency and unwarranted distortions in income distribution.

F. THE TRADE SECTOR

2.36 Both foreign and domestic trade are strictly regulated by the authorities. The exclusive reliance of the foreign trade system on administered mechanisms of licensing and allocation of foreign exchange and the unsatisfactory performance of the foreign trade enterprises have been major causes of inefficiencies and disruptions in the productive sector and in the supply of consumer goods to the population. Shortcomings in the network of internal trade have also been a source of serious economic difficulties.

2.37 In 1976, the authorities established a state monopoly on foreign trade. Initially, almost all imports and exports were handled through a few state enterprises, most of which specialized in certain products. Some enterprises fully or partially owned by the private sector were also engaged in foreign trade but they accounted for minor shares of total imports and exports. In view of the inefficiency of some of the public enterprises involved in foreign trade, the Government was forced to introduce more flexibility in the organization of imports and exports. A large number of enterprises were allowed to import, and several private enterprises are now directly engaged in import activities. However, there is still no significant competition in the foreign trade sector.

2.38 All imports and exports are subject to licenses. The import licenses are issued by the Ministry of Foreign Trade on the basis of ceilings established for different sectoral units and enterprises, in accordance with the foreign exchange budget included in the national plan and the priorities given to different categories of products. Due to insufficient coordination between the Ministry of Foreign Trade and the central bank, the enterprises having an import license have not always been automatically entitled to the allocation of corresponding amounts of foreign exchange.

2.39 The network of internal trade is based essentially on state enterprises. Most of the goods, imported or produced domestically, are supplied and transported to wholesalers through two centralized national distributors: one for foodstuffs (EDINBA) and another for industrial goods (EDINBI). Wholesale trade is concentrated basically in three enterprises: one for foodstuffs (EGROSBAL), another for industrial products (EGROSBIND), and another for other goods (EGROMISTA). A large proportion of the retail outlets are integrated in four state enterprises (EREMISTA, EREBIMO, ENCODIPA and DINAPROPE). The wholesale and the retail enterprises have subsidiaries at the provincial level. There are also other categories of state shops, including shops specializing in a particular product (for instance bread or fish), or focusing on a particular consumer group (for instance, personnel of the upper echelons of the party and public administration). Municipal markets and private traders also play a significant role. According to the National Register of Enterprises, in 1984 the internal trade sector included 50 private commercial enterprises, employing 3,800 workers, as compared with 48 public enterprises, employing about 20,000 workers. There are, however, many enterprises in the trade sector which are not included in that register.

2.40 Commercial enterprises operate either on the basis of fixed prices or margins fixed by government regulations. These margins, the specialization of enterprises, and the severe scarcity of practically all goods exclude any form of competition. Private traders do not compete with public enterprises or with each other because the range of their activities is regulated by the government and because they are severely constrained in their opportunities to obtain more merchandise. Complaints concerning difficulties created in the economy by inefficiencies in the commercial sector are widespread. That sector is often blamed for scarcities of goods which are not its fault. However, since there is practically no competition, it is probably true that in many cases the operating costs of commercial enterprises are excessive, that the enterprises do not respond to the requirements of their clients, and that their contribution to domestic production is far from satisfactory.

2.41 Agricultural production has been particularly affected by shortcomings in the trade system. During the colonial period, bush traders played an important role in stimulating peasant farmers to produce more, by seeking to exchange agricultural products for the industrial goods needed in rural areas. The disappearance of the bush traders after independence has been a major cause of the drastic decline in marketed agricultural production. A few years ago, the authorities tried to revive that production by introducing a special program of commerce in the rural areas. That program gave high priority to supplying the countryside with goods which are of particular interest to farmers. These goods were sold at official prices against the delivery of agricultural products, also at official prices. However, implementation of the program has been disappointing. In many cases it was not possible to achieve half of the established targets. In view of the inefficiency of state trading enterprises, private traders were called upon to participate in the program. However, their activities have been comparatively limited, not only because there are so few of them, but also because the allocation of industrial goods for exchange is decided administratively and is far from adequate.

G. THE FINANCIAL SYSTEM

2.42 The financial system consists of two banks which have branches across the country. The most important bank is the Banco Nacional de Angola (BNA) which serves as the country's central bank and until very recently, as the only commercial bank. It is also the sole legal holder of foreign exchange and all official foreign exchange transactions pass through it. The other bank, the Banco Popular de Angola (BPA) was until very recently simply a deposit taking bank whose assets were deposits in BNA. Since BPA did not make loans, it did not play a role in the determination of the money supply. As part of the SEF reforms, BPA has been authorized to make short term loans to small enterprises. However, these loans, in total, are not to exceed 20 percent of its demand deposits. Thus, BNA will continue to be by far the most important bank.

2.43 Prior to the SEF, BNA was the only source of domestic credit and as discussed above, it continues to be the only source of credit for most enterprises. The vast majority of its loans are to the government and state enterprises. BNA credit has been provided to the government whenever government expenditures exceed receipts. This credit is for an indefinite period. BNA loans to enterprises are almost exclusively short-term: up to 180 days to finance acquisition of commercial goods and up to 30 days to finance wage payments. By law, BNA can make longer term loans to enterprises, but in practice it does not. However, in the case of some high priority enterprises, such as the Benguela railroad, exceptions have been made to this rule and credit has been provided for extended periods. Medium- and long-term investment projects have been financed by government appropriations.

2.44 Within the BNA, decision making on loans to enterprises is decentralized, but provincial branches are restricted to making smaller loans than those which are made at the headquarters in Luanda. Provincial bank credit limits can be extended with the approval of the Governor of BNA. BNA interest rates on its loans to enterprises are set administratively. The current interest rate structure, which has not changed since independence, is broadly based on colonial practices and is as follows:

Up to 180 days	8.5%
180 days to 1 year	9.5%
1 year to 5 years	10.0%
5 years to 10 years	8.0%

2.45 The Government and all enterprises are required to deposit all cash holdings (except petty cash) in BNA. However, it is reported that this requirement has not been strictly enforced for enterprises in recent years. Interest is not paid on deposits, with two exceptions to this rule: cooperatives and agricultural and fishing enterprises receive 1% interest on their deposits, and BPA receives 2 to 3.5% interest on its deposits. All payments between enterprises and the government are made by drafts which are cleared through BNA. Enterprises can make cash withdrawals to pay salaries.

2.46 The Banco Popular takes deposits of individuals and some organizations. Demand deposits pay no interest, but time deposits pay the following interest rates: 6 months to 1 year - 4%; 1 year or more - 6%. To attract deposits, BPA also offers depositors the possibility of winning prizes in well-publicized lotteries. BPA has difficulty in attracting deposits because people are not accustomed to using banks for savings. In addition, people fear that the authorities might ask how they obtained any large deposits. Also, checks cannot be written without visiting the bank to obtain certification of sufficient funds, and interest rates are not attractive.

H. THE STATE ENTERPRISES

2.47 The modern sector of the Angolan economy is dominated by state enterprises. The only significant exception is the oil industry in which foreign private companies play a key role. The departure of the Portuguese at independence deprived numerous enterprises of most of their managers and technical and administrative staff. Inevitably, the operations of many of them virtually came to a standstill. The government stepped in and took over the abandoned firms in an effort to restore production levels and maintain employment. In October 1976, the Central Committee of the MPLA declared that the state would acquire 70% of the equity of all banks. It further legalized the nationalization of enterprises of strategic importance in the economy and of those abandoned by their former owners. The Party made it clear that enterprises of foreign companies, including Portuguese companies, which were willing to work with the government, would not be expropriated. Subsequently, on the basis of policies formulated in October, 1976, the Government nationalized all banks on February 25, 1978, and in April 1978, established a state monopoly in insurance. By mid-1977, more than 85% of enterprises were under state control. However, all non-Portuguese foreign concerns and capital remained untouched. By the end of 1978, the government owned 51% of the oil industry, 100% of sugar processing, textile manufacturing, bicycle and motorcycle manufacturing, paper, pulp and plywood production, the only steel plant in the country, all ship repair and maintenance facilities, all motor vehicle assembly works and 85% of the brewing industry. Since the late 1970s there has been little change in the proportion of economic activity conducted by public enterprises, which is roughly estimated to be about 60% at present.

2.48 In March, 1976, the government issued a decree which assigned operational responsibility for many of the relinquished assets to worker collectives. However, the disruption in production caused by strikes and other conflicts between workers and management proved too harmful to the economy. In 1977, a new law, (17/77), was promulgated stipulating the authority, responsibilities, organizational form and operational characteristics of state owned enterprises (Unidades Económicas Estatais). The implementation of law 17/77 was slow. By 1980, when the first census of companies was undertaken, only 41 enterprises had been converted into state enterprises out of a total of 1,900 registered companies.2/ However, four years later the number of public enterprises had risen to 397. By that time the total number of registered companies had shrunk to 687 as a result of liquidations, mergers and consolidations (See Table 2.2). Thus, by 1984, almost 60 percent of corporate enterprises were state owned and led by government appointed managers. In addition, 18 enterprises were jointly

---

2/ Registered companies include enterprises with 25 or more workers. The total number of firms, including those with less than 25 workers was around 4,000.

owned by the state and private interests. In most of these, the government had a majority stake.

Table 2.2: NUMBERS OF PUBLIC AND PRIVATE ENTERPRISES-1984 (a)

	Public Enterprises	Private Enterprises	Mixed Enterprises	Total
Industry	139	91	11	241
Petroleum	2	10	0	12
Energy	5	3	1	9
Fisheries	21	15	1	37
Construction	24	12	4	40
Agriculture	65	14	0	79
Transportation	64	21	1	86
Internal Commerce	48	50	1	99
External Commerce	9	18	0	27
Other Sectors	24	33	0	57
Total	401	267	19	687

(a) Includes only firms employing 25 or more workers.
Source: Minister of Industry, General Registry of Enterprises, April, 1984

2.49 In terms of the number of employees, public enterprises are considerably larger than those in the private sector. Altogether, they account for three quarters of employment in registered enterprises (Table 2.3).

Table 2.3: SIZE DISTRIBUTION OF PUBLIC, PRIVATE AND MIXED ENTERPRISES

	Percentage of Total number of enterprises		
Number of employees	Public	Private	Mixed
1-49	17.4%	43.6%	5.5%
50-99	12.5%	24.7%	16.7%
100-249	25.3%	21.9%	16.6%
250-499	17.1%	6.2%	16.7%
500-999	14.8%	3.1%	22.2%
1000-2499	9.7%	0.3%	11.1%
2500 and more	3.1%		11.1%
Total	100.0%	100.0%	100.0%

Source: The same as Table 2.2

Nearly 60% of public enterprises employ more than 150 persons, compared to less than 25% of private companies. The average company in the public sector employs 480 people, almost five times as many as the average private firm. It should be noted, however, that the public sector figure may be inflated because of over-staffing. The bulk of employment in public enterprises is in manufacturing, with substantial employment also in 3transport, trade, and agriculture (Table 2.4). Roughly 40% of the state enterprises operate on a national scale.

Table 2.4: EMPLOYMENT IN PUBLIC, PRIVATE AND MIXED ENTERPRISES-1984 (a)
(Thousands of workers)

	Public Enterprises	Private Enterprises	Mixed Enterprises	Total
Industry	52.2	9.7	23.1	85.0
Petroleum	3.2	3.2	-	6.4
Energy	2.5	0.2	0.6	3.3
Fisheries	6.9	1.2	0.2	8.3
Construction	12.0	2.1	2.0	16.1
Agriculture	63.6	3.3	-	66.9
Transportation	26.2	2.3	6.0	34.5
Internal Commerce	20.0	3.8	0.4	24.2
External Commerce	0.5	1.1	0	1.6
Other Sectors	5.7	0.8	0	6.4
Total	192.8	27.7	32.2	252.7

Source: The same as Table 2.2
(a) Includes only firms employing 25 or more workers.

2.50 The Government exercises control over the state enterprises through the technical (or sector) ministries as well as through the Ministries of Planning and Finance. Each state enterprise is directly responsible to a ministry or similar body. A third of all state enterprises are supervised by the Ministry of Industry. The Ministries of Agriculture and of Transport together account for another third (Table 2.5).

Table 2.5: CLASSIFICATION OF PUBLIC ENTERPRISES BY RESPONSIBLE MINISTRY

Ministry/Institution	Number of State Enterprises
Industry	135
Agriculture	65
Transport	65
Internal Commerce	47
Construction	24
Fishing	21
External Commerce	9
MPLA	9
Others	22
Total	397

Source: The same as Table 2.2.

The ministerial assignment does not always coincide with the nature of the activity of a state enterprise. Thus, for instance, many agro-industries report to the Ministry of Agriculture although they are engaged in manufacturing. Virtually every ministry is responsible for one or more state enterprises. In addition, nine state enterprises are supervised by the Party, and one by the Secretariat of the Council of Ministers.

2.51 Under law 17/77, which until recently constituted the basis for the organization, staffing, and operation of state enterprises, enterprises must prepare annual plans and budgets, in which all inputs and outputs are detailed. These should identify capital requirements, foreign exchange needs, the size of the subsidy to cover losses or, if the enterprise is profitable, the amount of the quarterly profit transfer to the Ministry of Finance. The plans and budgets are reviewed by the supervising ministry as well as by the Ministries of Planning and Finance. Regular reports on a company's performance in terms of the approved operational plan are to be submitted to the ministry to which it belongs. The appointment of the chief executive of a state enterprise requires the approval of Party structures. The MPLA is also formally represented on the board of directors, as is the Workers' Union. A new law on state enterprises was issued in 1988, with the basic objective of providing more autonomy to those enterprises and of reducing the interferences by the Government in their management (see Chapter 5).

2.52 In practice, the control of state enterprises by the government is often less strict than is apparent from formal requirements. First, meaningful planning of the operations of state enterprises in an economy that is seriously disrupted by war and suffers from a severe shortage of administrators has not been feasible. Thus, the actual performance of enterprises may differ significantly from what has been planned. The performance reports submitted by the enterprises are often late and incomplete, and their usefulness as an instrument of control is extremely limited. A second factor that introduces a measure of flexibility into the operations of state enterprises is the personal relationships among the small group of Angolan managers, politicians, and administrators which play an important role in the allocation of scarce resources to enterprises and in bypassing the cumbersome decision-making process. Nevertheless, bureaucratic planning mechanisms and the direct interventions by ministries in the operations of state enterprises remain important obstacles to their efficient operation. The performance of these enterprises is closely dependent on administrative decisions concerning the allocation of foreign exchange, prices, financing, wages, labor relations, etc. With such widespread administrative interference, it is impossible to evaluate the managers of the public enterprises and to make them accountable for the results achieved.

2.53 The efficiency and profitability of public enterprises have been highly unsatisfactory. It is extremely difficult to assess the performance of these enterprises in view of the heavy distortions produced by the unrealistic exchange rate, controlled prices, labor regulations and also by such factors as the disruptive effect of the war and the unequal impact of protection provided by import restrictions. An analysis of the financial performance of state enterprises is also hindered by the fact that many do not produce financial statements and balance sheets, and those that do, generally produce documents that are unreliable due to poor accounting standards.

2.54 Financial flows between the government budget and the state enterprises nevertheless provide some useful information about the operating results of these enterprises. As the Government covers the losses of state enterprises and, at least until 1986, the profits of state enterprises had to be transferred to the state, government accounts should reflect the operating results of public enterprises. Table 2.6 shows that over the period 1980-85 the two flows, the profit transfers and the payments to cover state losses (including price subsidies), were roughly equal. Subsidies exceeded profits in the years 1980, 1981, 1984 and 1985, while in the other years the balance was positive.

Table 2.6: FINANCIAL FLOWS BETWEEN GOVERNMENT AND PUBLIC ENTERPRISES, 1980-87 (Kz billion)

	1980	1981	1982	1983	1984	1985	1986	1987*
Profit Transfers	7.86	8.98	9.20	8.49	8.04	10.28	7.49	9.49
Subsidies	8.25	9.18	8.67	8.44	9.50	14.14	6.03	4.00
losses	8.25	8.25	8.26	7.79	9.23	11.57	5.11	..
working capital		0.67	0.30	0.12	0.14	1.84	0.15	..
price subs.		0.27	0.11	0.52	0.12	0.72	0.77	..
Depreciation	1.72	1.73	1.83	1.65	1.86	1.89	1.88	..
Investment	18.12	34.17	17.67	9.48	12.47	9.33	7.69	13.00

* (budget)
Source: Ministry of Finance

However, table 2.6 presents too favorable a picture of the financial performance of the state enterprises for a number of reasons: (i) the profits are gross profits, i.e., no tax has been paid on them; (ii) the losses are larger than indicated by the budgetary subsidies, as they have been partly financed by other means, such as non-payment of suppliers; (iii) profits that exist on paper may reflect claims that are unlikely to be paid and provisions for bad debt are inadequate; (iv) profits are not always genuine operating surpluses; and (v) the total profits figure includes a large contribution from the National Lotteries.

2.55 While it is estimated that about half the state enterprises report a profit, the conclusion from the above discussion must be that, taken together, the public enterprise sector probably generates a net loss. Thus, that sector requires resource transfers to cover its net losses as well as to finance its capital expenditures. The latter are in part covered by depreciation, 70% of which had to be transferred, until recently to the Government.

2.56 Access of the state enterprises to sources of finance other than the government has been extremely restricted. BNA provides only a limited amount of short term credit. Some enterprises do receive external credit directly, via BNA, though in principle this should pass through the budget. The extent of this extra budgetary funding is not known. Table 2.6 shows the extent of budgetary financing of the investment of state enterprises-all in the form of capital grants--as well as depreciation transfers by enterprises.

2.57 Substantial amounts are owed by the state enterprises to each other and to the government, as well as by the government to those enterprises. Though details on these debts are not available, a sectoral breakdown of the total amount owed indicates that the principal enterprises with net claims outstanding are engaged in external trade, energy and petroleum, and industry (Table 2.7). Agricultural enterprises are large debtors, as are the state enterprises engaged in internal trade, though the latter also have large claims outstanding. Table 2.7 shows also that the public enterprise sector as a whole is a net creditor to the tune of more than Kz 20 billion. Almost all of this is owed by the Government. The Ministry of Defense is the principal debtor among the ministries.

Table 2.7: CLAIMS AND DEBTS OF STATE ENTERPRISE BY SECTOR, END 1986
(Kw billion)

Sector	Owed by UEE	Owed to UEE
Agriculture	8.6	1.4
External Commerce	7.5	14.2
Internal Commerce	15.1	16.8
Energy and petroleum	.6	7.5
Industry	3.3	9.6
Other	6.0	12.0
Total	41.1	61.7

Source: Ministry of Finance

I. PRIVATE ENTERPRISES

2.58 The private sector in the official market consists largely of enterprises which were not nationalized after independence. As shown in Table 2.2, in 1984 there were 267 private enterprises and 19 mixed enterprises, which are joint ventures between the private and public sectors. Those enterprises had 60,000 employees, corresponding to about a quarter of the total labor force in the modern productive sector. More than half of the jobs provided by private and mixed enterprises are found in manufacturing industries. On the basis of the number of employees, the private and mixed enterprises are also comparatively important in the oil sector, in construction, in transportation, and in internal trade (See Tables 2.2 and 2.3).

2.59 Private enterprises have, by and large, been operating under legislation that dates from pre-independence days. Such legislation refers to licensing and registration, to corporate income tax and, for foreign owned enterprises, to profit and capital repatriation. The activity of private enterprises is strictly dependent on government decisions with regard to import licenses, allocations of foreign exchange, supplies of raw materials and other inputs, prices, operating margins, purchases by the public sector, etc. The influence of administrative decisions on the operation of private enterprises means that the autonomy of those enterprises is very limited. They are not subject to the stimulus of market forces or to the constraints of competition. The allocation of foreign exchange and other decisions affecting the private sector depend on the degree of priority accorded to a particular enterprise, and on personal relations between company management and the authorities.

2.60 In spite of the constraints resulting from government interference and regulations, many private enterprises have been profitable, especially because they benefit from comfortable operating margins under the regime of controlled prices. However, several private enterprises have shown significant losses, primarily resulting from a lack of foreign exchange, raw materials, and other inputs. Some enterprises have been kept alive on the basis of expectations that better opportunities will arise in the future.

2.61 Mixed private/public companies were formed immediately after independence in industries where not all shareholders had abandoned a particular company. The abandoned part of the shareholding was taken over by the Government, while the shares of owners who remained were left intact. Often, remaining private shareholders later entered into managerial and technical assistance contracts with their own enterprises. Apparently, the remuneration for these services is accepted by both the managing partners and, tacitly, by the Government, as an indirect means to reward the private shareholders. Actual capital repatriation or dividend remittance abroad has, as far as could be ascertained, not taken place from mixed companies.

2.62 The country has maintained a relatively open policy on cooperation with foreign companies, including major multinationals. The foreign investment law, passed in 1979, permits foreign equity in Angola provided that the country's independence and interests are respected. Foreign firms are under a special obligation to train as many Angolans as possible. Foreign investments are not allowed in defense related industries, banking, insurance, telecommunications, and water supply. These restrictions do not apply to foreign technical assistance (see Chapter 5 on new foreign investment legislation).

2.63 Foreign companies, operating as enclaves, play a central role in the oil industry and, therefore, in the Angolan economy. These companies operate under special regimes or on the basis of joint ventures and production sharing agreements with SONANGOL, the national oil company. Diamond mining companies and the most important hotel in the country also operate as foreign enclaves. Enclave enterprises are free from most government interference and regulation. They especially benefit from their ability to use their foreign exchange revenues to satisfy their import needs (including those of consumer goods for their workers), without being submitted to the normal import licensing process and without having to compete for allocations of foreign exchange from the central bank. Some large foreign contractors in the building industry share this benefit.

J. PARALLEL MARKETS

2.64 Severe shortages of goods and services at official prices have led to the rapid development of parallel markets, in which prices are freely determined by demand and supply. Transactions in the parallel markets escape all government regulations. Technically, these markets are illegal but in fact they are tolerated by the Government. In the past, the authorities took some initiatives to repress these markets by confiscating merchandise, imprisoning traders, and destroying sales stands. However, the effect of such moves on the development of the parallel markets was transitory and not very significant. The markets have grown continuously and are now quite diversified. Most of the traders and producers in the parallel market operate on a very small scale, but some of them have evolved into fairly sophisticated enterprises, with a substantial turnover.

2.65 Parallel markets play an important role in the Angolan economy. They provide most consumers, and even many producers with the only opportunity to obtain goods and services which are not available in the official market. They reduce the gap between aggregate demand and supply, although at much higher prices than in the official markets. They contribute to the welfare of consumers by making it possible to reach a better adjustment between their patterns of consumption and their preferences. They encourage the production of goods and services which would not take place at official prices (for instance, the production of horticultural products by individual peasants around the main cities). Parallel markets are also the source of many services that are difficult to obtain through official markets, such as repairs by skilled workers, transportation in private cars within Luanda (unofficial taxis), and cargo transportation by truck between different regions of the country.

2.66 At present it is possible to find a wide variety of goods and services in the parallel markets, including agricultural products, beverages, fish, manufactured foodstuffs, textiles, clothing, shoes, household appliances, radios, TV sets, watches, construction materials, agricultural instruments, etc. The goods come from different sources: (i) from the production of foodstuffs, handicrafts, and services by individuals or families, which are not channelled to the official market; (ii) from sales of "self consumption" goods obtained by workers in industrial enterprises; (iii) from sales of goods purchased in special shops, in shops of enclave companies or in foreign currency shops; (iv) from contraband; and (v) from sales of goods stolen from enterprises, ports, and some departments of public administration.

2.67 Competition in parallel markets is fairly active. Prices of commonly consumed goods tend to be very similar in the different parallel markets of Luanda. There are, however, large disparities between prices in the parallel markets in different regions of the country. Such disparities, which in several cases exceed the ratio 1:5 and may even reach the ratio 1:10, are explained by regional differences in the balance between demand and supply and by difficulties in the transportation of goods between different regions (due mainly to the war). Thus, foodstuffs tend to be much cheaper in the agricultural region of Lubango than in Luanda, and they tend to be far more expensive in the region of Lunda, which has insufficient agricultural production and which to a large extent must be supplied by air.

2.68 While information on parallel market prices is far from satisfactory, available evidence shows that differences between parallel market prices and the controlled prices in the official market are enormous and have increased continuously in recent years. A rough indication of the difference between official and parallel market prices in Luanda is provided by the data in Table 2.8. It should, however, be stressed that parallel market prices show substantial seasonal fluctuations. Differences between the US dollar exchange rate in the parallel and in the official market provide some indication of the evolution of the gap between parallel and official market prices for many common goods. The official price of the US dollar has been maintained at 29.92 Kz without any change since 1975, but the parallel market price for that currency has increased from about 600 Kz in October 1984, to 1,200 Kz in February 1985, to 1,800 Kz in July 1986, to 2,100 Kz in November 1987, and to 2,500 - 3,000 at the beginning of 1989. Thus, the average ratio between prices in the parallel market and in the official market in Luanda seems to have risen from around 20:1 at the beginning of 1985 to at least 50:1 in November 1987. Interestingly, many parallel market prices have not increased very much from November 1987 to the beginning of 1989 because the authorities substantially increased imports of consumer goods, notwistanding the increase in arrears on external payments.

Table 2.8: PRICES IN OFFICIAL AND PARALLEL MARKETS IN LUANDA
(Kwanzas)

	Official price		Parallel market	
	1985	1987	1985	Nov.87
Egg (one)	5	5	300	500
Beans (1Kg)	45	45	2,000	1,000
Rice (1Kg)	35	35	1,000	1,000
Potatoes (1Kg)	27.5	27.5	1,000	2,000
Maize flour (Kg)	17.5	17.5	1,800	1,000
Beef (1Kg)	90	90	2,500	3,500
Chicken (1Kg)	110	110	2,500	4,000
Beer (1 can)	50	50	1,500	1,500
Powdered milk (1Kg)	90	90	1,600	3,200
Bread (1Kg)	17	17	500	1,000
Cooking oil (1l)	55	55	1,000	2,000

Source: National Price Office and Mission estimates.

2.69 The extreme discrepancies between parallel and official market prices, which go far beyond that found in most other countries with shortages and black markets, create very serious distortions in the Angolan economy: (a) they encourage the diversion of goods from the official to the parallel market, (b) they are a main cause of contraband and of the high incidence of theft in enterprises and other institutions in the productive sector, and (c) they lead to arbitrary differences in the real incomes of the population. The real significance of nominal wages is very limited as compared to access to "self-consumption" goods. For example, because of "self-consumption" benefits, a worker in a brewery receiving a nominal wage of 10,000 Kz a month, has in fact an income four times higher than a skilled worker or technician who earns 35,000 Kz a month but has no access to special shops or to "self-consumption".

K. THE SUBSISTENCE SECTOR

2.70 The subsistence sector involves about two thirds of the Angolan population and it provides a major proportion of agricultural production. Peasants living in the subsistence sector have few contacts with the market, either to sell their products or to buy the goods and services which they need. The relative importance of the subsistence economy has probably grown substantially since independence. This is a result of the departure of bush traders, difficulties of internal transportation, and drastic reductions in the supplies of industrial goods to the countryside. Moreover, the peasant population may have increased with the return to their villages of many workers who lost their jobs on commercial farms and in other enterprises owned by Portuguese settlers. The return of the refugees who emigrated to Zaire during the period of the colonial war may have also increased the proportion of the population living in the subsistence sector. In recent years, however, problems of insecurity in the countryside have exerted an opposite influence. Because of the war situation, many subsistence farmers were forced to leave their villages and to seek refuge in urban areas.

CHAPTER 3

MACROECONOMIC PERFORMANCE

A. CAUSES OF THE ECONOMIC CRISIS SINCE INDEPENDENCE

The Deterioration of the Economic Situation since Independence

3.01 As mentioned in Chapter 1, the economy of Angola was severely disrupted during the transition to independence. The level of output declined sharply in 1975 and 1976. While there was some recovery in the period 1977-81, GDP is estimated to have practically stagnated in subsequent years until 1986 when aggregate output again fell significantly. In spite of the growth of the oil industry, GDP per capita is certainly much lower now than at the end of the colonial period.

3.02 Food production has been insufficient to feed the cities. Oil exports, which account for about 95% of total exports, have been unable to simultaneously finance the war effort and meet the demand for imports of spare parts, equipment, and intermediate and consumer goods. This situation has resulted in high levels of idle capacity in the industrial sector. The transportation system linking the provinces has collapsed, leaving the cities isolated from rural areas. The trade system has to a large extent regressed to one of a barter economy.

3.03 These serious difficulties are largely explained by three factors: (a) the war in which the Government has been involved during the entire post-independence period, against UNITA guerrillas and against repeated South African invasions; (b) disruptions created by the massive exodus of Portuguese settlers during the period of transition to independence; (c) the inadequacy of economic policies and economic management. These difficulties have been partially offset by the rapid growth of the oil sector, but the decline of international oil prices in 1980 deepened the economic crisis.

The Economic Disruptions Created by the War

3.04 The guerrilla war waged by UNITA, which has persisted since independence, is creating serious disruptions in a large proportion of the territory of Angola. Moreover, South Africa, besides providing active support to UNITA, has invaded Angola several times, attacked important economic targets, and has repeatedly occupied large areas in the south of the country.

3.05 The burden imposed on the Angolan economy by the guerrilla war and the South African aggression has been very heavy:

(a) The insecurity in many areas of the country has severely affected production, especially in agriculture. At the end of 1987, it was roughly estimated that only about 20% of the territory was relatively safe from war disruptions;

(b) The war has intimidated foreign technicians, many of whom have been captured, and has forced the exodus of more than 600,000 peasants (according to estimates of the International Red Cross) into the urban areas, where many depend on international relief assistance;

(c) Many important infrastructure facilities and productive units have been destroyed, including bridges, hydroelectric dams and power pylons, railway tracks, mines, manufacturing plants, coffee plantations, etc;

(d) A large proportion of the road and rail transportation network has been disrupted, including in particular the Benguela Railway, which served the hinterland of central Angola and provided an important access route to the sea for Zambia and southern Zaire;

(e) The supply to urban areas of domestic agricultural products from the countryside has been severely affected, forcing a heavy reliance on imported foodstuffs. At the same time, enormous obstacles have been created in the transportation of industrial products to rural areas;

(f) The defence effort has absorbed very large resources and accounts at present for more than 40% of total budgetary expenditures, and for a large proportion of the foreign debt;

(g) A high percentage of the limited supply of technicians and skilled manpower has had to be diverted to the armed forces.

The Consequences of the Exodus of Portuguese Settlers

3.06 During the colonial period, public administration, social and educational services and the productive units in the modern sector of the economy were run almost exclusively by Portuguese settlers. Those settlers, whose number had increased from 173,000 in 1960 to 340,000 in 1975, held practically all skilled jobs and a large proportion of semi-skilled jobs. The level of education of the Angolan population was extremely low. In 1973, 85% of that population was illiterate. The number of students in secondary and higher education accounted for only 1.2% of the school age population (5 to 24 years) and a high proportion of these were white settlers.

3.07 In the transition to independence, during the years 1975 and early 1976, about 300,000 Portuguese settlers fled from Angola. This exodus of practically all technical and administrative personnel, teachers, traders, managers, craftsmen and skilled workers created a situation of chaos in public administration and in the economy generally. Few Angolans had the professional qualifications to run the enterprises which had been abandoned and to fill the skilled and semi-skilled jobs previously held by the Portuguese. Most services and the activity of practically all enterprises were seriously disrupted. This situation explains to a large extent why, in many sectors, the level of economic activity is still much lower than in the years before independence. In spite of the progress made by Angola in developing human resources, there are still huge difficulties in recruiting the skilled people needed. It is estimated that at present 92% of civil servants in central and local government have less than 9 years of schooling. Foreign technical assistance has filled only a small proportion of the need for skilled workers.

Inadequate Economic Policies

3.08 The decline in production, scarcities in the supply of consumer goods and of inputs for industry, and distortions in the distribution of income can be attributed to a significant extent to inefficiencies in economic management and to inadequate economic policies. As explained in Chapter 2, the economy has been run essentially by administrative decisions. The market has not been allowed to play a significant role, and prices have been maintained at artificially low levels. The overvalued exchange rate has implied that all foreign exchange must be rationed and that exports of non-oil products have been severely discouraged. Public and private enterprises have had little autonomy and have depended on government decisions with regard to supplies of essential inputs, prices, and operating margins. The efficiency of public enterprises has been affected by labor indiscipline, overstaffing, lack of responsibility of some managers, and absence of adequate performance incentives. Distortions in relative prices have made economic calculations almost impossible. Low official prices for agricultural goods and the scarcity of supplies of consumer and industrial goods at official prices in the countryside have eliminated almost entirely the willingness of peasant farmers to supply foodstuffs through official markets. The large gap between demand and supply at official prices has led to the rapid development of parallel markets.

The Contribution of the Oil Industry

3.09 Without the contribution of expanding oil production, the economic crisis in Angola would have been far more serious. In 1985 the oil industry contributed about 30% of official GDP, almost 53% of government revenues, and 95% of total export earnings. However, since the petroleum sector is an enclave sector, it is isolated from other sectors of the economy, and its impact on GDP growth is limited by the way in which oil revenues are spent by the Government.

3.10 Given the financial drain imposed by the war (military expenses, etc.) and taking into account the momentum of large-scale spending programs launched in the late 1970s, the Government had no choice but to capture the oil windfalls rather than to give them away (e.g., by reducing taxes). However, the net benefits of the Government expenditure of oil revenues proved disappointingly low, even though the opportunity cost of taxing windfalls was marginal. Most oil earnings were spent for current consumption (including military expenses) or sunk into unprofitable investments. As a consequence, the effect of oil income on medium-term GDP growth was limited.

3.11 On the other hand, oil revenues had a strong short-term impact on the government's fiscal stance and on the balance of payments. In fact, the rise or fall in total government revenues was closely related to changes in tax receipts from the petroleum sector. Since some government expenditures proved inelastic with respect to the fluctuations in oil income, large budget deficits were incurred between 1979 and 1986 (totalling Kz 33 billion) which in turn put a heavy pressure on the country's external current account. In addition, oil revenues have supported the Government policy of real exchange rate appreciation, leading to a squeeze on tradables in favor of non-tradables and, in particular, reinforcing the market isolation of the agricultural sector. This, in turn, has increased the country's dependence on oil for foreign exchange. In this context, it should be noted that the "Dutch disease" effect of the oil windfalls might have been even more pronounced if military spending had not absorbed a considerable share of the export revenues from oil.

3.12 The fact that petroleum windfalls have encouraged the government to maintain public expenditure and domestic absorption at unsustainable levels has contributed to the inflationary pressures exerted by the country's steadily growing money stock. Since the credit overhang caused by a general lack of fiscal and monetary discipline has increasingly fuelled parallel market activities, the oil revenues' "secondary" spending effect let demand spill over into the parallel market and, thus, deepened the sectoral disintegration of the economy.

3.13 In sum, it can be concluded that out of Angola's oil income little was returned to taxpayers or saved for the future. Because of the lack of experience in economic management, the lion's share of the oil windfall was channelled into unprofitable ventures or spent for current consumption (i.e., expenditures for defence and consumption imports). Though the latter expenditure categories may have alleviated the oil revenue's direct impact on the real exchange rate and the relationship between tradables and non-tradables, it was the financial leeway provided by the oil income and the (incorrect) prospect of ever rising oil revenues which made the Government feel quite free from borrowing constraints.

3.14 The large margins of manoeuvre in the expenditure policies of the Government provided by the petroleum boom were severely affected by the declines in oil prices in 1985/86. In the face of such declines, the crisis in the Angolan economy was deepened to a considerable extent. In spite of a 25% increase in the volume of crude oil exports from 1985 to 1986, the value of those exports fell from US$1.90 billion to US$1.15 billion. As a consequence, foreign debt rose substantially and some arrears emerged in external payments. At the same time, the value of imports in dollars had to be cut by about 25%, adversely affecting industrial activity, investment, and supplies of consumer goods.

B. STRUCTURE AND EVOLUTION OF GROSS DOMESTIC PRODUCT

The Growth of GDP

3.15 Aggregate statistical data on the Angolan economy are incomplete and of dubious reliability. National output estimates exclude parallel market activity and are incomplete in their coverage of official markets. In addition, value added and factor income estimates are based only on official prices that bear almost no relationship to market prices. Compounding these shortcomings are the lack of satisfactory comprehensiveness and reliability of the data on public finance, foreign trade, the balance of payments, domestic credit and external debt.

3.16 Changes in real GDP are closely related to oil production. Available information points to a slow recovery in real GDP following the sharp fall in 1975-76. However there was a marked setback in 1981, when real GDP decreased 10%, mainly because oil production fell 15%, and another in 1982, when South Africa and UNITA intensified their attacks and sabotage operations. It was only in 1985 that production again reached the 1980 level. In 1986 GDP increased 6.8% in volume mainly because oil production increased 22%, but GDP expressed in current dollars fell 11%, as a result of depressed international oil prices which fell from US$ 26 a barrel in the previous year to US$12.5. In 1987, the increase of 25% in the volume of oil production and the recovery of oil prices to US$ 17.1 a barrel, resulted in an increase of 14% in GDP measured in current dollars.

3.17 The distribution of value added by sector using 1980 official prices for the period 1980-87 is presented in table 3.1. The paragraphs below summarize the main developments in the various productive sectors since independence. 1/

1/ Chapter 4 provides more detail on sectoral development.

Table 3.1 GDP BY SECTOR, 1980-87
(Kz Billions at 1980 Official Prices)

	1980	1985	1986	1987	Average shares in GDP 1980-87
Agriculture and Fisheries	37.0	32.9	33.1	28.1	21.0
Industry	19.2	13.8	11.5	14.7	9.9
Oil	37.7	54.3	66.1	84.2	30.5
Construction	10.7	8.1	10.3	6.5	4.3
Transport and Communications	5.5	6.7	6.2	6.4	3.9
Commerce	16.8	11.9	10.5	11.1	8.7
Services	34.9	34.0	32.5	34.1	21.7
GDP at Factor Cost	161.8	161.6	170.2	185.0	100.0
GDP at Market Prices	167.6	165.6	176.8	192.1	104.0
GNP	167.0	161.3	172.4	182.9	101.6

Source: Statistical Appendix, Table C.3.

Agriculture and Fisheries

3.18 Agriculture accounts for about 20% of GDP, 15% of which is subsistence farming. Production of most agricultural crops marketed through official channels declined rapidly after independence and, in several cases, reached negligible levels. Thus, by 1987, the output of coffee, a commodity in which Angola had been the fourth largest world producer, had dropped to less than 6% of its pre-independence level. Comparable percentages in other crops were 1% for sisal, 3% for maize, 17% for sugar, 36% for bananas, and less than 1% for cotton and rice. At present, the country is significantly dependent on food imports.

3.19 The state farms and trade enterprises set up to replace the previous system failed to reactivate agricultural production due to constraints in administrative and technical capability, the collapse of the transportation system, and lack of security in rural areas. The later introduction of farmers' associations and cooperatives, the gradual reactivation of private farms, and the creation of a network of rural services were attempts to reorganize the system, but these failed to increase production because the guerrilla war isolated most rural areas from the cities. In addition, the foreign exchange constraint did not allow enough imports of inputs and consumer goods to be traded with farmers as an incentive to produce for the market.

3.20 The contribution of the fisheries sector to value added is modest, about 1% of GDP. This is despite the sector's large potential, especially in the southwestern cold waters of Namibe and in the tropical waters of the Benguela coast. During the period of transition to independence, the modern processing plants were destroyed and the best fishing boats left the country packed with Portuguese refugees. An effort to rehabilitate the sector with external assistance has been plagued by organizational problems.

Mining and Oil

3.21 Although mineral resources are varied and substantial, diamonds constitute the only significant mineral production. While diamond mining was interrupted after independence, marketed production of diamonds recovered rapidly from 333 thousand carats in 1977 to 1,479 thousand carats in 1980, when it reached about two thirds of the output in 1973. It subsequently fell again by about 50% because of the insecurity created by UNITA attacks and growing theft and smuggling. A new strategy adopted in 1986, based on production sharing agreements, has led to a recovery in output. In 1987, production reached 870 thousand carats.

3.22 The enclave oil industry has been an important exception to the general decline in economic activity. The output of crude oil declined from 172,000 barrels per day in 1977 to 130,000 b/d in 1981, but subsequently increased rapidly to 359,000 b/d in 1987. The planned production for 1990 is 450,000 barrels per day.

3.23 The continuous growth of oil production was in part achieved through a successful association of the state enterprise Sonangol with foreign firms. In the rich Cabinda area, which supplies 70% of national oil production, a joint venture system was adopted, while in the new promising offshore areas of Zaire province a system of production sharing prevails. Sonangol is the only concessionary for oil production and has an internal monopoly in the distribution of refined oil products. The State is the sole owner of oil and gas deposits.

The Manufacturing and Construction Sectors

3.24 Value added in the manufacturing sector is less than 10% of GDP. In 1976, in order to overcome the paralysis of production created by the exodus of Portuguese managers and technicians, the Government created state enterprises to run manufacturing firms. However, the limited availability of skills, foreign exchange limitations, inadequate supplies of agricultural inputs, and the lack of a disciplined work force seriously hampered the reactivation of industrial activity. In spite of these obstacles, total manufacturing production at constant prices doubled in the period 1977-83, but has stagnated since. Despite the 1977-83 recovery, output of manufacturing industries corresponds at present to only about two-thirds of the 1973 level.

3.25 Construction expanded in 1985-86 but its value added is less than 5% of GDP. The sector has been unable to meet the large demand for investment in infrastructure, to repair the war damage, and to build a significant number of houses. Most new houses in the rapidly growing urban areas are small and rudimentary, and have been built by their owners with the partial help of workers with some experience in construction. The development of the building industry is constrained by the limited domestic capacity to produce construction materials, but plans exist to double cement production capacity in Luanda.

Services and Transportation

3.26 The tertiary sector accounted for 34% of total value added in 1980-87. The Central and Provincial Governments are the major components of this sector. Value added of public administration accounts for more than one-fifth of GDP and consists mainly of the salaries of the Ministries of Education, Health, Culture, Social Welfare and Defence. Commerce and transportation together account for almost 13% of GDP. This percentage does not include the commercialization margin of oil exports and the value added in the important parallel market activities in commerce and private transportation.

C. GROSS NATIONAL EXPENDITURE

3.27 There are no official estimates of national accounts from the expenditure side. The figures shown in Table 3.2 were based on data provided by the government and on mission estimates. (See an analysis of the Angolan system of national accounts in Annex IV). Total investment was estimated on the basis of available information on imports of capital and transport goods and the value added by the construction sector. Private consumption was derived as a residual.

Table 3.2 EXPENDITURES OF AVAILABLE RESOURCES, 1982-87
(Kz Billions at Current Official Prices)

	1982	1985	1986	1987	Percentage of GDP 1987
Private Consumption	108.5	88.2	97.9	90.3	40.6
Public Consumption	44.1	63.4	66.0	67.2	30.9
Private Investment	26.1	36.7	39.5	35.1	19.8
Public Investment	2.4	2.3	4.7	3.6	1.6
Total domestic expenditure	181.2	190.6	208.1	196.1	88.2
Exports of goods and NFS	67.0	93.7	60.5	100.7	45.3
Imports of goods and NFS	81.3	82.5	72.7	74.5	33.5
GDP at Market Prices	166.9	201.8	195.9	222.3	100.0
Net Income sent Abroad	-5.6	-7.0	-3.6	-10.4	-4.7
GNP	161.3	194.8	192.3	211.8	95.3

Source: Statistical Appendix, Table C.5

3.28 In spite of the data limitations, some trends can be observed in the evolution of consumption expenditures. First, government consumption grew more rapidly than GDP in the period 1982-85. As a result, the share of government consumption in GDP increased from 26% in 1982 to 30% in 1985. At the same time, the share of private consumption fell from 65% to 41%. However, in the following two years, reflecting the adjustment effort, there was practically no increase in government consumption. Increases in private consumption have also been very modest; in real terms private consumption in 1987 was lower than in 1985.

3.29 The level of investment after independence has been very low (about 18% of GDP in the period 1982-87). Moreover, it has been concentrated in the oil industry and was undertaken mostly by the international oil corporations. Until 1980, investments in oil exploration and development were inadequate and, as a result, production fell in the period 1980-82. After 1980, new exploration and production arrangements were established with the international oil companies and, as a result, investments in the sector increased from US$201.6 million in 1980 to US$326.3 million in 1981. Total petroleum sector investments in the period 1981-86 attained US$2,522 million, or an average of US$420 million per year. However, the official

GDP estimates do not include value added under the production sharing agreements, and the corresponding goods and capital flows are not recorded in the balance of payments. These omissions lead to underestimates of the amount of private investment in national expenditures.

3.30 On the basis of available data, public investment spending appears to have been less than 2% of GDP in 1982-87. These expenditures are well behind the needs for infrastructure reconstruction and development. Public investment has been low primarily due to a lack of foreign exchange.

3.31 Exports of goods and non-factor services increased from US$ 1,810 million in 1982 to US$ 2,344 million in 1985 and corresponded to about 43% of GDP over this period. In 1986 however, the sudden collapse in oil prices brought exports of goods and non-factor services to US$ 1,406 million. In 1987, due the recovery of oil prices and a 27% increase in oil production, exports of goods and non-factor services attained the peak level of US$ 2,355 million. Imports of goods and non-factor services have been determined mainly by the availability of foreign exchange provided by oil exports. They averaged US$ 2,044 million in the period 1982-85. However, due to the crisis in international oil prices, imports fell to US$ 1,689 in 1986. In 1987 the increase in exports, combined with an apparently very modest increase in imports of goods and non-factor services, resulted in a substantial improvement in the balance of goods and non-financial services, from a deficit of US$ 283 million in 1986 to a surplus of US$ 612 million in 1987. However, as discussed in paragraph 3.65 below, in view of the very large negative errors and omissions entry for 1987, some skepticism about this turnaround is warranted.

D. EMPLOYMENT AND WAGES

Employment

3.32 A comparison of the 1970 census and the official estimates for 1985, based on the census conducted in 1983 in Luanda and in 1984 in the provinces of Cabinda, Zaire and Namibe, shows an important change in the population structure and labor force. The population of working age (between 14 and 59 years old for men and 14 and 54 years old for women) decreased from 63% of the total population in 1970 to 44% in 1985 and the proportion of the economically active population fell from about 32% to 24%.

3.33 The war induced peasants to migrate to the cities, reducing the labor force in rural areas from 74% of the economically active population in 1970 to an estimated 37% in 1985. Most of the population of the rural areas remains in the subsistence sector. The increase in the urban population forced the Government to absorb the migrants in the public sector and in state enterprises. According to official estimates, employment in industry, commerce, transport and administration increased from about 10% of the economically active population in 1970 to 35% in 1985, in spite of sharp declines in production in all sectors except the oil industry.

3.34 Despite serious weakness in the data on public sector employment, it is estimated that the Government employs about 150,000 workers in civilian activities, of whom 25,000 are in local administration. In addition, there are about 90,000 - 100,000 persons engaged in military and security functions or whose status is not clear.

Table 3.3 ECONOMICALLY ACTIVE POPULATION, 1985

Sector	Thousands of employees	Percentages
Total	2,109	100
Agriculture	756	35.8
Industry	238	11.3
Construction	155	7.3
Services	403	19.1
Non-productive sectors	485	23.0
Unemployed	71	3.5

Source: Statistical Appendix, Table B.1.

3.35 There is also no reliable estimate of the number of salaried workers in the economy. The number of affiliated workers in the official trade union organization UNTA (Uniao Nacional dos Trabalhadores de Angola) in 1985 was 666,000 workers or 32% of the economically active population, of whom 83% were employed in state enterprises, 12% in private enterprises and 5% in mixed enterprises.

Wages

3.36 The general labor law established a uniform salary scale. While this could, in theory, create rigidities in the labor market by not considering differences in economic activities, in practice official wages are only a small part of total remuneration. Real income is mainly determined by access to goods at official prices and by the value of income in kind. Thus, wage differentials are misleading as an indication of differences between categories of workers.

3.37 According to the UNTA statistics (See Tables B.3 and B.4 in the Statistical Appendix), the average monthly salary in 1985 was 9,758 Kz, equivalent to about US$325 at the official exchange rate. Wage differences among professional categories were rather narrow, fluctuating from a minimum of 5,761 Kz for agricultural workers to 18,000 Kz for technicians. In public administration, there are four occupational categories: laborers, with salary scales from 4,500 to 19,800 Kz; administrative workers, with monthly salaries between 5,000 and 15,700 Kz; technicians with salary scales from 10,000 to 35,000 Kz; and directors and managers, earning from 10,000 to 30,000 Kz.

3.38 In 1986, the average wage increased to 12,049 kwanzas for the 410,000 workers' wage bill controlled by the National Bank of Angola (BNA).

The average monthly salary in 1986 is reduced to 11,754 Kz if corrections are made to exclude the high incentives given to the workers in the sectors of wood, manufacturing, and mining. Comparing the UNTA and the BNA samples, the increase in the average wage was about 23% in 1986. The average monthly wage controlled by the BNA increased 20% in 1987, reaching 14,444 Kz.

3.39 The purchasing power of salaries and fringe benefits is very low because the supply of goods at official prices is limited. In November 1987, an average worker was able to spend only about 300 Kz in the official market. Since prices in the parallel market were about 30-50 times official prices, the purchasing power of nominal salaries is extremely low. However, higher level employees have the opportunity to purchase larger quantities of scarce goods at official prices (3,000, 6,000 or 8,000 Kz worth of goods per month according to their position in the hierarchy). Similarly, in order to remedy the low purchasing power of salaries, many state enterprises make payments in kind to their workers (auto-consumo). The exchange in the parallel market of goods received through "auto-consumo" introduces an unequal real wage distribution that does not reflect workers' productivity. "Auto-consumo" consists basically of the gift or the sale at official prices of goods produced by the enterprise. The value of those goods in the parallel market corresponds to several times the official wage. Thus, for instance, workers in the beer factory in Luanda, who are certainly among the greatest beneficiaries of auto-consumo, earn on average a nominal monthly wage of 10,000 Kz, but the parallel market value of the beer which they receive as auto-consumo raised their total earnings to an estimated 140,000 Kz per month in 1988. In such conditions, it is clear that the system of real wage formation precludes economic rationality in the distribution of the available supply of food and other consumer goods.

E. GOVERNMENT FINANCE

Introduction

3.40 The public sector dominates economic activity in Angola. Since independence, a large and growing part of the official economy - nearly two thirds in 1986 - has been financed through the government budget. State controlled enterprises account for an additional large share of GDP. The prominent position of the central government is partly a consequence of the rapid growth of the oil sector as a source of government revenue over the past 15 years. It also reflects the government's wish to control key sectors of the economy. The practice of incorporating the financial results and investment expenditure of public enterprises in the budget further adds to the central role of the government.

3.41 The government's finances since independence have passed through two phases. The first phase extends from independence through 1981. It is characterized by buoyant revenue performance, an even faster growth in expenditure and, at least since 1978, large overall deficits. The second phase, which follows the initial fall in oil prices in 1981 and continues through the present, is marked by large fluctuations in both revenue and expenditure, and continuing deficits.

3.42 These two prominent features of the Government's finances -- rapid growth in resources and subsequent instability - are related to the heavy dependence on revenue from oil and the volatility of the oil price. They have posed special problems for fiscal policy. First, the rapid rise in available resources has put the system for allocating and utilizing these resources under severe strain. Secondly, the revenue instability has made budgetary management difficult, and carries some responsibility for the persistent budgetary deficits. The problems of how to establish a better balance between revenue and expenditures and how to improve the use of resources are the most important fiscal issues to be addressed.

Revenue

3.43 Revenue collection has expanded greatly since independence, largely as a result of the development of oil exploration and events in the world oil market. The increase in revenue took place mainly during the period 1974-81 when total revenue quadrupled. Since 1981 budgetary resources have been marked by considerable instability. Revenue fell by almost a third in 1982, recovered gradually through 1985, but declined again over the next two years. The 1989 budget foresees another improvement in the resource position. Income from oil has been the principal source of revenue. In 1981, taxation of petroleum operations accounted for 61% of total government revenue, and 71% of tax revenue (table 3.5). The dependence is even stronger when the indirect effect of oil sector activity on tax revenues is taken into account. Oil exports determine the level of imports. Consequently they determine not only the revenue from import taxes, but also the level of economic activity and thus the revenues from direct and indirect taxes in general. Given this dependence on oil, revenue fluctuations are largely explained by changes in Angola's oil production and in world oil prices.

Table 3.4 SUMMARY OF GOVERNMENT FINANCE 1985-89
(Kz billion)

	1985	1986	1987	1988 (Budget)	1989 (Budget)
Revenue	78.5	71.2	64.4	89.5	78.1
Taxes on petroleum	41.7	30.1	35.8	35.8	41.5
Other taxes	24.5	21.7	18.9		23.2
-on income & property	(14.9)	(12.0)	(10.3)		(9.0)
-on domestic goods and services	(5.6)	(5.0)	(5.1)		(7.4)
-on international trade	(4.0)	(4.7)	(3.4)		(6.8)
Non Tax Revenue	12.4	19.5	9.7	26.4	13.4
Total Expenditure	90.5	86.2	87.4	106.0	112.7
Recurrent expenditure	81.2	75.7	76.4	87.8	92.6
Capital expenditure	9.3	10.5	11.0	18.2	20.1
Overall budget deficit	12.0	15.0	23.0	16.5	34.6
Statistical discrepancy	-9.2	7.3	-4.0	-	-
Financing	2.8	22.3	19.0	16.5	34.6
Domestic: BNA (net)	2.8	22.3	19.0	14.0	24.1
non-bank	-	-	-	-	5.0
External: loans	n/a	n/a	n/a		3.0
grants	-	-	-	2.5	2.5

Source: Ministry of Finance: Reports on the Execution of the Budget

3.44 The performance of non-oil taxes during the 1980s has been poor. In 1987, they were only slightly above the level in 1980, implying a substantial decline in real terms. Of the three main types of non-oil taxes, those on domestic production and consumption have performed better than those on income and on international trade (table 3.5). The principal revenue components are discussed in more detail in Annex VI.

3.45 The ratio of non-oil taxes to non-oil GDP in Angola averaged 10% during 1985-87, compared to an average ratio of 17% for lower-middle income countries.2/ The comparison is even less favorable for Angola when allowance is made for the effect on the ratio of distortions in the

2/ World Development Report, 1987.

economy.3/ The low tax/GDP ratio indicates that due to the large contribution of the oil sector to revenue, the cost of government expenditure to the Angolan taxpayer is relatively modest (details on the tax system are included in Annex VI).

Table 3.5 GOVERNMENT REVENUE - 1981 and 1987
(Percentages)

	1981	1987
Taxes on petroleum	61	56
Other taxes	25	29
- on income	(15)	(16)
- on domestic goods	5	8
- on international trade	4	5
Non-tax revenue	14	15
Total	100	100

Source: Statistical Appendix, Table D.2.

Recurrent Expenditure

3.46 Government administration is highly centralized in Angola. The budget covers not only expenditure by the central government but also spending by provincial authorities and, in part, by public enterprises. On the other hand, some government outlays are not included in the budget but should be, such as expenditure financed through external grants. Moreover, it appears that in several years a significant amount of public spending, including some investments, military expenditure, and interest on the external debt, were undertaken without budgetary authorization.

3.47 Recurrent expenditure grew rapidly after independence, and in 1980 amounted to five times the pre-independence level. Despite the subsequent revenue instability, current expenditure maintained an upward trend during the 1980s, notably from 1983 to 1985. It has tended to increase when revenues improved, and to remain stable in years when revenue declined. However, this trend in spending masks important changes in its composition. There has been a major shift towards expenditure on defence and internal security since 1980, in particular from 1982 to 1985. As a result, military outlays doubled between 1980 and 1985, and in 1987 defence accounted for 48%

3/ GDP is understated as it does not include a major part of the substantial parallel market activity; transfers to government of the entire non-oil public enterprise profits have been included in non-oil taxes.

of total recurrent expenditure. Given the overall budgetary constraint imposed by the revenue position, this increase was achieved at the expense of nonmilitary expenditures. While fluctuating considerably, these expenditures had in 1987 dropped below their level in 1980. Real spending for civilian purposes has thus suffered a sharp decline over the years.

3.48 Expenditure on personnel accounts for the bulk of the recurrent budget. Salaries and other personnel related expenditure absorbed 66% of recurrent spending in 1987 (table 3.6). This includes the cost of military personnel. The personnel cost is equally high in the civilian sector, reaching an estimated 64% in 1986, up from 43% in 1981. The rise in the wage bill appears to have accelerated in recent years. In the absence of data on civil service employment and pay it is hard to identify the factors contributing to this increase. A general salary increase was granted in 1986 and a job evaluation exercise was started in the same year. The latter is gradually being implemented, and its impact on the budget will be spread over several years. The government is aware of the inflexibility which the large civil service wage bill imposes in terms of budgetary management. It is undertaking a survey of the civil service in order to improve its control over personnel expenditure.

Table 3.6 ECONOMIC CLASSIFICATION OF RECURRENT EXPENDITURE IN 1987

	(Percentages)
Personnel	66
of which: salaries and benefits	(62)
other costs	(4)
Goods and services	17
Subsidies	7
Transfers	5
of which: interest on ext.debt	(-)
Other expenditures	5
Total	100

Source: Ministry of Finance: Report on the Execution of the Budget, 1987.

3.49 Until 1986, subsidies to public enterprises absorbed around 25% of the non-defence recurrent budget (30% in 1985). While these subsidies comprised mainly payments to cover operating losses, they also included specific price subsidies and provisions for working capital. Between 40% and 50% of the subsidies were in support of agricultural enterprises. With effect from 1986, public enterprises were required to be financially more autonomous. Budgetary transfers were to be restricted to cases where losses are war related or are due to specific social functions which the enterprises are expected to perform. As a result, subsidies dropped to 14% of non-defence spending in 1986 and 1987, and are down to 8% in the 1989 budget. While some enterprises were allowed greater flexibility to set higher prices for their products, others seem to have reduced their losses through increased parallel market operations, or were forced to finance them by not paying their suppliers and, in some instances, their employees.

3.50 A budgetary provision for payment of interest on external debt was made in some years, but only once, in 1986, was such a payment actually made by the Ministry of Finance. Interest payments in other years were made by the central bank (BNA) which is responsible for servicing the external debt. However, these payments were never recorded as budgetary expenditure and should account for part of the extra budgetary expenditure by BNA. No interest has ever been paid by the government on its domestic borrowing from BNA.

Capital Expenditure

3.51 The budget distinguishes between two kinds of capital expenditure: investment undertaken by public enterprises (so-called productive investment) and investment under the direct responsibility of ministries. The latter have been of minor importance until 1986. Public enterprise investment has relied almost entirely on the government for its financing as little bank credit is available for this purpose, and until 1986 obligatory transfer to the State of 90% of profits and 70% of depreciation left enterprises practically without financial resources.4/ Actual investment expenditure differs substantially from budgetary provisions due to the lack of coordination between the institutions responsible for preparing the investment budget (BNA and the Ministries of Planning and Finance). The size and composition of the public investment program is to a large extent determined by BNA which plays a key role in the allocation of foreign exchange for investment projects.

3.52 Capital expenditure grew rapidly after 1975: from Kz 2 billion before independence to Kz 34 billion in 1981. In the wake of the 1981 fall in oil prices, severe cuts were made in the investment program, primarily because of the foreign exchange constraint. As a result, budgetary expenditures on "productive" investment dropped sharply between 1981 and 1987, from Kz 34 billion to less than Kz 7.4 billion in nominal terms. In 1987, capital expenditures represented less than 10% of total government outlays. The decline in public investment is probably less drastic when extra-budgetary expenditures are taken into account. Thus, for instance, much of the expenditure on the Capanda dam is not included in the budget. Also, the lower figures for 1986 and 1987 may in part be due to changes in regulations governing financial relationships between public enterprises and the government. As a result of these measures, a larger part of the investments of public enterprises may have been financed by the enterprises themselves. Apart from a broad sectoral composition of public investment (Table D.4 in the Statistical Appendix) few details on actual investment expenditure are available.

4/ Exceptions include Sonangol, Endiama and a hotel, which have been given special status.

Fiscal policy and inflation

3.53 The overall budget has consistently been in deficit since 1978, the first post-independence year for which data are available. The deficit has persisted even in years when revenue was buoyant, as in 1981 and 1984. In recent years, the overall deficit has increased and reached 7% of GDP in 1987, up from 3.5% in 1984. The current account balance is also negative. Since 1985, revenue has been insufficient to cover recurrent expenditure, with the gap rising to 4% of GDP in 1987.

3.54 There are substantial discrepancies between BNA data on net credit to the government and the official deficit as presented by the Ministry of Finance. While these may in part be due to different accounting practices, they could also be explained by extra-budgetary expenditures. As mentioned earlier these might include certain investments, some military expenditures, and the servicing of the external debt. Such expenditure could in particular explain the item "other credit to government" in the BNA's accounts (as distinct from "budgetary financing"), which in 1987 amounted to Kz 22 billion. This would imply a much larger budget deficit than shown in the Ministry of Finance accounts.

3.55 Government borrowing from BNA to finance the budget deficit has been the principal source of growth of the money supply, and thus a major contributory factor to inflationary pressure and the expansion of parallel markets. Advances from BNA are under present procedures the only source of deficit financing. However, they include drawings on external loans which the BNA, as manager and administrator of Angola's external debt, channels to the budget, but which are not distinguished from domestic financing, and at present cannot be quantified. An analysis of the inflationary impact of the budget would require an improvement in the accounting procedures relating to budgetary financing. The 1989 budget, for the first time, identifies separately both BNA and non-bank domestic borrowings as well as external borrowing.

Planning, Budgeting and Control of Expenditure

3.56 Development of the budgetary system has not kept pace with the rapid growth in government spending. The present institutional structure and responsibilities, budgetary procedures and available accounting skills are not adequate for the formulation and implementation of a large and complex budget. As a result, serious deficiencies are apparent in the planning and preparation of the budget as well as in the monitoring and control of expenditure.

3.57 Financial planning. There is no satisfactory financial plan for the public sector which on an annual basis analyses resource availability, expenditure options and borrowing needs, and provides a framework for the budget. The budget is also not well integrated into the overall planning exercise. Particularly weak aspects are its links with the preparation and execution of the foreign exchange budget, and the preparation of the public investment program, which does not adequately relate to other budgetary aggregates. Financial planning is particularly important in a country like Angola where large swings in resources occur from year to year.

3.58 Budget preparation is seriously hindered by a lack of information. Because of the delays in the preparation of accounts, there is no feedback into the budgeting exercise of data on actual expenditure in the past year. Basic information necessary for budget formulation is often not available. Thus for instance estimates of the civil service wage bill are made without knowledge of the size and structure of government employment. The public investment program is drawn up on the basis of generally badly prepared proposals by the various ministries, at times no more than project ideas, which are rarely supported by proper feasibility studies. There is no capability to appraise projects, either in the Ministry of Planning or at the sector level, nor are uniform selection criteria used for inclusion of projects in the budget.

3.59 Monitoring and control. Maintaining financial discipline and monitoring expenditures has been difficult in the face of a shortage of accounting skills, inadequate expenditure and reporting procedures and poor coordination between agencies. Ministries currently do not need expenditure authorization before making specific commitments. The system of quarterly expenditure ceilings by ministry does not lend itself to effective control, in particular when accounts are delayed. The lack of control is most serious with respect to investment expenditure. When there are no realistic cost estimates and expenditure targets, as in the case of many projects, no control is possible. The situation is exacerbated by the apparently different priorities of the Ministry of Planning and BNA regarding implementation of the investment program.

3.60 The Ministry of Finance does not have a Treasury department, but plans for its establishment are well advanced. It will consist of three divisions: treasury operations, external finance and relations with public enterprises. This should constitute a major step towards improved control over expenditure.

F. MONETARY POLICY

3.61 The National Bank of Angola maintains a fixed exchange rate and finances government budget deficits, which severely limits discretionary monetary policy. As indicated in the lower half of Table 3.7, the annual growth rate of the money supply (M2) has been erratic, which is explained by large year to year fluctuations in net foreign assets and domestic credit. The data show that net credit to the government consistently contributed to the growth of the money supply while credit provided to other sectors has contracted in recent years. However, the contraction in non-government credit was insufficient to offset the expansion of government credit, and net domestic credit growth averaged about 15% annually over the past five years.

3.62 While there are not reliable data available to calculate growth rates of narrow and broad measures of the money supply (M1 and M2) prior to 1984, the data in Table E.3 of the Statistical Appendix show that the growth rate of currency in circulation averaged about 23% annually from 1977 to 1988. From 1983 through 1988, currency in circulation averaged a 19% annual growth rate, the narrow measure of the money stock (M1) grew at an average annual rate of 16%, and the broad measure of the money stock (M2) averaged an annual growth rate of 17%. With prices fixed in official markets and supplies limited, this growth of the money stock has fuelled inflation in the parallel market and created extremely large relative price distortions between official and parallel markets.

Table 3.7 MONETARY SURVEY, 1983-1988
(Billions of Kz, end of period)

	1984	1985	1986	1987	1988
Net foreign assets	(2.5)	0.0	(18.5)	(24.1)	(40.4)
Net domestic credit	188.7	207.0	236.5	273.9	318.9
of which					
Net claims on gov't	91.5	94.3	158.3	219.4	266.2
Claims on other sectors	97.2	112.8	78.2	54.4	52.8
Other net assets	(14.2)	(3.1)	2.3	8.2	34.6
Notes in circulation	71.9	80.0	92.3	117.0	140.3
Deposits (net of gov't)	100.1	123.9	128.0	141.0	172.9
Memorandum					
Broad money stock (M2)	172.0	203.9	220.3	258.0	313.1
Annual growth in M2	18.0%	18.6%	8.0%	17.1%	21.4%
Ratio GDP/money	1.12	0.99	0.89	0.86	NA

Source: Statistical Appendix, Tables E.1 and E.2.

3.63 As indicated in Table 3.7, the velocity of monetary circulation has fallen in recent years and stood at 0.86 in 1987. This could be taken as an indication of forced savings. However, given that much economic activity takes place in parallel markets at elevated prices and is not included in the measure of gross domestic product, the numbers reported in Table 3.7 probably understate actual velocity by a large margin. In view of the lack of any reliable measure of inflation, it would be impossible to estimate a reasonable money demand equation.

G. THE BALANCE OF PAYMENTS AND THE EXTERNAL DEBT

Balance of payments

3.64 Table 3.8 provides the balance of payments in recent years. In examining these figures, one should keep in mind that the data used by the authorities in constructing the balance of payments are often of poor quality. For example, as explained by the authorities, prior to 1988 debt service payments were generally not categorized according to whether they were interest or principal payments. In constructing the balance of payments, only specifically identified interest payments were recorded as such, resulting in a downward bias in reported interest payments. In addition, data on the financing of the global balance are incomplete; the figures shown in Table E.4 of the Statistical Annex are mission estimates.

Table 3.8 BALANCE OF PAYMENTS, 1980-87
(millions US $)

	1980	1984	1985	1986	1987	1988
Merchandise exports	1,883	2,033	2,238	1,303	2,269	2,466
Merchandise imports	1,368	1,575	1,415	1,097	1,316	1,385
Service and income exports	179	111	128	115	92	127
Service and income imports	604	811	864	828	729	1,767
Net unrequited transfers	21	26	20	139	51	32
Current account balance	110	(217)	107	(368)	368	(528)
M&L term capital						
Inflows	475	765	845	785	716	948
Outflows	189	367	404	549	674	1,169
Basic balance	396	181	549	(132)	409	(749)
Short term capital incl. errors and omissions	(309)	(124)	(558)	(187)	(676)	384
Global balance	87	57	(10)	(319)	(267)	(365)
Memorandum						
Gross International reserves	309	240	257	179	242	272
Reserves in months of import coverage	1.9	1.2	1.4	1.1	1.4	1.0

Source: Statistical Appendix, Table E.4

3.65 Examination of the balance of payments data in Table 3.8 indicates that Angola consistently runs trade balance surpluses and service account deficits, which generally exceed the trade surpluses. The data show Angola to have run current account surpluses in 1985 and 1987. However, since the errors and omissions and short-term capital flow entries for these years were negative and large relative to the current account balance, it is likely that more accurate accounting would reveal current account deficits occurred in these years as well. Moreover, as discussed above, since some interest payments were recorded as amortization payments, current account deficits may be understated for all of the years. Prior to 1986, capital inflows were sufficient to cover current account deficits, capital outflows, and omitted items. Subsequently, global balance deficits were large relative to reserve holdings and Angola was forced to accumulate debt service arrears and seek debt reschedulings.

3.66 As indicated in Table E.6 of the Statistical Annex, the most striking feature of Angola's export earnings is the large share accounted for by petroleum exports. Indeed, over 90% of Angola's export earnings come from oil and gas production. Moreover, the sharp fluctuations in Angola's merchandise export earnings in recent years is almost entirely explained by fluctuations in petroleum prices. From 1980 to 1988, the volume of crude oil exports rose every year, from 41 million barrels in 1980 to 154 million barrels in 1988. For most of these years, the rise in the volume of exports offset the decline in petroleum prices, and oil export earnings grew. However, in 1986, the price decline was so severe that despite a 25% increase in the volume of exports, earnings fell almost 40%. With the partial recovery of oil prices in 1987 and the continued growth of production, merchandise export earnings in 1987 recovered to 1985 levels.

3.67 Exports of diamonds, which provided substantial amounts of foreign exchange before independence, fell drastically from 1980 through 1986. In 1987-88, reflecting new arrangements for the mining of diamonds, there was a sharp recovery in diamond export earnings, and diamonds have risen to 7% of merchandise exports. Exports of other goods, especially of agricultural products which were important in the colonial period, declined steadily over the past decade and by 1988 accounted for less than 2% of exports. The deterioration in agriculture, especially coffee production, has been so prolonged and severe that, even with improved polices, the recovery of exports may take many years.

3.68 The 1986-88 depreciation of the dollar compounded the contractionary effect of falling oil prices. While Angola's export earnings are overwhelmingly dollar denominated, the United States is the source of less than 10% of Angola's imports, according to the IMF's _Direction of Trade Statistics._ Thus, the fall in the dollar added to the adverse shift in Angola's terms of trade.

3.69 Balance of payments data on merchandise imports are based primarily on exchange records at the central bank. More detailed data on the composition of merchandise imports from 1982 through 1986 are available from customs records, the source of the data in Table E.5 in the Statistical Appendix. However, the authorities warn that these data should be viewed cautiously since many imported goods are not recorded by customs or are recorded incorrectly. Nevertheless, it is worth noting that about 25% of import expenditures are for food and 50% are for capital goods.

3.70 In the balance of payments data, fluctuations in merchandise imports generally mirror fluctuations in merchandise exports, which reflects government efforts to attain a trade surplus sufficient to service external debt and cover nonfactor service imports. For example, following the decline in exports in 1986, the authorities enacted the following measures to limit imports: a sharp reduction in imported industrial inputs, especially of spare parts; a cut-back on foreign technical assistance; reductions in foreign travel; and tight limits on financial transfers by resident foreign workers and technical assistants. These restrictive measures were not without costs. Many directors of factories reported operating far below capacity for lack of spare parts and industrial inputs, and shortages of imported consumer goods contributed to inflation in the parallel market.

3.71 Exacerbating Angola's debt service difficulties was a decline in new external lending, forcing Angola to make substantial net resource transfers to its creditors. Thus, while the authorities' restrictive policies in 1986-88 did compress imports and produced trade surpluses, the surpluses were insufficient to cover the increase in required net resource transfers and substantial arrears accumulated.

External Debt

3.72 Responsibility for gathering and analyzing data on Angola's external debt as well as negotiating terms on new debts lies with the central bank. In many cases, the central bank also guarantees the external debt of Angolan importers. In the past, organizing and analyzing external debt data was not a priority within BNA and little attention was devoted to terms on new credits. The standard policy was to seek medium-term financing from commercial creditors under guarantees by export credit agencies. Recently, in response to Angola's severe debt service difficulties, the central bank established divisions to collect data on the external debt and handle debt negotiations, with a view towards harmonizing debt terms with debt-service capacity.

3.73 Table 3.9 presents estimates of Angola's total external debt as of the end of 1988, of which approximately two-thirds is non-military debt. Of the US$1,954 million of medium and long-term debt due western creditors, only about 7% is non-guaranteed commercial credits. The rest is intergovernmental or guaranteed commercial credits. With an estimated 1987 debt to GDP ratio 110% and a 1988 debt to export ratio of 244%, Angola's debt burden indicators are characteristic of the relatively heavy debt loads found in sub-Saharan Africa. Balance of payments data indicate that Angola would have had to devote 49% of its earnings from exports of goods and services in 1988 to fully meet its scheduled debt service obligations.

Table 3.9 TOTAL EXTERNAL DEBT STOCK, AS OF DECEMBER 31, 1988
(Millions US$)

Medium and Long-Term Debt	5,633
Western country creditors	1,954
Socialist country creditors	3,631
Official organizations	47
Short-term debt	691
Total	6,324
Ratios:	
Debt/GDP	NA
Debt/Exports G & S	244%

Source: Statistical Appendix, Table E.10 and mission estimates.

3.74 Table E.8 in the Statistical Appendix shows the evolution of the stock of civilian external debt from 1982 through June 1988. While data on Angola's debt prior to 1988 are less reliable than recent data and should be viewed cautiously, the table gives a rough idea of recent Angolan debt trends. Between 1982 and mid-1988, civilian external debt almost doubled. Moreover, the debt grew more rapidly than GDP or exports, leading to a deterioration in debt burden indicators. The debt service to export ratios in Table E.8 are based on actual debt service payments made, not debt service payments due. Since these data are derived from the balance of payments data, they should only be treated as broadly indicative.

3.75 With the sharp fall in its export earnings in 1986, Angola was unable to fully service its debt. Consequently, it largely limited its debt service to credit lines required for high priority imports, such as food, petroleum production inputs and defense. It accumulated arrears on its other debts. Angola also opened debt rescheduling negotiations with its medium and long term creditors. Bilateral agreements were reached with Portugal, Brazil, and the USSR. By late 1987, Angola and Paris Club members had established joint terms of reference for bilateral reschedulings of interest and principal on guaranteed debts contracted prior to 1987 and falling due before December of that year. The terms called for a 100 percent rescheduling of principal at commercial interest rates with a three year grace period and a three year repayment period.

3.76 Even with the 1987 reschedulings and a recovery in export earnings, Angola continued to accumulate debt service arrears. As shown in Table 3.10, at the end of 1988, Angola's arrears totalled US$1,122 million, of which approximately US$633 million was non-military debt. In addition,

Angola reported arrears of about US$261 million on suppliers' credits at the end of 1988.

Table 3.10 EXTERNAL DEBT ARREARS AS OF DECEMBER 31, 1988
(Millions US$)

I. Medium and Long-term Debt	952.5
A. Western Countries	260.5
1. Guaranteed rescheduled	11.8
2. Guaranteed non-rescheduled	168.1
3. Intergovernmental credits	8.2
4. Commercial	72.4
B. Socialist Countries	689.8
1. Non-military credits	201.2
C. International Organizations	2.3
II. Short term debt	169.0
Total debt service arrears	1,121.5
Total arrears, non-military debt	632.9

Source: BNA and mission estimates.

3.77 In 1989, Angola again sought to reschedule debts with major creditors. It concluded bilateral agreements with Brazil, Portugal, and the USSR and established terms of reference for reschedulings with Paris Club members. The Paris Club terms called for a rescheduling of 100% of the principal and interest on debts contracted before 1987 and falling due prior to October 1990. In addition, 100% of the principal and interest falling due from July 1989 through the end of 1989 on previously rescheduled debt was to be rescheduled, as well as 50% of that falling due between January 1, 1990, and September 30, 1990. The Paris Club agreement called for a 6-year grace period and a 4-year amortization period, beginning in October 1996.

3.78 Despite recent reschedulings and a recovery in export earnings, Angola continues to accumulate external debt arrears and must rely on short-term credits to finance many needed imports, making trade more difficult and costly. An assessment of whether such debt service difficulties are likely to persist in the medium term must be based on balance of payments projections. Table E.6(1) in the Statistical Appendix reports mission projections of major export earnings from 1989 through 1993. The petroleum sector projections are based on mission estimates and data provided by Sonangol. The diamond export projections are based on mission estimates and data provided by Endiama. The coffee export projections assume a constant volume of exports and a 4% growth rate in prices from 1990 through 1993.

3.79 Table E.7(1) of the Statistical Appendix presents a balance of payments forecast based on the export earnings projections of Table E.6(1). The projection assumes no major policy changes from those prevailing through 1988. In addition, if hostilities end in Angola, the composition and quantity of imports demanded could change significantly, but given the limited data available on imports and their uses it is difficult to predict these changes. Consequently, imports are assumed to remain the same fraction of exports as they averaged in 1986-88. Due to insufficient information on the 1989 debt reschedulings, the projection does not incorporate their effects. However, these recent reschedulings may substantially cover the 1989-90 financing gaps. The projection indicates that, without additional reschedulings, serious debt service problems are likely to re-emerge in 1991 and persist for several years.

3.80 Tables E.7(2) and E.7(3) in the Statistical Appendix present alternative balance of payments projections. The optimistic case in Table E.7(2) assumes export earnings from 1990 through 1993 are 20% greater than in the baseline scenario, while imports are held to only a modest increase above the baseline projection. In this case, Angola would face only intermittent moderate financing gaps, which it might be able to meet from reserve holdings. The pessimistic case, presented in Table E.7 (3) assumes export earnings from 1990 through 1993 are 20% lower than in the baseline scenario. It also assumes imports are tightly compressed throughout the period. Despite the import compression, very large financing gaps persist through 1993, suggesting a rapid accumulation in arrears. As these projections demonstrate, Angola's capacity to service its debt is highly dependent on petroleum prices and its ability to limit imports to high priority items.

CHAPTER 4

SECTORAL DEVELOPMENT

A. AGRICULTURE 1/

Agricultural Performance and Policy

4.01 Seventy to eighty percent of the population is rural and about 20% of GNP is generated by agriculture.2/ With an area of 481,000 square miles and diversified ecological setting, Angola can grow a large variety of tropical and semi-tropical crops. Arable land is plentiful, with estimates ranging from five to eight million hectares. Extensive areas are also suitable for grazing, the Southern regions being free form the tse-tse fly. There is potential for significant production of a broad variety of agricultural, livestock and fishery products; including corn, manioc, beans, sorghum, sunflower, millet, potatoes, coffee, citrus, cotton, sugar, tobacco, bananas, palm oil, sisal, beef, pork, poultry, forestry and fish. Agricultural production, including livestock and fishery products, grew steadily until the disruptions of 1975-76. Angola was self-sufficient in all major food crops. The production of maize, the basis of the diet in the heavily populated central zone, had reached 710,000 tons in 1971, sufficient to permit significant exports (112,000 tons). Surpluses of other food crops, notably bananas, rice, sugar and palm oil, were also exported. Angola produced enough tobacco to satisfy its own needs and, in addition to being the fourth largest exporter of coffee, it was also one of the world's major producers of sisal. Exports of forestry products were considerable and livestock resources were abundant. According to the 1971 census, the last census available, there were more than 2 million heads of cattle and nearly a million goats.

4.02 Since independence, agricultural output has experienced a dramatic decline which has affected virtually all products. The sudden departure of the Portuguese resulted in the abandonment of most of the Portuguese-owned and managed farms, and created a manpower vacuum in many areas that are crucial to the effectiveness of agricultural operations, such as agricultural marketing, transport, input supply and research. Another major cause of the poor agricultural performance since independence is the war. The limited access to the rural areas, the destruction of infrastructure, the disruption of families and communities, and the budgetary demands of the war have had an immense impact on agricultural activity. Finally, an equally important contributory factor has been the failure of agricultural policy and government intervention to provide producers with adequate incentives and the necessary support services.

1/ See also Annex VII: Agriculture.

2/ This includes only state controlled production, which is estimated to be 10 to 15% of total production.

4.03 The current situation in the sector is in stark contrast to both pre-independence production levels and to Angola's agricultural potential. Appendix Table F.1 presents estimates of current output levels for a range of agricultural products compared to pre-1975 figures. Production of the principal staple foods (maize, cassava, sorghum, millet) is estimated at 25-35% of the output reported in the statistics just before independence. Production of many other crops (tobacco, sisal, cotton, palm oil, groundnuts) does not even reach 10% of earlier levels. While the number of cattle declined by only about 20%, and the goat population actually grew by around 50%, the number of swine as well as beef production were well below previous levels.

4.04 Angola has been transformed from a country self-sufficient in food to one dependent on increasing food imports, including food aid, and on the verge of famine. The increasing dependence of Angola on food aid is shown in Table 4.1. Food aid requested for 1987/88 amounted to 200,000 tons of cereals, three times greater than the 68,000 tons requested in 1983/84. The ability of government to finance commercial food imports diminished from 238,000 tons in 1983/84 to 99,700 tons in 1986/87. In addition, 18,000 tons of meat were imported in 1987. Dependence on food aid has remained a serious problem in subsequent years.

Table 4.1 CEREALS DEFICIT
(tons)

April/March	Programmed Commercial Imports	Requested Food Aid	Actual Commercial Imports	Delivered Food Aid	Deficit: Commercial Imports	Deficit: Food Aid	Deficit: Total Deficit
1983/1984	254,000	68,000	238,000	63,100	16,000	4,900	20,900
1984/1985	242,000	82,000	196,000	70,500	46,000	11,400	57,400
1985/1986	210,000	120,000	192,600	44,300	17,400	75,700	93,100
1986/1987	120,000	143,700	99,700	52,762	20,300	90,938	111,238
1987/1988	100,000	199,200	122,300	79,440	22,300	124,260	101,960
1988/1989	222,600	179,300	137,200	91,050	85,400	88,250	173,650

Source: World Food Program, Luanda

4.05 Agricultural exports have virtually ceased. Production of coffee, until 1973 the principal foreign exchange earner, had fallen to 13,500 tons in 1987 as compared to 240,000 in 1974. Timber exports in 1985 were only 14% of the volume exported in 1973. A number of products that were previously exported are now imported (e.g., sugar, palm oil, beans).

4.06 Agricultural Policy. The massive abandonment of the Portuguese-owned and managed farms at independence created a vacuum with which the new government had to deal. With commercial private sector agriculture disintegrating, centralized organizational arrangements were introduced in an attempt to quickly fill the gap and establish a state controlled agricultural model. The central government institutions dealing with agriculture, have since formally administered prices, production, investment, marketing, distribution, exports, imports and all other aspects of the sector. They have attempted this in the face of severe technical, human resource, and administrative deficiencies and despite serious problems in internal transportation and trading in the rural areas. Central planning, price controls and other macro-economic distortions, together with the neglect of the peasant sector, which was the major producer of food, eliminated incentives. Prices at all levels have been centrally determined and rarely changed and consumer goods have become increasingly scarce in the countryside.

4.07 A plethora of agricultural agencies has been established in spite of severe deficiencies in qualified staff. Only 1% of the labor force under the jurisdiction of the Ministry of Agriculture is classified as technical and most agricultural schools are closed. Under the Ministry of Agriculture alone, there are more than 100 public enterprises and agencies. They include state farms and integrated agrarian complexes, as well as specialized forestry enterprises, service companies, etc. Under yet different bureaucratic jurisdictions, other public entities are responsible for agro-industries such as sugar cane and the production of agricultural implements and materials. Angola's initial experiment with centralization and administrative controls is understandable, in view of the post-independence disruption and insecurity, the harshness of the Portuguese system of private sector exploitation and the disarray following the massive exodus of Portuguese farmers and traders. Nevertheless, the maintenance of these policies despite the obvious constraints and failures is now recognized by many Angolan policy-makers as a mistake and a main cause for the declining agricultural performance.

4.08 In addition to the problems of security and inadequate policies, investment in agriculture has been limited and poorly planned and implemented. In 1986, for instance, of the US$12.6 million in foreign exchange equivalent originally approved for investment, only US$2 million was made available, in view of the severe balance of payments constraints. Moreover, while a cursory review of the 1986 investment performance shows a level of implementation exceeding 100%, it appears that 69% of the total investment for agriculture went to build 900 residences in Kuanza-Bengo, a questionable project not contemplated originally in the Ministry of Agriculture plan. In contrast, only 47% of the planned investment for training and support services took place.

Rural Structure

4.09 Producer Organization. Policies regarding the organization of agriculture since independence have emphasized state or collective ownership. However, some private commercial farms continue to exist and the SEF program encourages the expansion of private commercial farming and gives greater attention to the individual peasant producer. Official policy for agriculture established two main forms of organization:

(a) State Farms or AUPs (Agrupamentos de Unidades de Producao). Abandoned commercial farms were combined into state-owned production units with managers and workers as public employees.

AUPs depend on the Government for financial support and they have incurred substantial losses. In 1986 the reported losses of state farms were 1815 million Kz, or US$61.3 million at the official exchange rate; and

(b) Peasant Associations. Intended originally to be collectives, they have become agglomerations of peasant households making their own production decisions. Their presumed advantage is priority access to government services and inputs. Unlike state farms, peasant associations do not collectivize production.

4.10 Despite the effort to change the rural structure to conform to ideological considerations, the role of the peasant remains essentially the same as it was before independence. Today the rural structure consists of three major groups: (i) declining large-scale state farms; (ii) relatively small numbers of Portuguese farmers known as "cooperantes", and of Angolan farmers, who produce mainly fruits and vegetables; and (iii) a large and dominant sector of peasant (small holder) agriculture. The latter is made up of various types of producers: (a) pastoralists in the Southern regions engaged in nomadic herding; (b) small-scale farmers producing maize, sorghum and cattle in the transitional zones of the pastoral areas; (c) small farmers in the fertile and densely populated central plateau; (d) small farmers in the coffee areas; (e) small farmers growing cassava as their main staple in the Northern and North Eastern regions and in the tropical forest; and (f) a small number of hunters in the far South. The typical peasant family cultivates 1.5 to 2.5 ha with subsistence crops. Rotation and intercropping is the usual practice. Tools are rudimentary with the hoe most common. Animal traction is used in some areas, such as the fertile areas of Huila province. The number of peasant family units is estimated at about 800,000.

4.11 Whereas peasant agriculture remained essentially unchanged since independence, commercial farming, which flourished in colonial times, has almost disappeared. Colonial policy supported the cultivation of cash crops and livestock by settlers from Portugal with land grants and financial incentives. Substantial investments were made in infrastructure such as irrigation and transport in support of commercial farming. Farm sizes varied, with some farms as large as several thousand ha. Commercial livestock production is estimated to have been as high as 40% of the total.

4.12 Marketing and Parallel Market. The Ministry of Internal Commerce (MIC) is responsible for the supply and distribution of goods in both urban and rural areas. In rural areas, MIC is expected to supply consumption goods in exchange for agricultural products. The distribution of meat, however, is under the control of the Ministry of Agriculture. The goods to be supplied are planned annually at the central level in what is known as the "Fundo da Mercadoria para a Populacao". Before independence, merchants, estimated at between 20,000 and 30,000, performed the marketing in rural areas. Most were not specialized traders but combined trading with farming and cattle raising. The variety and flexibility of the large number of private traders and entrepreneurs responded to the local conditions in a way the present centralized trading system is not able to.

4.13 Government stores have very few goods to offer. It is estimated that up to 90% of family income in Luanda is consumed in the parallel market. Most peasants have sufficient cereals and food they produce but have no access to imports. The imported food goes to meet urban demand, the needs of the armed forces, and the displaced. In the absence of price incentives, the availability of consumer goods and access to them by the peasantry determines the size of the rural surplus available for exchange. Since the present system is failing to provide most of these needed goods (both consumer goods and agricultural inputs), the majority of peasants no longer produce for the market, but only to meet their family needs.

4.14 It is difficult to estimate how much of domestic agricultural production moves through official channels. For instance, in 1986, maize production through official channels was 18.6 thousand tons, whereas total maize production is estimated to be about 300 to 350 thousand tons, having been as high as 700,000 tons previously. Consumer goods, when available in rural areas, can be purchased up to the value of the produce the peasant supplies the store at official prices. The shelves of these stores, however, are empty and what goods become available move quickly to the parallel markets. More reliance on market forces is needed, not because such reform is in and of itself sufficient for agricultural development but because the flexibility and adjustment which markets allow, are prerequisites for a successful implementation of other measures promoting long-term agricultural development. Important steps in that direction were taken with the liberalization of many agricultural prices in 1988, though policy towards agriculture is still far from being adequate.

Agricultural Support Services

4.15 Services. Agricultural support services come under the Ministry of Agriculture, with the exception of ENCODIPA which deals with marketing. Excessive centralization and severe limitations of qualified staff generally inhibit their effectiveness. The Ministry of Agriculture, within the guidelines and objectives of the S.E.F. program, is reviewing agricultural policy and ways by which to improve agricultural services. At the provincial level, the Ministry of Agriculture is represented by a branch (Delegacao) with "directorates" to support peasant associations, livestock, conservation, etc. There is no institutionalized rural credit system and all services to agriculture are provided by state agencies. With no alternatives in the private sector, these agencies are the conduits of all supplies. Even when seeds can reach the provincial level through official channels, there are no local and intermediate marketing links. It is indicative of conditions prevailing in Angola and in particular of price distortions, that as much as one-third of seeds destined for planting are used for human consumption despite being chemically treated.

4.16 Security problems and problems of infrastructure, especially of transport, affect the provision of agricultural services. However, structure and organization of the support system diminishes its effectiveness and creates distortions. In fact the emerging emphasis on the neglected peasantry is mistakenly perceived as requiring another layer of costly official institutions. The recently introduced agricultural development stations (EDAs), are already burdened with Departments of Planning, Finance, Human Resources, Technology, Supply, and others (i.e., yet another cumbersome bureaucracy). Agricultural policy and organization should move in the opposite direction and become less dependent on the public sector. Government institutions have an important role to play in supporting production and some public services, such as agricultural research and training, should clearly be strengthened. However, the extreme scarcity of human, organizational, and financial resources has made excessive reliance on government a risky course. Some of the agricultural support services provided are described further below but it should be noted that at the beginning of 1989 the Angolan authorities were preparing substantial changes in the structure and in the range of activities of the agencies and of the public enterprises operating in the agricultural sector. It is nevertheless doubtful that such reforms can succeed to reverse the declining performance of agriculture without comprehensive economic policy reform.

(a) Mechanization: ENAMA (Empresa Nacional de Mecanizacao Agricola) provides mechanical services to agriculture. It is involved in ground clearing, leveling, and construction of earthworks for reservoirs. In 1986, less than 2% of the work force of ENAMA was classified as technical and more than 70% of its tractor fleet was inoperative due to lack of spare parts and maintenance problems. The parts problem is aggravated by lack of uniformity in makes of equipment, partly due to the fact that donors promote their own brand of equipment.

(b) Fertilizers and Implements: DINAMA (Distribuidora Nacional de Materiais Agricolas) is responsible for the procurement and distribution of implements, fertilizer and insecticides. It procures and distributes these materials on the basis of the national master plan for the agricultural sector. But even when fertilizer and other inputs are available, transportation is a major constraint. Seventy percent of the transport fleet of DINAMA is out of commission. Even when the security situation permits, transport of supplies over long distances and poor roads is problematic.

(c) Seeds: ANGOSEMENTES is responsible for the purchase and distribution of seeds. Seed distribution is given high priority by the Ministry of Agriculture and the amounts of seed distributed have been increasing in recent years. The distribution of maize seed increased from 773 tons in 1984 to 1,668 tons in 1985, and 1,994 tons in 1986. Foreign exchange limitations, the cumbersome process of import approval and problems with transport often delay the arrival of seed in time for planting.

(d) Marketing and Distribution of Goods: ENCODIPA (Empresa Nacional de Comercializacao e Distribuicao de Produtos Agricolas), under the Ministry of Internal Commerce, is responsible for providing consumer goods to rural areas in exchange for agricultural products. It operates through commercial outlets in both urban and rural areas. Although allocations are determined annually by the national economic plan, actual allocations are usually different. ENCODIPA's stores in the countryside are almost empty.

(e) Extension Services: Dinamizadores rurais (rural mobilizers) can be considered a type of rural extension service. It is estimated that approximately 1,000 dinamizadores have been trained since independence with attrition around 30%. However, only about one-third receive any training in agriculture and there are no linkages between the dinamizadores and the other services. As with the other services, the development of extension is costly. In the face of enormous human resource gaps, extension should focus on grass roots support and organization rather than on formal institutions and agencies. The authorities are preparing a plan of rural extension with the objective of assisting 1 million families. A pilot project included in that program will start to be implemented in the Huila province in the years 1989-90. The organizational structure of the program appears to be heavy. Apparently it will involve some functions (including in particular rural trading) which should preferably be transferred to private enterprises.

(f) Agricultural Development Stations: Estações de Desenvolvimento Agricola (EDAs) are a recent introduction and constitute a response to the failures of the other institutions serving agriculture. The intention is to transform the state farms into peasant associations which do not collectivize production. The EDAs were designed to fill the gap between services which DINAMA and AGROSEMENTES provide and the peasant. EDAs, as pointed out earlier, are already heavily bureaucratized and it is doubtful that they will be able to be of significant support to the peasantry.

4.17 Agricultural Education and Research. The institutions which serve agriculture, depend on human resources. The scarcity of trained people at all levels is enormous. The colonial regime provided little training to Angolan nationals. Decolonization and the withdrawal of trained persons depleted all sectors of the skills needed to manage agriculture at the most basic levels. The few qualified individuals are drawn into administrative positions where the demands are perceived to be more immediate. In spite of Government efforts to improve agricultural education, most agricultural schools under the supervision of the Ministry of Agriculture are either closed or only partially operating, mainly because of security considerations and lack of food. There are two secondary technical schools in Huila and Huambo and another is being built in Malanje. The school in Uige was closed down for security reasons. The faculty of Agronomy is in Huambo. Even when institutions (e.g., for extension and research) are considered critical to agricultural development, simple and very selective forms of organization should be encouraged rather than the wholesale transplant of institutional models from environments with ample human resources. Institutional development should recognize the extremely limited human resources in Angola. An attempt at better understanding already existing peasant systems and their improvement might be a better approach to rural development in these circumstances. The Instituto de Investigacao Agronomica is the entity responsible for agricultural research in Angola. It has a staff of six agronomists, five of whom work at Huambo. Before independence, the institute had 60 professionals, some with graduate training. With the Portuguese exodus only one remained. The lack of trained people and the dismantling of the limited agricultural research at independence left Angola with no capability in this area. Only sporadic contacts with international research centers (CYMMYT, ICRISAT) and national programs (mainly EMBRAPA in Brazil) have taken place.

Policy Reform

4.18 Agricultural Policy Adjustment and Supply Response. The memory of colonial exploitation and the identification of that period with a liberal market-based agricultural policy, should not prevent the return to greater market reliance. The objectives of SEF are an indication that Angolan economic policy makers are beginning to realize this. The distribution of power and land ownership are now different from that in the colonial period. The possible adverse effects of market-based agricultural policy can be dealt with through corrective measures and selective controls. The balance between social and economic objectives in agriculture does not have to preclude incentives for individual production, especially for the peasantry.

4.19 Government authorities, and the Ministry of Agriculture, in particular, recognize the need for urgent reform of agricultural policy. Policy reform is seen as a prerequisite to the needed technical assistance, institution building and agricultural investment for the country's long-term-agricultural development. Present production levels are so distant from production possibilities and past performance, that an initial positive response is assured. A program of agricultural policy adjustment should draw from experience elsewhere in Africa and should include: (a) production incentives through improved prices and the availability of consumer goods and inputs in the countryside; (b) institutional reforms encouraging local intermediaries and private transport for marketing and distribution; (c) investment for rehabilitation of storage and transport; and (d) coordinated and focused technical assistance and training to strengthen selective support services for agriculture, such as research and policy analysis.

4.20 The Angolan authorities have already liberalized the prices of a certain number of agricultural products. Agricultural supply response to price incentives has been shown to be positive throughout Africa, and the results already achieved since the liberalization of prices confirm that Angolan agriculture is not an exception. The recent experience in Huila province also illustrates that response. Improved availability of goods in the countryside of that province has brought about a significant increase in marketable supply. The total production of maize moving through official channels reached 17.5 thousand tons in 1986, of which one third was produced in Huila. Though this performance reflects better security conditions in this province, it is also an indication of peasant response to incentives. This production increase is still modest when considering that in 1970 Huila marketed 50,000 tons of maize.

4.21 Even though a short term production response can come from the available labor and land, the long term development of Angolan agriculture will require improved practices and technology inputs and trained people. Increasing the financial and human resources, and improving the institutional organization necessary for such development is a long-term process. Use of improved seeds, fertilizer, insecticides and animal traction should raise yields significantly. Increasing agricultural production will require institutional reform in order to reduce centralized state control and provide for more reliance on the peasantry. Such a reform is not as radical as it might appear since in practice production and distribution of the bulk of agricultural output already takes place outside formal institutions and controls and the underlying structure of the peasantry appears not to have been severely damaged by the centralized policy model or the war. This is also the case with regard to institutional support to agriculture, i.e., the gap between the official, controlled and planned actions and what actually happens is considerable.

4.22 The political economy of adjustment. A broad liberalization of agricultural production, marketing and distribution for all agricultural and food products within the context of SEF, is a prerequisite to reversing the dangerously declining food situation in Angola and realizing the country's agricultural potential. The major part of the economy has operated in the parallel informal sector. As the contribution of agriculture to Government revenue is marginal (with the exception of coffee) the liberalization of agricultural policy will have no adverse effect on current public finance. Rather, with appropriate policies, the increased agricultural production will improve agriculture's contribution to public revenues. The short-term effect of price liberalization will be adverse for those who presently benefit from access to agricultural products through official channels at controlled prices. But only a small share of the population has access to this limited supply and the percentage of income spent on price controlled goods is small. A senior public servant family in Luanda, with two members working, consumes about 5% to 10% of its monthly income on "the circuito official"--Government stores at official prices - unless he has access to special shops. What the agricultural policy reforms will accomplish is to legitimize what has been the parallel economy. An indirect benefit of more reliance on the market would be the reduction of corruption which the large discrepancies between official and parallel market prices is fomenting.

4.23 Potential response. While the security situation limits the potential for raising agricultural production throughout the country, there are secure areas that could provide an immediate response to policy adjustment. The following regions, which constitute about 20 to 25% of the national territory, are relatively secure and could produce considerably more for the market.

(a) S-SW Region. From the city of Lobito on the Atlantic coast to the town of Tambor in the South to the valley of the river Cunene, about 300 km inland, where three areas can be distinguished:

- an arid strip, where only irrigated agriculture is possible, limited to the plains of the main rivers;

- a semi-arid strip, where rainfed agriculture is possible, based on drought-resistant grains such as massambala (sorghum) and massango (pearl millet), as well as cotton, while irrigated agriculture also offers attractive possibilities;

- inland plateau, where rainfed agriculture is fully viable.

(b) N-NW Region. Including Cabinda Province in the North and the coastal area south to Sumbe (capital of Cuanza Sul province), extending to the interior from Soyo and along the transport corridor Luanda-Dondo. The following agricultural areas can be delineated in this region:

- Luanda region, between the Dande valley and the Cuanza; suitable for fruits and vegetables and also cassava, sweet potatoes and maize. Considerable potential and adequate infrastructure exist in this region to supply most of the food needs of the 1.2-2.0 million people of metropolitan Luanda.

- Region south of the Cuanza, between the Cuanza valley and Sumbe, capital of Cuanza Sul province; cattle raising, cotton, food crops.

- Region north of the Dande, between the Dande valley and the Soyo (course of the Zaire); food crops, inland fishing.

- Cabinda region, comprising the province of Cabinda with considerable forestry potential.

Appendix Table F.7 gives estimates of the potential response for major products over a three-year period if appropriate policies and incentives for agriculture are introduced.

B. FISHERIES

4.24 The 1,600 Km long coastline of Angola, particularly to the south off Namibe and Benguela, is rich in fishing resources. The meeting of the cold Benguela current and the warm Agulhas current creates favorable conditions for plankton, which attract sardine and horse mackerel, the two principal commercial species, accounting for about 90 per cent of the catch. Other species include tuna and shellfish, whose commercial potential the government is now beginning to develop. The fishing industry is based mainly in the Southwestern ports of Namibe, Tombwa and Lucira and the port of Lobito in Benguela province. Before Independence, the industry was relatively well-endowed with fish processing capacity for canning, freezing, drying and salting, and the production of fish meal and fish oil. At that time, most of the commercial catch was exported, mainly as fish meal or frozen fish. The fishing fleet was estimated at 700-800 boats in the early 1970s but many of these vessels departed following the outbreak of the 1975-76 war. Industrial installations were abandoned, and often sabotaged, by their Portuguese owners, and the situation was exacerbated by the exodus of managers, technicians and trained seamen. Rehabilitation of industrial processing capacity has been slow, reflecting shortages of skills, limited foreign exchange, and delays in the delivery of equipment and spare parts, as well as excessive centralization and control by the Government. This procurement function is the responsibility of the National Enterprise for Assistance to the Fishing Industry (ENATIP). The Ministry of Fishing has overall control of the industry from fish capture to distribution, and supervises the activities of separate State Economic Units (UEE) operating in individual sectors.

4.25 Delays in the re-equipment of the national fleet and in the delivery of new vessels ordered from Spain have impeded the recovery of domestic fishing output. In recent years, the Angolan fleet has landed between 65,000 and 75,000 tons annually, significantly below output levels in the late colonial period. However, domestic fish supplies are supplemented by foreign fishing fleets operating under licence in Angolan waters, which land a portion of their catch in Angolan ports in payment of fishing fees. This payment in kind rather than in foreign exchange increases domestic fish supplies for local consumption by some 120-130 thousand tons annually. For example, the total foreign fleet catch in 1987 was 295.7 thousand tons, of which 122.7 thousand tons or 41.5% were landed in Angola. The total foreign catch in 1987 was considerably below 1985 (403.5 thousand tons) and 1986 levels (373.3 thousand tons), due mainly to the termination and consequent winding down of agreements with Spain and USSR. Several agreements with foreign fleets are likely to be revised in the near future in order to incorporate the higher operating capacity of the domestic Angolan fleet due to the arrival of new boats purchased from Spain and Italy. In 1987, the national fishing fleet numbered 466 motorized craft, excluding artisanal fishing boats.

4.26 In common with other state-owned productive sectors, the fishing industry is now caught up in the process of decentralization and reform launched by the SEF/PRE. The present organization of the industry is under review and the Ministry of Fisheries is evaluating the possibility of privatizing certain activities or forming mixed enterprises. Further broad policy objectives include higher production and better distribution facilities in order to increase domestic fish consumption, and the reinvestment of a higher proportion of the foreign exchange earnings generated by the industry in modern installations and equipment. In addition to continued support for "industrial fishing", the Ministry will give greater priority to the development of artisanal fishing, particularly in the Southwest region. This region has the richest fishing areas and considerable international assistance, mainly from EEC governments, already has been received to restore the capacity of the national fishing fleet and rehabilitate fish processing activities. The Ministry of Fisheries is now incorporating individual investment projects in a Master Plan (Plano Director para as Pescas). This Plan identifies delays in supplies of parts and vital equipment as major obstacles to rehabilitation, together with shortages of trained staff and skilled labor, especially in the fishing fleet. Inland fisheries, which are under the Ministry of

Agriculture, are also receiving attention and merit support in view of their potential as an easily accesible protein source for the rural population.

4.27 In the medium-term, the Ministry intends to promote the development of higher value species, notably shellfish. There is also some concern to avoid increases in the quotas allowed to foreign fleets on the grounds that fish stocks may be excessively depleted. There also are unconfirmed allegations that the fishing methods utilized by foreign fleets are reducing plankton supplies, thus threatening the sustainability of this valuable natural resource. Properly managed, the expansion of Angola's fishing industry would provide increased supplies of protein for domestic consumption and an important source of export earnings. The SEF/PRE reforms promise to bring this objective closer by increasing the financial autonomy of state firms, giving a greater role to the private sector, and by allowing firms to retain a larger share of foreign exchange earnings, which would relax the main constraint to the rehabilitation of the industry.

C. MINING

Introduction

4.28 The geology of Angola was comparatively well explored and mapped in colonial times. Additional information has been gained from prospecting for oil and from more recent work carried out with foreign technical assistance. The most important mineral occurrences are the diamonds in Luanda Norte Province, the iron ore at Cassinga, and the phosphates in Cabinda and in Zaire Province. There are also small deposits of copper and associated minerals in various places, the possibility of development of small gold mines at M`popa and Lombige, as well as known deposits of mica, kaolin, asphaltic coal, rare earths and uranium, which might merit further exploration. Quartz, marble and granite are found in the south and are mined on a small scale. The only significant mining activity at present is that for diamonds. The iron ore mine is being held on care and maintenance, potential exploitation of phosphates has not gone ahead and exploration of other known deposits of various minerals is at a virtual standstill.

4.29 The prospecting for and development of mineral deposits in Angola is governed by law 5/79 which vests the mineral wealth of the country in the State, provides for the State to carry out all prospecting and for State mining enterprises to develop mineral deposits (with the assistance of outside agencies where necessary). Amendments to the law, which are expected to be published shortly, will permit foreign companies to prospect for minerals in Angola, and will remove the provision whereby mining companies must be 51% owned by the State. Law 10/79 governing foreign investment in general is also under review. The Direccao Nacional de Geologia e Industria Mineira (DNGIM or Geominas) which is part of the Ministry of Industry, is the Government agency controlling prospecting and mining and recommending the issue of prospecting licences and mining leases. It is also responsible for geological mapping. Development of mineral deposits has been left in the hands of State enterprises especially formed for this purpose. Thus, the Empresa Nacional de Diamantes de Angola (Endiama) controls the diamond industry and the Empresa Nacional de Ferro (Ferrangol) the iron ore mine at Cassinga. Other state enterprises exist for developing phosphates (Fosfang), granite and marble (Roremina), quartz (Minoquartz), and underground water (Hydromina).

Diamonds

4.30 Development until 1987. Diamonds were first discovered in Angola in 1912. They exist in Angola in three environments--in gravels found in rivers and on river banks, in conglomerates known as Colonda resulting from old river beds subsequently disturbed and distributed, and in old volcanic pipes known as Kimberlites. The known deposits of alluvial diamonds are spread over very considerable areas, extending southwards from the Zaire border along the main rivers for some 400 kilometres in the northeast corner of the country and to the west a similar distance from the border along the Cuango River. While in general it is clear that considerable reserves of alluvial diamonds remain to be exploited, the detailed information available on proven reserves is unreliable. Complete records were not handed over by previous managements and in recent years prospecting has been hampered by insecurity and by lack of staff. In 1979, Geominas estimated the reserves of diamonds in Luanda Norte, as shown in Table 4.2 below. Since then some 8.5m carats of alluvials have been mined from the river banks, beds and terraces, and there has been an unquantified deterioration in reserves due to illicit mining. Moreover, some of the reserves are located at a considerable distance from existing plants.

Table 4.2: ESTIMATED RESERVES OF DIAMONDS IN LUNDA NORTE, 1979

	Proven (carats)	Grade (ct/m3)	Implied (carats)	Grade (ct/m3)
Alluvial & Terraces	40m.	1.0	130m.	0.6
Kimberlites	50m.	1.2	220m.	1.0

Source : Geominas.

4.31 The Companhia de Diamantes de Angola (Diamang) was founded in 1917 with its principal shareholder the Societe Generale de Belgique, the Ryan-Guggenheim group from the USA and various French and Portuguese banks. In 1921 it received the right to prospect for and mine diamonds throughout the whole of Angola, with only part of the coastal strip being excluded. Early developments concentrated on rich and easily available gravels. By the late 1940s production had risen to 800.000 carats a year.

In the early 1970s production was coming from some 42 different areas, each with its own washing plant, and had reached just over 2m carats a year. After coffee, diamonds were Angola`s most valuable export until they were surpassed by oil in 1971. In 1971, Diamang's concession was reduced to 50.000 sq.km. in the Luanda Norte area and the remainder of the old concession was granted to the Consorcio Mineiro de Diamantes (Condiama), a consortium consisting of the Angolan Government, De Beers and Diamang. This was part of the effort at that time to extend mineral development over wider areas of the country.

4.32 In the aftermath of Independence almost all of Diamang's skilled expatriate labor force of 2.500 left and the overall labor force fell from 20.000 to 6.000. In 1976, Diamang`s head office was moved from Lisbon to Luanda, when the Angolan Government took over the Portuguese State`s 38% interest in the company. This interest was increased to 77% by nationalising the holdings of small shareholders in 1977 and 1979. Societe Generale and Sibeka remained the principal other shareholders with 17% and a management agreement was signed with them. The Diamond Corporation, a De Beers subsidiary, and minor shareholder, continued to market the production through the Central Selling Organisation (CSO).

4.33 Production fell to 333.000 carats in 1977 and in an effort to improve the situation a new management agreement was signed with Mining and Technical Services Ltd. (MATS), a company indirectly owned by De Beers or its associates. This company managed to double production in 1978 and to increase it further to nearly 1.5m carats in 1980. Meanwhile, in line with law 5/79, a state enterprise, Endiama, was incorporated in 1981 to take over the State's holding in Diamang. It also was given the right to market all diamonds produced in Angola and to prospect for diamonds throughout the country. The contract with MATS was not renewed in 1985 for several reasons, including: (a) attacks on installations in the Cuango area and on the company's supply routes, which affected the provision of consumer goods to workers and required the airlifting of diesel fuel and spare parts; (b) the deterioration in security against theft in Lucapa and Andrade; (c) the fall in diamond prices; and (d) dissatisfaction on the part of Endiama with the performance and cost of MATS. In 1986, shareholders decided to put Diamang into liquidation due to the accumulation of operating losses, whereupon the State assumed the responsibility for the liabilities of Diamang, while Endiama assured the continuation of the operations.

4.34 Following a drop to only 267.000 carats ($16m.) in 1986, output recovered to around 871.000 carats ($107m.) in 1987. Endiama achieved this by opening up the Cuango mining area again under a contract mining arrangement with RST. Under this arrangement Endiama seconded local staff to RST and allowed it the use of its equipment. In return RST supplied the necessary expertise and expatriate staff to operate the concession. RST meets all foreign exchange costs and Endiama meets the local costs. RST receives a fixed monthly payment in foreign exchange and a variable bonus based on its attainment of an agreed production plan. The contract is being renegotiated for a further two-year period, and will involve RST investing US$3 m. mainly in spares and earthmoving equipment, to be matched by a similar investment by Endiama. In 1987, a second contract mining arrangement was entered into for the Lucapa area with the Sociedade Portuguesa de Emprendimentos (SPE), a Portuguese group with access to staff previously employed by Diamang and in which Sibeka has an interest. This arrangement is for a two year period with phase one being the rehabilitation of the infrastructure in the area. It includes a prospecting component and provides for SPE to invest $3 m. in the first year. An unidentified third company is negotiating to enter into a further contract mining arrangement for the areas around Luo and Catoca. Negotiations with the De Beers group took a significant step forward after a letter of intent was signed between that group and Endiama, that could pave the way to the required investment in the kimberlites. If all goes according to plan on the mining side, Endiama will give the CSO in due course exclusive marketing rights to their production again.

4.35 A major concern of Endiama is the limited amount of prospecting that it is able to carry out at present, since this means that it is impossible to tailor operations to the average grade of the deposit, with the result that high- grading is almost certainly taking place. Given peace and stability a further major investment would be required from return the mines to the sort of high volume low grade operation that will make the most economic use of the remaining reserves. Through the years, Diamang, and its successor Endiama, built up and maintained a considerable social infrastructure in the Luanda Norte Province. The company provided power and water, schools and hospitals, bus services and sports facilities for the entire province, and developed ranches and fruit and vegetable farms to supply its requirements.

4.36 Government Control and Policy Making Framework. The organisation and control of the diamond mining industry has always been different to that of the rest of the mining industry. In colonial times Diamang was very much a law unto itself, particularly in the mining areas. Now, although nominally responsible through Geominas, Endiama's management effectively reports directly to senior Government levels through the Minister of Industry. It also has a direct relationship with the National Bank of Angola. Hence, the company continues to have a special position due to its economic and social importance. In October, 1986, the Economic Commission of the Council of Defence and Security decreed that the newly constituted management of Endiama must run the company without recourse to further loans of foreign exchange or local currency and that the company must survive on its earnings. Since then Endiama's management has been allowed to get on with the job. Endiama controls the operations of its contractors through agreed mining plans which are part of the basic agreement with them. However, due to the weakness of the data base on proven ore reserves, these plans have tended towards overmining in the past. Endiama is working to overcome this by including prospecting commitments in the more recent agreements.

4.37 Marketing and financial performance. Until December 1985, Angolan diamond production had always been sold through the Central Selling Organisation (CSO), which sells 80% of world production. Since 1986, the diamonds have been sold through the open market, first directly to diamond dealers, and subsequently by tender. Being a small producer, Angola has been able to ride on the back of the CSO's marketing monopoly. Endiama was able to sell its diamonds at higher prices than it would have obtained from the CSO, mainly because it was selling into a rising market, and its buyers required much lower mark-ups than the CSO. The CSO normally requires a mark-up of 11.1% on the diamonds it markets to cover expenses of its worldwide advertising for diamonds (some US$110m in 1987) and from its role in running a buffer stock for diamonds, which at times has reached a value of US$2 billion. In comparison, an independent diamond merchant with low overheads and the ability to achieve a rapid turnover will only seek a margin around 3%. Endiama is aware of the possibility that the tender system may not prove so profitable in a weaker market and has also been concerned that it is not building up any longterm relationships with the dealers involved in the tenders nor providing any training in diamond marketing for Angolan nationals. Consequently, since October 1988 it has been experimenting with a system of selling direct to selected diamond merchants upon the basis of its independent preevaluation with provision for the merchants involved to share excess profits with the company and for them to have Angolans in their offices to monitor the sales and to learn about diamond marketing. This arrangement seems likely to continue until Endiama returns to an exclusive arrangement with the CSO, perhaps early in 1990, if serious progress is made with an agreement with De Beers to develop a major kimberlite mine. In the meantime the CSO is unwilling to buy only part of the production, but will market any diamonds that it itself produces.

4.38 In the absence of proper financial accounts, Endiama's profitability can only be assessed on the basis of its provisional accounts. As shown in Table 4.3, Endiama's foreign exchange earnings in 1987 amounted to about US$16 million. Deduction of domestic expenses running at Kz 117m. a month leave a monthly operating loss of Kz 66m. The Government provides a subsidy to make up to the company the added costs arising from the war and obligations to provide services to the people of the Lunda Norte Province, including payments to workers who are unemployed but still remain housed, paid and fed by the company. Hence, Endiama is left with monthly losses of around Kz 80m. As to the net foreign exchange earnings of the company, after net losses of US$52m. in 1985 and US$33m. in 1986, there should be a net surplus of some US$23m. in 1987. The debts taken over by Endiama from Diamang amount to some Kz 18bn, of which Kz 2bn is due to the National Bank of Angola, and of the remaining Kz 8bn, Kz 2bn is due to local suppliers and Kz 6bn is owed in foreign exchange. Endiama pays a 5% royalty on sales to the Government as well as paying normal income taxes when it makes a profit.

Table 4.3: ENDIAMA'S RECEIPTS AND DISBURSEMENTS IN FOREIGN EXCHANGE, 1985-88

	1985	1986	1987	1988 (9mths)
Receipts				
Sales	$33.937m	$16.808m	$97.280m	$125.431m
Disbursements				
Goods	38.025	13.862	10.099	27.394
Services				
Overseas salaries	9.043	6.384	9.400	4.717
Transport	23.432	16.627	20.947	12.950
Technical services	14.128	7.430	22.345	15.928
Royalties*	.598	-	8.204	10.080
Brussells office	.305	.125		
Lisbon office	.280	.160	.276	.230
Other financial costs	.143	4.847	.116	4.940
Total disbursements	$85.954	$49.435	$71,387	$76.239
Capital Expenditure			9.913	9.119
Net gain (loss)	($52.017)	($32.627)	$15.980	$40.073

* Royalties paid to contractors - payable to MATS in 1985 and to RST in thereafter.

Notes:

1. Goods included 43% foodstuffs in 1985 and 56% in 1986.

2. Other financial costs in 1986 includes expenditure that has not yet been allocated to other categories.

3. Capital expenditure is not included in this schedule for 1985 and 1986 when some $5m was spent in 1985/86.

Source: 1985 Ministry of Industry
1986, 1987 and 1988 Endiama

4.39 It is estimated that some US$50m worth of diamonds leave Angola unofficially every year, either smuggled across the Zaire border for sale in the open market in that country or smuggled to Lisbon. A small part of this arises from illicit mining that takes place near the Zaire border and on the fringes of the various areas mined by Endiama, but the major part comes from direct theft by people working on the mines. The authorities in Angola are well aware of the problem that exists. Security in the mining areas is the joint responsibility of Endiama and of the mining police which reports to the Minister of State Security. Steps have been taken to improve cooperation between them and to tighten physical security at the plants. Nevertheless, enormous pressures exist on everyone in the area to obtain diamonds as they are the sole means of paying for both necessities and luxuries available only through traders from Zaire. The situation cannot realistically be expected to improve until consumer goods are available to workers and security personnel in Lunda Norte.

4.40 Prospects. The future of the diamond mining industry in Angola lies with the successful development of the kimberlite pipes known to exist there. There are over 638 of them in all, 300 of which have grades better than .04 carats per cubic metre. Four are especially interesting, as shown below:

Name	Size	Grade carat/m3	Diamond Type
Catoca	66.2ha.	1.0	Low quality
Camatue	19.8ha.	.24	Good quality
Camatchia	22.5ha.	No firm information	
Camafuca-Camazombo	150.0ha.	.10	Diverse

In size alone the pipes are amongst the ten largest in the world. Despite the limited information available, there would seem to be a strong chance for developing at least one major diamond mine from amongst them, given peace and stability. Endiama is currently discussing possible steps to develop these kimberlites with the De Beers group and also has offers of cooperation in this area from the USSR. In addition, other major mining finance groups with experience in diamond mining are showing some interest. The first requirement is for a desk study to pull together all existing information and to decide what further drilling and sampling is required before a full feasibility study is undertaken. Full development of a mine would take at least five years and it is unlikely that a development of this magnitude could be attempted before peace has been restored.

4.41 The contract mining arrangements entered into by Endiama should ensure that production is maintained at around a million carats a year in 1988, and expands steadily thereafter over the next five years, provided there are no serious attacks on mining installations. A major investment in the development of one or more kimberlites could boost production in 1992. The following estimates of future production (shown in Table 4.4 below) are based on a range of assumptions including, in the worst case, further attacks in mining areas, and in the best case, a major additional mine coming into production in 1992. Whatever happens, some production from the kimberlites is expected in 1992. It is not expected that Endiama will achieve higher prices in 1988 than in 1987, but thereafter prices are expected to rise with inflation as the De Beers CSO continues to use its control of the market to achieve this.

Table 4.4: PROJECTED DIAMOND PRODUCTION, 1988-92
($million)

	1989	1990	1992	1995
Low	160	160	175	200
High	220	260	310	500
Best guess	180	210	230	360

Source: Mission estimates

Other Minerals

4.42 Iron Ore. The iron ore deposits at Cassinga were discovered in 1910 but serious exploration did not commence until 1954 when development by the Companhia Mineira do Lobito began. By 1967, 130m tons of ore with 63% fe had been proven and a further thousand million with 35% to 53% fe was indicated. A US$93m project was developed in partnership with Krupp, including a 94 km branch line from the main railway, a pier for berthing bulk carriers of up to 160.000 dwt, and ship loading facilities capable of handling 5.000 tons per hour at Mocamedes (now Namibe). Exports began in 1967 and early reports showed the ore specification to be extremely acceptable. Between 5 m. and 6 m. tons a year were exported annually from 1968 to 1973. With the best of the high grade reserves depleted and the general situation uncertain, the mine was closed in 1974 before independence. Plans to reopen the mine in 1981 were disrupted by attacks on the power plant and the railway line. The mine is now held on a care and maintenance basis. However, it will not be economically viable at current international prices, taking into account the enormous investments which would be needed in the railway and in the port and considering that the best ore reserves seem to have been depleted. Ferrangol also controls extensive iron ore deposits at Cassala-Kitunga and manganese in Kwanza-Norte.

4.43 Phospates. Large deposits of phosphate occur in Cabinda at Mongo-Tando and in Zaire Province at Kindonacaxa. Reserves of 10m tons have been proven at Kindonacaxa and a 15.000 ton a year pilot plant was built in 1981. Tests show that the crushed phosphates produced are suitable for domestic use as fertilisers, but further development has been delayed mainly, it is understood, due to expected difficulties in transporting the fertilisers because of the war. A State enterprise Fosfang controls the production in the Zaire province and is studying the possibility of using the phosphate ores as a new material for the production of phosphoric acid. The deposits in Cabinda were prospected by Cofan, a consortium of Portuguese, US and British companies, which spent over a million dollars, but gave up when their concession expired due to lack of funds and discouraging results. Fosfang is reviewing the possibility of developing these deposits with the help of Bulgargeomin.

4.44 Other Minerals. The only other mining taking place in Angola at present is the quarrying of granite, marble and quartz. In colonial times more than 22 companies were involved in the quarrying of granite, marble and ornamental rocks mainly in Huila and Namibe. Angolan black granite is highly regarded in world markets. Roremina (Empresa Nacional de Rochas Ornamentais) has recently chosen a partner for a joint venture company which will operate the two best granite quarries. The project will require an investment of about US$2.5m. and will earn about US$3m. a year in foreign exchange. Expansion is envisaged if the project is a success. Its location means that there will be no interference from the war. Minquartz, another state company, controls the mining of quartz in Kuanza Sul, but because of security problems its production has been very low. In 1988 exports amounted to only 301 tons, worth US$ 336 thousand. Since the development of small gold deposits is fashionable in the mining world at present, it is possible that outside interest may be aroused in the small deposits at M`popo near Cassinga and at Chipinde in Huila/Huambo. the resources of Kaolin are also of significant economic interest. An investment of about US$ 25 million will be made in a project to explore those resources in the province of Huila.

Potential Constraints

4.45 The extent of mineralization, the fact that some 240 mining and exploration concessions existed in 1959 (although many of them were undoubtedly speculative), and the fact that 27 companies were actively prospecting and mining in Angola in 1970 are all indicative of the mineral potential of the country. Furthermore, most of the south east remains to be explored. The principal constraint on further development of the mining industry is without doubt the continuing war in Angola. Mining installations and essential infrastructure have been attacked, workers have been kidnapped, transport routes are seriously disrupted, and it is impossible for geologists to travel safely about the business of prospecting. As a result, the cost of running the diamond mines is vastly inflated. Diesel oil and essential spares have to be flown in to the mining area and it is difficult to get staff. The iron ore mine is closed following an attack on its power station and due to the insecurity of the railway; phosphates are not mined because the fertiliser product cannot be transported to the agricultural areas.

4.46 The development of the mining sector will be helped by the geological map (scale 1: 1 000 000) and by the geomorphological map (scale 1:1 200 000) of Angola. However, since independence, with the exception of the oil industry, little has been done to encourage foreign investment, but with the proposed changes to the mining law and the policy changes expected to occur as a result of SEF, the way should now be clear for foreign interests to participate in the industry. Moreover, the experience of the oil companies will demonstrate that the Government is willing to allow those who do participate a good return on their investments. However, one major obstacle still stands in their way and that is the weakness of the local currency. Ways around this problem can be found by operating through unincorporated joint ventures, with the foreign investor assuming foreign exchange costs in return for a share of the foreign exchange earnings of selling the production. A local partner, usually the Government in some form, would meet local costs and receive its reward from the rest of the production revenue.

4.47 Another constraint that is difficult to quantify in the present circumstances is the lack of management expertise and of capable artisans in Angola, as a result of the almost total failure of the colonial power to train local people rather than use labor imported from Portugal. In the diamond mining areas, the lack of artisans has been partly overcome by employing people from the Phillipines who are willing to work for pay and conditions below those required by Europeans. However, this must be necessarily a temporary solution and any major development in the future will have to incorporate a high training component. It should be noted that this lack of management skills is also likely to hinder the Government in its dealings with prospective investors. If peace and an improved economic situation lead to a wider interest from outsiders in investment in Angola the Government will need assistance to enable it to find the right balance between encouraging investment and controlling those providing it.

D. MANUFACTURING INDUSTRY

Structure and Performance

4.48 At independence Angola had, for a country of its size and level of income, a relatively large and broadly based manufacturing sector. By 1974, there were almost 4000 registered manufacturing enterprises in the country employing 200,000 workers and producing the equivalent of US$650 million. Production ranged from processed food to shoes, textiles and metal fabrication, and was larger and more diversified than in most other African countries. The influx of settlers from Portugal during the few decades before independence had helped create a market for a range of consumer goods, and constituted a source of entrepreneurial, technical and administrative skills. In 1962, exchange controls were imposed to avoid large scale capital flight after the outbreak of the liberation war in 1961. This measure led many large Portuguese trading companies and agricultural enterprises to invest in manufacturing activities.

4.49 The situation changed radically at independence when the massive departure of the Portuguese settlers caused numerous enterprises to be abandoned. While some of these maintained limited operations under government control, many others ceased to function altogether. The Portuguese exodus also deprived the sector of many of its human resources and affected the demand for manufactured goods. The outcome was a sharp drop in manufacturing activity. Out of a total of 687 enterprises listed in Angola's company registry, 280 (41%) are currently considered to be engaged in manufacturing, as compared to almost 4000 in 1974. Industrial production also declined dramatically. In 1977, industrial output had dropped to 28% of the level achieved four years earlier (table 4.5). Mining in particular was hit very hard, with mineral output, mainly diamonds, down to as low as 10% of production in 1973. The subsequent partial recovery was uneven. Though the index of industrial output masks shifts in the composition of production within each of the branches, it appears that light industry, which in 1987 produced 62% of its 1973 output, is furthest on the way towards regaining pre-independence levels of output. To a large extent, this recovery is attributable to two new textile plants, a medium scale one that started operations in Benguela in 1979, and the large Textang II plant in Luanda, which came on stream in 1983. The figures indicate, however, that production in most branches stagnated from 1983 to 1986, and then fell quite sharply in 1987. It appears that this is the result of a progressive deterioration of assets that have not been adequately maintained, and of the increasing scarcity of foreign exchange to purchase raw materials and other inputs.

Table 4.5: INDEX OF INDUSTRIAL PRODUCTION, 1973-87
(1973 = 100)

	1973	1977	1983	1986	1987	Weight in 1987
Food processing	100	37	48	48	42	33
Light industry	100	31	87	88	61	45
Heavy industry	100	24	45	52	36	15
Mining	100	10	28	13	17	7
Total	100	28	57	56	43	100

Source: Statistical Appendix, table H.5

4.50 Employment in manufacturing was also seriously affected by the widespread closure of companies and the decline in the level of activity after independence. Employment in registered manufacturing enterprises in 1984 amounted to 85,000 (representing a third of total employment in enterprises) compared to 200,000 ten years earlier. Having taken over many of the abandoned enterprises, the state has acquired a dominant position in the sector. This is reflected in its share of 78% of manufacturing employment, with a further 6% in state controlled joint ventures. (Table 4.6).

Table 4.6: EMPLOYMENT IN MANUFACTURING ENTERPRISES, 1984

Ownership	No. of firms	Total number of workers	Percent of Total	Average No. of Workers
UEE	163	65,908	78	404
Mixed	13	5,330	6	410
Private	99	13,764	16	139
TOTAL	275	85,002	100	309

Source: Angola, Company Registry

4.51 The principal industrial branch in terms of output is light dustry. In 1987, it contributed an estimated 45% of total output, followed by food processing (33%), heavy industry (15%), and mining (7%). Before independence the structure of industry was somewhat different, with mining playing a more important role (17%). In spite of the deteriorating trend in production, Angola's industry remains broadly based with a wide range of products. In 1987, the food processing subsector produced, among other products, beer and soft drinks (over 500,000 tons), corn meal and wheat flour (over 55,000 tons), cooking oil and margarine (over 4,500 tons) and a number of minor products. The light industry sector produced a variety of textiles and clothes, shoes, matches, plywood, soap, paint and glue, plastic ware, etc. Heavy industry produced tyres, bicycles and motorcycles, dry batteries, refrigerators, radios and televisions, metal furniture, etc. Although amounts produced are increasingly modest, production capacity for a wide range of consumer goods still exists. 3/

4.52 Financial Performance. According to data collected by the Ministry of Industry, the manufacturing sector as a whole has been turning in a net loss at least from 1978 onwards. These losses have ranged from 9% to 18% of the value of gross output. While both the food processing and heavy industry branches have consistently operated at a loss, light industry as a whole has been profitable between 1981 and 1985. Obviously, within each branch of industry results vary a great deal. Until 1981, mining also showed a profit, but since then results have deteriorated rapidly. The combined loss of the manufacturing sector in 1987 was estimated at the equivalent of 17% of gross output. This figure would rise to 31% if mining were included. It should be stressed that, given the severe price distortions, the financial results are not a reflection of economic efficiency. Several reasons account for these losses. They include an overvalued exchange rate, price controls, low capacity utilization, and the inability to lay off workers when they are not needed. For example, the large deficits of Diamang (now Endiama) are a direct consequence of the unrealistic exchange rate. The inflexibility of the wage bill is illustrated by a comparison of the results of 1986 with those of 1987. Although the value of output fell by 25% in 1987 (in constant prices), payments for wages and salaries increased by 3%. The large losses could only be sustained over such a lengthy period due to government subsidies. These subsidies, which included specific price subsidies and grants for working capital as well as the coverage of operating losses, reached Kz 3,270 million in 1985 for enterprises under the supervision of the Ministry of Industry (Table 4.7). Although government policy since 1986 stresses greater financial autonomy of public enterprises, the budget for 1987 still included Kz 1,800 million as subsidies for industry.

3/ Direct observations in plants visited would indicate that plant utilization is, on average, below 20% of nominal capacity (including auto-consumo and theft).

Table 4.7: FINANCIAL FLOWS BETWEEN GOVERNMENT AND INDUSTRIAL PUBLIC ENTERPRISES, 1980-87 a/
(Kz. million)

	1980	1981	1982	1983	1984	1985	1986	1987
Profit transfers	287	814	552	623	796	701	862	
	1122	906	1505	1763	1976	3270	1428	1800
-losses	1122	864	1055	1161	1251	1660	760	750
-working capt.				31	28	50	27	300
-price subs.		42	450	571	697	1560	641	750

a/ Relates only to enterprises supervised by the Ministry of Industry
Sources: Ministry of Industry and Ministry of Finance.

4.53 Investment. Public sector investments in manufacturing industry since 1980 have been erratic. The following table shows the pattern for the industries under the jurisdiction of the Ministry of Industry, subdivided into four categories usually considered in Angola, i.e., industries engaged in food processing, other light industry, heavy industry and mining. Heavy industry is somewhat of a misnomer, since apart from a cement factory, the petroleum refinery and a moderately sized steel plant, truly heavy industry does not exist in Angola. The investment figures listed in Table 4.8 have usually covered a combination of civil works, equipment, technical assistance, studies and financing costs. The relatively large investments in the light industry sector in 1981 and 1982 were mainly for the textile plant Textang II in Luanda and for the forestry and plywood producing operation of Panga Panga. A large part of investment in heavy industry, notably in 1981, has been dedicated to rehabilitation of the steel plant. Total annual investments averaging the equivalent of about US$44 million appear small compared to total original investments in the manufacturing sector in Angola, which have been estimated at over of US$ 1 billion.

Table 4.8: PUBLIC SECTOR INVESTMENT IN INDUSTRY, 1980-86
(Kz. million)

	1980	1981	1982	1983	1984	1985	1986
Food Proces.	167	700	700	n/a	n/a	n/a	229
Light Industry	158	1328	1038	n/a	n/a	n/a	304
Heavy Industry	330	1721	408	n/a	n/a	n/a	283
Mining	0	468	116	n/a	n/a	n/a	324
TOTALS	655	4217	2262	1064	672	463	1140

n/a = not available
Source: Ministry of Industry.

4.54 Government control. Within the established centralized system of close guidance and control of economic activities, each industry, irrespective of ownership, is assigned a tutelary Ministry. The majority of firms (219) come under the Ministry of Industry, with several other ministries, notably those of Agriculture, Fisheries, and Construction also supervising some. A key responsibility of the tutelary Ministry is to develop, together with each enterprise, its yearly production plan, identifying *inter alia* financing needs for both working capital and investments, the level of subsidy (if necessary) and foreign exchange requirements. The enterprise relies upon its tutelary ministry for the disbursement of operating subsidies and for the all-important foreign exchange allocation. Within the prevailing system, there is an incentive for the industry to keep the production target low, so as to avoid subsequent pressure for better performance. Profitability of operations, or even minimization of costs, have hitherto not been emphasized. The ministry on the other hand will make efforts to increase planned production. As a result of these opposed interests, the planning process becomes a negotiating process rather than a process to plan and optimize production *per se*.

4.55 A considerable number of firms under the tutelage of the Ministry of Industry are privately owned (36%), while a few others (5%) are joint ventures of public and private capital, though with the former usually having a controlling stake. Private firms are considerably smaller than public manufacturing enterprises, at least measured in terms of number of employees. The average state owned company employed almost three times the number of workers as the average private firm. Each publicly-owned industry has a board of directors with representatives of both the party and the unions. In the period immediately following independence, many workers, with the aid of local committees and some support in the party, tried to take control of day-to-day management operations. Experiments with collective management, including workers commissions, were abandoned in late 1976. Enterprise directors are supposed to be selected from party ranks and have to be approved by the political bureau.

4.56 Public sector industries are supposed to obtain their raw materials and inputs from other government owned companies. Imports are made exclusively through the state import monopoly and non-payment for these supplies is used as a common means to finance industrial operations. This, in effect, forces government to subsidize industry indirectly by footing the bill for a large part of industrial inputs through its own trading companies. In theory, total production has to be handed over to state distribution companies at pre-determined prices. In practice, a substantial part of production goes into other channels, including barter trade between enterprises, workers' auto-consumo, the enterprise's own auto-consumo, and theft. The latter has been estimated as high as 35% for certain producers of much sought after consumer articles, such as plastic toys and sandals.

Industrial Policy

4.57 Despite the MPLA's commitment to the establishment of a socialist economy, its leaders have apparently taken a pragmatic approach with respect to nationalization and foreign investment. Legalization of state intervention in the economy, including nationalization of industry, was laid down in law 17/77 and by mid 1977, 85% of the abandoned enterprises were put under state control. It was made clear, though, that foreign companies, including Portuguese, who were willing to work with the government would not be expropriated.

4.58 The Government's industrial development efforts have been marked by an absence of clear objectives. The early Central Committee resolution of October 1976 stressed a revival of production as a short term tactical aim, but did not indicate priorities. Relatively large investments were made in a few projects, notably in the production of textiles and steel, with the latter possibly reflecting an emphasis on heavy industry. The foreign exchange shortages during the 1980s have been felt acutely in industry, which is heavily dependent on imported inputs. The deteriorating situation in the manufacturing sector led to new guidelines for industrial development after the second party congress in 1985, which stressed the need to conserve foreign exchange. These gave priority to the production of mass consumer goods in order to reduce imports as well as to the provision of incentives for increased agricultural production. Diversification of exports was also supported. However, the fundamental question of the economic viability of existing industrial activities has not been addressed. There is at least a strong presumption that the relatively large and broadly based industrial sector Angola inherited at independence does not represent an efficient use of resources. This is in part due to the changes in the economic environment following the departure of the Portuguese settlers. Thus, a principal long-term aim of the government should be to restructure Angola's industrial base so that it better reflects relative scarcities of resources.

4.59 The existing system of incentives, as determined by policies affecting external trade, prices, interest rates and labor, does not help to achieve this industrial restructuring. The highly overvalued Kwanza, and the unrealistic official prices and interest rates are giving producers and consumers of manufactures the wrong signals, and have created a large gap between demand and supply of foreign exchange, credit and most consumer and intermediate goods. This has required government intervention in the form of rationing, costly subsidization of many industrial activities, and tight control over operations and investments of public industrial enterprises. However, such intervention has been unable to correct for the price distortions. For example, the state controlled marketing system has failed to overcome the disincentive effect of unattractive prices on agricultural supplies to agro-industry. With regard to exports, the foreign exchange retention scheme which is supposed to partly offset the disincentive effect on exports of the overvalued Kwanza, only applies to a few exporters (e.g., Sonangol, and one hotel). Thus, a major adjustment of the system of incentives is a prerequisite for the establishment of a more viable industrial sector.

4.60 Policy changes with respect to industry are, among others, reflected in the proposals that are part of the SEF program. In principle, more operational autonomy will be granted to state enterprises, with the concomitant responsibility to operate profitably. Direct subsidies to offset operational losses are being restricted. While past policy was one of complete dependence of the enterprises on the government for funds, the new rules allow 50% of earnings to be retained. Companies were also promised increased leeway to set prices and to hire and fire personnel. These policy changes are predominantly of importance to state enterprises and will have less impact on private or mixed companies. Those private companies that remained in operation after independence have, by and large, been operating within the framework of pre-independence laws and regulations. Private industry has been left to fend for itself, though within the realities of a socialist economic system. Access to foreign exchange appears to be the main problem of these industries. Many of them operate, at least in part, through the parallel market. Repatriation of profits is allowed for private foreign investment up to an annual limit of 25% of the original foreign equity, but this rule is not automatically applied.

Prospects and recommendations

4.61 Numerous industries have been kept in operation after independence in spite of fundamental changes in the market and in the economy in general. Limited resources, both material and human, are spread too thinly over a diversified industry whose broad range of production should be questioned. There are no indications of systematic efforts to restructure this industry with a view to using resources more efficiently. The wisdom of producing motorcycles while nuts and bolts have to be imported, should be questioned. An industrial sector study, focusing on the value added at international prices of major manufacturing sub-sectors and enterprises, should be undertaken. In those cases in which this value added is proportionately small and involves a high cost in domestic resources, it will in general be preferable to abandon the existing production. Such a move would contribute positively to the development of other domestic productive activities by releasing scarce resources, including skilled personnel and foreign exchange spent on imported inputs. Trained manpower being a major constraint, dedication of some of the country's financial resources to training of technical shop floor personnel should show good returns in the long run. Angola urgently needs more of the type of trade school that exists at the steel plant in Luanda. Not only will such schools generate the technical cadre that is indispensable for the operation of industry, but from the ranks of these same technicians will spring the future entrepreneurs of small new industries.

4.62 The establishment of a more appropriate incentive framework is an essential step towards the creation of a more viable industrial base in Angola in the longer run. Policy measures relating to the exchange rate, prices, interest rates, import licensing and marketing are discussed elsewhere in this report as part of a general economic reform program. Together, these would gradually lessen the need for administrative controls and provide incentives to more efficient industrial activities. As these reforms will take time to become effective, the government should at the same time undertake a review of the major public enterprises in industry with a view to phasing out those enterprises that clearly lack long term economic viability. The remaining industries should be given greater operational autonomy, with tutelary Ministries focusing on monitoring and control of performance rather than on prescribing production levels. In the next few years, investments should be concentrated mainly on the recovery of those industries which appear to be viable in the long run, rather than on new projects. In addition to re-establishing the trade schools, the training of skilled operators should be encouraged by creating adequate salary differentials between skilled, semi-skilled and unskilled workers. There is also a need for an incentive and support system to encourage the growth of small entrepreneurs. Seed capital, foreign exchange allocation, pertinent legislation and fiscal incentives are among the measures needed.

E. CONSTRUCTION AND BUILDING MATERIALS

Introduction

4.63 Angola's infrastructure, industrial and urban sectors all require significant levels of new investment to rehabilitate systems, improve output, and raise the quality of services. The successful implementation of such investment programs requires the availability of an appropriate mix of funding, materials, human resources and construction enterprises. In the early 1980s, the infrastrutural planning focus has been on financing issues, with less emphasis on the physical inputs and production elements. However, in recent years, it has become increasingly obvious that the national construction sector, which includes all activities from design to building services, was incapable of even meeting routine needs, let alone the consequences of any new investment packages. Many such programs would require quantities of materials (sometimes large) which could be reliably supplied against tight construction schedules, while meeting minimum standards of quality at reasonable cost. The national construction materials sector is presently incapable of meeting these conditions and this represents a serious obstacle to the success of general recovery programs like SEF and to specific sectoral programs like urban renewal.

4.64 The Ministry of Construction (MC) is the apex sectoral planning entity and has managed its operations by categorizing activities geographically (province, region and national) and by type of output (building, engineering and materials). However, productivity has continued to fall throughout the 1980s. In 1986, only about half (52%) of the MC planned output was achieved by the 34 companies directly under its control - Kz 4,7 billion out of a targeted Kz 9.1 billion. Furthermore, global production expenses for the sector were double the sales income received, although 23 companies were reported as financially self supporting during the same period. There are 12 companies (almost all state entities) responsible for the construction of buildings, 8 for infrastructural projects, 10 supplying materials and 4 providing specialist services like geo-technical work.

4.65 While building and engineering companies are generally under the direct responsibility of the Ministry of Construction, in the materials sub-sector the Ministry of Industry (MI) largely controls metal, plastics, paints and electrical products. As an example, in a study of building materials in the Luanda region, consultants found four separate organizations involved in the operation of companies and production units in the sub-sector. These were:

(i) Ministry of Construction: 17 companies and 40 production sites.

(ii) Ministry of Industry: 18 companies and 21 production sites.

(iii) Commissar: 15 production units, and

(iv) Ministry of Agriculture: 2 production units

This highlights a potential problem of coordination within the sub-sector and points towards recognition of the heterogeneous nature of the sub-sector when considering much needed policy reforms. The study of the building and construction materials industry identified over 80 production sites in Luanda and Bengo alone, and there are likely to be many more small units working in the parallel or informal market. However, it is the commercial strength of the larger companies that will either help or hinder economic recovery in the short to medium term, and these should be the initial focus of sub-sector investment.

Performance of the Sector

4.66 Table 4.9 shows construction output for 1985 and 1986, by category of company. It is noted that output in the building sector has fallen

Table 4.9: BUILDING AND ENGINEERING CONSTRUCTION OUTPUT, 1985 AND 1986
(Kz million)

Categories	Building		Engineering		Total		% Achieved of Planned Output
	1985	1986	1985	1986	1985	1986	1986
Provincial Delegations	42	77	410	394	452	472	55
Provincial Companies	1,226	373	47	122	1,274	495	65
Regional Companies*			611	862	611	862	87
National Companies	1,817	1,254	174	198	1,991	1,452	35
Total Sector	3,086	1,705	1,243	1,576	4,329	3,281	49

* Not operating in building sub-sector

Source: Annual Report: Construction Sector, MC.1987

back in 1986, while the engineering groups have generally shown some growth. However, total sector production fell by 25 percent. Equally importantly, the full sector was operating at less than half capacity. Contracting with international construction companies is generally a second-best solution, and the long term policy which accords most effectively with economic reform programs is one which would strengthen the national sector and enable it to provide a good proportion of the required services on schedule, within estimated cost, and at a profit. Recent data confirm that the sector continues to weakean, adversely affecting productivity and financial strength. Sub-sector performances are briefly detailed below.

4.67 Engineering - In 1986, this sub-sector employed over 6000 workers, and produced an output valued at Kz 1.6 billion, with one company responsible for half of that value. In the balance sheet for that year, total expenditures for the sector exceeded revenues by over 40 percent. In general terms, mixed companies fared better than public entities. Total revenues were dominated by general work (74%) followed by the maritime sector (10%), bridges (7%), and water/sanitation (2%). The small size of the latter category is rather surprising given the rapid growth of urbanization, which must have created a significant demand for basic utilities throughout the country.

4.68 Building - This sub-sector accounts for 46% of the MC budget and over 60% of its foreign exchange budget. It employed over 10.000 workers in 1986, most with low levels of education and skills. The need to augment the work force with specialized foreign personnel (730) contributed to the size of the foreign exchange needs, and this is likely to be a feature of building operations over the short and medium term. As with engineering sub-sector, overall financial performance was very poor, and expenses exceeded revenues by almost 50%. Gross output, at Kz 2.6 billion, was only that of 1983, showing that despite the need for various rehabilitation in recent years, output has failed to respond and meet this demand. A few companies dominate the sub-sector and 3 entities were responsible for over 60% of the revenue generated.

4.69 Materials - In terms of the MC budget, this sub-sector is relatively modest in its financial needs, accounting for 15% of MC costs and 14% of its foreign exchange allocations. Nevertheless, it is critical in any recovery strategy for the building and engineering sub-sectors. In addition, there are excellent job creation and foreign exchange saving opportunities which strengthen the attractiveness of investment in materials production. In 1986, actual revenue reached Kz 1,436 million, which was about 6% of planned targets.

Investment Proposals

4.70 In the southern region, a number of measures have been proposed to carry out emergency rehabilitation of existing infrastructure, together with new buildings and facilities required as part of the economic recovery program, including low cost housing and community infrastructure. To accomplish these objectives, it is proposed to: (i) develop appropriate building and construction techniques, taking into account technical skills and materials availability; (ii) improving the capacity of local production units, especially for brickmaking, cement, wood products and carpentry activities; (iii) promote small scale labor intensive construction projects (irrigation, rural roads); and (iv) improve technical assistance and organization to meet the extensive construction needs. No costs are given for the program, though the labor intensive program is estimated at around US$0.5 million per year, including payments in food for salary. Technical assistance costs, including key personnel and equipment for a single, large five year program totals out at US$ 3.3 million.

4.71 In the Luanda region, consultants selected 46 factories to assess what actions could be taken to raise productivity, currently averaging only 16% of installed capacity. They concentrated attention on the production of clay bricks, wooden door and window frames, and steel reinforcing bars, and found that major factors affecting output were shortages of foreign exchange for raw materials and spare parts, lack of manpower skills and poor staff incentives. They recommended a five year program of 44 projects which would cost US$22 million plus Kz 159 million (1988 prices) local currency to fund (a) US$10.2 million technical assistance, (b) US$ 9.8 million equipment purchases and (c) US$2 million plus Kz 159 million for civil works. In addition, they recommend linking financial incentives to productivity for salary payments. Management techniques (like setting production targets) and accounting practices also need improvement and strengthening.

4.72 It is currently unclear how ministerial staff intend to schedule these programs and integrate them into overall sector planning. Most production entities are struggling with a complex series of problems, some operational and others completely out of their control. At this moment, the size and economic significance of the informal market is unknown, except that it dominates the private housing construction sub-sector. However, MC staff are correct in attempting to improve the productivity of the larger formal companies so that short and medium term planning can be strengthened. Since the production methods of many building products and materials do not lend themselves to small scale units, MC staff should identify those entities more suitable for private/mixed operations and separate them from those where government finance and technical assistance would have a high impact. It needs to focus on those key materials related to proposed investment projects, and try organize and support the sector so that material centres (of whatever ownership pattern) supply as much of the related demand as possible.

Conclusions

4.73 The main points to emerge from this review of the building and construction materials sector are the following:

(i) the national construction sector, covering activities from design to building services, is currently incapable of meeting routine demand for products and services, and output has continued to fall throughout the 1980s.

(ii) output in the government controlled sector is dominated by few companies, while many other units contributing little value continue to absorb budgetary resources.

(iii) the work force is difficult to motivate, education and training skills are low, and absenteeism is increasing. Part of this is related to very low salary purchasing power.

(iv) equipment needs are often specialized; public companies have a worse record of equipment maintenance and availability than mixed entities, and spare parts availability for all the sector is poor causing frequent breakdowns in production. In addition, the irregular supply of materials, both from local and imported sources, combines with production difficulties to affect productivity.

(v) poor stock, accounting and inventory controls are noted in the sector, leading to waste, losses and theft of costly items, which therefore contributes to a lack of cost control.

(vi) low availability of transport services severly constrains the supply of raw materials, operational capabilities and the distribution of final products.

(vii) the security situation continues to limit operations and raise costs.

4.74 Within the overall context created by the security situation and macroeconomic policies, sector policies should focus on strengthening the sector and improving operational capabilities. Specific measures might include:

(i) calculating the demand for products and services on a regional basis, and avoiding the necessity of importation wherever possible. This requires a five year plan, covering both existing demand patterns and those arising from investment in construction programs of all types.

(ii) reducing the number of government controlled entities by focusing on the key production centers and cutting those absorbing resources without prospect for improvement.

(iii) strengthening the role of mixed and private enterprises,

(iv) rationalizing public enterprises in the sector by setting achievable targets, payment by results, adequate salary levels and improved access to foreign exchange where appropriate to production needs, implementing cost control and introducing appropriate accounting system to manage costs, help set prices and determine investment requirements.

The current situation creates a grave hindrance to economic recovery and labor employment prospects. Production does not meet demand levels, at official prices, and is highly erratic as a consequence of both input difficulties and production problems. If sector forecasting can be coordinated with other sector needs, like demand from infrastructure, transport and urban renewal, bottlenecks can be identified. These can then be analyzed and alternative strategies developed to correct deficiencies, and determine alternative local and regional sources of supply, before international sources are employed.

F. ENERGY 4/

Introduction

4.75 By African standards, Angola is well endowed with energy resources, including a large hydro potential, ample biomass stocks and substantial oil and gas reserves. In terms of its proven oil and gas reserves, Angola ranks first among the African countries with medium-scale hydrocarbons. Furthermore, based on both the crude oil reserves which have been discovered so far (more than 1.4 billion bbls. equivalent to about 17.5 million tons) and the current level of domestic petroleum product consumption (about 1.5 million tons p.a.), Angola's long-run position is that of self-sufficiency in oil (assuming that the rate of time preference is positive).

4.76 In 1986, Angola's primary energy supply amounted to 19.7 billion toe which, on a per capita basis (2.2 toe), is an exceptionally high figure. However, if adjusted for crude oil exports, the non-energy use of natural gas (reinjection) and the losses involved in charcoal production, final energy consumption proves moderate (see Table 4.10 below). In 1986, final energy consumption worked out at 229 kgoe per capita, of which about 102 kg were commercial energy (petroleum products and electricity). For comparison, in 1985 final commercial energy consumption in Gabon and the Congo (two other African countries with medium-scale hydrocarbon endowments) amounted to 602 kgoe and 151 kgoe, respectively.

Table 4.10: ENERGY BALANCE OVERVIEW, 1986
(in '000 toe)

	Fuelwood/ Charcoal	Natural Gas	Crude Oil	Electricity Hydro	Petroleum Products	Total
Total Domestic Supply of Primary Energy	2,074	3,418	14,102	173	-	19,765
Final Energy Consumption	1,180			49	879	2,108

Source : Energy Sector Assessment Report.

4/ This section provides an overview of the energy sector, based on the forthcoming Energy Sector Assessment report, which should be consulted for further details on the sector.

4.77 Figures on commercial energy consumption indicate that in the 1980s there was hardly any correlation between energy demand and the overall performance of the economy. As real GDP declined between 1980 and 1986, the consumption of electricity remained almost constant (-0,5%) while the consumption of petroleum products showed a strong upward trend (+6.6%), as shown in Table 4.11 below. In fact, given the extremely low level of electricity tariffs and refined product prices (measured in terms of the purchasing power of parallel market income), commercial energy demand (dominated by household and military use) did not face constraints other than those set by the supply capacity and the availability of end-use devices. Accordingly, the regional and sectoral distribution of commercial energy became heavily distorted, reflecting the drawbacks of the civil war and the depressed and disintegrated state of the economy.

Table 4.11: SELECTED INDICATORS ON ANGOLA'S ENERGY SECTOR

	1986	Average Annual Rate of Change a/ 1980-1986 (%)
Crude Oil Reserves (million bbl)	1,418	-
Crude Oil Production (1,000 b/d)	282 (b)	+14.70
Natural Gas Reserves (TCF)	5	-
Petroleum Product Consumption (1,000 toe)	879	+ 6.63
Electricity Consumption (GWh)	588	- 0.49
Electricity Generation (GWh)	753	+ 0.57

a/ Least square estimates.
b/ In early 1988, oil output had increased to about 450 000 barrels per day and the reserves to production ratio had dropped to below 10 years.

Source : Ministry of Energy and Petroleum and mission estimates.

4.78 Woodfuels contribute significantly the country's energy balance, even though the supply from rural areas is frequently disrupted. However, the high degree of urbanization and the constraints imposed by the war have led to regional and local supply/demand imbalances, particularly in urban coastal areas. Moreover, in nominal terms woodfuels, which are almost exclusively traded in parallel markets, prove to be the country's most expensive source of energy, a fact which is attributable to temporary, war-dependent shortages and inefficiencies (particularly in the distribution systems), rather than to a general lack of biomass resources.

The Role of Petroleum

4.79 As explained in Chapter 2, the petroleum sector has been of crucial importance to the economy of the country. While Angola has not been in a position to optimally use its oil revenues, it managed to develop the petroleum sector in a fairly efficient way. Large investments undertaken in the 1980s (financed by foreign private capital) laid the groundwork for a continuous increase in oil production since 1982, and except for 1986 output growth even offset the fall in international petroleum prices. So far, a non-distortionary (but tight) tax regime (which concentrates on net profits rather than on royalties), favorable geological conditions and comparatively low production costs have attracted the foreign capital required to keep the petroleum sector prospering. Between 1980 and 1986 the average annual investments in crude oil exploration and development amounted to US$390 million, and for the period 1987-90 the expenditures in upstream activities are scheduled to exceed US$500 million per annum (see Appendix Table G.3). However, the deterioration of Angola's balance of payments in 1986/87, the financial burden of loss-making downstream operations and growing debt service requirements of SONANGOL (the country's state-owned oil company), coupled with the fact that part of the old SONANGOL management has recently been replaced with relatively inexperienced technocrats, will make it difficult to maintain the high level of investments required to ensure that crude oil production continues to rise in the 1990s.

4.80 Clearly, as long as the war continues, Angola's primary concern will be the development and exploitation of its oil reserves at the fastest pace possible. Moreover, if petroleum prices remain in the vicinity of US$18/bbl until the early 1990s, there is a strong economic incentive to deplete the producing fields as quickly as feasible (and to convert the oil into more profitable assets). However in the medium term, the more relevant question will be the country's absorptive capacity for oil revenues, particularly if output continues to increase as rapidly as in the past. Broadly speaking, in the event of peace, it might become more advisable to slow down the expansion of the petroleum sector and to give priority to the development of other sectors, such as agriculture and industry. In fact, the removal of the war constraints would favor the implementation of a structural adjustment program envisaging a reduced dependence of the economy on oil.

4.81 For the next three to four years, however, the crude oil production rate is by and large determined by the level of past and current investments in field development on the one hand, and the pressing revenue needs of the Government on the other hand. In 1987, petroleum output increased significantly to 351,000 b/d. Output growth continued in 1988, but will probably slow down by 1990. Crude oil export revenues recovered from US$1,150 million in 1986 to US$2,000 million in 1987 and climbed further to around US$2,600 million in 1988 (see Table 4.12 below). However, since production from Cabinda is expected to stagnate at the end of the 1980s (due to delays in investment and the shifting of priorities towards Block 3), export earnings will remain below the US$3,000 million level until the early 1990s (unless oil prices happen to rise considerably).

Table 4.12: PROJECTED CRUDE OIL EXPORTS, 1987-1991

	1987	1988 a/	1989	1990	1991
Oil Production (million tons)	17.55	21.70	22.25	22.40	22.50
Exports (million tons)	16.05	20.02	20.75	20.90	21.00
International Price of Oil (US$/bbl)	17	18	18	19	19
Export Revenues (milion US$)	1,992	2,631	2,727	2,899	2,913

a/ Actual oil production in 1988 was 22.5 m.tons.
Source: Sonangol and mission estimates.

4.82 Apart from the planned investments (by foreign oil companies) in oil exploration and development, which are required to prevent the reserves-to-production ratio from falling significantly below the level of 10 years, there is no need for additional heavy investment in up or downstream operations of the petroleum sector. In particular, the Government should refrain from any attempts designed to integrate the oil enclave into the economy on the basis of large downstream projects such as fertilizer production or refinery modernization/expansion. In the medium-term the economic prospects for the proposed ammonia/urea plant are far from favorable. Moreover, the recent de-bottlenecking of the Luanda refinery (which seems to run profitably) will make a broadly satisfactory supply of the domestic market feasible (with excess fuel oil being exported and deficit fuels being imported at the margin). This is particularly the case if two minor, economically viable LPG recovery projects which could substitute for household LPG imports come on stream in the immediate future.

The Power Sub-Sector

4.83 In the power sector, the main task will be the rehabilitation of the existing infrastructure (and the financial recovery of the utilities) rather than the provision of additional capacity. Power demand projections indicate that new capacity (above and beyond the existing capacity which is susceptible to rehabilitation) will not be required until the mid-1990s. However, developments over the next decade will be conditioned by the Capanda project, which involves a 4x130 MW hydroplant at an estimated total cost which could reach US$2.0 billion. This project will not contribute to the solution of the most pressing problems of the power sector. Rather, it will add considerable generating capacity for which there is no need (until the end of the century) and which could not even be used because of the limited and outworn transmission and distribution facilities of the country. It will also greatly inflate Angola's external debt and, at the same time, create very little additional revenue for the utilities, thus aggravating the financial difficulties of the sector. In part in response to these problems, the Government has decided to slow down the completion of the project by installing only two of the four generating units. While this will save more than US$100 million, the civil engineering costs will remain essentially the same (except for some small savings which are expected from using some innovative techniques in laying concrete) while the capacity will be halved. This will raise both the economic and financial costs of the energy to be generated at Capanda. A study is about to begin (with ESMAP assistance), which will review, among other key elements the power subsector, the phasing and scheduling of the Capanda project as well as a future role for GAMEK (the executing agency of the Capanda project), possibly as a river valley development authority or as a contractor for other projects.

Bio-mass Resources

4.84 The country's vast biomass resources (with an aggregate sustained yield exceeding 150 million tons per year) would, under normal conditions, easily meet rural and urban woodfuel demand. Hence, there is also no need to launch expensive afforestation programs. On the contrary, Government is well advised to continue its "hands-off" policy in order to avoid additional disruptions in the supply of firewood and charcoal, particularly to urban concentrations on the coast (the main shortage areas). However, with the return to peace, measures will be required to improve the efficiency and competitiveness of both woodfuel charcoal production and trade so that woodfuel supply costs become more reasonable relative to "commercial energy" counterparts such as LPG and Kerosene. Until then, government policy should restrict itself to selected activities in a few areas (e.g., introduction of improved stoves, agro-forestry trials in rural areas).

Energy Policies

4.85 The key to a more rational use of Angola's energy resources are major improvements in the energy sector's incentive framework, combined with substantial efforts to upgrade the organizational and managerial capabilities of the institutions which are involved in the supply and distribution of energy commodities. In particular, measures should be taken to:

(a) reduce wasteful and low priority consumption of petroleum products through the establishment of a more efficient pricing scheme which eliminates subsidies on the refinery's crude oil supply and petroleum product output and brings the domestic price structure in line with import and export parities;

(b) privatize at least part of the petroleum product distribution system, currently a Sonangol monopoly;

(c) adjust the electricity tariffs to a level at which the financial cost (and in the longer run, the economic cost) of supply can be recovered, and improve the management and revenue collection/ accounting system of the utilities by means of technical assistance, training efforts and a decentralization of responsibilities; and

(d) develop policy instruments that may help to increase the competitiveness of woodfuel markets, to be implemented as soon as the civil strife comes to a halt.

4.86 In view of the currently prevailing distortions in energy production and consumption, it is difficult to predict what changes in demand and supply are likely to result from the proposed policy measures. Moreover, much depends on when and to what extent the economy will recover from the present recession and what role agriculture and industry are going to play. Without resumption of growth in agriculture and industry and as long as the civil strife continues to disrupt the basic infrastructure of the country, the short-term demand impact of the measures will certainly be limited to the (urban) household sector. A more reasonably structured pricing system for household energy (in particular the prices of commercial energy compared to traditional energy sources) is likely to curb the future increase in electricity, LPG and kerosene consumption. However, industry's demand, which is dominated by a few energy-intensive operations using boiler fuels (cement, refinery, extraction) as well as government consumption which is biased towards transport fuels, will show little response unless major structural changes take place.

4.87 On the supply-side, the above-mentioned measures may lay the groundwork for a gradual financial recovery of the country's utilities and the fuel distribution system, so that future increases in demand can be met on a more viable basis. However, any sustained success in restoring the efficiency of the energy sector (excluding the oil enclave) is conditional on the design and sequencing of the overall policy reforms required for structural adjustment, on both the macro and micro levels.

G. TRANSPORT

Overview

4.88 Angola's basic infrastructure has strong colonial antecedents and its present configuration, though not its condition, is essentially unchanged since Independence (see map I). In 1975, the system had a comprehensive modal mix which included rail, highway, air, cabotage and shipping and provided an excellent opportunity for potential transit facilities to match or facilitate economic development. The modal pattern was dominated by a distinctive, lateral three rail-port corridor system (north, central and southern), supported by feeder road networks. Additional highways provided very basic north-south provincial links, as well as access to national borders. The air sector, which then linked all key provincial cities, has subsequently become the only dependable means of passenger and light freight transit over much of the country, due to the security situation.

4.89 In 1987, Angola's transport infrastructure comprised 72.000km of roads, 2.500km of railways, 3 international and 3 cabotage ports, and a hierarchy of 31 airports. An estimated 30.000 non-military trucks and 400 buses, 40 locomotives, 11 long distance ships, 10 cabotage vessels, and 21 aircraft operated infrequent modal services at low levels of efficiency. Rail and port systems form distinctive corridors, which previously ran eastwards from Luanda to Malange (a distance of 430km) in the north, Lobito to Luau (1.350km) in the central heartland and Namibe to Menongue (750km) in the south. Regions are linked to these corridors by 9.000 km of paved highway and 66.000 km of secondary and feeder roads, which together with the air services provide the main means of north-south travel. Cabotage currently accounts for 180.000 tons of freight between the four main ports and has potential for substantial growth. The Cabinda enclave is dominated by the oil industry and the non-petroleum infrastructure is small.

4.90 Output from 1985 to 1987 for the system under the Ministry of Transport and Communications' (MINTEC) control is shown in Table 4.16 below. Total freight traffic for 1986, at around 3 million tons, is about three quarters that of 1985, with the road and maritime sectors compensating to a limited degree for the continuing decline in rail traffic. In 1987, the number of passengers carried fell below 25 million, following a decline in bus services which offset improvements in rail and air transit demand. The total value of MINTEC-controlled transport and communications services in 1987 was estimated at Kz 17.631 million, of which 31% was attributed to road services, 30% to air and the remainder split fairly evenly between the other modes and communications. The data for the period 1980 to 1987 show a significant decline in road activity, especially urban bus services, with rail and maritime holding constant, and port output rising slightly then falling back. The communications and air travel sub-sectors both showed consistent growth, although both faltered in 1987. In spite of the progress made in the sector, it is sobering to note that the value of total sector output in 1987 was less than half that achieved in 1974.

Table 4.13 ANGOLA: OUTPUT OF MINTEC CONTROLLED TRANSPORT SERVICES (1985 - 1986)

	Freight a/			Passengers b/		
	1985	1986	1987	1985	1986	1987
Road	996	1,309	1,100	29,475	19,546	16,203
Rail	521	465	517	7,200	7,980	6,398
Maritime	512	598	53	-	-	-
Air	43	35	42	926	1,098	815
Ports	1,739	1,551	1,172	-	-	-
Totals	3,812	3,958	2,884	37,602	28,623	23,516

a/ Thousands of tons.
b/ Thousands of passengers.

Source: MINTEC, 1987.

4.91 The security problem has disrupted all transport modes and severely constrained corridor operations. Services have been cut, investment programs cancelled and overall domestic transit efficiency lowered. Destruction of at least 45 bridges and key sections of track has virtually paralyzed regional rail movement and only 20% of the system can be operated normally. Mineral shipments have ceased and port activities, 1.2 million tons in 1987, are concentrated on handling import commodities for urban consumption, especially food, for which rail transit is not well suited. Road transport to autarchic regional centers is only possible with armed convoys, operating irregularly and at great cost. The road system has not been systematically maintained since Independence, over 200 bridges need rehabilitation, and 5 400 Km (60%) of paved surfaces need rehabilitation or reconstruction.

4.92 In 1987, the truck fleet was estimated at 30,000 units but many of these are not operational or are severely under-utilized. For example, in 1987, only 37% of the heavy vehicles controlled by MINTEC were operational, their output had fallen 12% over 1986 and vehicles averaged just 11,500 km a year. The state trucking sector has been very successful in channeling imported vehicles into their operations and this is reflected in a fleet profile which is technically sophisticated and young in age. The private sector, in comparison, operates vehicles generally at least ten years old and of simple, robust design. Fortunately, they are well suited to current Angolan conditions where journeys are rarely longer than 50 km and vehicle trip speeds are low. Urban passenger transport is concentrated in Luanda where advanced bus designs are operated over extremely rough roads in overloaded conditions, resulting in service lives less than 20% of those for normal use. Urban bus service levels during 1987, in terms of route kilometers offered, had fallen to 19% of that achieved in 1981, which partially explains the growth in private taxi and light truck urban services. Demand still far exceeds supply, however, and all urban areas have experienced large growth rates in pedestrian flows which add to the problems of congestion and safety. All vehicles are affected by chronic spare parts supply problems which appear intractable under current distributional arrangements.

4.93 Port operations fell dramatically at Independence and in 1986 were less than a fifth of their 1973 level, which was 6.4 million tons. Furthermore, the flow of goods has been reversed, with imports dominating the freight business (representing 90% of the 1.7 million total 1986 port tonnage). Facilities originally designed for large bulk exports are not adequate for the type of import products currently handled and the lack of warehousing, cold storage, secure areas, equipment and transport facilities result in an inefficient physical distribution system. Shipping is subject to costly delays, cargo is damaged and pilfering rampant. Angolan-controlled shipping accounts for about a third of port tonnage, divided equally between the three national agencies. Containers have not been a success due to a combination of ineffective and costly use within Angola and poor transshipment facilities. Operations at Luanda port have improved over the past 18 months only because traffic has declined over 60% as a result of falling oil revenues. Privatization of container work is being openly discussed and a number of shipping agencies and companies are interested in taking on this business. Cabotage has failed to attract passengers or increase freight traffic, although MINTEC has given coastal transport a key role in their short term investment proposals.

4.94 Air transport has grown consistently since 1975, assisted by attractive tariffs and greater security from attacks and sabotage. Aircraft are operated by Angolan Airlines (TAAG), which is nominally profitable due to cheap fuel, low wages and high load factors. The fleet is currently operating at about half the number of annual hours considered efficient for its operation. Six Boeing 707s are used for international flights, though they are banned from a number of European airports because they no longer meet 1988 European Community noise requirements. Domestic traffic is carried by a mixed fleet of 15 aircraft, including five Boeing 737s, though the marketing of domestic services is weak (for example, daily service schedules are published in the newspaper and not in easily distributed passenger time-tables). Airport activities are the reponsibility of the Airport and Navigation Company (ENANA), and airport facilities form the main constraint to improved subsector domestic operations. Most regional airports are unable to take the 737, cannot offer refuelling facilities and lack radio navigation and other safety aids. As a result, TAAG has to operate its domestic flights during daylight hours, which severely limits utilization and schedules. The need to fly planes with adequate fuel reserves and also meet high seat demand and carry urgent cargo, results in overloading. The reduction in safety margins is reflected in the loss of three 737s since 1977.

Issues and Recommendations

4.95 The sector was found to be in urgent need of restructuring at all levels of modal activity. It is characterized, inter alia, by the following constraints:

(i) inadequate fleet sizes of vehicles, trains, ships and airplanes;

(ii) short service lives of road vehicles, railway engines and mechanical handling equipment of all types;

(iii) distorted tariffs, leading to inefficient modal distribution of passengers and cargo;

(iv) unreliable, ad-hoc and inconvenient service schedules;

(v) the failure of urban passenger transit systems to meet the needs generated by rapid urbanization, and a consequent growth in pedestrian trips;

(vi) chronic lack of foreign exchange to purchase all modal spares and poor support from the commercial section of the National Bank of Angola;

(vii) weak transshipment capabilities, especially at port facilities;

(viii) inadequate modal maintenance facilities and insufficient numbers of technical staff;

(ix) the large size of transport parastatal entities has created management and manpower staffing problems which are overwhelming administrators;

(x) poor management, remuneration, and control of staff; and

(xi) inconsistent road vehicle licensing arrangements.

These constraints result in costly passenger and cargo rates in real terms and an inefficient demand for modal services. In general, the supply of services is totally inadequate to meet the demand at official price levels and parallel pricing of maintenance and services is present in the road subsector, together with queuing and time delays in other modes.

4.96 If the Government of Angola wants to take corrective action, it is important to note that the transport sector has limited capacity to absorb large investment programs. Limitations include inadequate local complementary services, lack of experience in managing large projects at Ministry and Provincial levels, and potential difficulties in meeting targets for locally produced and financed inputs because of irregular supply of locally manufactured materials and budgetary constraints. In these circumstances, a sector program focusing on short term, high impact projects with modest financing requirements seems to be the most appropriate response, supported by policy changes. Large single projects should be evaluated separately, taking into account their consequences in terms of sectoral absorptive capacity.

4.97 MINTEC's programming and evaluation unit has proposed a series of investment programs based on a hierarchy of provincial, regional and national/ international transport needs. The plans are modest and pragmatic and recognize the dual problems of security and budgetary constraints. In the short term, it is considered desirable to reduce the demand for air services, both cargo and passengers, by raising service levels in other modes, particularly highways and cabotage. In addition, MINTEC controlled tariffs are grossly distorted, do not reflect real resource costs and require urgent review and upward revision.

Modal Development

4.98 Roads. The key issues and options in the road sub-sector are as follows:

(a) Supply of Services. The numbers of operational vehicles must be increased and useful life in kilometers extended through easier access to spare parts, training mechanics and improving maintenance facilities. In addition, stricter control of drivers and loads, and improved road conditions would contribute significantly to prolonging vehicle life. There should be an efficient private sector to complement State transport enterprises. Regulation should be very carefully evaluated, as excessive control has rarely had the desired effect in other African countries and vehicle licenses should be freely available as long as applicants meet required operational standards. Tariffs should be determined by market forces and efficient operators should be allowed to have more than one vehicle. A variety of vehicle types, providing different levels of service at different prices, will determine the appropriate price levels, as long as excessive regulation is avoided. In urban transport, bus fleets need to be expanded and the surface roughness of the route network needs to be improved to reduce vehicle damage. The desirability of companies and parastatals operating bus services for the sole benefit of their employees should be reviewed and the private sector, comprising taxis, pick-ups and mini-buses, should be allowed to grow.

(b) Highway Infrastructure. The Ministry of Construction (MC) has the responsibility for the design, construction and maintenance of the highway network. It is currently operating with a severely constrained budget. Highway infrastructure needs to be regularly monitored to implement a needs program, related to a revised highway maintenance system. Such a program could have an important regional employment potential. There are five rehabilitation projects which, with the exception of Malange to Saurino, are located along the more secure coastal belt. Three relatively short construction projets are currently being undertaken, with an equal number being evaluated for their economic viability. Critical links which would complete the north-south coastal highway are also being put forward to international agencies for possible funding and should generate high rates of return. Finally, there are several lateral network sections identified by MC engineers that link the coastal highway with interior provincial regions, but there is no current prospect for their funding. In discussions with MC staff, it was determined that there was little chance of significant improvements to the network while the present administrative structure was retained. MC staff favored the creation of an autonomous highway authority, directly funded from road users and beneficiaries, charged with operation and maintenance of the network. The Junta Autónoma de Estradas de Angola which existed until independence could be a role model for such an operation, with suitable modifications for current socio-economic conditions. In planning terms, road investment is appealing because its flexibility permits regional impacts to be finely tuned and the sector also has attractive employment prospects, particularly in the areas of road construction and maintenance. As part of the proposed reorganization, consideration may also be given to determining a system of vehicle user charges to cover infrastructural investment and maintenance.

4.99 Cabotage. Regional development requires that goods and produce from an area be transported to major markets without delay and at low cost. Cabotage has an excellent potential for providing services over part of the regional transport link from the producer to consumer, though its present performance is dismal. MINTEC is proposing programs for both passenger and cargo cabotage investment, principally in the ship fleet which is presently old, unreliable and incapable of providing the desired level of service. Two new 320 passenger ships are operating between Luanda and Lobito but facilities at all ports need to be improved to allow coastal ships to be promptly berthed, unloaded and serviced. The existing arrangements represent a serious obstacle to efficient cabotage operations.

4.100 Railways. Investment requirements for Angolan railway systems are considerable. There is a need to rehabilitate the permanent way, replace damaged bridges, renew rolling stock, rebuild non-operational locomotives, renovate signalling and communications, improve transshipment facilities, develop adequate numbers of technical staff and ensure a regular supply of spare parts for the entire operation. The analysis of the Benguela corridor should be treated separately, using standard evaluation criteria and an assessment of security to determine the desirability and timing of rehabilitation. Railway projects that promote short-term sectoral impacts should be favored, such as improving rail transit in the Luanda port and hinterland, providing technical assistance to adequately maintain existing engines, rebuild engines and rolling stock in all three systems and plan sequential investments within selected corridors. Such corridor projects should include passenger traffic where appropriate. Finally, demand forecasts need to be carefully examined to avoid the unwarranted assumption that pre-Independence traffic levels can be easily regained once the military and political obstacles are removed. This may simply not be the case, given the growth of competing modes and routes in Southern Africa.

4.101 Air. The evaluation of TAAG's long distance aircraft should be a separate project and only measures to improve domestic services should be considered in the proposed program. The company currently operates a severely under-utilized fleet which needs rationalization. In 1986, over

5,400 staff were employed at high nominal salary levels by African standards, given that most had no technical or managerial skills. Personnel numbers need to be cut, and management improved (perhaps by the privatization of cleaning and catering) in an effort to bring about immediate improvements in productivity. TAAG presently carries a large and costly eight-month inventory of spare parts because of difficulties in obtaining foreign exchange. Also if ENANA airport safety and communications could be improved within the domestic system, TAAG could operate its aircraft over a longer daily period and thereby improve utilization. Finally, due to tariff distortions and the fixed exchange rate, TAAG is subsidizing all its activities in real resource terms. A sequential adjustment to the tariff structure is urgently needed to allow TAAG to operate on a sound financial basis.

4.102 Technical Assistance. All transport modes could benefit from assistance to develop and train good management, retrain experienced and responsible operators and develop the competence of technical staff. Technical assistance should be targeted on critical areas within selected projects, like installing a highway inventory and condition system as part of a revitalized provincial network. An improved equipment maintenance capability is required for most modes and highway maintenance could well be a prominant feature of technical assistance. Training programs at all levels in all modes are also highly desirable and should result in higher utilization and productivity, to the benefit of the economy.

4.103 Communications. The transport sector, in common with other sectors, would benefit from improved public communications at all levels. Communications in general have failed to attract sufficient investment to match demand and to maintain standards. The number of subscribers doubled to over 50,000 since 1975. Companies were nominally profitable in 1986 but tariffs do not reflect resource costs and the whole subsector needs reorganization in terms of tariffs, salaries, mail transport, maintenance, technical training and management control of staff and operating producers. The mail system is essentially a low technology operation while telecommunications is characterized by high technology, with substantial investments and good potential profitability. The reform of the mail service can be achieved by concerted Government action, with little help from external agencies. A number of projects in the area of telecommunications have been proposed by MINTEC and technical assistance and equipment could be provided in some areas.

H. HUMAN RESOURCES [5]

Characteristics of the Labor Force

4.104 According to the latest census data,[6] 44% of the total population in the mid-1980s was of working age (table 4.17), the labor force participation rate was 53%, and the official unemployment rate was 3%. In Luanda, the proportion of working age was higher, and the labor force participation rate lower than the national average. As shown in Table 4.17 below, the proportion of those employed who work in the primary sector has dropped sharply since 1970. The change reflects less a structural development than the problems agriculture is facing as a result of the war and the lack of adequate incentives. About half the workers in the tertiary sector in Luanda are thought to work in government administration. In the other provinces, the sectoral composition of workers varies widely.

5/ The structure and growth of the Angolan population are discussed in Chapter 1.

6/ The census information relates to 1983/84 for the provinces of Luanda, Cabinda, Zaire and Namibe (covering only 15% of the country's population). The results for the latter three provinces were combined and the relative distributions were taken to be representative of the other 14 provinces.

Table 4.17: LABOR FORCE DATA, 1985
(Percentages)

	Total 1970	Total 1985	Luanda	Other Provinces
Population of working age	62.6	44.0	47.5	44.8
Labor force participation rate		53.3	48.0	54.2
Unemployment		3.3	3.9	3.2
Percentage employed in:				
- primary sector	74.5	37.1	5.5	41.6
- secondary "	7.7	19.3	33.3	41.1
- tertiary "	17.8	43.6	61.2	17.3

Source: Anuário Estatístico and Census of 1983 (Luanda) and 1984 (other provinces).

4.105 The educational level of the labor force in Angola is extremely low, as shown in Table 4.18 below. The sum of illiterates and those with incomplete basic education was 88% in Luanda and as high as 97% in Namibe, indicating that the vast majority of the labor force can be considered functionally illiterate. Less than 10% of the labor force completed basic education, and the proportion receiving education beyond that level is very small indeed. The educational level of the labor force in the provinces is substantially lower than in Luanda. As a result, the shortage of skilled workers is very acute. In Luanda, the percentage of workers in jobs requiring at least secondary education is estimated at 14%, whereas only 3% meet that requirement. In the other provinces, the situation is worse; the number of jobs requiring secondary education compared to the number of workers that have achieved that level was 2,857 versus 103 in Cabinda, 1,830 versus 47 in Zaire, and 1,478 versus 78 in Namibe. Assuming that the jobs in the administration's higher echelons require a university degree, the number of these jobs (1,319) vastly exceeds the number of those holding such degrees (177).

Table 4.18: EDUCATIONAL LEVEL OF THE LABOR FORCE, 1983/84
(Percentages)

Educational Level	Luanda	Cabinda	Zaire	Namibe
Illiterates	15.5	43.7	47.9	42.8
Basic Education				
- incompleted	72.0	50.6	47.9	53.7
- completed	9.6	5.2	3.9	3.1
Secondary Education	2.8	0.5	0.2	0.4
Higher Education	0.01	0.01	0.005	0.02
Total number	201,918	21,228	19,868	16,858

Source: Census of 1983 (Luanda) and 1984 (other provinces)

Structure and Organization of the Educational System 7/

4.106 Regular Education. Regular Education is divided into three levels: basic or primary education, secondary education and higher education. The first two levels have regular courses offered to students in the normal age group. Apart from regular education, vocational training and adult education are offered to older students. Primary education lasts eight years, and is also divided into three levels, in addition to one year of pre-school. The first level lasts four years and is compulsory. The second and third levels last two years each. Secondary education is open to students who have completed the third level of primary education and offers three alternatives: pre-university, a two-year course leading to entrance in the university; secondary technical education, which offers different specializations and lasts four years; and a four year teacher training program. The pre-university course has proved too short and has been extended, on an experimental basis, to three years. There are 14 pre-university schools, of which only three have their own facilities. The teacher training course for primary education teachers is given by the National Institute of Education, located in 14 provinces. Besides these institutes, there are the Luanda National Institute of Physical Education and the Pedagogical Industrial Institute in Huambo. Secondary technical education offers specializations for technicians in areas such as agriculture, electricity, health, mechanics, fishing and finance.

7/ For a more detailed account, see Annex IX: The Education Sector.

4.107 The Agostinho Neto University, established in November 1976, is the sole institution of higher education in Angola. It has three sites: Luanda, Huambo and Lubango. In Luanda, there are faculties of Law, Economics, Science, Engineering, Medicine; in Huambo, faculties of Agronomy, Medicine, Economics and Law (although these hardly function); and in Lubango, there are courses in Economics and Law as well as the Institute for Educational Science. The Institute trains teachers for the National Institutes of Education. It also offers correspondence courses in Huambo and Luanda, and so it does not have resident teachers. University courses consist of two levels: a first level of three years and a second level of two years, except for medicine which lasts a total of six years. Only the completion of the second level provides a diploma. Most students have full time jobs, and those from other cities receive free board and lodging.

4.108 Adult Education and Vocational Training. Students who are too old for regular primary education have other options. Adult education is offered at levels corresponding to levels I, II and III of primary education. Each level is a two-year program divided into four semesters. Adult classes are given at night using the facilities of regular schools. Literacy programs equivalent to the first semester of Adult Education are carried out by the National Center for Literacy. The Center conducts one year programs using volunteer teachers, and the program and manuals used are specifically designed for the students' needs. The literacy programs are managed by the party (MPLA). Provisional schools offer a four year course to children older than 10 years and to dropouts, concentrating on rural areas. The first two years are spent learning vocational skills such as farming, carpentry, masonry, shoe making, printing, etc. Provisional schools are boarding schools. Finally, the Centers for Vocational Training provide regular courses under the direct control of MED or offer courses for a firm's employees, financed by the Ministry that controls these firms. There are 11 Centers operated by MED and 107 within firms. The Centers controlled by MED offer two cycles. The first cycle corresponds to level II of primary education and takes two years. The second cycle, which has few students, offers courses equivalent to level III of primary education.

4.109 Education Sector Objectives, Organization and Resources. The main objectives of educational policy are formulated through the MPLA-PT Congresses and resolutions, and through government legislation. Important among the former are the First Congress of MPLA held in 1977 and the Second Congress in 1985. The First Congress set the nature and goals to be followed by the educational system, including nationalization and secularization of schools, compulsory primary education, free education and cooperation between community and school. The First Extraordinary Congress of the Party (1980) and the Second Congress expressed concern about the issues of quality and efficiency, and recommended a diagnosis of the educational system. Recently the Party's Central Committee approved two documents containing the diagnosis, and expressed its concerns for more effective action to pursue the existing priorities.

4.110 Government responsibilities and resources related to education are with some exceptions centralized in the Ministry of Education (MED). This organization has four administrative levels: the central administration, the provincial delegations, the municipal delegations and the communal units. The central administration coordinates educational policies, sets the guidelines, allocates the resources, determines curriculum changes, buys school materials, sets teacher wages, supervises schools, organizes teacher training programs, etc. It has two Vice-Ministers, each responsible for various Departments or Directorates. Under the reorganization of MED in 1987 (Decree 9/87), the responsibilities of the Vice-Ministers were changed. One Vice-Minister now handles all matters related to secondary, technical, and vocational education and the other is responsible for general education, mainly primary education. The main purpose of the organizational change was to charge the MED with the responsibility for the coordination of vocational training, which is facing a major crisis. However, MED has its hands full with planning and administering regular education. The organization of the provincial delegations is similar to that of the Ministry of Education, with supporting units and executive departments, although their number is smaller. Contacts between the provincial delegation and the municipal delegations and communes are severely affected by difficult communications, large distances and poor roads. The autonomy given to the school directors is minimal.

4.111 Over the period 1980-87, the proportion of the government budget allocated to education has varied between 9.6% and 13.7%. Apart from the budget of the Ministry of Education, separate budgets exist for the Agostinho Neto University, the National Center for Literacy, and the National Institutes for Languages and for Scholarships. While budgeted expenditure has fluctuated considerably from year to year, the overall trend until 1987, even in nominal terms, has been downward. In 1985, the education budget was 12% below the level in 1980. Given the increases in the cost of goods and services, the decline in real terms was much greater. Available data about actual expenditures are limited, but indicate that they fall substantially short of budgeted figures.

4.112 Many of the critical problems affecting the education sector are related to poor management capacity of MED or to poor government organization. For example, MED lacks responsibility for the coordination of the budgets of the Provincial Delegations, which is carried out by the Ministry of Finance; in school construction, which is the task of the Ministry of Construction and in the production of equipment, supervised by the Ministry of Industry. For imports, the foreign exchange allocated to Maquimport (about US$ 6 million) was not used in 1987 and the arrival of the imports was delayed for more than one year. As a consequence, in 1987, half of the required textbooks and the whole supply of pens, stencils, etc. were not available. Domestic production has also been below the planned levels. Thus, only 12% of the textbooks and 19% of notebooks were produced in 1987. For student desks, the percentage was less than 2%.

4.113 <u>Primary Education</u>. Enrollment in primary education almost tripled between 1976 and 1979, then declined by nearly 50% between 1980 and 1986. This dramatically shows the consequences of the war and of trying to increase access to education without a major investment in education facilities, teacher training and supplies and materials. The war has disrupted educational activity and absorbed scarce human and financial resources. The drop in enrollment can be attributed to several factors: a decline in the number of teachers and classrooms, inadequate school inputs, transportation difficulties, linguistic problems and parental illiteracy. The gross enrollment rate declined from 76% in 1980 to 44% in 1984. Low internal efficiency, as reflected in promotion rates well below 50% and a productivity index of 22% for Level I, indicate serious wastage which reduced net enrollment rates from 70% in Level I to 1% in Levels II and III.

4.114 Secondary Education. Secondary technical education has grown rapidly. Enrollment increased at an average annual rate of 23% between 1978 and 1985 in the face of serious difficulties which affected the quality of education. Problems include a lack of equipment, inadequate and insufficient teaching materials, and a high proportion of part time teachers and "cooperantes" among all teachers. The effectiveness of the latter is impaired by language problems and cultural differences. Though internal efficiency is generally low, there are signs that it is improving. The National Institutes of Education present similar problems, and each year less than 5% of the stock of primary education teacher graduates, which is insufficient to even cover the normal attrition rate. Moreover, most graduates are already teaching. A high proportion of teaching staff at the Institutes consists of "cooperantes". Enrollment at pre-university courses has been growing at an annual rate of 13%. The high proportion of both part time teachers and "cooperantes" poses a problem here as well. It is also generally agreed that two years are insufficient to prepare students for university.

4.115 Higher Education. Enrollment in higher education is now nearly twice as high as before independence. The University offers a wide range of specializations, despite the limited availability of resources, suggesting high unit costs. Students are often not adequately prepared for university and the quality of education is affected by a serious shortage of teaching materials, laboratory equipment and qualified staff. Higher education, including board and lodging, is free. A significant part of non-personnel expenditures on higher education is devoted to food. There are also questions about the relevance of curricula. The University Council has approved new curricula for all fields of study in January 1989. The final decision is to be made by higher government levels. However it is expected that the new curricula will be introduced in the coming school year (September 1989). This reform is very important for the Faculty of Economics, which will offer a new specialisation (Business Administration) and, possibly, Agricultural Economics.

4.116 Reorganization of the educational system. There is a proposal for the reorganization and rehabilitation of the educational system, which involves substantial investments. This Emergency Program deals with construction and maintenance of school buildings, increasing teacher's wages and improving their recruitment, and increasing the local capacity to produce school materials. In primary education the construction of 29 schools (404 classrooms) and the repair of 8 schools (25 classrooms) is planned only in Luanda because of acute problems in the supply of construction materials in the remainder of the country. The total cost is estimated at US$ 22 million, although it is not clear whether the budget will provide these resources. In technical secondary education, it is expected that the Institute of Economics in Luanda will be completed in 1989 and that the Institute of Agriculture in Huambo will be completed in 1990. They are both being funded by a loan from the African Development Bank. The projected construction of the Institute of Agriculture in Malange and the Institute of Education in Lubango will also use resources provided by the ADB. In higher education, investments are planned for the Higher Institute of Educational Sciences in Lubango (US$25 million) with financing from ADB and there are also plans for opening a branch in Luanda (US$1 million). The Faculty of Agriculture in Lubango (to be created) will receive resources from the ADB (US$ 35.7 million) and the existing Faculty of Agriculture in Huambo requires resources estimated at US$ 3 million which have not yet secured. The Faculty of Law is negotiating a loan from Spain (US$10 million) to build its facilities in Luanda.

4.117 The Emergency Program also provides for an increase in the wages of all teachers of 60%, starting in 1989. Although this increase is necessary to reduce the number of teachers who leave their jobs and of part-time teachers, the impact of this measure may prove to be small because it will be unable to compensate for the absence of non-pecuniary benefits for those who work for MED. Finally, the Emergency Program has given attention to the domestic production of school materials, first through investments to rehabilitate existing plants and secondly, by expanding production capacity. Initial investments are estimated at US$ 10 million.

4.118 According to the program, important changes in the educational system should start to be implemented after the phases of preparation, testing and evaluation. Compulsory education will be extended to six years and the second and third levels of primary education will be eliminated. After primary education, there will be a three year course - the secondary first level - which will branch out in general technical and teachers courses. The secondary second level will be the equivalent of the existing secondary offering four-year technical and teachers courses and a three-year general course to replace the pre-university (two-year) course. Higher education will offer short-duration courses (three year) in addition to the five-year courses. Adult education will have courses corresponding to primary education and secondary first level education; professional training will have courses corresponding to primary education and both levels of secondary education. At the moment, it is hard to judge the impact of the proposed changes. The extension of compulsory education to six years and of primary and secondary education to 12-13 years will have to be accompanied by other changes for the system to be able to retain the students longer. Whereas the secondary first level teachers course will train the teachers for the first four grades of primary education, it is not yet clear, aside from differences in the students age, what will be the differences among the secondary first level technical courses and the corresponding adult courses and professional training courses. The short-duration university diploma may be refused by the market, if there is an attractive private rate of return for the additional two years.

Priority Areas for Possible Technical Assistance in the Education Sector

4.119 Basic Education. Basic education is in a state of disarray and requires concerted action in three main areas:

(a) School Materials. Most textbooks and other school materials are imported even though a domestic supply is feasible, especially at an equilibrium exchange rate. There is a need to identify the existing plants which could increase production without subsidies, their need for additional investments and for required inputs, including skilled labour. The reduction of the import content of school materials should allow a larger availability, per student, of textbooks, pencils, notebooks, etc. There is also a need to examine ways to improve the existing distribution facilities. Technical assistance should be extended to INIDE, the agency of MED which is responsible for curriculum design, textbook elaboration and other areas of research related to the learning process. At the moment, the lack of trained personnel is the major cause of its abysmal performance.

(b) School Construction. The absence of school construction and maintenance in recent years and the intensive use of the existing facilities have caused severe deterioration in the buildings and their equipment. For the required construction in the coming years, it is necessary to: (i) carry out an inventory of the school buildings, their availability and use and the maintenance and enlargement work required; (ii) study the construction materials available in the country, especially those locally produced; (iii) train the personnel for an agency to be established within MED, responsible for the design and supervision of school construction; and (iv) secure foreign assistance to start school mapping studies.

(c) Teacher Training. To increase the number of qualified teachers, a two-pronged strategy is required: (i) increase the number of full-time Angolan teachers at ISCED, which provides college training level for teachers at the Institutos Normais de Educação (INEs); (ii) improve the qualifications of the stock of teachers in basic education through better designed in-service training. UNESCO has been active in this area. Both of these teacher training programs will require additional financial and technical assistance.

4.120 Educational Planning. Decision-making at MED is deficient and its improvement is essential to increase the efficiency of the system. Three areas, in particular, require attention:

(a) Educational statistics. The existing educational data is limited and there are large delays in its availability. There is a need to expand the statistics to cover relevant indicators and to improve the data collection system. Other information such as actual educational expenditures, cost studies, teacher qualifications, is also missing.

(b) Educational planning. The ability to plan the educational system at the central administration level is very weak. Both training abroad and foreign experts are required to bring that ability up to acceptable levels.

(c) Coordination and decentralization. The coordination tasks both at central and provincial levels suffers from the lack of qualified administrative personnel and of facilities. Also there is a need to further decentralize tasks. Technical assistance could help in the organization of courses for the administrative staff of MED (both in the central administration and in the provinces) and in providing resources to buy the equipment (vehicles, telex, etc.) required for improved communications.

4.121 Manpower demand. The shortage of qualified administrators both in the government and in public enterprises is a serious constraint for the implementation of policies and the sound management of firms. In this regard, two studies are recommended:

(a) Identification of skills needed in the higher and middle administrative echelons of government and public enterprises. The requirements would be expressed in terms of the educational content (formal, at secondary and university levels, and short training courses).

(b) Identification of the need to expand enrollment, change curriculum, train teachers and provide adequate textbooks and other school materials to the students in the fields of economics and administration. At the moment, a major change of the economics curriculum both at secondary and university levels is being proposed, but a course in administration does not exist. Short training courses are being offered by many public institutions. A better knowledge of the type of courses required, and their organization and desired content, is needed to design their expansion.

Recommendations for the Education Sector

4.122 The following recommendations emerge from the analysis of the education sector's structure, performance and constraints:

(i) High priority must be given to teacher training, starting with the highest institutions. Thus, an increase in the number of teachers to eliminate the need for correspondence courses and to replace most of the "cooperantes" at the Institute for Educational Sciences in Lubango is vital. The approach suggested places emphasis on quality of education and institution building. Measures with more immediate impact on basic education are changes in the curriculum and improvement of teaching materials and in-service training. The issue of teachers' wages must also receive attention.

(ii) Reorganization of MED should have four goals: transfer of the responsibility for vocational training to an agency outside MED; placing of the National Center of Literacy under MED; strengthening educational planning and management and improving the flow of information; and decentralizing decision making, to reduce delays and inefficiencies in the use of resources.

(iii) Additional resources should be made available to avoid further deterioration of school buildings, replace equipment, increase teaching materials, and improve teachers' salaries. Cost recovery could make an important contribution, initially through charges for board and lodging.

(iv) The economy's lack of qualified policy analysts and management personnel requires urgent measures such as curriculum reform in the economic courses, both in secondary technical schools and at the university, as well as the creation of administration courses. For this purpose, better coordination of INORAD with the university is required, as well as technical assistance to be provided by a reputable university.

(v) In primary education, and in other levels as well, the emphasis should be on improving quality. Improved maintenance of school buildings, better teachers and educational materials and changes in the curriculum are the main steps needed to reduce wastage. It is further recognized that expansion of the number of classrooms is required to reduce the number of daily shifts and of students per classroom. The increase in efficiency will have desirable consequences on access as well. In some cases, it may be possible to meet the demand for places.

(vi) The future expansion of enrollment in secondary education should be predominantly in general education courses rather than technical ones. It is desirable that the training of the students be achieved in courses of short duration or in firms. In this way, most costs of the technical component will not overburden the education sector. This redirection is already apparent in the conception of the Secondary Technical School, which relies on training provided by firms. In the short run, ensuring that these centers for vocational training have adequate facilities is necessary in order to provide for the over aged students.

(vii) In higher education, the increase in the proportion of full-time Angolan professors requires higher wages and increased opportunities to study abroad. Presently, the available resources are spread too thinly through the various courses and specializations, resulting in low efficiency. In some cases, it would be better to send students abroad. Another way to increase efficiency of resource use is to widen the common core curriculum.

(viii) Technical assistance should play an important role in teacher training, in educational planning and administration, in school construction and maintenance and in the improvement of the supply of textbooks and other school materials.

The Health Sector

4.123 The Ministry of Health is responsible for activities related to the organization, coordination and control of the health sector. It comprises the offices of the Minister and the Vice-Minister; supporting units (Consultative Council, Planning Office, National Institute of Public Health and Office of International Affairs) and the Provincial Delegations. The organization of the health network is in line with the administrative division of the country (18 provinces, 163 municipalities and 532 communes). Medical service in the communities is provided by Health Posts, Village Health Workers and Traditional Birth Attendants. Further up the scale are Health Centers and Municipal Hospitals, Provincial Hospitals and National Hospitals. Table 4.19 presents the number of these facilities in 1973, in 1985 and in 1987. The number of inhabitants per health post increased by 82% between 1973 and 1985, indicating a serious deterioration in the assistance provided by these facilities. The ratio of inhabitants per hospital has risen by at least 47% over this period. The situation improved slightly in 1987.

Table 4.19: HEALTH FACILITIES BY TYPE - 1973 AND 1985

Type	1973 Number	1973 Inhabitants per Health Facility	1985 Number	1985 Inhabitants per Health Facility
Health Posts	1,318	4,651	1,036	8,450
Health Centers and Municipal Hospitals	671	23,852	225	38,907
Provincial Hospitals			17	514,941
National Hospitals			7	1,250,571

Source: UNICEF

4.124 The number of beds in national and provincial hospitals in 1985 was 8,018, of which 2,388 were in Luanda. For health centers and municipal hospitals, the number of beds is 6,478, of which 146 in Luanda. The ratio of beds per 1,000 inhabitants, which was 3.0 in 1973 had dropped to 1.7 in 1985. The availability of medical personnel is also far from satisfactory. There were 554 physicians in Angola in 1985, the majority of them foreigners (406), as compared to 561 physicians in 1973. The ratio of inhabitants per physician increased from 10,927 in 1973 to 15,521 in 1985 (by 42%), declining to 12,770 in 1987 (723 physicians). The number of paramedics in 1985 was 8,553, of which 204 were foreigners, with a ratio of 1,000 inhabitants per paramedic. This ratio remained the same in 1987.

4.125 The training of health personnel poses major questions. At lower levels, training initially focused on meeting the urgent demands arising from the massive exodus of health personnel in 1975/76. Courses lasted for 2 years and the prerequisite was Level II, or six years of primary education. It is estimated by UNICEF that about 10,000 basic health technicians were trained in these courses in the last 10 years. In 1986 there were 21 schools providing this training, at least one per province. At the intermediate level, there are 3 secondary technical health institutes in Bie, Huambo and Luanda. In 1989, Cabinda will have its institute. The number of graduates from these institutes in the period 1982/83 - 1985/86 was 217. The course lasts four years and requires 8 years of primary education. Finally, there is one Faculty of Medicine, in Luanda and a nucleus in Huambo, offering a six-year course. In the period 1975/76 - 1984/85, a total of 230 physicians graduated. It is expected that about 45 doctors will graduate every year. The two major problems of health manpower training at the secondary and university levels are an insufficient number of graduates and deficiencies in the curriculum. Also, there is a need to upgrade basic level technicians, which is not being met.

4.126 Government expenditures in the health sector in 1985 amounted to Kz 650 per capita. In the period 1981/89 an average of 6.2% of budgetary resources was spent on health. However, real expenditures declined considerably in the same period because of inflation. This decline was partly compensated by foreign assistance provided by bilateral and multilateral agencies, such as the Swedish International Development Agency (SIDA), the World Health Organization (WHO) and UNICEF, which funded various health programs. For example, SIDA will provide, in the period 1988/91, US$ 24 million for various programs; the European Economic Community is expected to provide US$ 27 million for hospital construction and the Italian government will provide US$ 16 million also mainly for construction. Cuban and Soviet aid consists of doctors and nurses.

4.127 Health policy is directed mainly towards assisting children in the 0-5 age group and pregnant mothers, and towards reducing the incidence of communicable diseases. A primary health care strategy underlies the provision of health services. Health posts, village health workers, and traditional birth attendants provide care at the lowest level. Cases in which the health posts cannot provide adequate care are directed to Health Centers or Municipal Hospitals first. If medical care is not feasible in these facilities, use is made of Provincial or National Hospitals. In this way, better use is made both of installations and available human resources. There is limited information about the use of health facilities. In 1987, there were 6.5 million consultations and 247,700 admissions to hospitals. The proportion of assisted births was 17% in 1987. Figures available for vaccinations against infectious and contagious diseases in 1987 indicate that the highest coverage is for measles (37%) and the lowest for polio (3%).

4.128 There is only circumstantial evidence about health conditions. Infant mortality is very high, although precise estimates are very difficult to obtain, ranging from 200 per thousand, according to United Nations figures, to 325-375 according to a recent UNICEF study, both for children under five in 1985. For infants under one, UNICEF estimates mortality at 200, while U.N. figures show a decline from 193 per thousand for 1960-70 to 166 per thousand for 1980-85. For Luanda, the infant mortality rate increased, from about 107 per thousand in the years before Independence to 130 per thousand in 1980 and to 186 per thousand in 1984. UNICEF has found rates in the 240-300 per thousand range in emergency areas directly affected by the war. The proportion of born children weighing less than 2,5Kg was 21% in 1986. Life expectancy has increased from 35 years in 1960-70 to 42 years in 1980-85 but remains quite low.

4.129 War-related problems, aside from disrupting roads and destroying medical supplies and health posts, are reflected in the 650,000 refugees, 80% of which are mothers and children. In addition, the destitute people, mostly migrating peasants, who live in the periphery of the cities demand health services in already congested facilities or are not served at all.

Finally, there were about 11,000 disabled people in 1987 as a consequence of the war, 85% of them with leg disabilities. The serious health conditions which prevail are difficult to deal with because of a variety of causes, and the fact that many of these causes cannot be addressed by the health authorities. One of the main causes is the war. Another important cause of the serious health conditions is the precarious supply of water and the lack of any sewage system or other sanitation facilities in the periphery of many cities, as well as inadequate shelter and the absence of solid waste collection and disposal services (see Section I of this chapter for more details on urban services). Under these circumstances, it is not surprising to find that communicable diseases are the most important causes of death, including acute diarrheal diseases, tetanus, measles, tuberculosis, malaria, sleeping sickness and infectious hepatitis. These problems are aggravated by other factors, such as the high proportion of illiterate mothers and malnutrition. There is a heavy concentration of health services in favor of Luanda and Cabinda and, generally, of the urban areas. Thus, only 28% of the municipalities have a physician. In Luanda and Cabinda, the ratio of physicians per 10 000 inhabitants (1,9) was almost five times larger than the ratio in the other regions.

4.130 Faced with budgetary, health personnel and other constraints, the design of a viable and effective health policy is a major challenge, particularly in the context of war-related destruction and insecurity. One major difficulty is the lack of reliable statistical information, which is necessary for more effective targeting of actions. High priority should be given to better vaccination campaigns, at least in the secure areas, dissemination of information to mothers about the prevention and control of diarrheal diseases, improvement of nutrition standards and maternal and child health programs generally. The limited government resources must also be complemented by the effective use of foreign and community resources.

I. REGIONAL AND URBAN DEVELOPMENT

Spatial Development Patterns

4.131 Regional development and planning in Angola is inextricably linked to the continuing war and changing conditions of internal security. Since only 10-20% of the national territory is estimated to be sufficiently secure to permit normal economic activity, regional development planning on a national scale is clearly impossible. Spatial development patterns since Independence in 1974 have been shaped largely by the volatile security situation rather than economic forces. The security situation determines the nature and intensity of regional economic activity and the possibilities for interregional trade. Although its spatial impact varies considerably, the disruptive effects of the war are felt in some measure in all regions. The continuing conflict has provoked significant population movements of displaced people seeking greater security and reliable supplies of food. These movements have been an important source of urban population growth in the unplanned, self-built communities on the periphery of such centres as Luanda, Huambo, Kuito, Malange and Benguela. It is estimated that the displaced population currently numbers 534,000 people, roughly 9% of the rural population.

4.132 Although the war and terrorist activities against the civilian population are the principal cause of economic disruption in rural areas, this has been aggravated by the inefficiencies of centralised planning and administrative controls. Thus, the State distribution system has proved an extremely poor substitute for the colonial bush traders, resulting in a pronounced decline in levels of marketed agricultural surplus. Consequently, even in areas where normal economic activity can be pursued, rural trading networks have atrophied, reducing commercial flows between the countryside and towns. These institutional factors have accentuated the withdrawal of agricultural producers into a self-provisioning or subsistence economy and direct barter transactions. Since this regression has occurred in all regions, it is often difficult to disentangle the disruptive effects of the war from other causes.

4.133 The security situation effectively precludes the application of regional economic analysis and only the "relatively secure" South-Southwest provinces of Huila, Namibe and Cunene constitute what meaningfully can be described as a 'region'in economic and institutional terms. Even then, the boundaries of this region are ill-defined and change with the security situation. A second spatial category comprises pockets of relatively stable economic activity on the coast, which form small "enclave regions". The security perimeter of these enclaves is variable, however, depending on the frequency of attacks, and may be as little as 30-50 miles. These enclaves include (i) the province of Luanda and the coastal area extending north to Soyo; (ii) the area around the coastal towns of Benguela and Lobito, and (iii) the oil producing province of Cabinda. The third spatial category which can be distinguished includes strategic provincial capitals, such as Huambo, Kuito Bie, Malange, and Uige, which have significantly smaller rural hinterlands than the "enclave regions". Lacking seaports, these strategic interior towns and other protected urban settlements have precarious economic links with the rest of the country, as road and rail transport require military support. The areas most affected by the war are those which border the zone that has been occupied by insurgents and South African forces in the provinces of Kuando Kubango and Cunene. Elsewhere, the regional impact of the war varies according to such factors as (i) proximity of sources of infiltration from the occupied territory in the South and from foreign bases; (ii) the frequency and intensity of guerrilla activity, (iii) population density and concentrations of displaced people, and (iv) logistical difficulties which, in practice, depend on ease of communication with the coastal port cities.

4.134 The Eastern provinces of Lunda Norte, Lunda Sul, Moxico, and Kuando Kubango are the most severely affected by the current conflict. Kuando Kubango has suffered large-scale military exchanges which have caused direct damage to economic and social infrastructure and forced the local population to flee from the war zone. There are an estimated 70,000 displaced people in Moxico, and thousands of others have taken refuge in emergency camps established in nearby provinces. Guerrilla operations and the occupation of the southernmost area of the country by South African forces have brought economic activity there to a standstill. The local economy has been crippled by the systematic destruction of dwellings, roads, bridges, dams, wells, schools and health facilities. Relief supplies are transported mainly by air. Also, the provinces of Lunda Norte and Lunda Sul are both seriously affected by guerrilla activity. As indicated in an earlier section of this chapter, the diamond mining area operated by Endiama, in the north-east of Lunda Norte, is now supplied mainly by air. Security conditions in the northern provinces, comprising the provinces of Zaire, Uige, Malange, Bengo, Kwanza Norte and Kwanza Sul, have reportedly worsened significantly in the past year or two. This is particularly the case in Uige and Malange, where guerrilla operations have seriously disrupted agricultural production. The railway between Luanda and Malange has only operated irregularly since mid-1986. Several of these provinces have relatively large concentrations of displaced persons, as shown by 1988 United Nations African Emergency Task Force estimates for Malange (15,000), Uige (28,000), Kwanza Norte (38,000) and Kwanza Sul (114,000). In addition, an estimated 60-80,000 Angolans have returned from Zaire since 1985. The northern enclave province of Cabinda has not suffered significant war disruption as its economy is dominated by the offshore oil industry and this sector is protected by a strong garrison of Cuban troops.

4.135 Outside the immediate war zones in the south, the central highland provinces of Huambo, Bie and Benguela are the worst affected by the current conflict. In the colonial period, this region was Angola's "granary", while the city of Huambo was the country's second manufacturing center. These activities have been severely disrupted by guerrilla operations and economic sabotage, which have resulted in large contingents of rural migrants and displaced people. Rising levels of emergency relief aid are now required to support the population in this former agricultural heartland of Angola. Road and rail links with the port of Lobito and Benguela have become increasingly precarious, essentially cutting off Huambo and Bie from other regions of the country. In these heavily populated central provinces, the guerrilla conflict and the attendant insecurity have had a devastating impact on all sectors of economic activity. The disruption of agricultural production, together with the impaired transport links with the coast, has created an emergency situation with thousands of people lacking basic needs and suffering from malnutrition. Health conditions also are deteriorating due to the increasing scarcity of food and essential medical supplies, as well as guerrilla attacks on health posts. NGO survey data indicate that in Huambo province 40-45% of children under six were malnourished and 5-6% presented clinical symptoms of severe malnutrition. Red Cross surveys in Huambo in 1985 revealed infant mortality rates of 250-350 per thousand in badly affected areas, as well as maternal mortality exceeding 10 per thousand live births. In response to this situation, the provinces of Huambo and Bie are receiving priority under the Emergency Assistance Program administered by the United Nations Emergency Operations Group (UNEOG) and the Angolan Interministerial Commission for Coordination of Emergency Assistance (CIMCAE).

4.136 As indicated above, the South-Southwest Provinces of Huila, Namibe and Cunene form the largest area in Angola where the security situation permits a significant measure of normal economic activity. This large, semi-arid region, with an estimated 1.1 million inhabitants and population density of 5.3 per km2, has a strong agricultural vocation, notably for beef cattle and corn production. The possibility of rehabilitating the regional economy in order to generate an exportable agricultural surplus endows the South-Southwest with special importance in the present context of widespread economic disruption and Angola`s increasing dependence on food imports. The security of the South-Southwest region is only relative, of course, and varies within the region. For example, the rural areas in the northern and eastern parts of Huila province are considerably less secure than the area in the vicinity of the provincial capital, Lubango. Cunene, in turn, is even more dangerous and virtually the whole population, mainly nomadic or seminomadic pastoralists, has been badly affected by the war. Economic and social infrastructure in Cunene has been devastated by the South African occupation and subsequent hostilities. An estimated 89,000 people in Cunene depend on emergency relief, and a further 25,000 live in camps in Huila, which also has roughly 37,000 deslocados in temporary camps. The emergency needs of this displaced population and the reconstruction of the regional economy have become the focus of assistance from several multilateral and bilateral donors.

Regional Development Policies

4.137 In line with the general trend towards greater decentralization of economic decision-making espoused by the SEF, the new Planning Legislation (Lei de Planificação, Lei nº. 12/88) issued in July 1988 explicitly acknowledges the importance of regional planning. National Plans should elaborate measures to correct regional disequilibria (Article 4) and Multiyear Plans are expected to formulate spatial planning and regional development policy (Article 6). The new legislation provides for the preparation of regional plans and the creation of corresponding administrative structures, although these activities are subordinated to the National Plan and require the prior approval of the Council of Ministers (Article 18). Particular emphasis is given to the elaboration and coordination of local plans by provincial and municipal government institutions. Planning at the local level is to focus mainly on meeting basic needs, and specifically in the areas of housing, health, and other public services (Article 17).

4.138 Since the new planning legislation was issued in July 1988 preliminary steps have been taken to establish more appropriate institutional structures. However, this work is largely formal in content and so far there has been little concrete improvement in the administrative capacity of regional and local institutions. Within the Ministry of Planning and the National Institute of Physical Planning, spatial analyses of the Angolan economy are being undertaken in order to establish the appropriate divisions for regional planning purposes. It is anticipated that eight regional planning areas will be created, together with Luanda province, which will form a separate region. Following the example of the

Southwest region, each area will have a Regional Planning Office (GPR) which, under the direction of the Ministry of Planning, will be responsible for the preparation and coordination of regional plans.

4.139 At the local level, it is proposed to strengthen the capacity of municipal agencies to plan and execute small infrastructure projects to meet basic needs for urban and social services. The restoration of local administrative and management capacity is regarded as an essential foundation for effective regional planning. In this respect, it seems that the colonial local government structures of municipal councils (camaras municipais) may be revived in some form. This possibility also is suggested by current proposals to decentralize public finances in order to restore some measure of financial autonomy to municipal and provincial governments. These institutional proposals have yet to be implemented, however, and a pilot project involving some 50 municipalities has been mooted as possible first step. Within the context of the SEF, such decentralization potentially can make an important contribution to the revival and reconstruction of regional and local economies.

4.140 Institutional changes currently underway in the Southwest region of Huila, Namibe and Cunene illustrate how regional development planning may evolve in the immediate future. In order to ensure consistency, final preparation of a reconstruction program for this region has had to await the more detailed elaboration of the SEF and formal approval of the PRE. On the basis of the UNDP-sponsored report by Dar Al-Handasah Consultants, which identified well over 100 large and small projects in infrastructure sectors and productive activities, and incorporating SEF/PRE priorities, a regional investment plan will be announced in the first semester of 1989. This plan will provide the basis for project submissions to donor countries, and a donor conference is likely to be held in the second half of 1989.

4.141 A detailed assessment of the regional investment plan for the Southwest region must await publication of the project proposals and policy recommendations. Nevertheless, some preliminary observations are made here. After the destructive and destabilizing effects of the war, it is only to be expected that priority should be given to the immediate relief needs, the resettlement of displaced families, and economic reconstruction. In addition to the rehabilitation of basic economic and social infrastructure, the revival of agricultural production and the mobilisation of increased marketed surpluses hold the key to regional economic recovery. Reforms of the pricing and distribution system to ensure that there is an adequate supply of manufactured goods available on favorable terms to rural producers are therefore of crucial importance. While this point is recognised by the regional authorities in Huila, the nature and timetable of these reforms has yet to be determined. Obviously, the response of the international donor community is also critical to the success of the program, in view of the absence of local resources or earmarked central government revenues. The regional authorities are aware that the key to recovery of the productive sectors, particularly peasant agriculture, is the revitalisation of trade and commerce. However, the full resolution of this problem requires basic policy and institutional reforms at the national level.

4.142 The issue of institutional decentralisation is a central one in the context of regional development, and involves a complex mix of national and local considerations. First, there are no national guidelines which define relationships between institutions operating in a provincial or regional context and the provincial branches of the vertically-organized central government ministries. Routine coordination at the regional level therefore is effectively non-existent. Given the highly centralised structure of public administration in Angola and the acute shortage of administrative cadres, there are no local or regional institutions which at present are capable of taking over decentralised activities. While decentralisation must be preceded by national administrative reforms, the weakness of local institutions presents a major obstacle to its realisation, at least in the short term. A case in point is the Regional Planning Office (GPR), which was established to coordinate the planning effort in the South-Southwest region. With its small and inexperienced staff, the GPR is ill-equipped to perform this role. Its operational weakness also reflects the lack of effective complementary government agencies to collaborate with the GPR in planning and implementation. In large measure, the GPR is operating in an institutional vacuum.

4.143 These institutional limitations qualify the view that the South-Southwest relief and reconstruction program is a major exercise in decentralisation. Rather, it represents no more than an initial step in this direction. Far more fundamental reforms are required, including the creation and strengthening of regional institutional structures, if this process is to gain momentum. For example, the budgetary process must be decentralised to give provincial authorities a real voice in setting priorities and coordinating the expenditures at the local level of national state enterprises and central government ministries.

4.144 When announcing the reconstruction program for the southwest, the Minister of Planning is expected to provide further details on the general framework for regional planning, including the creation of regional planning offices (GPRs). Depending in part on the experience of the Southwestern reconstruction program, and particularly the response of donors, it is expected that at least one other program, and possibly two, will be under preparation by late 1990. The leading candidates are the Central region of Benguela, Huambo, Bie and Moxico and the Middle North region, comprising the provinces of Kwanza norte, Kwanza Sul, Malanje and Bengo. Clearly, economic and social reconstruction in these provinces can only be contemplated if there is a significant improvement in the security situation.

Urban Development and Basic Urban Services

4.145 Introduction. Patterns of urban development in Angola since Independence have been determined mainly by the disruptive effects of the war. Guerrilla warfare and economic sabotage, including the widespread use of antipersonnel mines, have destabilized agricultural activities and forced the rural population to seek safety in protected urban sites. Rural urban migration in response to economic factors is thus heavily distorted by these war-induced population movements. The urban population is estimated to have risen from 15% of the total population in 1970 to 23% in 1985, although it should be noted that there are no recent Census data at the national level. However, most observers agree that urban population growth has been rapid since 1974. This is particularly evident in the capital city of Luanda, whose population has risen from 450,000 to 1.3 million in the period 1975-85.

4.146 The large influx of migrants has overburdened the capacity of urban infrastructure and public utility systems and led to a marked decline in both service standards and service coverage. Lack of managerial and technical cadres, limited equipment, and the precarious financial condition of public utility companies have resulted in the deterioration of the systems inherited from the Portuguese in 1975. These same factors, in combination with rapid and unplanned urban settlement, have caused service coverage to fall. With only limited investment since Independence and grossly inadequate maintenance, the basic urban services of water supply, sewage and sanitation, and refuse collection are now in a critical state. This situation is exacerbated by the virtual absence of any urban planning, or sites and services provision. Urban expansion since 1975 has been characterized by the proliferation of self-built housing in unplanned, and largely unimproved, communities (musseques) on the fringes of the main urban centres. The neglect even of elementary urban planning can be attributed to the vertical structure and power of the central government ministries and state enterprises. This has resulted in the absence of routine working relationships at the provincial level which would provide the basis for coordinated programs embracing several interdependent sectors of activity.

4.147 The institutional framework of urban development. The most striking feature of the urban institutional framework in Angola is that, although formal structures have been established, the operational capacity of the component institutions is in most cases extremely weak. The sources of this weakness include the departure of Portuguese managerial and technical staff, the loss of significant local financial autonomy, and the decision to replace the municipal utility agencies by national companies under central government ministries. Before Independence, urban management and basic services provision were undertaken by the municipal councils and public utility companies. These activities were financed to a large extent by local revenues. This financial autonomy effectively was eliminated following Independence and these revenues now accrue to the central government. Fiscal centralisation was accompanied by the reorganization of the municipal public utility companies under the 'super-ministry' of Construction, Housing, Transport and Public Works and, in the case of electric power, under the Ministry of Energy. The municipal companies were consolidated to form national companies in the respective public utility sectors, such as the National Water and Sanitation Company (ENAS). Operational difficulties caused by the excessive degree of centralisation eventually were recognized in 1986, when the "super-ministry" was reorganized. This reform included the creation of a State

Secretariat for Urbanization, Housing and Water but this new institution has no operational capacity at present.

4.148 With the abolition of colonial municipal administrative structures, those functions not transferred to central government ministries were vested in Provincial Commissariats. These have considerable formal powers, including planning, budget preparation, and project implementation at the provincial level. In practice, however, these powers are significantly diluted by the independence of the provincial delegations of central government ministries and state enterprises. The activities and budgets of these entities are controlled by the respective ministries, and their expenditures are included in the provincial budget simply for formal accounting purposes at present. The Provincial Commissariats thus neither control nor coordinate the bulk of public sector expenditure at this level.

4.149 Urban water supply. Before Independence, responsibility for water supply was vested in the municipal councils and, in the case of Luanda, delegated to the municipal water and electricity company. Following the dismantling of these councils, water supply and electricity became the responsibility of the Ministries of Construction and of Energy. The municipal water companies were replaced by provincial companies, whose activities would be coordinated by the National Water and Sanitation Company (ENAS). ENAS was established in 1978 but its statutory duties have never been properly defined. It failed to execute a coordinated national water supply program. It may also have aggravated the acute shortage of managerial and technical cadres as it was staffed mainly by transferring personnel from the municipal water company in Luanda.

4.150 In 1986, some of the functions previously attributed to the Ministry of Construction, including urban water supply, were assumed by the newly-created State Secretariat for Urbanization, Housing and Water (SEUHA). This new agency has only a handful of staff, and no effective operational capacity. The position of ENAS following this reorganization remains in some doubt. At present, the national coordinating functions of ENAS are being exercised by the Luanda Provincial Water Company (EPAL). The institutional framework of urban water supply is therefore extremely weak and lines of responsibility between national and provincial agencies are poorly defined.

4.151 As in the other main cities of Angola, the physical infrastructure of the water supply system in Luanda is deteriorating rapidly due to the large backlog of routine maintenance work and lack of investment in equipment. Rehabilitation requirements extend to all segments of the existing system - collection, pumping stations, treatment, and distribution - although distribution is perhaps the most critical area. Apart from rehabilitation, it is necessary to extend the system to serve the rapidly growing population living in unplanned settlements in semi-urban areas. The present system supplies an estimated 87% of the population, with 20% having water connections and 67% with access to public fountains. This latter figure must be heavily qualified, however, as a large proportion of the public water fountains in the musseque communities are out of order due to damage or lack of maintenance or because the supply has been turned off to avoid excessive water losses. Also, public fountains frequently fail to work because of insufficient pressure due to clandestine or 'pirate' connections made to supply private households.

4.152 Although the combined capacity of Luanda`s two water supply systems is 200,000m3 per day, actual production does not exceed 50-60% of this total. This poor performance is due principally to lack of maintenance and essential spare parts. As a rule, the distribution system operates for only 6-8 hours each day in order to allow storage capacity to be restored. In addition, there is insufficient pressure to raise water to even the second floor of multi-story buildings in Luanda. Service standards in Luanda also are reduced by the significant level of water loss, including frequent burst water mains and long delays in repair, which may amount to half the total water produced.

4.153 Operational inefficiency is aggravated by the administrative and financial weakness in ENAS/EPAL. Tariffs were last revised in 1954, with the result that EPAL requires an extremely large subsidy from the Budget, roughly estimated to cover 85-90% of operating costs. A complete set of accounts was last submitted in 1979. Billings and collections are substantially in arrears, and water supply is effectively free to many consumers. Billings are made every six months but many meters are defective and the installation of new ones is slow. The large omissions in billings are compounded by the low rate of collection, amounting to no more than 50% of billings. An immediate revision of the level and structure of tariffs clearly is required if EPAL is to reduce its deficitary position. The current charge is a flat rate of three kwanzas per cubic meter. There is no differentiation between household and industrial consumers. As to administration, like most enterprises, in Angola, EPAL has serious staff shortages. Most of the professional engineers and middle-level technical personnel departed at Independence and have not been replaced. There is also a lack of semi-skilled and unskilled labour to undertake routine repairs and maintenance, as well as a shortage of meter readers and bill collectors. Rates of turnover and absenteeism are high.

4.154 Public utility pricing. Mission discussions of the PRE indicate that there is still considerable uncertainty about precise details of implementation. This also applies to basic urban services but the issue of public utility pricing is now much more prominent than in December 1987. In order to restrict the drain on general budgetary resources, it appears that efforts will be made under the PRE to reduce the operating deficits of public utility companies and their recourse to central budget financing to cover investment expenditures. At present, these enterprises have only formal financial autonomy and virtually all their revenues go directly into the central budget. As a first step towards greater autonomy, it is proposed to raise user charges by an across-the-board increase of some 300 per cent. These charges have been little changed since the colonial period. This increase will be accompanied by other measures intended to stimulate greater managerial initiative and responsibility. Specifically, it is proposed that the present system of financing operating deficits and expenditures indiscriminately will be replaced by a flat rate of subsidy per unit of production. This unit subsidy is expected to increase the utilization of installed capacity and to raise managerial efficiency as, for example, by encouraging more effective billing and collection practices. However, although the revision of user charges and growing awareness of the importance of cost recovery represent important steps forward, these proposals have yet to be implemented. Indeed, the planning authorities seem prepared to continue subsidizing basic urban services so long as they can achieve greater control over the absolute amount of subsidy. This may be done by creating a Price Compensation Fund to subsidize public utilities but in close coordination with fiscal policy. This position is defended on the grounds of the "special characteristics" of basic urban services and the alarming shortfall in service provision.

4.155 Sewage, surface drainage and solid waste. Following the abolition of the municipal councils, management of the systems of sewage, surface drainage, and solid waste collection was taken over by the Provincial Commissariat of Luanda (CPL). Responsibility for sewage and surface drainage subsequently was transferred to ENAS in 1978 before reverting to the CPL in 1983. In the course of these transfers, the size of the original CPL staff engaged in this sector fell from almost one hundred to 10-15 workers. The construction of new sewage and surface drainage systems and major repair works was assigned in 1977 to the newly-created Basic Infrastructure Construction Company (ENCIB), which was subsequently split into Provincial Commissariats. The ENCIB inherited by the CPL has practically no operational capacity due to an acute lack of administrative, technical and financial resources. This degree of disorganisation is indicative of the problems and difficulties of improving service in this sector.

4.156 Luanda has a long history of inadequate sewage and sanitation services and the situation was already considered serious in the 1950s. To keep pace with the housing boom during the 1960s, and following the destruction of many mains and pipelines by landslides, the colonial authorities drew up a master plan to reconstruct and extend the existing system over a 15 year period. This program was only very partially implemented before Independence, and since then the system has experienced a long and continuous decline. Falling service standards have been accompanied by lower service coverage. Current estimates suggest that only 13% of Luanda's urban population has sewage connections and 16% has septic tanks. However, all types of existing facilities - sanitary installations in buildings, main sewers, and septic tanks - have deteriorated for lack of cleaning, maintenance, and repair. The problems found in the household sector extend to industrial wastes. The situation regarding the disposal of industrial effluents is said to be critical due to the saturation of existing septic tanks and the lack of maintenance.

4.157 Collection and treatment services for solid wastes are also extremely deficient in Luanda, particularly in the unplanned *musseque* settlements. Even in the central urban zones, waste collection is inadequate due to the insufficient capacity of public containers and the lack of vehicles to empty them. The untreated garbage is dumped on open ground and there are no facilities for landfill. Solid waste collection services in Luanda urgently need an infusion of financial and technical resources to rehabilitate existing equipment and increase overall capacity. Proposals for improvement made in 1987 by a Ministry of Health Working Group include the immediate purchase of an additional 18 collection trucks and, in the medium term, the construction of a proper landfill site.

Urban Housing

4.158 The State Secretariat for Urbanization, Housing, and Water Supply (SEUHA) is responsible for public housing programs and urban settlement planning, but this agency has only a skeleton staff and very limited operational capacity. These limitations are exacerbated by the disorganisation of the provincial Basic Infrastructure Construction Companies (ENCIBs), which are meant to undertake the construction work required for basic sites and services provision. As a consequence, public housing programs and urban planning policies effectively are nonexistent at both national and provincial level. Zoning regulations intended to direct the spontaneous urban settlement process in Luanda have not been enforced. Areas designated for self-construction and future site and service provision have been invaded by squatters, replicating the haphazard patterns typical of earlier musseque settlement. Apart from selected higher income residential areas, the housing stock in the "formal" sector in Luanda is in a poor and degraded state. Many apartment blocks built during the late 1960s were abandoned at Independence and subsequently occupied by Angolans, including rural migrants and people displaced by the war. This housing now suffers from chronic overcrowding and disrepair. Some apartment buildings were left unfinished without water and sewage services, but in many others the installed services no longer function. These overcrowded high-rise blocks have been described as 'vertical' musseques. These conditions are also found in the 'popular'34 story apartment buildings constructed with Cuban assistance after 1975. Several schemes to resettle musseque communities in modern apartment blocks were proposed in the late 1970s before the focus shifted to self-construction and site upgrading as reflected in the Auto-Construcao legislation.

4.159 It is estimated that over 900,000 of Luanda's 1.3 million inhabitants live in musseque settlements. In addition to these areas of improvised, extremely high density housing, there is also a limited number of bairros populares or native townships which were established towards the end of colonial rule. These bairros were endowed with a planned network of serviced streets but, following the deterioration of basic urban services since 1975, conditions now are approaching those found in the musseques. Most musseque inhabitants live beyond the `formal` urban structure in unplanned and poorly serviced communities on the periphery of the city. A high proportion of the housing stock in Luanda thus consists of self-built units with no access to the piped water or sewage systems. Most houses have only very primitive sanitary facilities, typically shallow latrines, and sewage and surface drainage channels are open and close to dwellings in many cases. In areas subject to flooding during the rainy season, the danger to public health from these sanitation conditions becomes acute. Only very initial steps have been taken to formulate a policy of musseque upgrading. These include the recent creation of the office for Musseque Renewal and Rehabilitation (GARM). Though it is premature to attempt an evaluation of GARM, the weakness of other urban planning and executive agencies does not augur well for its future. Nevertheless, the housing conditions of the urban poor in Luanda would be improved significantly by an effective programme of musseque upgrading and sites and services provision.

Investments in urban infrastructure and housing

4.160 Public utilities, including water supply, sanitation, and electricity, figure prominently in the investment priorities of the PRE. However, only the general guidelines of the PRE investment program and priority sectors had been established at the beginning of 1989. Sectoral investment allocations, and especially foreign exchange allocations, will be determined at a later stage. Emphasis will be given to projects which allow existing installed capacity to be utilized more fully.

4.161 The shortages of construction materials, especially of bricks, tiles, ceramics, pipes and metal structures, are critical. These shortages represent a serious bottleneck to urban reconstruction programs, and imply a corresponding increase in their foreign exchange requirements. For example, a pilot project in self-help housing to build 1500 dwellings with very basic specifications in the industrial suburb of Viana in Luanda has absorbed US$ 5 million in imported tools and construction materials.

4.162 The priority given to basic urban services in the PRE investment program apparently reflects concern at the highest level about the deterioration and critical state of urban infrastructures notably in Luanda. In February 1988 the President established a Commission of Inquiry into Sanitation and Water Supply in the city which identified seven priority projects for the immediate rehabilitation of Luanda's infrastructure in these sectors. Although these projects have not been implemented due to funding constraints, several recent initiatives should be noted. Solid waste collection services have improved by subcontracting these to a German firm. The main garbage disposal site has been moved away from its close proximity to housing and the principal parallel market ("Roque Santeiro") but its new location and the continuing lack of treatment of solid waste are considered unsatisfactory by the provincial authorities. Discussions are underway with the African Development Bank to finance a further re-siting of the city's main garbage dump. The seven priority rehabilitation projects identified by the 1988 Presidential commission with an estimated cost of US$30 million have also been submitted to this source. The Provincial Commissariat is seeking assistance from the European Community estimated at 10 million ECUs for an emergency program to rehabilitate the sewage system. France and Portugal are assisting in the rehabilitation of Luanda's main water pumping station on the Bengo River. The Canadian government apparently has expressed interest in musseque upgrading projects, which might allow the newly-created Office for Musseque Renewal and Rehabilitation (GARM) to extend its activities beyond the stage of pilot projects.

4.163 It remains to be seen whether this flurry of activity and emergency relief proposals will produce concrete results. The physical degradation of Luanda's water supply and sanitation systems remains critical and nothing short of a major long-term rehabilitation program, including institutional reforms to restore administrative capacity and greater financial autonomy, is likely to bring lasting improvements in service provision.

4.164 Despite the avowed intention of the SEF/PRE to pursue administrative decentralization, there are as yet only very incipient signs of progress in this direction in the Provincial Commissariat of Luanda. However, the Commissariat is reviewing all local tariffs and charges in anticipation of these changes in local government finance. In some cases, penalties and fines have been reinstated (eg., litter laws), the building licence system is being updated, and rents for public housing are under review.

CHAPTER 5

REFORM OF ECONOMIC POLICIES

A. THE PROGRAM OF ECONOMIC AND FINANCIAL RESTRUCTURING

Introduction

5.01 Although the difficulties of the Angolan economy are, to a large extent, due to problems created by decolonization and the continuing war, the authorities recognize that the failings and deficiencies of their economic system and policies are also important causes of the existing situation. Consequently, in 1987 they announced an ambitious program of Economic and Financial Restructuring, usually designated as SEF (Programa de Saneamento Economico e Financeiro), oriented toward the following two main objectives:

(a) stabilization of the financial situation, by reducing internal and external disequilibria, which are reflected in inflationary pressures, large budgetary deficits, excessive losses and indebtedness of many enterprises, serious deterioration of the financial situation of the banking systemn, accumulation of arrears in foreign payments, and difficulties in servicing the external debt;

(b) reform of the economic system, in order to increase productivity, improve the allocation of resources and create the conditions for a faster rate of economic growth and equitable development in the future.

5.02 The authorities established a Technical Secretariat charged with the task of preparing proposals for new legislation and of taking other initiatives required to implement the policy changes set forth in the SEF. During 1988, the Government approved several laws and discussed several drafts of new legislation, with the objective of establishing the new basic framework for the economic policies and economic reforms to be undertaken under the SEF in specific areas (foreign exchange controls, development of the private sector, restructuring of public enterprises, foreign investment and issue of securities). At the beginning of 1989, the authorities approved a "Program of Economic Recovery" (Programa de Recuperacao Economica), known as PRE, oriented to the two main objectives of starting the process of macro-economic adjustment and of promoting the rapid recovery of production. The PRE, which in principle will initiate the implementation of the economic reforms announced in the SEF, covers the period 1989-90 and defines the main guidelines, objectives and priorities for macro-economic policy and for the investment projects to be implemented at the sectoral and regional levels.

5.03 The legislative initiatives already taken by the government under the SEF have to be completed by regulations before they can be implemented. Though implementation of the PRE is expected to extend over a period of at least two years, the authorities have not yet taken the key decisions which are foreseen in the SEF and the PRE in such areas as the adjustment or liberalization of controlled prices, the depreciation of the exchange rate, more effective control of public finances or the money supply, etc. The process of implementation of the SEF will thus have to reach a more advanced stage before it is possible to know to what extent the program will be sufficient to deal with the serious problems of stabilization and development faced by the Angolan economy. The description and analysis of the present chapter show, however, that there are good reasons to believe that, if adequately implemented, the SEF will bring very substantial improvements to the management of the Angolan economy and to the efficiency of the productive structures.

5.04 The following sections summarize the main changes in economic structures and policies announced in the SEF and in the PRE, in some of the laws already published and in documents produced by the Technical Secretariat. Annex V to the present report includes an analysis of the main laws already published under the SEF: the law on the control of foreign exchange, the law on economic activities, the securities law, the foreign investment law, and the law of state enterprises).

The Stabilization Measures Announced in the SEF

5.05 The most important measures of financial stabilization announced in the SEF include: (1) the reduction of the deficit of the state budget; (2) the adoption of new solutions to finance the budget deficit; (3) the restructuring of the financial situation of public enterprises; (4) the reform of domestic credit policies; (5) the rescheduling of external debts; (6) adjustments of controlled prices; and (7) adjustments in the exchange rate. Those measures are expected to contribute not only to a reduction in the external disequilibrium and domestic inflationary pressures, but also to the structural adjustments required to achieve higher productive efficiency and faster economic growth.

5.06 Reduction of the Deficit of the State Budget. In order to achieve a reduction in the budget deficit, the SEF envisages both a reform in the tax system and stricter control of budgetary expenditures. The devaluation of the kwanza will also contribute to a significant extent to improving the public finances. According to the guidelines established in the PRE, several tax rates will be raised and exemptions from customs duties will be sharply reduced. Taxation of the profits of enterprises will be extended to public enterprises and to the activities of the parallel market. At the same time, stronger incentives will be granted to tax collectors in order to stimulate their efficiency. The SEF also announces the intention of the authorities to initiate studies for a reform over the medium term of the Angola taxation system, including an analysis of possible benefits from introducing a tax on value added and a unified income tax.

5.07 The possibility of cutting budgetary expenditures is constrained by the financial requirements of the war effort. However, the authorities expect that a major contribution to the more effective control of expenditures will come from reductions in subsidies and other transfers to public enterprises. These reductions will be achieved by improvements in the profitability of public enterprises and by the introduction of a new system for financing their investments. Such investments will be financed by the retained earnings of public enterprises and by bank credits obtained directly by them, rather than by budgetary transfers. In addition, the PRE announces planned increases in the prices charged to the users of public utilities and services provided by the public sector (housing rents, transportation, post and telecommunications, water, electricity, etc.). A reduction in the level of expenditure may also be achieved through the proposed reform of the system of project evaluation and approval, which aims at establishing better screening procedures and criteria for investment projects.

5.08 According to the PRE, the authorities will take initiatives to strengthen the mechanisms of control of public expenditures. They envisage the reorganization of the services of Public Accounting and the Treasury, which will control the public debt and all cash payments and receipts of the government. The PRE also announces that a survey will be undertaken of all the personnel in the public administration, in order to ensure a more satisfactory control of budgetary expenditures on wages.

5.09 New Solutions to Finance the Budget Deficit. Until now, the budget deficit has been financed mainly by monetary creation and also partly by foreign credits. In order to avoid the inflationary effects of money creation, the authorities intend to finance a larger proportion of the deficit by domestic borrowing from households and from enterprises with large cash balances. For that purpose, they intend to develop a market for public debt securities with attractive returns for private savers. The SEF also envisages the possibility of issuing a compulsory war loan to be subscribed by wage earners.

5.10 In 1988, the government approved a law on securities (law 8/88) which regulates the issue of savings bonds with maturities ranging from 12 to 18 years, to be subscribed by individuals, of development bonds to be subscribed by enterprises and other collective entities and of restructuring bonds to be used in the settlement of the arrears of the Government and of public enterprises. The PRE announces plans to issue 5 billion kwanzas of savings bonds and 90 billion kwanzas of restructuring bonds. It is the intention of the authorities to issue the savings bonds at a price above par and to reimburse them totally or partially in foreign exchange.

5.11 Restructuring of the Financial Situation of Public Enterprises. The authorities will seek to reduce the losses of enterprises in the public sector by restructuring some of them, privatizing others, and closing those that do not appear viable in the long term. The profitability of the enterprises kept in the public sector will be improved by the liberalization or increase of their prices and by the introduction of measures designed to increase their productivity. The financial situation of existing public enterprises will be restructured by cancelling part of their debts or by converting such debts into equity. The rescheduling of debts through the issue of restructuring bonds, involving the extension of their amortization periods, is also envisaged. Finally, the SEF announces a stricter ex-post control of the financial operations and payments of public enterprises. The Government has initiated a number of studies aimed at restructuring the financial situation of the public enterprise sector.

One of these involves an analysis of the indebtedness between public enterprises as well as between those enterprises and the government, with a view to establishing a more rational financial structure of existing enterprises. Work is also proceeding with respect to the development of a methodology for assessing the viability of existing public enterprises.

5.12 Strengthening of the Financial System. According to the SEF program, the arrears of public enterprises will be identified and rescheduled by means of restructuring bonds. Those bonds will replace bad and doubtful debts in the portfolio of the National Bank of Angola (BNA). The cleaning of the balance sheet of that bank will be followed by a revision of its intermediation margins, in order to improve its profitability. The interest rates on both deposits and bank credits will be increased. The authorities envisage the introduction of more flexibility and more competition in the banking sector. As discussed in Chapter 3, legislation has already been enacted to enable the Popular Bank of Angola (BPA) to begin making loans. The possibility of further expanding the powers of BPA or establishing other banks in the future is admitted.

5.13 Reform of Domestic Credit Policies. The SEF envisages not only a reduction of the proportion of credits from the banking system channelled to the Treasury, but also an improvement in the allocation of credit to the productive sector. To this end, the National Bank of Angola (BNA) is being administratively separated into central banking and commercial banking departments. In addition, legislation has been enacted to permit the introduction of securities, to be sold by firms to other enterprises and the public, as alternative sources of financing. Interest rates on deposits and loans will be increased to make bank deposits more attractive and to discourage the unnecessary use of credit. BNA will begin to provide medium and long-term credits to enterprises to finance investment and banks will become more independent from government instructions in their credit decisions. Unless there is an explicit government guarantee, approval of credit to public or private enterprises will depend on judgments by bank management on profitability and risks of the operations to be financed. BNA will closely monitor the use of credit by enterprises to ensure that the funds are used for projects with a reasonably high probability of generating sufficient resources for enterprises to reimburse their debts. Longer term SEF plans call for credit to be allocated increasingly on the basis of interest rates and less on mandatory rules of selection.

5.14 Rescheduling of External Debt. One of the main purposes of the SEF is to provide the basis for negotiations concerning the rescheduling of Angolan external debt. The authorities are interested not only in a solution to the current arrears problem, but also in extending the maturity of existing debt, so as to alleviate the debt service burden in the next few years. At the same time, they intend to introduce more discipline in the management of their external debt in order to avoid the resurgence of new debt crises.

5.15 Liberalization and Adjustments in Controlled Prices. According to the SEF, among the main economic reform measures to be enacted, is the key role to be attributed to the liberalization or adjustment of controlled prices, in order to reflect changes that have taken place in wages and input costs, particularly imported inputs. Many agricultural prices were already liberalized in 1988, with clearly positive results as far as the supply response is concerned. The objective of the liberalization and of the adjustments in controlled prices is to create conditions for the adequate profitability of enterprises.

5.16 The PRE announces the intention of the authorities of maintaining price controls at the national level on a certain number of essential goods and services, including in particular water, electricity, oil, gas and transportation. In the agricultural sector, the government will introduce guaranteed minimum prices for the producers of some key products. In most productive sectors, the elimination of the existing system of price controls will allow enterprises more autonomy in their pricing decisions, giving them more opportunity to adapt their prices to changing conditions of supply and demand. Regulations will, however, continue to be applied regarding the maximum margins charged by trading enterprises and the prices of enterprises which enjoy a monopoly position. In view of the gradual liberalization of prices, the control of the aggregate price level will tend to rely essentially on macroeconomic policies.

5.17 Adjustment of the Exchange Rate. The SEF explicitly envisages a devaluation of the kwanza. Under discussion is an initial 100 percent devaluation to be followed by a second devaluation of similar magnitude within a year. An explanatory text about the SEF suggests that, in the external debt rescheduling negotiations, creditors will probably press for a larger devaluation than considered appropriate by the authorities. The same text states that "the exchange rate will not be the most important instrument of stabilization." According to the authorities, the reduction of the budget deficit and adjustments in the price level will to some extent replace the role of the exchange rate in restoring equilibrium. The SEF admits that, in a second stage of the reform process, a crawling-peg system for the exchange rate may be introduced if it is considered necessary to stimulate exports. It should be emphasized that the reference to a devaluation of the Kwanza represents a fundamental change in the economic thinking of the Angolan authorities. Until 1987, the authorities persisted in maintaining a fixed exchange rate against the dollar, without acknowledging the enormous distortions created by such a policy.

5.18 Foreign Exchange Control. The allocation of foreign exchange has probably been the most important factor determining the volume and the structure of consumption and investment and the level of activity in all productive sectors which depend strongly on the availability of imported inputs. Even after the devaluation of the exchange rate, the allocation of foreign exchange will continue to be based essentially on administrative mechanisms. A new exchange law (law 9/88) was issued by the government with the objective of improving those mechanisms.

5.19 The exchange law establishes the obligation of delivering to the exchange authority the foreign exchange received by the residents, forbids compensation of debts and credits between residents and non-residents, and limits the ability to carry out exchange functions to the entities so authorized by the exchange authority. The Central Bank is responsible for managing foreign exchange holdings. All foreign exchange operations, regarding capital movements, current invisible transactions and payments related to goods, will continue to be subject to controls. All such transactions require authorizations or licenses. In the particular case of imports and exports of goods, the licensing authority is the Ministry of Foreign Trade. According to the new foreign exchange law, the first fortnight of each month, the Central Bank will inform the ministry of the maximum amount of foreign exchange available for licenses to be issued the next month. Priority in the issuance of licenses is to be given in accordance with the objectives of the national plan.

Structural Reforms in the Economic System

5.20 In order to increase the efficiency of the productive system, the SEF announces, among other measures, a more important role for the private sector, more autonomy for public enterprises, a revision of the law on foreign investment and improvements in the planning system.

5.21 Enlargement of the Role of the Private Sector. Recognizing the shortcomings and inefficiencies of public enterprises, the SEF envisages the establishment of more favorable conditions for the development of the private sector. It explicitly admits that smaller public enterprises will be transferred to the private sector and that state ownership will be concentrated largely in key enterprises with strategic roles.

5.22 In 1988, the authorities issued a new law (law 10/88) which defines the regimes for the different types of ownership of enterprises. That law recognizes four categories of enterprises: (1) Public enterprises; (2) mixed enterprises owned jointly by the public sector (the state, public enterprises or other public entities) and by private capital (national or foreign); (3) cooperatives; and (4) private enterprises (including individuals, partnerships and corporations). No economic activity can be performed without previous authorization by the authorities. A number of activities, including those of central banking, military industry, distribution of electric power, basic sanitary services, telecommunications, transport (except short range maritime transport) and port and airport administration will be reserved exclusively for public enterprises. However, the Council of Ministers may exceptionally authorize private enterprises to undertake economic activities reserved for public enterprises, except for central banking and military industry. Natural resources owned by the State, as specified in terms of constitutional law, may be explored only through concessions or other regimes not involving the transfer of ownership. The Council of Ministers was charged with revising the legislation on the establishment and functioning of private enterprises and cooperatives, nationalization and expropriation, intervention of the State in private enterprises, and licensing of economic activity. In the meantime, any intervention of the State in private enterprises on the basis of the existing legislation requires authorization by the Council of Ministers. A major objective of the new legislation on economic activities is to establish clear rules and guarantees for private enterprises and to enlarge substantially the productive sectors in which those enterprises will be allowed to operate. A special emphasis will be given to the development of private activities in retail trade. It is expected that private traders will make an important contribution to the development of closer economic relations between the countryside and the cities, thus stimulating the marketable production of agricultural crops. Private enterprises will also be especially encouraged in the sectors of internal road transportation, building, repair services, and handicrafts. Enterprises which are currently operating in the parallel market in those sectors will be legalized.

5.23 Increased Autonomy for Public Enterprises. A new law on public enterprises (law 11/88) was published in 1988 with the major objective of providing more autonomy to the management of those enterprises. The activities of the enterprises will be based on their budgets and on their annual and medium term plans, which will be integrated in the macro-economic targets and guidelines established in the national plan. According to the principles announced, the ministries will establish general regulations for the different productive sectors and will plan the activities of such sectors, but will not intervene in specific management decisions at the enterprise level. The law states that, except as provided in specific legal regulations, no organism of the State or other third party has any right to interfere in the conduct of these enterprises. It is foreseen, in particular, that enterprises will have more autonomy in their price and labor policies, although within constraints established by the government for the protection of consumers and workers. Public enterprises will face more active competition, not only because of their greater autonomy but also because of the encouragement of private sector activities.

5.24 Public enterprises will be subject to the same tax treatment as private enterprises. The supervision of the enterprises is the responsibility of the ministry responsible for the sector (Ministro de Tutela), and the Minister of Finance. The sectoral ministry guides and supervises the activities of state enterprises by defining the development policy of the economic activity concerned, approving the multi-year plans and budgets proposed by the enterprises, evaluating directors and approving enterprise accounts. In the case of large companies, the Council of Ministers may require approval by the Minister of Planning of the multi-year plans and budgets and of the investment programs of the enterprise. Public enterprises are to be given greater financial autonomy. The State is not liable for their obligations. Enterprises will retain their depreciation, though its use will still be subject to control, as well as 50% of their profits. Part of the profits may be allocated to workers on the basis of their individual performance. Enterprises will be urged to operate along commercial lines, and will be told that they can only expect government subsidies if their performance is affected by circumstances beyond their control, such as the war. Also, SEF raises the prospect of liquidating non-viable companies as well as privatization of others. However, in practice it appears that fairly close ministerial control, in terms of both planning and execution of operations, is still being maintained. Questions remain about the operational freedom that management of public enterprises will have, for instance in terms of selecting their supply sources and their markets.

5.25 Revision of the Legislation on Foreign Investment. A new law on foreign investment (law 13/88 of June 16, 1988) was approved with the objective of improving the authorization, encouragement and supervision of foreign investments by the Government, and of simplifying the process of negotiation and approval. The new system is aimed at ensuring that foreign investments will contribute effectively to the economic development of Angola and correcting important distortions and shortcomings of recent years in that area. Another major objective is to establish more attractive conditions for potential foreign investors. The creation of a new Institute for Foreign Investment was announced. That Institute will promote foreign investments in Angola including, in particular, joint ventures with Angolan enterprises. Among other functions, the Institute will evaluate foreign investment projects, centralize negotiations with foreign investors, and assist them in all the initiatives and formalities concerning their proposed investments.

5.26 There will be a substantial enlargement of the sectors of economic activity in which foreign investment is permitted. The law excludes investment by non-residents only in the areas of defence, central banking, education, health, water supply and sewerage, electric power, postal services, telecommunications, social communications, administration of ports and airports, air transport, and long range maritime transport. This list notwithstanding, the Council of Ministers may authorize specific investments in areas complementary to those so listed. Limitations on the percentage of foreign ownership of the capital of enterprises will be reduced and foreign investors may be allowed to establish new enterprises fully owned by them. They will also be permitted to acquire Angolan enterprises which are not producing or which are highly inefficient and could be turned around.

5.27 The law specifies that investors are to receive just and equitable treatment and, in particular, it guarantees the repatriation of profits or of the foreign investor's share in case of liquidation or sale of the enterprise. In both instances, the prior authorization of the Minister of Finance is required. In case of expropriation, the investor will be given "just compensation". In case of disputes between the foreign and local investor which cannot be resolved amicably, the parties may have recourse to arbitration according to UNCITRAL rules. It should be emphasized that the disputes which may be subject to such arbitration are not those involving the State but only those between the local and foreign partners. Thus, in the case of expropriation, there would not be the possibility of submitting a dispute regarding compensation to arbitration.

5.28 Foreign investments under this law may be given certain incentives, such as exemption from or reduction of income taxes and customs duties on inputs or outputs. They may also benefit from other incentives available under existing legislation in cases in which they reinvest profits, develop activities of a social character, and train and use local labor and management.

5.29 The law leaves a number of matters to future regulation. These include areas of priority for foreign investment, compensation in case of expropriation, guarantees which might be required from the investor, terms of the contract to be signed between the investors after approval of the investment, and obligation of employment of local labor.

5.30 Improvement of the Planning System - A new law on economic planning (law 12/88) was published on July 9, 1988. The new law states that national plans will continue to be a major instrument of economic management. However, it is recognized in the preamble of the law that the system of economic planning has relied too much on administrative mechanisms and bureaucratic methods and that it will be necessary to assign a more important role to the operation of market forces. The authorities intend to improve the system of planning by changing some of its more important characteristics and mechanisms and by better recruitment and training of experts charged with the planning tasks at the central, sectoral and enterprise levels. In view of the unsatisfactory experience with detailed quantitative planning, the authorities will reduce substantially the number of annual targets for the production and supply of important goods and services. Annual plans will be based to a larger extent on projections of key economic variables and will put more emphasis on the macro-economic policies required to ensure internal and external equilibrium at very aggregate levels. Macro-economic management will be based essentially on the level of public expenditures, the average level of taxation, the exchange rate, interest rates, the average rate of increase of wages, and the average rate of increase of controlled prices. However, most prices will be determined by market forces. The allocation of resources, especially as regards the volume of investment and the structure of output, will be determined essentially by the price mechanism and by market competition. The plan will influence the activities of major productive sectors mainly through broad guidelines, incentives, public investments, taxes and tax credits and the accountability of managers, rather than through output targets.

5.31 The authorities will seek to achieve better coordination between the Annual Plans, the State Budget, and the Foreign Exchange Budget. The State Budget and the Foreign Exchange Budget will be more effectively subordinated to Annual Plans. Investment programs which are being executed at present will be reviewed and some large projects may be slowed down or stopped. Domestic financial constraints and the availability of foreign exchange will have a greater weight in decisions concerning new investments. Enterprises will have more autonomy in their investment decisions if they can finance them internally or if they can obtain domestic credits without government support. Finally, there will be more decentralization of planning activities from the Planning Ministry to the planning organizations at regional levels.

B. THE SEF AND PROSPECTS FOR ECONOMIC REHABILITATION

Introduction

5.32 As mentioned above, the general thrust of measures envisaged in the SEF seems to be appropriate. However, since the actual implementation of most of those measures has not yet started, it is not possible to present precise comments on their expected contribution to the adjustment of the Angolan economy. Nevertheless, an evaluation of that contribution will require:

(a) a definition of the key objectives to be pursued;

(b) a discussion of the strategies to be adopted in implementing the reforms envisaged;

(c) an analysis of institutional constraints to implementation of the SEF program and of the measures which will be needed to ease such constraints;

(d) a discussion of the main reforms in macro-economic policies and economic structures to be introduced under the SEF, including in particular:

(i) the development of a network of competitive enterprises, providing a basis for the operation of the market system;

(ii) the reduction of the budget deficit;

(iii) the reform of the price system and the adjustment of wage levels;

(iv) the adjustment of the exchange rate and the policy of foreign exchange allocation;

(v) monetary and credit policy.

(e) an assessment of the social problems which may be created by the implementation of the policies of economic adjustment and reform envisaged in the SEF;

(f) an assessment of shortcomings in the availability of key statistical data required for the conduct of economic policy; and

(g) an analysis of a scenario based on the end of the war.

5.33 The following sections deal in turn with each of the foregoing points. In order to provide some useful information about the difficulties and the achievements to be expected from the SEF and the PRE and from the policies recommended in the present report, the last section of this chapter summarizes experiences with the implementation of similar programs undertaken in recent years by Ghana and Mozambique. Both of these countries were facing serious economic difficulties similar to those of Angola and tried to respond to such difficulties with economic policies similar to those that Angola has been contemplating. The experiences of Ghana and Mozambique are thus highly relevant for the discussion of the SEF.

Definition of Key SEF Objectives

5.34 As mentioned repeatedly in various parts of this report, the development of the Angolan economy over the next few years is closely linked to the evolution of the war. The analysis of the following sections is implicitly based on the assumption that substantial improvements will be achieved as regards the war situation and that Angolan authorities will have the opportunity and the international support to divert a substantial volume of resources from the war effort to the tasks of economic reconstruction and improvement of social conditions. The results expected from the SEF would, of course, be almost entirely frustrated if the Angolan Government is forced to allocate a high share of available resources to defence activities, if there is not a significant enlargement of the areas of the country enjoying reasonable security, or if there are frequent attacks against installations of strategic economic importance.

5.35 The behavior of international oil prices will also be an important factor influencing the success of the SEF. If those prices drop to significantly lower levels, it would be extremely difficult for the SEF reforms to offset the negative effects of the tighter external constraints on the economy. However, if oil prices rise very substantially, there might also be risks that the authorities would reduce their commitment to the SEF reforms, and would return to some of the inefficient and wasteful economic policies of the early 1980s.

5.36 As mentioned in paragraph 5.02, the SEF reforms are oriented towards two main objectives: (1) stabilization of the financial situation; and (2) reform of the economic system. The analysis of the following paragraphs is based on an alternative formulation, probably more significant from the operational point of view, which identifies the following priorities for the economic reform program in Angola: (a) ensure adequate control of domestic demand; (b) stimulate domestic supply; and (c) improve the allocation of resources.

5.37 Control of Domestic Demand. The control of domestic demand is indispensable to reduce the inflationary pressures reflected in the generalized and growing scarcities at official prices of consumer goods and inputs for productive activities. Such control is also essential to keep the current account in balance and the external debt within sustainable limits, without excessive recourse to rigid and inefficient schemes of administrative allocation of foreign exchange. The control of domestic demand will have to rely primarily on efforts to reduce the budget deficit, the main source of inflationary pressures. However, effective control of the expansion of domestic credit to the productive sector will also be necessary in order to avoid excessive growth in the money supply and in the demand for imports.

5.38 Stimulation of Domestic Supply. The rapid recovery of domestic production is one of the basic objectives of the PRE. That recovery will have to be based mainly on agriculture. There are good reasons to believe that agricultural production by peasant farmers in the areas not affected by the war (mainly in the provinces in the southwest and around Luanda) will respond very quickly and substantially to adequate incentives. Such incentives should include: (i) more favorable prices for agricultural products, some of which have already been introduced; (ii) development of a network of private bush traders; (iii) greater availability of consumption and agricultural input goods for purchase by peasant farmers; (iv) better transportation and storage facilities for agricultural crops; and (v) improved support services and technical assistance. Other areas in which a supply response is much needed and could be rapid and quite important are those of repair services, private truck transportation, small-scale consumer goods industries and construction. Efforts aimed at stimulating the production of manufacturing industries and of large scale agricultural activities should be more selective. Resource constraints will limit new investments and the rehabilitation of existing capacity. Severe scarcities of managerial and technical skills will also create serious obstacles to a rapid and easy recovery of production in many of the larger enterprises.

5.39 Improvement in the Allocation of Resources. In view of the extremely large distortions in the Angolan economy, improvements in the allocation of resources can increase the welfare of consumers and correct arbitrary inequalities in income distribution that are not justified by reasons of productive efficiency. A better allocation of resources can also increase productivity in most sectors of the economy and improve the efficiency of investments. The achievement of these objectives will require, among other measures: (i) the reduction of administrative interferences in the economy and more reliance on market forces; (ii) the stimulation of competition in the productive sector; (iii) substantial changes in price policies and the exchange rate; (iv) the progressive unification of the official and parallel markets; (v) a review of public expenditure priorities; (vi) the reform of public enterprises; and (vii) an improvement in the mechanisms for evaluation and selection of public investments.

Strategies for Reform

5.40 The reform process in Angola will require very drastic transformations in the economic system, in the methods of economic management, and in economic policies. In principle, two strategies can be conceived for the implementation of such transformations:

(a) a shock adjustment, under which the most important changes would be made within a very short period; or

(b) a more gradual or staged approach, under which the required transformations would be introduced progressively, in partial steps taken over a period of several years.

5.41 In the case of Angola, a full shock adjustment does not seem to be feasible for a number of reasons. In theory it would be possible to introduce measures of advanced liberalization and stabilization within a comparatively short period (elimination of controls over prices and imports; introduction of a market-determined floating foreign exchange rate; introduction of strict controls on the expansion of credit to the public sector; introduction of market-determined interest rates; etc.). However, in practice there is the risk that, given the state of development of Angolan economic structures, the extent of the distortions and the constraints created by the war, a strategy of very rapid liberalization would produce new economic disequilibria, different from those which exist at present, but not necessarily less serious. Similarly, attempts to stabilize the economy over a short period of a few months would involve very harsh decisions. The shortcomings and insufficiencies in existing administrative and productive structures would compound the adverse effects which would certainly arise.

5.42 On the other hand, a gradual approach involves dangers if it is extended over too long a period. There is no doubt that the new economic policies required in Angola will only be effective if they are supported by structural adjustments. If these cannot realistically be achieved in a few months, the gradual approach will be unavoidable, although its results will appear only slowly. At the same time, a gradual approach will reduce the risks of big mistakes and will provide more opportunities to learn through experience and to introduce corrections in the course of the adjustment and reform process. A gradual approach will, however, tend to fail if it starts with weak measures and if it is extended over an excessive long period. Weak measures produce weak effects, undermine the credibility of the reform program, and may be counterproductive. In addition, if the implementation of the program is extended over an excessively long period, there is the risk that the political commitment that it requires will become progressively weaker and that the resistance of adversely affected groups will become progressively stronger.

5.43 In view of the considerations and circumstances prevailing in Angola, a <u>combination of shock treatment with a gradual approach</u> should be considered. The existing economic distortions are so serious that a rapid reduction of many of them is urgently required. That reduction cannot be achieved without the introduction, even in initial reform stages, of radical changes, involving adjustments in price and wage policies, the depreciation of the exchange rate, more flexibility in allocating foreign exchange, and more autonomy and accountability for public enterprises. Initial reform measures should also include improvements in taxation, better control of public expenditures, stimulation of competition, more attractive incentives to private enterprises and less government interference in productive activities. Such measures must be integrated into a <u>consistent</u> package, conceived so as to reinforce the total positive impact of the various measures and to neutralize the undesirable effects of some of them.

5.44 Further work and discussions will be needed to formulate the required changes with precision. It is clear, however, in light of the analysis and discussion presented here, that the process of reform should begin with decisive steps involving:

(a) a very substantial adjustment of the exchange rate;

(b) the liberalization of a high proportion of administered prices (including not only the prices of agricultural products, many of which have already been liberalized, but also the prices of goods and services in which the volume of transactions is comparatively small or which at present are mainly supplied in the parallel market);

(c) substantial increases in the prices which will continue to be controlled;

(d) the introduction of incentives to stimulate exports of agricultural goods;

(e) the adoption of solutions to reduce the rigidity of the administrative allocation of foreign exchange for some key imports (spare parts, inputs for agriculture, etc.);

(f) increases in tariff duties, elimination of a large number of tariff exemptions and increases in some indirect taxes;

(g) adjustments in wage levels (as far as possible combined with a reduction in self-consumption facilities and privileged access to goods and services at official prices);

(h) the enlargement of the autonomy of public enterprises, the financial restructuring of the most important of those enterprises and the closing of public enterprises which are not viable;

(i) the legalization of a substantial proportion of the activities in the parallel market and, more generally, improvements in the legal framework for private enterprises and the introduction of incentives for the development of small scale enterprises, especially in the areas of trading, truck transportation, repair services and construction;

(j) the revision of the methods and mechanisms of economic planning with a view to introducing more flexibility and reducing bureaucratic interference in productive activities.

5.45 The initial changes in economic policies would have to be complemented by additional reforms to be introduced gradually in subsequent stages. These reforms should involve further steps towards the reduction of administrative controls and the elimination of existing economic distortions. They should be based to a large extent on structural transformations aimed at increasing the efficiency of taxation and public expenditure control systems, public enterprises, the banking sector, the educational and training system, urban services, the transportation sector, etc.

5.46 The impact of a reform program like the SEF on the level and efficiency of production may not come about very quickly, even if the initial package of adjustment measures is strong. Many existing difficulties will persist in the medium term and new problems will certainly emerge. Thus, for instance, even if the output of marketable agricultural products responds rapidly to new incentives, scarcities of essential consumer and intermediate goods are not likely to disappear in the next few years. Changes in economic structures, including, for example, the development of an internal market with a reasonable degree of competition, cannot be achieved in a short period. Similarly, drastic changes in economic policies, including in particular the liberalization of prices, will not produce the expected results if they do not take into account the constraints and conditions imposed by shortcomings in economic and administrative structures. It is for all these reasons, that the implementation of the SEF should be based on a combination of shock treatment and a gradual approach: the initial package of adjustment measures should introduce drastic transformations in economic policy, but the implementation of the structural reforms and the additional adjustments in economic policies will have to be undertaken over a period of several years.

5.47 The success of an economic adjustment and reform process extended over several years will depend on the proper sequencing of the measures to be undertaken. A given measure, introduced too early, before the basic conditions for its success are created, may aggravate the problems of disequilibrium instead of correcting them. Thus for instance, in the Angolan context, a policy of full liberalization of domestic prices and a depreciation of the exchange rate sufficient to permit the liberalization of imports could create risks of a vicious spiral of inflation-devaluation -inflation if the budget deficit is not previously reduced to levels which could be financed without excessive monetary creation. Similarly, the adoption of a new system of prices to stimulate agricultural production can only produce its expected positive effects if transportation to rural areas and trade in those areas are allowed to develop unconstrained by bureaucratic decisions and controls.

Institutional and Training Requirements

5.48 As mentioned in various sections of this report, many difficulties in the Angolan economy result not only from inadequate economic policies, but also from institutional constraints, including serious shortages of management capacity and skilled personnel, as well as a generalized lack of discipline at various levels. It is thus evident that the preparation and approval of a well conceived program of economic reform will not by itself be sufficient to achieve the objectives mentioned in the preceding sections. The success of such a program will depend crucially on the capacity of the Angolan authorities to implement the program. The following paragraphs deal briefly with some of the key requirements for a reasonably adequate implementation of a program of economic reform. The points to be analyzed include: (i) political commitment; (ii) decentralizing economic decision-making; (iii) reduction of the prevailing lack of discipline; and (iv) the availability of skilled personnel.

5.49 Political Commitment. In view of the arguments presented in the preceding sections, the success of the SEF will depend to a large extent on the commitment of the Angolan authorities to implement it over a period of several years. The strategy of rehabilitation and reform will fail completely if the Angolan authorities do not persist for a sufficiently long period in the implementation of the SEF policies, even in the face of disappointing initial results and resistance against the transformations to be introduced. Such resistance may come from two sources: those who will argue that the policies envisaged are not appropriate in the specific Angolan context; and those who fear that such policies will affect adversely their privileges and power. For these reasons, without a strong political will, it may for example be extremely difficult to develop a stronger role for market forces, given the natural resistance against such a change in a country which until now has been so closely managed by bureaucratic decisions.

5.50 Decentralization of Economic Decisions. The decentralization of economic decision-making would certainly reduce many of the inefficiencies, contradictions, overlaps, and delays created by the existing system. Another important justification for economic decentralization is that it would economize on scarce resources of qualified manpower. At present, a substantial part of those resources are absorbed in tasks such as preparing detailed regulations (which often are not observed), granting a multitude of authorizations and licenses, and intervening in minor decisions of enterprises and departments at the lower levels of public administration. A more decentralized system would make it possible to concentrate scarce managerial and technical capacities on the design, implementation, and control of general economic policies and on the more important decisions. If detailed decisions of less importance were taken on a more decentralized basis by a large number of economic agents, lower level decision-makers could develop expertise in specific areas. In addition, under a decentralized system, the greater dispersion and smaller impact of possible mistakes would reduce the seriousness of their consequences. Such a decentralization of economic decision-making must be primarily based on: (i) a more important role for the market; (ii) greater autonomy for public and private enterprises; and (iii) more delegation of decision-making powers in the public administration, including regional and local authorities. These measures are envisaged in the SEF, but their implementation will not be easy and will require a strong commitment from the authorities.

5.51 Reduction of the Lack of Discipline. As mentioned in several sections of the present report, there is a widespread lack of discipline at various levels of the public administration and within the enterprises in Angola. The manifestations of such lack of discipline include decisions that are contrary to existing regulations, decisions taken by some authorities which encroach upon the jurisdiction of others, high absenteeism of workers, theft of a substantial proportion of the production of some enterprises, theft from the ports, etc. Part of that lack of discipline is due to existing economic difficulties, such as the scarcity of essential consumer goods, difficulties experienced by the workers in getting transportation to their jobs, and bottlenecks created by the war. The program of economic reform will undoubtedly ameliorate some of the fundamental causes of loose discipline but, to be effective, decisive efforts by the authorities to combat the generalized lack of discipline will be required, starting at very high levels of the political and administrative structure. Without such efforts, there is the risk that the objectives of the reform program will be frustrated to a large extent.

5.52 Availability of Skilled Personnel. The scarcity of skilled personnel is one of the main constraints to improving economic policies and to increasing economic efficiency in Angola. As mentioned above, decentralization of economic decision-making will economize on scarce human capital resources. However, there are many areas in which management at the central level will have to be maintained and improved: for instance, in the control of budgetary expenditures, in tax and customs administration, in the credit system, in the administration of justice, in the organization and functioning of the education and health systems, etc. At the same time, the need to train personnel at intermediate skill levels for public sector administration and for enterprise management and production is critical. For example, there is a pressing need for accountants, mechanics and foremen. The recourse to foreign technical assistance, in the framework of economic aid programs or on a commercial basis, will continue to be necessary on a large scale. However, the efficiency of foreign technical assistance has not always been entirely satisfactory, mainly because of bad choices in priorities, inadequate efforts to follow up the work started by foreign experts, and insufficient interaction and knowledge-transfer between foreign and Angolan experts. In such conditions, the implementation of a program of economic reforms in Angola will require action in the following areas: (i) the allocation of existing human resources; (ii) training; and (iii) the utilization of foreign technical assistance.

5.53 Allocation of Existing Human Resources. The existing allocation of skilled personnel should be reexamined, taking into account the objectives of the program of economic reform. The changes to be introduced in economic institutions and policies will create the opportunity and the need to transfer a substantial number of experts and administrators from functions whose relative importance will decline (especially bureaucratic regulations and controls) to other functions that will become more essential (for instance, management of large enterprises and administration of incentives and support schemes for medium and small enterprises). The reallocation of scarce human resources in the public administration and in the productive sector will depend essentially on the structure of incentives. That structure includes at present not only the level of wages, but also payments in kind (self-consumption in manufacturing enterprises) and the possibility to acquire goods and services at official prices (access to special shops, possibilities of buying or renting houses, priorities in purchases of cars, air tickets, etc.). The complexity of the existing structure of incentives creates strong distortions and rigidities. It will thus be essential to: (i) define priorities for the allocation of the scarce supply of managers, administrators and experts; and (ii) review the existing structure of incentives for skilled personnel in order to simplify them and adapt them to the requirements of the new mechanisms and institutions of economic policy to be introduced in the next few years.

5.54 Training of Skilled Personnel. In the medium- and long-run, the availability of skilled personnel at the different levels in public administration and in the productive sector will depend primarily on the development of the educational system. As explained in Chapter 4, and in Annex IX, the Angolan authorities have made substantial efforts in the area of education, particularly at the level of secondary and higher education. However, important improvements are required in educational policies, including in particular: (i) more emphasis on vocational training at the secondary level; and (ii) changes in the "curricula" in higher education, in order to give more priority to applied techniques. The authorities are studying transformations in line with these proposals. They are for instance studying the introduction of substantial changes in the curriculum of the Economics Faculty at the University of Luanda, with a view to increasing the relative importance of courses in applied economics. In connection with these transformations, it would be important also to emphasize courses in management (accounting, financial management, project evaluation, marketing, etc.). In parallel with the development of the educational system, there is a strong need for training courses for experts, managers and skilled workers in the public administration and in productive enterprises. The precise definition of the programs and priorities for such courses can only be determined after further studies, but it is known that they are required in many areas and at different levels (including, for example, courses in accounting or in the repair of machinery and transport vehicles). Also, one of the first priorities should be to organize specialized seminars on the Economic Reform Program for economists and managers.

5.55 Technical Assistance. Substantial amounts of money have been spent on technical assistance provided to Angola either on a commercial basis or in the context of bilateral and multilateral programs of international cooperation. In the coming years, Angola will continue to depend very heavily on foreign technical assistance. For that reason, it will be essential to define priorities and to install mechanisms which will ensure more efficiency in expenditures on technical assistance. The preparatory work should start with a survey of technical assistance experience in recent years, assessing the results achieved in relation to the costs, the follow up of the studies and recommendations made by foreign experts, the transmission of knowledge to Angolan nationals, etc. That survey would provide the basis for a medium-term program, subject to annual revisions, defining the priorities and the guidelines for expenditures on technical assistance and taking into account the resources available both from internal and from external sources.

Development of a Network of Competitive Enterprises

5.56 One of the fundamental reforms of the Angolan economic system should be to introduce a more important role for market forces. However, it will be extremely difficult to achieve that objective with existing structures. A predominant part of productive activities in the official market is based on public enterprises which operate at low levels of efficiency, with very little autonomy and without competition. Private enterprises in the official market are also so strictly regulated and dependent on government administrative allocations that the influence of the market on their decisions is very weak. Peasant farmers, who, in principle, can provide the main basis for the expansion of agricultural production, are isolated in subsistence activities and have few links with the market. The only area in which market forces operate freely is that of the parallel market. Given this situation, deep structural changes in the organization of the productive sectors are needed, especially to develop more autonomy for public enterprises, to liquidate or sell off some public enterprises, to stimulate competition and develop incentives for the establishment of small private enterprises.

5.57 More Autonomy for Public Enterprises. According to the SEF and law 11/88, more autonomy will be given to public enterprises, an undoubtedly very important objective. However, the central economic plan will apparently continue to play a major role in the activities of public enterprises. Those enterprises will still prepare, for at least a year ahead, business plans and budgets, in which all their inputs and outputs will be detailed quantitatively and financially. The plans will continue to be sent to the Ministry of Planning through the ministry that oversees the enterprise in order to be integrated into the national plan. A council, comprising the Ministers of Finance and Planning and the overseeing ministries, will revise these plans if necessary, and return them to the companies for implementation. Public enterprises will still be responsible for keeping detailed performance records, which will be submitted periodically up the chain of command for scrutiny. These do not appear to be changes that will stimulate very much autonomy for public enterprises.

5.58 The authorities recognize that the degree of control over management decisions inherent in the hierarchical command structure has in the past invited too much political interference in what are essentially economic activities. To rectify this situation, law 11/88 envisages a much wider separation between the supervisory ministries and management. However, the planning process, which will remain intact, will continue to limit managerial initiatives because the plan instructions, which must be observed in order to qualify for foreign exchange allocations, will limit short-term flexibility. The relaxation of the pervasive system of government price controls will enlarge opportunities for producers of goods and services to charge whatever they believe necessary to reach profitability. The Government, however, reserves the right to place a ceiling on any price in the interest of consumer protection. It is clear, however, that for the present steps towards financial autonomy to be effective, progress has to be made in liberalizing a broad range of prices, in adding flexibility in the allocation of foreign exchange, and eliminating other constraints imposed by government policies on the management of public enterprises.

5.59 Public enterprises are expected to enjoy greater financial autonomy. Access to bank credit will remain unchanged, but to compensate for the withdrawal of unlimited government budgetary support, these enterprises will be able to accumulate extra investment and working capital, beyond the original equity (Fundo de Constituiçao) provided by the State. This new source of financing is to come from retained depreciation and presumably a larger share of operating profits. Public enterprises will also be allowed to raise money through debt issues.

5.60 Apart from the need to establish an economic environment that encourages a more efficient allocation of resources, which is an essential condition for the efficient operation of any enterprise, the key to a successful rationalization of the state enterprise sector is having capable managers at the enterprise level and ensuring ex-post control of their performance. Without able managers it will not be easy to set up a system of arms-length ministerial control and reduce the current interference in operations. To find good managers, it will be necessary to reform the present pay structure in order to offer adequate incentives. Law 11/88 envisages a quite complex management structure for the large enterprises consisting of: a Board of Directors with 3 to 5 members, one of whom will be appointed by the workers; an Auditing Board, with 3 members appointed by the Government; a Managing Board, consisting of the chief Executive Manager, appointed by the Board of Directors, and several senior executives of the enterprise; and an Advisory Board to the Management, with consultative functions and composed of the Managing Board, a representative of the trade unions and a representative of the official party. According to the same law, the management structure of the smaller public enterprises will be more simplified. In those enterprises, there will be no Board of Directors, the Auditing Board may be replaced in some cases by a single auditor, and the Managing Board may consist only of the Managing Director. However, in smaller enterprises the composition and the functions of the

Advisory Board to the Management will be similar to those of large enterprises. In order to strengthen the autonomy of the managers, it is foreseen that they will be appointed for periods of 3 to 5 years with opportunities for renewal, and that they can be dismissed only under conditions specified in general regulations. Solutions of this type are probably not well adapted to the constraints imposed by the scarcity of managers and professional skills in Angola. It would certainly be more realistic to envisage less elaborate management structures, except in very few large enterprises of key importance in the economy (Sonangol, TAAG and a few others). The effective autonomy of public enterprises and the efficiency of their management will depend mainly on the process of selecting managers and their allocation among enterprises. Enterprise autonomy and efficiency will also depend on the extent of interference by political structures and by ministers in the day-to-day activities of the enterprise, as well as on training programs in management skills, management performance evaluations, incentives for good performance, and penalties for incompetence or neglect.

5.61 Liquidation or Transfers of Public Enterprises. Constraints on the availability of imported inputs, equipment and managerial capacity and professional skills make it extremely difficult to ensure the viability of a significant number of public enterprises. The maintenance of some of these enterprises absorbs scarce resources which often could be used more productively elsewhere. Very often these enterprises provide jobs without a proper corresponding contribution to the gross domestic product. They tend, therefore, to impose a burden on the economy, instead of helping its development. In such conditions, the Angolan authorities face the challenge of having to close some public enterprises which offer no encouraging prospects of becoming viable. In a few cases, they will have to transfer such enterprises to the private sector (by total or partial privatization, leasing, management contracts, etc.).

5.62 The existing law on public enterprises recommends that management of public enterprises pursue operational efficiency and maximize operating profits. However, the practice has been to permit those enterprises that for one reason or another have shown losses, to resort to either an annual state budget subvention or to obtain long-term loans from the central bank. According to the intentions of the authorities, public enterprises which do not show a profit are presumably to be terminated by liquidation or sale. This discipline will undoubtedly be beneficial for the economy, but it is uncertain whether it can be uniformly enforced because of political resistance and the adverse effects on urban employment.

5.63 While the private sector can accomplish some productive activities more efficiently than the state sector and letting it do so would relieve the Government of an unnecessary burden, there is clearly a significant role for state enterprises. Some public enterprises operate in naturally monopolistic areas (e.g., public services) and others in areas considered vital to state security (e.g., air transport and telecommunications). These will definitely not be privatized or liquidated. It is, moreover, possible that the operational management of some of private companies will not be allowed to be more than executors of pieces of the national plan. Some of the larger trading companies, and many of the local public enterprises which are logical candidates for privatization, may not move in that direction rapidly for lack of available entrepreneurial talent and capital. In addition, the scope for privatization is limited by problems of insecurity, labor relations, lack of skilled personnel, narrowness of the domestic markets, difficulties in internal transportation, irregularities in energy supply, etc.

5.64 Stimulation of Competition and Incentives for Medium-sized and Small Private Enterprises. The market cannot provide efficient mechanisms for the operation of the Angolan economy unless there is a sufficiently large number of enterprises competing actively against each other in a large proportion of the productive sectors. In order to fulfill that condition, it will be indispensable to stimulate actively the development of medium and small scale private enterprises in several sectors. This raises several considerations:

(a) The possibility of rapid growth in agricultural production in the next few years will depend primarily on the contribution of peasant farmers. That contribution may be very significant if it is stimulated by appropriate price policies and by the development of adequate trade and transportation facilities. A limited number of large commercial farms, of which some exist already, can also make a useful contribution, especially as regards the introduction of new technologies.

(b) The development of diversified structures in the trade sector should be a cornerstone of the reform of the Angolan economic system. These structures should be based on a large number of small and medium enterprises in all levels of trade, including imports, exports, domestic distribution, and wholesale and retail trade. Encouraging the establishment of traders in rural areas (bush traders) is particularly important, given their potential role in stimulating agricultural production;

(c) To support the development of the trade sector and agricultural production, it will also be essential to stimulate the creation of small private enterprises in transportation (e.g., in trucking and bus services);

(d) There is also considerable potential for the establishment of small-scale private enterprises and artisans in several manufacturing activities, services, and the construction sector (mechanical and electric repairs, cloth and shoe-making, food processing, furniture, restaurants, etc.).

5.65 A major reason for encouraging the development of a large number of new private enterprises should be to create a climate of active competition in the economy. Competition is indispensable to ensure efficiency in production and in the allocation of resources and to avoid high levels of concentration of wealth and economic power. In order to achieve more competition the authorities should avoid imposing specialization on enterprises. Rather, they should encourage the establishment of new trade and transportation enterprises in branches and regions in which there are already similar enterprises and activities. They should avoid granting special benefits in favor of specific enterprises which could lead to distortions in competition.

5.66 The creation of conditions by the authorities for the establishment and development of new enterprises in competition with each other should involve a number of steps:

(a) The authorities must clearly define the legal conditions for the operation of private enterprises, specifying the guarantees offered to them and ensuring that they will not be subject to arbitrary interventions not specified in the law. The legislation should also provide for adequate legal protection against crimes, breach of contracts, etc. The strengthening of the judiciary system will be particularly important for that purpose.

(b) The authorities must develop adequate flexibility in policies concerning price controls, wages, labor, credit, allocation of foreign exchange, etc. If these policies continue to be based almost exclusively on administrative decisions, risks involved in the creation of new enterprises would be much higher and new initiatives would be stifled.

(c) The authorities need to quickly legalize enterprises which at present operate in the parallel market. The legalization process should not be unduly restricted beyond requiring the enterprises involved to comply with adequate regulations concerning taxation, protection of health and security, enrollment of labor, etc.

(d) The system of licensing the establishment of new enterprises should be liberalized. The creation of new enterprises complying with existing general regulations should be authorized without great formalities and with a minimum of restrictions.

5.67 The authorities should give high priority to the creation of incentives for the development of small enterprises in different sectors of economy. The incentives to be introduced could include: (a) tax holidays; (b) assistance for professional training of selected categories of skilled workers (mechanics, electricians, construction workers, accountants, etc.); (c) technical assistance to small enterprises, based on the support of foreign technicians; (d) adequate credit facilities; and (e) provision of adequate infrastructure (warehouses for storing agricultural products, rental of shops and industrial buildings owned by the State, supply of water and electricity, etc.) In addition, specific programs for the development of small enterprises in priority sectors (trade, transportation, mechanical repairs, etc.) should be prepared and implemented, if possible with the support of technical and financial foreign assistance. It should be noted that the authorities are considering at least some of these measures and that the authorities envisage the preparation of "Sectoral Programs for the Promotion of Small Enterprises".

Reduction of the Budgetary Deficit

5.68 Two basic means are open to the government to reduce the 4gbudgetary deficit. These are increased mobilization of non-oil tax revenues and containment of the growth of public expenditure.

5.69 Mobilization of Non-Oil Revenues. At present, the bulk of government revenues are derived from the oil sector, and the domestic tax burden is thus light. There are good reasons for making an effort to exploit the domestic revenue potential more fully. Widening the revenue base would not only contribute additional fiscal revenues but would also lessen the inherent instability in the government's finances due to their dependence on the international oil market. The main components of a tax reform package should include changes in the tax system as well as improvements in tax administration. Changes in the tax system should include: (a) the simplification of the import tariff and the elimination of most existing tariff exemptions; (b) an increase in tariff duties on less essential consumption goods; (c) an increase in indirect taxes on petroleum products, tobacco, beer, alcoholic beverages and other consumer goods; and (d) the introduction of a unified profit tax on all (including public) enterprises. Adjustments in the exchange rate and internal prices recommended in the present report would contribute to a substantial increase in the base for indirect taxation. The Government is already considering reforms in these areas, and in some instances (e.g. with regard to the import tariff and the unified profits tax) they are well advanced.

5.70 Better tax administration and collection would require more and better qualified staff, which in turn depends on satisfactory pay levels, on proper training, and on adequate physical facilities and equipment. An improvement in tax administration is certainly necessary but it is unlikely to yield the expected benefits until some of the major distortions in the economy have been removed. Such distortions create strong incentives for evading taxes. On the other hand, the growth of non-oil revenues depends significantly on the integration of parallel markets into the official economy. Such integration would help to raise the tax base of both direct and indirect taxes. The authorities should proceed with the simplification and rationalization of the tax system, as it would contribute to the establishment of a more efficient incentive system.

5.71 Utilization of Budgetary Resources. The SEF appears to put more emphasis on tax reform than expenditure restraint. However, priority should be given, at least in the short to medium term, to measures aimed at controlling the level of spending. Such measures are likely to contribute more quickly to a reduction in the budgetary deficit than efforts to increase non-oil revenues. There is also considerable scope for improving the efficiency of resource use in the public sector through better allocation of resources as well as through stricter controls and reduced waste.

5.72 In the area of recurrent expenditures, it is essential to curb the growth in the wage bill. This requires a strengthening of personnel and salaries administration. A first step has been taken through the start of a census of all employees in the public sector, which would help to verify the existence of all staff on the government's payroll. Strict controls should also be imposed on recruitment. The increased autonomy of public enterprises, price adjustments, and the greater flexibility of labour policies will help to cut losses of public enterprises and thus reduce budgetary expenditures on subsidies. Most urgently needed, however, is a rationalization of the process of formulation and implementation of the public investment program. This will involve a wide range of actions, including strengthening of project preparation, creation of adequate project appraisal capacity, the introduction of clear and uniform project selection criteria, improvement in reporting procedures to monitor implementation, and establishment of clearly defined responsibilities for formulating and executing the investment program.

5.73 Effects of Exchange Rate Depreciation and Price Adjustments. In principle, devaluation of the kwanza and the adjustment of controlled prices would contribute to reduce the budget deficit. Devaluation would result in increases in kwanza terms of both budgetary expenditures and revenues. For example, there would be increases in the revenues from the oil sector, customs revenues and other sources. There would be increases in expenditures which involve payments in foreign exchange (service of the external debt, imported equipment, war material, external technical assistance, diplomatic representations, etc.), in expenditures on wages, to the extent that these are adjusted after a devaluation, and expenditures on goods and services produced domestically (mainly tradeable goods, to the extent that their prices would be adjusted). While the final net effect would depend very much on the level of international oil prices as well as salary adjustments and their factors, in the present situation, a devaluation would contribute to a significant extent to reduce the budget deficit.

5.74 Similarly, the adjustment of controlled prices would be one of the most decisive factors for reducing the budget deficits. First, the increase in prices would in principle contribute to a reduction in losses of public enterprises and their need for budgetary subsidies. Second, the base for indirect taxes would be raised by the increases in controlled prices. The net budgetary effects of price adjustments would depend on the specific rates of increase of the prices of different goods and services and on the weight of those goods and services in public expenditures and on the base for indirect taxation.

5.75 Monitoring and Control. The comments of the preceding paragraphs show how important it will be to strengthen the management of the budget. The budget should become a major instrument of economic policy, particularly with regard to the allocation of resources of the public sector. This requires effective coordination between the planning process, foreign exchange management, and budget formulation. While the overall responsibility for the size and financing of the budget should be shared by the Ministries of Finance and Planning, the former should be solely responsible for external borrowing and the management of the external debt, with the central bank in charge of its administration.

Price and Wage Policies

5.76 On the basis of the information available it is not yet possible to evaluate the likely impact of the changes in price policy envisaged in the SEF. According to the announcements made, the authorities intend to maintain a system of generalized price controls during the first stage of implementation of that program. At the beginning of 1988, the authorities had the intention of increasing the average level of controlled prices by 44 percent. The fundamental question which needs to be clarified is whether the price adjustments involved in that increase will be of sufficient magnitude to significantly correct for the extremely serious distortions and inefficiencies created in the Angolan economy by the existing system of controls.

5.77 Apparently, the adjustments of controlled prices envisaged by the authorities will be decided largely on the basis of the objectives of covering the costs of production and reaching satisfactory levels of profitability for public enterprises. These objectives will, however, be far from sufficient to correct all the important shortcomings of the present price policies. If prices are determined on a cost plus basis, they may protect productive units with very low inefficiency, but they will create problems for consumers and for other enterprises. Moreover, prices based on costs, which in turn are based on artificial prices of foreign exchange and domestic inputs, will not reflect the strength of demand and will not solve the problems created by the existing system of administrative allocation.

5.78 However, it is apparent that the situation is not yet ripe for the introduction of a drastic transformation of the price system of Angola, involving the removal of most price controls and a high degree of liberalization of prices. A system of free prices would only operate satisfactorily if there were active competition in most markets. Even if there were sufficient competition, the rapid transition to a generalized system of free prices would probably create serious disruptions and difficulties: the equilibrium in the price levels would not be found quickly, and there would be risks of overshooting and speculation as shown by the experiences of other countries.

5.79 In such conditions, price controls will probably continue to play an important role in Angola during the initial stages of implementation of the SEF. It must recognized, however, that remaining price controls will continue to create serious economic distortions, given the insufficient administrative capacity of the state bureaucracy and the enormous shortages of essential consumer goods and inputs. In such conditions, it will be essential to introduce important changes in the existing system: first, the average level of prices which remain subject to controls should be raised very substantially; second, the authorities should envisage the liberalization of many specific prices, already in the first stage of implementation of the SEF; and third, the adjustment of controlled prices should take into account the need to correct the most glaring distortions in relative prices.

5.80 The need for very large increases in the level of controlled prices is obviously justified by the large gaps existing at present between aggregate supply and demand. The devaluation will be a key parameter in determining the average increases to be introduced in domestic prices. As mentioned above, increases in controlled prices should reflect not only the objective of covering the costs of imports and of domestic production, transportation and marketing, but also the objective of reducing the severity of the scarcities which led to highly inefficient mechanisms of administrative allocation. The hesitation of the authorities to accept sufficiently high increases in prices are based mainly on two types of arguments: they fear the effects of price increases on the acceleration of inflation; and they consider that price increases would reduce the standard of living of consumers with lower incomes.

5.81 The risks of inflationary effects depend on the budgetary, monetary, and wage policies to be followed in the future. By themselves, increases in controlled prices would only reflect the existing repressed inflation which is made so obvious by scarcities in the official market and high parallel market prices. On the other hand, increases in controlled prices could contribute to reducing inflationary pressures, by cutting the budgetary deficit and the losses of public enterprises. Moreover, increases in controlled prices would in principle tend to reduce prices in parallel markets.

5.82 The argument about the negative effects of price increases on the standard of living of the poor is also of doubtful validity. As explained in other chapters of the present report, scarcities of goods and services supplied at official prices are so severe that the poorest groups of the population get very small quantities of those goods, or none at all. Those groups must satisfy their consumption needs by self-sufficiency production and by participating in parallel markets. The existing system of administrative allocation at low official prices involves such important privileges for some categories of workers and consumers that apparently it contributes to widening income inequalities rather than to reducing them. Increases in the controlled prices of many products would probably improve the situation of the poor, by raising the income of peasant farmers, by reducing scarcities and by lowering prices in the parallel market.

5.83 In some cases, price subsidization may be used to resolve conflicts between adequate profitability for producers and low prices for consumers. However, in Angola, extended price subsidization would be incompatible with the objective of balancing the Government's budget. Moreover, its effects on income distribution would be negative, unless a system of rationing would ensure a fair distribution of goods with subsidized prices among all the consumers, especially consumers with lower incomes. Schemes of social assistance targeted to specific groups of the poor (including in particular children and refugees) would probably be more efficient, from the point of view of a more equitable distribution of income, than generalized price subsidies. It must, however, be recognized that there are important administrative difficulties in implementing schemes of that type, as there are in implementing effective rationing mechanisms.

5.84 With regard to a large number of goods and services, the authorities should go beyond the objective of increasing controlled prices. In markets in which there is enough competition, they should consider introducing full price liberalization at an early stage. The prices of some foodstuffs produced by small farmers or fishermen (especially horticultural products, fruits, fresh fish) have already been liberalized. With the liberalization of prices which have been subject to controls, the production of agriculture, small scale industries and of services will certainly be stimulated. Recourse to systems of direct barter to encourage agricultural production (such as the Market Program in the Countryside - Programa de Comercializaçao no Campo) cannot satisfactorily fulfil all the needs to stimulate agricultural production, as experience has amply demonstrated.

5.85 The correction of distortions in relative prices should also be a major objective of the new price policy. As described in other chapters, the losses of efficiency resulting from the existing pattern of relative prices are enormous. For tradable goods, the structure of relative prices prevailing in the world market should provide a benchmark for the determination of relative prices in Angola. Of course, the structure of relative prices in the world market should not be transferred rigidly into the structure of Angolan prices for tradable goods (in view of transportation costs, etc.). But satisfactory improvements in economic efficiency, both for producers and consumers, cannot be achieved if extremely high distortions in relative prices are not substantially reduced.

5.86 The price policies recommended in the preceding paragraphs should be accompanied by some adjustment in wage levels. Increases in official prices will not require increases in wages of the same magnitude because for most workers the proportion of their wages spent in the official market is very low (often less than 10%). In correspondence with the proposed average increase of 44% in controlled prices, the authorities intend to increase wages by 20%. Both of these increases are low in the face of the existing distortions in prices and wages, but the difference between them does not seem to be unreasonable in relative terms. However, for some categories of workers, including in particular the technical and managerial staff who benefit from access to special "baskets" of goods at official prices, the adjustments in wages may have to be more substantial. In any case, adjustments in prices and wages should take the following points into consideration: (a) they should contribute to narrowing existing gaps between supply and demand; (b) they should not impede the objective of reducing the budget deficit; (c) they should contribute to a reduction in losses of public enterprises; (d) they should contribute to narrowing income differentials between the urban population and the rural population, in order to stimulate agricultural production and discourage the exodus of peasants to the cities.

5.87 The price policies recommended in the preceding paragraphs would certainly contribute to: (a) stimulate production in various sectors, especially agriculture and small scale industries and services; (b) improve the profitability of enterprises and reduce the budget deficit; (c) reduce inefficiencies in production and consumption which result from the existing system of administrative allocation in all official markets; (d) improve social equity; and (e) reduce the distortions resulting from the existence of separate official and parallel markets.

Exchange Rate Policy

5.88 As stated in Chapter 2, the exchange rate of 29.92 kwanzas per dollar, maintained without change since 1975, has involved very tight rationing of foreign exchange. It was also indicated that together with price controls, this exchange rate policy has been an important factor in the decline of agricultural exports and in the enormous distortions in relative prices. As noted earlier in this Chapter (para. 5.17), current SEF plans envisage the devaluation of the kwanza. However, while such a devaluation would be substantial in percentage terms, it is unlikely to reduce significantly the severity of the existing system of administrative allocation of foreign exchange. It is, of course, extremely difficult to determine even approximately the devaluation required to arrive at an equilibrium exchange rate. The price of the dollar in the black market (around 2,500 Kz in February 1989) is not necessarily an accurate or precise indicator, although it suggests that a very large devaluation is in fact required. Following a substantial initial devaluation of the kwanza, a strategy of successive steps will probably be necessary in order to arrive at an equilibrium rate.

5.89 There are two additional reasons why this approach to exchange rate adjustment should be preferred. First, many of the expected effects of devaluation will only be produced if domestic prices are sufficiently flexible. In principle, the prices of tradable goods should increase by approximately the same percentage as the price of foreign currency. Otherwise, the devaluation would produce no significant effect on agricultural production nor would it significantly improve the allocation of foreign exchange, correct existing distortions in relative prices, or create conditions to stimulate the development of competitive markets.

5.90 Second, an attempt to jump instantly to an equilibrium exchange rate would create risks of an inflationary spiral if it is not accompanied by an adequate control of the money supply. Thus, following the first-stage devaluation, the equilibrium rate should be approached gradually in conjunction with substantial cuts in the budget deficit, which are required to slow down considerably the rate of expansion of the money supply. While reductions in the budget deficit are necessary to ensure the success of devaluation, the devaluation can in turn contribute to those reductions as explained in para. 5.73 above.

5.91 Until the equilibrium exchange rate is reached, foreign exchange would continue to be rationed. The licensing of all imports and the allocation of foreign exchange by administrative methods currently in effect would continue to be a source of distortions and production bottlenecks, with serious consequences for productive efficiency. In order to reduce the negative impact of these consequences, the authorities should consider introducing partial solutions for the difficulties created by the existing system. Such solutions might include import surcharges, export subsidies for agricultural products, export retention schemes, auctioning of import licenses, or a system of dual exchange rates. All of these solutions are unsatisfactory, but they may be preferable to the existing system of administrative allocation and, therefore, deserve careful consideration. If any of these solutions are introduced, they should be gradually abandoned as the exchange rate moves to equilibrium.

Monetary Policy

5.92 The improvements in monetary and credit policies embarked upon and envisaged in the SEF will certainly increase efficiency in the use of scarce financial resources and ensure a better control over the money supply. In implementing the changes envisaged in the SEF, the following points deserve special attention.

5.93 Policies to reduce inflationary pressures and the growing discrepancy between official and parallel market prices must include slowing the growth rate of the money supply or increasing the public's demand for monetary balances. A reduction in the growth rate of the money supply depends on the Government budget reforms recommended earlier in this chapter. The central bank should possess adequate instruments to control the money supply, including in particular the power to regulate the liquidity of the banks through cash reserves and rediscount quotas. A policy of ceilings on the expansion of credit to enterprises may be necessary in the next few years.

5.94 While there is no reliable price index in Angola, it is clear that current interest rates on bank deposits are negative in real terms. Increasing interest rates on individual deposits would encourage financial savings and alleviate inflationary pressures. However, in view of the multiple reasons for peoples' failure to use the banking system (discussed in Chapter 3), one should not expect a quick and dramatic increase in bank savings in response to such interest rate increases.

5.95 Currently, much of the financing of investment projects by enterprises is provided by government grants since the fixed price structure does not allow many enterprises to generate sufficient resources for investment nor to borrow on commercial terms. Conditional on the enactment of the price policies recommended in this chapter, medium and long term investment financing should be provided on the basis of sound financial considerations. However, before proceeding with this step, careful thought should be given to additional measures that may be required to establish financially viable independent enterprises out of industries with insufficient capital and antiquated equipment, long accustomed to receiving direction and financial infusions from the Government.

5.96 In line with the above policy measures, increasing loan interest rates to more closely reflect market conditions is advisable. If, as proposed in the SEF, a new price policy is introduced and enterprises are encouraged to operate financially independent of the Government, setting interest rates to reflect demand conditions would reduce the administrative burden of allocating scarce credit. Concessional lending should be limited to high priority industries or industries where externalities distort the price structure. Moreover, for administrative and accounting reasons, it would be preferable to remove this subsidizing role entirely from the banking system and place it explicitly under the state budget.

5.97 An increase in the autonomy of banks and an enlargement in their responsibilities for financing the investments of enterprises, which until now have been financed by the Government, can improve efficiency in the allocation of financial resources. These objectives of the SEF will require, however, that: (a) banks possess adequate authority to refuse loans to enterprises which do not offer adequate guarantees and satisfactory prospects for repayment; and (b) the growth of credit to enterprises be limited in accordance with monetary policy requirements and the objective of reducing the rate of inflation.

5.98 Efforts under way to administratively separate the commercial banking functions of BNA from its role as a central bank should be continued. Such a separation will clearly delineate the dual functions of the bank and allow the authorities to separate monetary policy from commercial loan activities. The change will also provide the authorities with better information on monetary developments and improve control of policy measures.

5.99 Priority should be given within the BNA to improving the accounting system and administrative controls. Given the shortage of trained personnel within the banking system, it is advisable for BNA to contract a team of accountants to help in cleaning up its balance sheet. Such a project would give the authorities a clear picture of developments in the monetary sector. In addition, as the banking system's role in financing enterprises' investment projects grows, it is vital that the bank have in place trained personnel to enact administrative controls that will protect the financial integrity of the commercial banking division. Development of such a staff will require a substantial commitment to personnel training programs.

5.100 At a later stage it would be advantageous to promote competition in the area of commercial banking through the establishment of two or three independent banks. Creation of a medium and long term credit department in the BNA should also be considered. Such a department could later be transformed into an independent investment bank.

Social Impact of Economic Adjustment and Reform Policies

5.101 The implementation of the policies envisaged in the SEF and recommended in the present report is expected to have significant positive effects on the average living standards of the Angolan population. By stimulating the recovery of economic activity, the improvement of productivity and the faster growth of output in several sectors, especially in agriculture, the SEF policies will contribute to increase the volume of goods and services available for consumption and investment. At the same time, they will create conditions for a better allocation of the available resources and for the correction of some serious distortions in income distribution. These results will be achieved mainly by reducing the inequities associated with rigid mechanisms of allocation and with the operation of parallel markets.

5.102 The expected benefits from economic liberalization will be reaped to a large extent by some of the poorest strata of the population. In particular, many peasant farmers, who together with their families account for a significant majority of the Angolan population and whose standards of living tend to be worse than those of urban dwellers, will benefit from increases in their real incomes. With the liberalization of prices, the improvement of transportation facilities and the development of commerce in rural areas, peasant farmers will find better opportunities for marketing part of their output and purchasing the industrial consumer goods and agricultural inputs that they need.

5.103 However, in spite of their probable net positive impact on social conditions, the economic reforms recommended in the previous sections are likely to create difficulties for specific groups of the population, especially in urban areas. Those difficulties will result mainly from: (a) the reductions of the real incomes of the employees of the public administration and of public enterprises who enjoy valuable advantages of access to special shops or to systems of payment in kind (auto-consumo); (b) the problems of unemployment which may be created by the liquidation or the restructuring of unprofitable public enterprises; and (c) the scarcity of budgetary resources to finance social programs, especially in the areas of health and education.

5.104 Reductions in the Real Income of Employees in the Public Sector. As stated in the preceding paragraphs, the policies of adjustment and reform of the Angolan economy require that the increases in controlled prices exceed the increases in wages by a significant margin. However, as already explained, the difference between the rates of increase in controlled prices and in wages does not imply a corresponding decline in the levels of living of workers, because for most of them the proportion of wage income spent in goods and services at official prices is very low. If prices in the parallel market increase less than wages, as is to be expected, there may be even an improvement in the real incomes of large segments of the population, including in particular workers with lower wages and those who are not employed in the formal sector.

5.105 The workers who enjoy preferential access to special shops or to special "baskets" of goods and services at official prices, and those who benefit from "auto-consumo" would, however, tend to be negatively affected to a very significant extent. Their privileges would be reduced as a consequence of the liberalization or adjustments in controlled prices and the reductions which should be introduced in the preferential schemes of allocation through special shops, special baskets and "auto-consumo". The reduction of such privileges would not necessarily be undesirable from the point of view of social equity or economic efficiency. The existing schemes of preferential allocation of scarce goods and services at the very low prices of the official market create huge inequalities in the distribution of real incomes which in many cases have no relation whatsoever to the social productivity of the beneficiaries. Thus, for instance, unskilled workers of a beer factory or a tobacco company get real incomes from "auto-consumo" which in most cases are several times higher than those of teachers or of skilled employees in public administration or firms that do not provide the same opportunity to acquire scarce goods at official prices.

5.106 The reform of the price system and the introduction of market mechanisms in the distribution of goods and services must however be combined with important reforms in the structure of nominal wages. At present, nominal wage differentials are so low that they have to be compensated by differentials in access to special schemes involving the purchase of scarce goods and services at low prices. The reduction of the importance of these schemes should not affect the real incomes of the officials, experts and managers who play key roles in the public administration and in public enterprises. It is for that reason that their nominal wages should be increased far more than those of workers at lower levels of skills, as recommended in paragraph 5.86.

5.107 Problems of Unemployment. The liquidation of nonviable public enterprises will create problems of unemployment for their workers. Similar problems will result from the restructuring or privatization of public enterprises which are over-staffed. In order to reduce the difficulties created by unemployment, the Government has prepared draft legislation creating an "Unemployment Fund" which will pay unemployment subsidies to workers who lose their jobs. At the same time, the Angolan authorities have the intention of establishing training facilities for recycling workers into other industries and other skills. Finally, the recovery of productive activities which is expected to result from the reform of the economic system and policies should create new employment opportunities for workers laid-off from public enterprises. Some direct measures to create jobs for laid-off workers could also be undertaken by the Government (e.g., through the enrollment of these workers in public works projects financed by the public sector or by foreign funds). There will in principle be many opportunities to implement such a solution. The rehabilitation and construction work needed in urban infrastructure, roads, railroads, bridges, electric transmission lines, housing and social infrastructure, will require the employment of large numbers of unskilled workers.

5.108 Resources to Finance Social Programs. The reduction of the budget deficit must be one of the cornerstones of the program of economic adjustment in Angola. However, this cannot be achieved without strict discipline in public expenditures. In principle, it will be possible to combine the reduction of total budgetary expenditures with the maintenance or even some growth in selected expenditures that may contribute more strongly to long term economic growth or an improvement in the social situation. In fact, cuts in budgetary expenditures can be concentrated to a large extent in the reduction of subsidies to loss-making enterprises, in expenditures on surplus personnel in public administration, and in defence expenditures if there is an improvement in the war situation. The Government should, therefore, be able to reduce significantly its expenditures, while avoiding reductions in expenditures on social programs, especially in the areas of health and education.

Improvements in Statistical Data

5.109 In the past year, the Angolan government has made commendable efforts to improve the statistical data on the economy. However, a firm conclusion that should be drawn from this report is the continued high priority that these efforts should command. Such an improvement is essential for effective management of economic policy. Better economic data would enable the authorities to analyze the causes of economic deficiencies, project and monitor the effect of policy reforms and also strengthen Angola's position in its interactions with external creditors and agencies. While data on economic conditions are deficient across most sectors of the economy, this section identifies some of the highest priority needs for improving macroeconomic data.

5.110 In the area of national production, it should be a short-run priority to improve data on the quantitative output of the most important goods and services in the economy by ensuring that firms reporting to the various ministries report conscientiously and promptly. The ministries could assist this effort by devising reports that clearly define the requested data and that can be completed reasonably quickly by personnel with modest technical training. In the longer-run, surveys should be conducted to estimate the extent of small-scale production and the percentage of production channeled to official markets.

5.111 Development of national price indices should also be a high priority. The authorities should collect monthly or quarterly data on (a) producer prices of a selected number of the most important goods and services, (b) official retail prices for goods and services with an emphasis on private consumption goods, and (c) representative prices of the most essential goods traded in parallel markets. In addition, a survey should be undertaken of typical household consumption spending patterns, at least in urban areas, specifying not only the quantities of goods purchased but also the percentage of these products that come from official and parallel markets. The results of this survey should be used to construct a consumer price index. The weights of different goods and services derived from the surveys might have to be corrected periodically, in order to reflect important changes in the availability of specific consumer goods in the official and parallel markets.

5.112 With regard to government finance, an improvement in data is needed in the following areas. With regard to both the format for presentation of the budget and the classification of revenues and expenditures, it is recommended that the IMF's Manual on Government Finance Statistics be followed. This would distinguish between revenue, recurrent and capital expenditures and financial flows; with regard to revenue a distinction would be made on the one hand between tax and non-tax revenue, and on the other hand between oil and non-oil taxes, as well as between major categories of non-oil taxes (taxes on income and property, on domestic goods and services, and on international trade). The Manual also gives guidance on establishing an economic classification of expenditure. In addition to providing more up-to-date information on actual expenditure (now 3 years delayed) the authorities should improve the information on capital expenditure, reduce the amount of extra-budgetary income and expenditure (notably external grants and loans, capital expenditure and external debt service), and strengthen personnel and salary administration.

5.113 In the monetary sector, there are three clear priorities in terms of improving the data. First, efforts should be made to clean the balance sheets of the Central Bank, writing down assets that have little or no value. Second, the data on monetary statistics should be organized and classified according to well defined accounting standards (following IMF guidelines in this regard would be advisable). Third, monetary statistics should be prepared on a monthly basis without long delays. Without these improvements, it will be practically impossible to conduct monetary policy on a satisfactory basis.

5.114 In the area of balance of payments data, the major effort should be to ensure that the data are as all-inclusive as possible and that the categories agree with the guidelines established in the IMF's Balance of Payments Manual. The advantage of using these guidelines is that they are well-defined, compatible with most other countries' procedures, and would be immediately comprehensible to external creditors and multilateral agencies. Second, given the overwhelming importance of the oil sector, efforts to create two measures of the balance of payments, one for the oil sector and the other for non-oil sectors, should be continued. Third, there is a pressing need to improve data on imported merchandise. Currently these data are reported to be highly unreliable.

5.115 Finally, the major efforts that have been made to collect and centralize data on the source of outstanding external credits and the terms of these credits should be continued. However, better coordination between the departments responsible for medium and long term debt and those responsible for short term debt would aid in the effort to provide up to date assessments of the overall external debt obligations of the country.

5.116 It must be recognized that given the shortage of trained personnel in Angola and the scale of the task, improving the quality of economic data in the short run will probably require contracting outside experts to aid in the effort. Besides assisting in the above projects, foreign experts could assist the National Statistical Institute (INE) in collecting other basic statistics required for effective economic policy making. Some priorities here include: creating a central register of enterprises; classifying activities, goods and services, and occupations which will be needed in compiling and presenting data; collecting basic demographic data; developing the technical capability to gather reliable survey data; and establishing in-house training programs for collecting and analyzing descriptive statistics. In the longer run, it is desirable that Angolan nationals replace any outside experts that are employed. This process can be accelerated through formal training programs and the assignment of high quality counterpart personnel to assist the experts.

A Scenario Based on the End of the War

5.117 If the war ended in the near future, the prospects for the recovery of the Angolan economy and for the success of the economic reform program would become much more encouraging. The end of the war would create conditions for: (a) improving the confidence of domestic economic agents and of foreign partners in the future of the economy; (b) diverting substantial financial and human resources from the defence effort into productive purposes; (c) reducing the budget deficit and the current account deficit of the balance of payments more rapidly; and (d) improving the utilization of existing natural resources and of productive installed capacity. If the war ended quickly, a special plan for economic recovery should be prepared. Such a plan would emphasize, in particular, the rehabilitation of the productive capacity and infrastructure damaged by the war (including dams, transmission lines, manufacturing plants, farms, bridges, roads, railway lines, etc.). The areas of transportation, regional development, and resettlement of displaced persons would deserve special attention.

5.118 The Transportation Sector. Cessation of armed hostilities would have a dramatic effect on the economic performance of the transport sector. The impact of a return to internal security and peace would be greatest in the rail mode but would have the highest short-term benefit in the road sector. All rail corridors would require considerable investments in rehabilitation programs to bring them back to reasonable operating levels and the benefits would take time (often many years) to be realized. Corridor evaluations have been done on two of the three key networks (Benguela and Moçamedes) and all have emphasized the regional development benefits, while stressing the corridor impact rather than the rail impact. Fortunately, there are a number of bilateral and multilateral agencies that stand ready to supply both capital and human resources for corridor rehabilitation once peace is established. In terms of sequencing, rail corridor rehabilitation should be considered as part of a medium-term recovery strategy.

5.119 Road investment, on the other hand, can be undertaken in modest increments and finely tuned to take account of the manner in which hostilities are ended. Calculations in Annex VIII demonstrate that war conditions are largely responsible for driving up real ton kilometer rates by 300 percent (and over 420 percent when the impact of poor highway maintenance is estimated). Even when allowances are made both for errors in estimation and the impact of non-security related influences on productivity (like lack of spare parts), it is clear that under more peaceful conditions the existing vehicular stock would become significantly more productive, to the benefit of related sectors like agriculture. Army vehicles and equipment could be transferred to state (or private) trucking enterprises to re-equip fleets and highway maintenance facilities. Human resources presently in the armed forces would be available to service equipment, repair vehicles and subsequently maintain existing infrastructure and develop new low-cost feeder road systems linked to the new agricultural programs. The plans of the Ministry of Transportation to develop the private trucking sector at provincial levels would fit well with this re-deployment scenario.

5.120 The desire to strengthen provincial transit links to ports and generally improve cabotage operations will enable that joint modal system to supply more inter-regional transport services in a relatively short time span, once hostilities cease. The rehabilitation of all these transport modes would affect both the flow of passenger traffic and of cargo, releasing pressure from the overloaded air sector.

5.121 Regional Development. An end to hostilities in Angola and the re-establishment of secure conditions in agricultural areas would allow the implementation of regional reconstruction programs to restore the economic and social infrastructure of regional economies. If the rehabilitation of road and rail corridors received priority in national reconstruction plans, the revival of regional economies would lead to the growth of trade and the gradual re-emergence of regional specialization along lines of comparative advantage (although some irreversible changes have probably taken place in the patterns of demand and supply from what prevailed in earlier periods). In the rural sector, self-provisioning strategies and barter would give way to production for local and interregional markets. That development should be supported by institutional changes in marketing and distribution systems.

5.122 Although peace-time conditions would increase resource availability, policymakers would still have to decide on the spatial priority and sequencing of regional reconstruction efforts. The central highland region of Huambo, Bie and Benguela would be a leading candidate for priority in any regional economic reconstruction initiative. As the country's "granary" in colonial times, this region possesses the productive capacity to make a significant contribution towards improving the domestic food situation. Assuming complementary changes in transport and distribution systems, the size of this region's potential agricultural supply response, and hence its quantitative impact on national food deficits and the external payments position, is a strong argument for priority. Other grounds include the relatively high concentration of population in these central provinces and the possibility of reviving industrial activities in the city of Huambo, formerly Angola's second largest manufacturing center. These considerations suggest that an end to hostilities would stimulate Angolan authorities and international donors to undertake a detailed review of regional development priorities, which are currently focused on the South-Southwest provinces of Huila, Cunene and Namibe (as discussed in Chapter 4).

5.123 <u>Resettlement of Displaced Persons and Urban Rehabilitation</u>. The end of the war is likely to result in some reduction of rural-urban migration, including the return of some displaced people to their communities. Although these changes may attenuate current pressures on urban infrastructure and services provision, the resettlement of large numbers of displaced persons will be a major task and many of the changes in population patterns which have taken place are not likely to be reversed. In the field of urban services, greater resource availability and security would allow a start to be made on the long-deferred rehabilitation of the infrastructure of Angola's towns and cities. Immediate priorities include institutional changes to restore the organizational capacity, financial independence, and morale of the agencies responsible for urban services. A major immediate effort is needed to replenish staffing levels, to eliminate the backlog of maintenance work, and improve the performance and coverage of existing service systems. In the housing sector, an immediate priority is for sites and services projects to improve service provision and housing conditions for the urban poor. Such projects should be integrated with urban planning efforts to arrest the current haphazard process of urban settlement, notably in Luanda.

Lessons from the Programs of Economic Reform in Ghana and Mozambique

5.124 Until a few years ago, Ghana and Mozambique were facing serious economic difficulties very similar to those Angola is experiencing at present. Both of these countries launched programs of economic adjustment and reform which, broadly speaking, have many elements in common with the SEF proposals and with the policy recommendations of the present report. Thus a summary of the experiences of Ghana and Mozambique can provide useful insights into the packages of policy measures which are needed in Angola, especially as regards the magnitude of some of the changes which may be required (for instance in the exchange rate and in controlled prices). Moreover, a review of the experiences in Ghana and Mozambique can suggest some of the difficulties which will be faced and the results which may be expected.

5.125 The Economic Recovery Program of Ghana. 1/ The Ghanaian economy experienced a protracted decline throughout the 1970s and the early 1980s, owing to a combination of adverse exogenous factors (mainly oil price shocks) and inappropriate domestic policies (expansionary fiscal and credit policies which led to a marked inflation, overvalued exchange rate, administrative allocation of foreign exchange, and an intensification of price and distribution controls). From 1970 to 1982, real per capita income declined by more than 30 percent and real export earnings fell by 52%. In addition, import values fell by one third, inflation accelerated to 44%, and arrears in external payments accumulated (amounting at the end of 1982 to 90% of export earnings for that year). Faced with this extremely serious situation, the authorities of Ghana introduced in April 1983 a comprehensive Economic Reform Program (ERP) whose key elements included the introduction of a new exchange rate policy, liberalization of imports, a reduction of price controls and the adjustment of controlled prices with a view to reduce subsidies. In addition, the program eliminated distribution controls, increased interest rates to positive real levels, and took steps to control domestic demand. Additional reform measures adjusted the wage policy to offset partially the erosion in real incomes and to reverse the severe compression between the top and bottom grades, and sought to rehabilitate the country's economic and social infrastructure.

5.126 The new exchange rate policy played a particularly important role in the ERP. Thus, the official exchange rate of the cedi was adjusted, in stages, from C 2.75 per U.S. dollar in April 1983 to C 90 per U.S. dollar in January 1986. Subsequently, in September 1986, a dual exchange rate system was temporarily introduced with the establishment of a second foreign exchange window where the rate was market determined in the context of a weekly auction. Initially, the auction rate applied to all external transactions through the official banking system, except for foreign exchange earnings from exports of cocoa and residual oil and except for import payments for crude oil, petroleum products, and essential drugs, as well as service payments on government debt contracted before January 1, 1986. Exports and imports of goods and services exempted from the market rate were effected at the first foreign exchange window, which maintained a rate of C 90 per U.S. dollar. However, effective February 21, 1987, official exchange rates were unified in the context of the auction market and, in March and September, access to this market was widened significantly. The exchange rate depreciated from 145 cedi per US dollar after the introduction of the weekly auctions to 176 cedi per US dollar at the end of 1987. The spread between the auction and parallel market

---

1/ Summarized from "Ghana: Policy Framework Paper, July 1988-June 1991", September 30, 1988, International Bank for Reconstruction and Development.

exchange rates fell to about 30%, compared with some 100% prior to the introduction of the new exchange system.

5.127 The reform of the exchange system was completed with the widening of access to the foreign exchange market. Most bids for foreign exchange to cover imports of goods and services and some current transfers are eligible for participation in the weekly auctions. To help meet the additional demand for foreign exchange resulting from the widening of access to the auction market, the authorities reduced the amounts of foreign exchange retained by the government or held outside the official banking system. The depreciation of the official exchange rate has made it possible to improve price incentives in the economy. In particular, the producer price for cocoa, which amounted to only C 12,000 per ton for the 1982/83 crop, was raised progressively to C 85,500 per ton for the 1986/87 crop year, and to C 140,000 per ton for the 1987/88 crop year, almost trebling the real purchasing power of cocoa farmers over the period.

5.128 The recovery effort was set back by the severe impact of drought and bush fires in 1982-83, as well as by the expulsion of over one million Ghanaians from Nigeria. However, with the expansion in agricultural, mining, and manufacturing output, real GDP grew by 8.7% in 1984, 5.1% in 1985, 5.3% in 1986 and 4.8 percent in 1987. The supply situation thus eased appreciably, as increased food crops, spare parts, and consumer items began to flow into the marketplace. Exports of cocoa, which fell to a low of 149,600 tons in 1984, have risen steadily to an estimated 195,200 tons in 1986. Meanwhile, demand-management policies have been effective in turning around the balance on government accounts (excluding capital expenditure financed through external project aid) from a deficit equivalent to 4.6% of GDP in 1982 to a surplus equivalent to 0.5% of GDP in 1986. These policies, together with the improved supply conditions, have resulted in a rapid deceleration in the average annual inflation rate, from 123% in 1983 to 25% in 1986, though inflation increased to 40 percent in 1987. The balance of payments deficit has also been reduced substantially, from US$243 million in 1983 to US$57 million in 1986. In 1987, in view of a sharp increase in net capital inflows, the balance of payments registered a major turnaround to an overall surplus of US$139 million in 1987. With such improvements, external arrears, which had reached US$601 million at end-April 1983, were brought down to US$100 million at end-December 1986, while at the same time external reserves increased to US$194 million, equivalent to ten weeks of imports.

5.129 The Economic Rehabilitation Program of Mozambique. 2/ The Mozambican economy experienced a marked and sustained decline in output and an aggravation of economic distortions and financial imbalances during the first half of the 1980s. These developments resulted from a combination of adverse exogenous developments, disruptions and insecurity spread by armed attacks in various parts of the countryside, and economic policies that proved inappropriate to deal with the economy's problems. Between 1980 and

---

2/ Summarized from "Mozambique: Policy Framework Paper, 1989 to 1991", February 24, 1988, International Bank for Reconstruction and Development.

1986, overall production fell by about 30% and exports by nearly 75%, while imports were compressed by more than one third from their 1980 level by 1985, before recovering somewhat in 1986. External imbalances, aggravated by an increasingly overvalued exchange rate, led to the rapid accumulation of external debt service arrears. Internally, due to large fiscal deficits and unconstrained bank financing of enterprise losses, the money stock tripled despite shrinking output. Extensive administrative controls on prices and allocation, while intended to promote efficiency and social welfare, introduced rigidities and disincentives that proved counterproductive. As shortages increased, barter, inflation, and parallel markets became widespread.

5.130 After the introduction in 1984-86 of partial adjustment measures which proved to be insufficient, the Mozambican Government launched a far-reaching Economic Rehabilitation Program in January 1987 intended to deal with the structural problems and widespread distortions in the economy. A comprehensive set of exchange rate, wage, and price measures have been undertaken since 1987. The metical was devalued in several steps from Mt.39 per U.S. dollar (buying rate) to Mt. 200 per U.S. dollar (buying rate) in January, 1987, and to Mt. 400 at the end of 1987 and to MT 620 per US dollar in October 1988. Fixed prices of commodities and services were raised by 100-500% after the January 1987 devaluation, and by 50-100% after the June 1987 devaluation. Subsequent large increases in controlled prices were introduced in parallel with the devaluation of the metical. Increases in conditioned (markup-regulated) prices were permitted by allowing enterprises to increase prices without prior approval, subject only to ex-post review in terms of established criteria and formulae. Moreover, the number of products subject to fixed prices was reduced significantly from 46 to 37 in 1987 and to 25 at end-1988. Following the devaluations in January and June 1987, general wage increases of 50% each time were awarded, together with additional selective raises and bonuses to reward higher productivity and retain valuable employees.

5.131 To supplement the price and distribution reform measures, the Government adopted restrictive domestic financial policies. In the fiscal area, the revenue base was strengthened through tax reforms and improvements in tax administration; recurrent expenditure was contained and steps were initiated to improve the financial discipline of the public enterprises. A substantial revision of the domestic tax code, including the widening of the base of domestic taxes, the rationalization of the income tax and simplification of collections, was enacted in January 1987 and led to a substantial increase in revenue. Recurrent expenditure was contained through putting a cap on consumer subsidies and on the budgetary transfers to meet the operating losses of public enterprises. Through these measures, the current budget deficit (excluding grants) as a share of GDP was reduced sharply while the overall deficit increased modestly as a result of the impact of the exchange rate changes on capital expenditure. Indications are that budgetary performance in 1988 led to further improvements. The Government's recourse to bank credit fell substantially in 1987 and 1988.

5.132 Money and credit policies for 1987 and 1988 were aimed at reducing the overhang of excess liquidity in the economy and improving the efficiency of credit utilization. Interest rates were raised sharply effective January 1987, from a range of 0-6 percent for deposits and 3-1 percent for loans, to 3-20 for deposits and 12-35 for loans. The interest rate on bank loans to the Government was increased to 8 percent in 1988, and the Government became current on interest owed to the banking system. Nonetheless, with substantial price adjustments being implemented, interest rates remained negative in real terms. New criteria for extending bank credit were developed that emphasized the application of commercial principles in the evaluation of new loan requests, within overall credit ceilings. A new system of accounts for the banking system was introduced in late 1988, and progress was made in separating the central and commercial banking operations of the Bank of Mozambique. In 1987, credit to the Government and to the economy (enterprises, etc.) was held to the programmed amounts and net foreign assets increased slightly more than assumed. The expansion of money and quasi money in 1987 thus amounted to about 50 percent, which, as planned, was less than one-third the rate of increase of nominal GDP. In 1988, monetary and credit aggregates remained within the programmed ranges, with the benchmark for public sector borrowing from the banking system being observed. Again, the pace of monetary expansion was below that of nominal GDP growth, although the increase in income velocity had decelerated markedly.

5.133 The implementation of the foregoing measures had a significant impact on the economy in 1987-88, despite the continuing dislocations in the countryside. In 1987, a modest recovery in gross domestic output of around 4% was recorded. This positive growth rate reflected a substantial rise in the agricultural production of the family and private commercial sectors resulting from the improved pricing incentives and the increased flow of consumer goods, and a pick-up in light industrial activity as a result of increased imports of inputs and spare parts. In 1988, GDP growth is again estimated at about 4%. In those areas unaffected by the problems of drought and insecurity, agricultural marketed output grew substantially, while elsewhere, production was severely hampered. For the country as a whole, marketed output of food crops grew by 15%, while aggregate agricultural marketed production grew by more than 5%. Industrial recovery was adversely affected in early 1988 by the inadequate flow of spare parts and productive inputs, but, in the latter half of the year, production revived, allowing a modest growth over the two years. The picture was also mixed in transport, with a reduction in traffic from South Africa only partially offset by increases from Zimbabwe, Malawi and Zambia. Increased aid flows, meanwhile, made possible a rise in per capita consumption and the maintenance of investment levels.

5.134 As a result of the exchange rate adjustments, together with the freeing of many product prices and the adjustment of fixed prices, consumer prices increased sharply in 1987 by 163%, but the rate of price adjustment decelerated considerably in 1988 to about 50%. These rates of price adjustments largely reflect the policy adjustments implemented under the ERP, particularly the exchange rate changes and the substantial reduction in consumer price subsidies. The underlying rate of inflation is estimated to be modest, as indicated by the price movements in the parallel market and of decontrolled prices. There was also a substantial reduction in the scope of parallel markets, with parallel-market prices for goods showing signs of stabilizing or easing and the parallel-market exchange rate declining by about one half from its level in late 1986 of around Mt. 1,800 per US dollar by late 1987; the end 1988 rate of around 1,250 was still considerably below the initial rate.

5.135 With regard to the balance of payments, there was a substantial recovery in exports, and imports expanded at an annual rate of 18 percent over the two years. Mozambique was also able to make substantial progress in regularizing its relations with creditors. Debt rescheduling agreements were reached in principle with London Club banks in May and Paris Club creditors in June 1987, and with other creditors in the course of 1988.

TABLE OF CONTENTS

Annexes and Statistical Appendix

ANNEX TABLES

<u>Annex VIII Cont'd</u>:

Annex IX: EDUCATION

ECONOMIC DEVELOPMENT DURING THE COLONIAL PERIOD

A. Introduction

1. Unlike the majority of former European colonies in sub-Saharan Africa, which became independent in the late 1950's and early 1960's, Angola has been an independent nation only since 1975. The length of the Portuguese colonial presence in Angola (over 500 years) and its particular characteristics left a colonial legacy which continues to constrain Angolan economic development. The unique nature of the Portuguese colonial system is that it was based on an indigenous labor system that was never "free." Domestic slavery was legal until 1870 when it was replaced by a brutal system of forced labor (euphemistically called "contract labor") until 1961 when it was abolished in the wake of the nationalist uprisings. Moreover, since the 1920s, Angolan development policy focused primarily on raising the number and prosperity of the white settlers and increasing the coffers in Portugal at the expense of the indigenous Angolan peoples. Angola's best agricultural lands were seized by Portuguese settlers. Angola became the dumping ground not only for hundreds of thousands of largely illiterate Portuguese but also became the repository for Portugal's key exports such as alcoholic beverages, in particular in the twentieth century. Prior to the outbreak of the armed struggle in 1961, Portuguese economic interests enjoyed a virtual monopoly over investments in the colony and, given Portugal's own economic under-development, this caused unique distortions in the Angolan economy not found in parts of Africa colonized by the British, French, or even the Belgians. Finally, the fact that over half of the 325,000 white settlers had never gone to school and the vast majority of the rest had less than four years of education, resulted in the Portuguese occupying almost every position in the modern economic sector from engineers and doctors to waiters and taxi drivers. Thus, shockingly few Angolans were trained in any skilled profession. The singularity of Portuguese overseas policy makes it particularly important to analyze the pattern of colonial development in Angola in order to understand the opportunities and constraints of the People's Republic of Angola fourteen years later.

2. Angola's colonial economy can be characterized through various stages or cycles of development. These cycles can even be named after the major export and its direction: slaves to Brazil, coffee to Portugal and oil to the United States, each cycle defining a period during which the external sector of the economy is dominated by a particular product, by a particular market or both. The analysis of Angola's development cannot neglect the interaction between economic dependence and colonial rule. For purposes of exposition, the colonial economic history of Angola can be divided into three broad periods. The first period includes the early alliance between the Portuguese and Congolese crowns, as well as the slave trade directed mostly to Brazil, (sometimes referred to as a South Atlantic link). The second period begins with the hundred years of transition from slaves to coffee, during which territorial occupation and settlement took place, and includes the emergence of a coffee export economy based on quasi-forced labor. In the forties, the Angolan economy initiated a growth process that involved considerable immigration from Portugal, in response to the coffee

boom. The white settler population increased from 44,000 in 1940 to about 325,000 by 1974. Generally favorable prospects for external trade were decisive in the evolution of internal conditions, reflected by changes in industrial regulation, in agricultural incentives, in labor laws and in monetary policy. A third period begins with the Portuguese military response to the 1961 armed revolt when some of the economic constraints of colonial rule where relaxed, allowing rapid industrialization to take place alongside the coffee economy and concludes with the beginning of the "oil boom" which immediately preceded the 1973 price increase by OPEC and the 1974 Portuguese revolution.

B. A South Atlantic Link

3. It is believed that in the thirteenth century Angola was inhabited primarily by Koisan-speaking groups who were forced to migrate by the push of Bantu-speaking peoples whose migratory patterns and developed (slash and burn) economies took them into the territory. Some were well developed kingdoms (e.g., Luanda and Kikongo) who moved southward into Angola during the thirteenth and fourteenth centuries in search of new areas to cultivate.

4. The first encounter between Europeans and Angolans occurred in 1483 during a voyage of Diego Cao on his way to find a sea route to India. The initial contacts between the Portuguese and Kikongo were quite egalitarian and included the establishment of diplomatic relations between the two Kingdoms. The Kongo royal family even urged Lisbon to send missionaries to facilitate the conversion of Kikongo to Christianity. Within a decade of the first contacts, however, Portugal focused almost all attention on the slave trade and by 1526 the situation had deteriorated to the point that the Kongo King wrote to his Portuguese counterpart that the slave traders brought "ruin to the country. Every day people are enslaved and kidnapped, even nobles, even members of the King's own family." 1/

5. At the time, the Congo occupied a vast region, including the parts south of the present Congo and Zaire and north of Angola, where the capital was situated. The region was densely populated. The population lived mainly on the cultivation of a certain number of food plants such as massambala, massango and luco. 2/ On a lesser scale, banana, vegetables, sugar-cane and the palm tree were cultivated, the latter being used to make a fermented drink called malufo. This spirit constituted on of the country's principle handmade products, besides weaving and metal-working. While malufo was produced by the peasants and satisfied an important dietary requirement, the rest of production was reserved for the nobility. Metal

---

1/ Paiva Manso, Historia do Congo, p. 54.

2/ W.G.I. Randles, _L'Ancien Royaume du Kongo des origines a la fin du XIX siecle_ (Ed. Mouton, Paris, 1968), p. 65. This book is the major reference for this period. A text from the end of the 16th century notes the sweet potato as the basic food.

-working (iron, copper and gold) was practised in this part of Africa from the first century B.C. 3/ In the same way as palm was used to produce malufo, the production of cereals also gave rise to a manufacturing process for obtaining flour. The first European chronicles also note the raising of beef cattle, sheep, and poultry, but animal traction and the weaving of wool were not practised. 4/ Except for the sowing of the land, agricultural work was the responsibility of the women. Overall, available tools were extremely modest, although despite periods of drought or plagues, production was described as abundant.

6. Land belonged to the kingdom. On the death of a particular farmer, all his fixed property reverted to the King or traditional chiefs, who then decide on the future of the estate. Inheritance was therefore dependent on royal consent. The recorded testimonies agree that this policy prevented private wealth accumulation, so that the differences between rich and poor were determined for each generation by the political process. The peasants paid taxes to the village chief, who paid the provincial governor, who in turn paid the King; at each stage of the process the receiver kept for himself a certain percentage. Although some testimonies report that the process was quiet harmonious, other testimonies report that the collection of taxes almost always implied (principally in the backward regions) the resort to violence, provoking occasional revolts. 5/

7. Long-distance trade was controlled by the King or by the governors of the provinces. Salt from the coast and from mines and raffia products form inland areas were two of the main products exchanged. Some Portuguese chronicles note that the zimbo (a small shell from Luanda island) served as currency. However there is no solid evidence of the use of zimbo for the acquisition of food; it is merely conjectured that the zimbo may have served, in certain cases, for long distance trade. Moreover, the zimbo together with other products and even slaves, were used to pay taxes. 6/

3/ R.P.A., History of Angola, p. 34. "The blacksmith enjoyed considerable economic prestige ... he was frequently soothsayer, judge and witch-doctor. The fact of possession of metal weapons made certain tribes and peoples superior in offensive power over their neighbors who had only stone weapons. This explains how the Bantu, who arrived in the territory inhabited by the Koisan, settled there."

4/ Op.cit., Randles, p. 69-70. This and the following section are based on citations of H. de Bolonha.

5/ Cavazzi, cited in Randles, p. 76.

6/ Felner, History of the Kingdom of the Congo, cited by Randles, Op.cit.

The King is reported to have fixed the prices of products. 7/ Indeed, the analysis of documentation from the various periods suggest that such prices remained relatively stable over four centuries.

8. The first attempt at white settlement occurred in 1575 with the arrival in Luanda of Paulo Dias de Novais who landed with the title of "donatario" of the Angolan coast, a method of colonization used in Brazil. Novais and his men were more interested in finding the fabled (but nonexistent) silver mines near Cambambe than in establishing permanent white settlements. They also brought the pursuit of slaves carried out among the Kikongo in the north to the area around Luanda inhabited by the Kimbundu. A period of wars and incursions followed, during which the rumors about the existence of silver mines in Cambambe proved to be false. 8/ This coincided with the Brazilian depression, and forced the colonial power to search for a new economic use for the former ally. For about three hundred years, this new use was going to be the slave trade, which became the basis of all colonial economic activity until the mid 19th century. Since Angolan slaves were mostly sent to Brazil, a South Atlantic link emerged between these two Portuguese colonies. Throughout, the international market conditions were highly rewarding for the slave trade. 9/

9. The Dutch conquest of Brazil, in the middle of the seventeenth century, led Holland to seek control of the source of the slaves, which were more numerous in Angola than anywhere along the West African coast. The Dutch made strategic alliances with key Angolan leaders, like the famous Queen Nzinga, who helped them drive the Portuguese from the coast in 1640. The Dutch did not accede to Queen Nzinga's admonition to eliminate all Portuguese in the area as they found the Portuguese to be useful middlemen in the slave trade. Luanda was reconquered in 1648 by a Brazilian fleet led by the Governor of Bahia. Once the area was recovered by the Portuguese, the Dutch were naturally forced to evacuate the important slave markets of Luanda and Benguela (founded in 1617), and other lesser ports in the north. The Sa expedition was almost entirely financed by Brazilian merchants and undertaken despite the clear policy of Dom Joao IV not to offend the Dutch in the difficult times following the Portuguese restoration. The King even threatened to punish Sa, who nevertheless was the initiator of a period of 12 years during which the governors of Luanda were Brazilians. During that period, the Brazilian slave trade became so predominant that there was a local revolt against the arrival of one of the governors in 1670, when appointing a new governor from Portugal, the Crown granted a Charter to the Luanda settlers for their protection.

7/ Proyat (1776) cited by Randles, Op.cit.

8/ D. Birmingham, Trade and Conflict in Angola, 1483-1790 (Oxford: Claredon Press, 1966), p. 62.

9/ Bernard Founou: Cours sur le Developpment de l'Afrique - Amorce du Sous-Developpment: La Traite Negrire, quelques donnes chiffres (IDEP - Dakar, March, 1979)

10. During the Brazilian consulate, the conflict against Congo and Matamba for the control of the inland trade continued. The African Kingdoms were defeated between 1665 and 1681 and both Kings accepted a truce, becoming vassals of the King of Portugal. However, the Portuguese continued not to control the slave trade, given that they had to pay a toll to the Imbangalas for the caravans coming from the Londa Empire. For that reason, it was necessary to return to the regime of exchange, with prices dictated by the English and French competition in the north. By that time, however, the sugar boom was over and Portugal was going through a severe depression. The volume of the slave trade decreased accordingly.

11. There are no reliable records on the number of slaves exported from Angola and Congo during the period from 1500-1700. There is some agreement on the slave imports into Brazil which total 625,000. It is thought that about half came from Angola. However many slaves exported from Angola were declared, for tax purposes, as having Brazilian destination, although they would go to Spanish America instead. 10/ North European competition for African slaves picked up after 1650, due to the sugar boom in the Caribbean, after the Dutch had been expelled from Brazil. In the 18th century, the English and French controlled over 80% of the West African slave trade. Portugal, however, handled about two-thirds of the south Atlantic trade. In the period 1700-1850, almost 1.8 million slaves were exported by Angola and Congo, whereas Brazil imported about 3.6 million. Almost all of Angola's exports went to Brazil, and taking mortality into account, the total number of slaves exported from Angola may have been as high as 2.5 million. The anticipation of the end of the slave trade led to enormous slave imports into Brazil in the late 1820's followed by a sharp drop in the early 1930s. However, the coffee related demand for labor maintained slave imports at a high level until the middle of the century. At the end of the period, there is little doubt that Angola and the Congo were severely depopulated as compared to the 16th century. Contrary to what seems to have occurred in West Africa, the increase in population brought by new food products like maize and manioc was not sufficient to offset the drain of the slave trade.

12. The colonial trade mechanisms lay basically in the relationship between the powerful coast merchants and the traditional chiefs inland or in the wandering activities of the hawkers, the small white, mixed race and black merchants, components of an incipient creole society. It is in this creole society that attempts at economic diversification were made several years before the abolition of slavery. In fact, from 1764 to 1772 an active economic policy was pursued in Angola under the governorship of Sousa Coutinho, leading, for example, to attempts at producing iron industrially in Nova-Oeiras, near Massangano. These efforts collapsed after Coutinho's departure but when the Brazilian demand picked up again, they were replaced by attempts to expand east and south. In 1830 the first coffee plantations

---

10/ Jorge Braga de Macedo, Colonial Development of Angola: The Rise and Fall of a South Atlantic Link (mimeo, Yale University, March 1978). Estimates of the total number of slaves shipped from Angola during this period range from 750,000 to 1 million.

appear in Massangano and Ambaca and cotton is grown in Golungo. At the same time, trading settlements like the Dondo, on the banks of the Cuanza, gained importance and Portuguese coming from Brazil settled in the Namibe desert where Mocamedes was founded. Most of Angolan foreign trade was with Brazil, the slaves being paid for by Brazilian cane liquor and gold.

13. Slavery was abolished in three phases, spanning over forty years. First, there was the prohibition of slave exports in 1836, followed by the abolition of slave trade under the Portuguese flag six years later; finally there was the abolition of slavery itself, in 1878. The prohibition was felt as a great loss and in the 1830's the idea of remaining associated to prosperous Brazil found many supporters in the local "comprador" class. Nevertheless, the pro-Portuguese faction won and some efforts were made to develop a tropical export economy. Wax, ivory, palm oil, and peanut exports came to the fore after the slave trade subsided. In 1870, the rubber boom spread through the territory and, until 1915, this product was to be Angola's first export, with yearly averages on the order of 2,000 tons. 11/

C. SETTLEMENT AND CONTRACT LABOR

Territorial Occupation

14. At the Berlin Conference in 1885, the principle of effective occupation was accepted over the Portuguese idea of priority of discovery. The partition of Africa imposed obliged Portugal to effectively occupy the territories it claimed to have discovered. This led to renewed interest in the exploration and the "pacification" of the interior, and to a debate over the use of the colonies. The debate was dramatized by an English Ultimatum in 1890 against the Portuguese idea of linking Angola and Mozambique by land (the so-called "pink map"). In Angola, Portugal had occupied Luanda and its immediate hinterland since 1575, and Benguela and surrounding districts since 1617. However, only in the 19th century can the Portuguese presence be considered stable in parts of the north (south of the Kingdom of Congo) or on the coast south of Benguela). In 1906, the settled area refers mostly to the zone of influence of the Benguela railway, built by the English with the purpose of transporting the minerals from Katanga and the Copperbelt and owned mostly by Tanganyika Concessions. The scant penetration and its pattern demonstrated the considerable dependence of the colony on external factors. Moreover, it suggested that after all these centuries, Portugal's colonial policy had been unable to secure an administrative occupation

---

11/ Joao Maria Cerqueira d'Azevedo, Subsidios para o Estudo Economico de Angola nos Ultimos Cem Anos (Luanda, 1950).

comparable with that achieved by the other partners in the Berlin Conference. This explains the statement that the effective Portuguese presence was limited to 65 years in about 80% of Angola's territory. 12/

15. At the end of the First World War, when various military occupation campaigns were in progress in the southern, central, and northeastern parts of the country, the international price of rubber fell. This trend continued and, in the 1930's, it forced the disappearance of rubber from the list of Angolan exports, where coffee already comes first in 1926. During this period of falling export prices, and national humiliation from the British ultimatum, some measures of colonial policy became relevant, such as the customs restrictions of 1892, which attempted to transform Angola into a closed market for Portuguese wines and textiles. Angola would thus be prohibited from manufacturing spirits which had become one of the main imports. In 1906, moreover, the native poll tax was introduced to alleviate the continuing crisis of the Angolan public finances and facilitate the recruitment of forced labor.

16. Simultaneously, important railway lines began to be built, linking the coast to the interior of the country. In 1909, the Luanda-Malange Railway was inaugurated, crossing a large segment of the territory where the commercial exchanges and the plantations had acquired considerable economic importance. The construction of the Benguela Railway (C.F.B.) was initiated six years earlier, though only in the 1930's does it attain the objective of reaching the eastern frontier to serve as the outlet for mining production from the Belgian and British possessions. A third railway was to connect the port of Mocamedes to Lubango, where the Portuguese had established a colony since the end of the 19th century. International investment in Angola was reflected not only in its use as a corridor by the Benguela Railway, but also by investments in the mining sector, especially in the diamond area of Lunda, where an association of English, South African, Belgian and Portuguese interests gave rise to Diamang in 1921. In 1929, the production of diamonds had reached 250 thousand carats and employed over 6,000 Africans as well as 155 Europeans. First attempts to win petroleum were made in 1917.

Monetary Reform

17. The negative effects of the Great Depression on the prices of raw materials, three successive locust plagues in the 1930's and budget mismanagement contributed to the colony's economic difficulties. A monetary reform designed to stabilize the Angolan currency was introduced in 1926. This was the origin of the "angolar" (which enjoyed fixed parity with the Portuguese escudo) as well as of the "Junta da Moeda de Angola" (Angola Monetary Authority), a Government Department controlling the matters dealing

---

12/ Gerald J. Bender, Angola Under the Portuguese- The Myth and The Reality, (Berkeley: University of California Press, 1978), Chapters 3 and 4. A map of the settled area in 1906 is reproduced in Randles, op. cit.

with currency circulation as well as the management of the Monetary Reserve Fund. The Authority supplied the colony with the amount of "angolares" to cover transfers from Portugal as well as Portuguese Escudos in Lisbon to cover transfers from Angola. The Bank of Angola began to issue angolares in 1928.

18. Despite this reform and the fact that the country's finances were kept under control until the end of the fifties, monetary difficulties plagued the colonial economy since monetary creation was directly linked to falling export revenues. The transfers of the settlers to the mother country and the slump in the export business opened a trade balance deficit in 1929, leading to the promulgation of the "Acto Colonial" in 1931, where the social, economic and financial policies of Lisbon for the colonies took constitutional form. In the face of the persisting crisis, the Portuguese government imposed credit ceilings, set up an Exchange Fund and restricted the transfer of funds, requiring the surrender of 75% of export receipts and a strict control of imports. These measures went against the objective of transforming Angola into a Portuguese settlement colony. Regarding authorization for transfer of profits, the restrictions were less severe, suggesting that the objective of attracting foreign capital was seen as instrumental in settling the territory. Government control, relaxed after the coffee boom in 1946 and again in 1963 when monetary integration of the so-called "Escudo Zone" was introduced, was to return forty years later with the restriction on payments in 1971. In the

meantime, the economic stabilization and recovery of the colony was initiated with the reduction of imports, thus allowing a trade balance surplus during the Second World War.

The Coffee Boom

19. During the war, Portugal increased its share of Angolan imports from 39% to 65%. At the same time, the occupation of land by the settlers increased rapidly, mostly in the north. Official statistics refer the share of the land controlled by the settlers as having increased from 12 to 40% in two years, probably an exaggeration. One of the means used to spread control over land was to demarcate the estates to encompass African coffee production as "natural growth". Production in 1946 can be considered the result of land occupations at the beginning of the decade, since the coffee trees needed five years before the first harvest. In 1945, diamonds were the principal export in value terms, but in 1946 despite a 40% increase in diamond exports, coffee exports became the main export, reaching over 46,000 tons. Coffee was to dominate the list of products exported by Angola from 1946 to 1972. The rise of coffee prices in the world market after the start of the Korean war in 1950, stimulated coffee cultivation further, and turned out to be a powerful attraction for the immigration of settlers from Portugal. The white population increased from 44,000 in 1943 to 173,000 in 1960, which together with the 53,000 of mixed race represented 5% of the total population of 4.8 million. In any event, demand for skilled labor in Angola was so strong that, from the mid - fifties, it was no longer

necessary to have a "letter of appointment", generally issued by the employer in the colony and guaranteeing that the settler/immigrant could find work there.

20. Besides coffee, whose share of total exports remained between one-third and one-half during the fifties, Angolan diamond and sisal exports normally made up the other half (Table 1). Lesser export products were sugar, cotton, manioc flour, fish-meal, dried fish and corn.After 1957, iron-ore began to be exported and in 1960, it already ranked as the fifth export. The forties were a decade of accelerated growth, due to the favorable trends in raw material prices, especially coffee and cotton. The subsequent stagnation starting in the mid-fifties coincides with the fall of raw material prices despite the increased quantities exported. During the same period, close to one half of imports was accounted for by wines and spirits, textiles, freight vehicles, bulk and work iron, industrial machinery and equipment, and railway material (Table 2).

21. Angola's principal customer in the fifties was the United States, with about one fourth of exports. The share of Portugal declined from about the same to less than one fifth, whereas the share of the United Kingdom and Holland rose from one quarter to one third during the same decade. Angola's main supplier was Portugal, with close to one half of the total, with the United Kingdom and Germany providing about one quarter of imports and the United States accounting for about 10%. The predominance of Portugal in Angola's imports, while exacerbated by the legislation reserving the Angolan market for certain Portuguese products, such as textiles and wines, was not as pronounced as in other European colonies, perhaps a reflection of the mother country's relative underdevelopment.

22. The rise in the value of coffee exports after 1946 helped the Angolan trade balance, which showed surpluses between 1950 and 1956, the largest one being recorded in 1953. From 1957 to 1960, the trade balance was in deficit, due to both the temporary fall in the price of some exports (coffee, sisal and maize), and a sustained growth in imports, mainly of textiles, wines and equipment. Nevertheless, the rate of growth of imports declined sharply over the period. This sharp drop in the pace of imports did not prevent a serious exchange crisis. Although some restrictions on the spending of foreign exchange earnings had been imposed already in 1955, more drastic restrictive measures were imposed by the Lisbon authorities in 1959. Residents were required to surrender to the territory's Exchange Fund approximately 90% of foreign exchange earnings, besides adhering to a list of priorities for imports. This situation remained in force until 1963, when a new system of payments came into force in the "Escudo Zone".

Colonial Policy of the "New State"

23. Integrating the colonies in a Portuguese economic union was one of the objectives of Salazar's "New State". Indeed, the Colonial Act mentioned the principle of "natural solidarity" between the metropolis and the colonies in article 34. This natural solidarity was said to be the foundation of the various economies, and stemmed from the "moral and

political links" between the metropolis and the colonies. In the fifties, Portugal exchanged manufactures for tropical materials with its overseas territories. However, the level of development of Portugal and its colonies, implied a pattern of trade for metropolitan Portugal which made it unlikely that the "Escudo Zone" would be able to exercise monopoly power in international trade, in line with the objective of collective self reliance desired by Salazar.

24. The Political Constitution of the Portuguese Republic was enacted in 1933, but it was not until 1951 that the philosophy of economic integration with the colonies was fully accepted. Article 34 of the Colonial Act was thus replaced by article 158 of the Constitution, and a paragraph was added which clearly stated the objective of national integration: "The economic reorganization of the overseas territories must integrate itself with the general economic organization of the Portuguese nation and participate through it in the world economy. To reach the aims stated in this article, the free circulation of products within the national territory should be facilitated by appropriate means, including the gradual reduction or elimination of tariff duties. The same principle will apply insofar as possible to the circulation of people and capital assets". In the same statute, the colonies were renamed "overseas provinces" - a traditional label which had been abandoned after the Republican revolution of 1910.

25. At the time, though, Portuguese attempts to establish an economic union with the colonies began to clash with the general European trend toward decolonization. Thus, in 1953, when countries like France and England were starting to prepare for the decolonization of their colonies, Salazar's government promulgated the Lei Organica do Ultramar (Overseas Territories Act), stating the objectives of Portuguese presence as "exploiting the resources and the peoples" together with "raising the living standards of the natives within the framework of social justice".

26. Steps were thus taken to facilitate trade between the various Portuguese customs territories, so as to move towards a customs union. A decree in March 1957 established free trade among the different overseas provinces as far as their domestic production was concerned. It was also decided that metropolitan imports from overseas would only pay 30 percent of the minimum tariff and some products -- such as tea, cattle, lumber, fruit and fish -- were free of duties. Moreover, imports from metropolitan Portugal were generally granted a 50 percent rate reduction in the tariff of the overseas provinces.

Contract Labor and International Factor Mobility

27. It was therefore in the fifties that the authorities in Lisbon created a framework that would justify their presence in African territories, despite the shifting international values and the increasing reluctance of international agencies to condone European colonialism. The number of home-based companies that began to invest in the colony increased, and many settlers whose prosperity derived directly or indirectly from the coffee

boom started a considerable number of small and medium-sized companies. In all cases the availability of local labor was the basic condition, whether by the practice of low wages or by the resort to so-called contract labor ("contratados").

28. Manufacturing industry, very incipient and geared to the local urban population, was based on the refining of sugar, treatment of tobacco, spinning and weaving, soap-making and fish derivatives (mainly fish-meal). The cement, beer and textile industries (those carrying largest weight in the manufacturing sector), the large agricultural companies and the import-export trade were tied to Portuguese capital, apart from the monopoly of all Angolan maritime freight, which was held by Portuguese companies. Foreign capital was dominant in the Benguela Railway, in the mining sector (mainly diamonds, copper, manganese and iron) and also in some agricultural companies such as Cotonang and SETA which had Belgian/Portuguese and American/Portuguese capital respectively. Industrial licensing continued to bar entry to the colonial economy for industries that might have generated competition with Portuguese exports into Angola. Hence the Angolan economy continued to be sustained by mining and agricultural activities.

29. The expansion of the plantations and the mines and the launching of work on infrastructure created a strong demand for labor, in part satisfied by the methods of recruitment already described. More specifically, recruiting officers provided forced labor in the diamond mines and plantations, while police raids provided the labor for public works, especially the opening of new roads. The vast majority of the contract labor was recruited among the farmers and herdsmen of the central provinces. Prior to the fifties, the number of forced workers is difficult to determine. Recruiters travelled all over the bush and managed to obtain the number of workers that had been promised to the companies. The methods ranged from capture for non-payment of taxes and for misdemeanors to the corruption of some tribal chiefs. An alternative form of recruitment was through the imprisonment, in the cities, of natives ("indigenas") who were not carrying a valid work permit. The use of forced labor was to diminish towards the end of the fifties, in the face of resistance from the population and the beginning of nationalist struggle and international pressures. In 1961, labor policy would be changed with the abolition of the Native Work Code (dating from 1928) and its substitution by the Rural Work Code, which defined working conditions in farms and mines. This was the first result at the armed struggle that started in 1961.

30. In the fifties, the majority of the indigenous population was employed in agriculture, and the commercial network, which extended from the principal markets of Angola to the hinterland, was rooted in the purchase of agricultural products and the sale of imported products. The white population which lived from agriculture possessed large estates or resided in the settlements. As the name indicates, these were zones in which the settlers' families were fixed, developing the agro-livestock potential of certain areas of the territory, which had been selected by the central government authorities. The regime of settlements was intended not only to provide an incentive for the immigration of Portuguese farmers, but also to

rationalize and improve farming production, bearing in mind the requirements of the export markets and domestic consumption (Table 3). The creation of new agricultural bodies - farm cooperatives - also began to be encouraged. Together with this associative movement, there was a growing intervention of the Provincial Agricultural Technical services, chiefly in the "campaigns for the stabilization of indigenous/itinerant agriculture, with the aim of organizing indigenous rural life, creating a class of small, settled farmers, which both facilitated technical and social assistance and protected the soil against erosion".

31. The prevailing social structure could be roughly described in terms of the following categories: (a) a dominant class whose representatives remained in the colony for the term of their "service commissions", useful even as a means of promotion in metropolitan public life (in a sense this was an "absentee" class, because most of its members did not reside in Angola); (b) an upper middle class consisting of resident Europeans (and their descendants) who became owners of medium-sized companies or attained top positions in business or public administration, thus controlling the economic life of the colony; (c) a lower middle class with mixed racial characteristics, though whites predominated (at the end of the fifties, it included about half of the 172,000 white inhabitants, almost all the 50,000 "assimilated" blacks and nearly all of the 53,000 mixed-race people); small proprietors, salaried employees and petty officials were included in this social layer, from which the forces behind the fight for independence were to emerge; (d) an urban proletariat, divided into two types according to race: a large number of white workers having a standard of living comparable to part of the lower middle class, and employed rural workers, entirely black, and with lower wage levels than the urban proletariat; and (e)in the four or five cities, and chiefly in Luanda, a kind of "lumpen-proletariat" became noticeable and included the majority of the black population who lived in the "muceques" surrounding the capital, as well as white street vendors and under-unemployed workers.

32. Although official statistics on earnings by race are unavailable, it is estimated that in the mid-fifties, Europeans earned a daily wage between US$100 and US$120, Cape Verdeans between US$60 and US$80 and black urban workers between US$10 and US$20. The wage differential, reflecting the lack of skills of the Angolan black worker as well as race, was even greater with agricultural workers, for whom daily wages ranged from US$6 to US$10. These wage differentials and the poor working conditions in rural areas led to internal migrations to the cities (mainly Luanda). In the civil service, the wage categories were practically the same as in Portugal, though fringe benefits were sometimes higher. Social stratification roughly matched racial differences. Thus, as a rule, management posts (even at the middle level) were held by metropolitan Portuguese; subordinate positions were occupied by Angolan whites, those of mixed-race and unqualified metropolitan Portuguese whites, while office boys and unskilled workers were black. Even jobs of the latter kind were also, to some extent, filled by whites towards the end of the 1960s.

Economic Causes of Nationalist Rebellion

33. In 1960, in the north of the country, the continuing coffee boom led many settlers to apply constant pressure to enlarge their plantations, disregarding the rights of the black owners. Simultaneously, deprivation and discontent in the countryside was attributed to the high prices charged by the traders in the hinterland and the low quality of the products they sold. While the resentment towards the bush traders was common in the whole territory, native property rights were more respected in the rest of the country than in the coffee growing region. The occupation of land by settlers was practiced on a smaller scale in the center, and was almost non-existent in the extreme south of the country, where the herdsmen kept possession of their cattle.

34. Perhaps because of the coffee boom, but certainly as a reaction to the drastic increase in the Portuguese population (up 570% from 1950 to 1960 in the coffee district of Uige), political/cultural movements espousing African nationalism grew during the early fifties. In 1952, 500 Angolan nationalists sent a petition to the United Nations requesting the end of Portuguese rule. In 1953 the Party for the United Fight of Angolan Africans, was founded and became the MPLA in 1956. The presidential elections of 1958 in metropolitan Portugal revealed also that a number of settlers were against Salazar, since the opposition candidate Delgado is thought to have won in Luanda. The campaign led to the arrest of 57 nationalists (the majority considered of mixed race) in December 1959. This political arrest set a course that would culminate in the beginning of an armed struggle for independence in February-March 1961, followed by a generalized insurrection in the northern countryside.

35. The lack of organization and technical means on the part of the northern rebels, their cruel treatment of the settlers and the prevailing tribalism obstructed the progress of the insurrection itself. The rebels controlled various agricultural and plantation communities in the then district of the Congo, causing damage to equipment and buildings, but leaving the coffee trees practically unscathed. The reaction to the rebels came with a vengeance: between 8,000 and 30,000 African Angolans were killed, the former being the Portuguese official figure and the latter being the one the United Nations committee accepted. According to the same source, by December 1961, another 150,000 inhabitants from the northern rural areas fled to the Republic of the Congo-Leopoldville.

36. The events of 1961 led to reformist measures, supported by a new reinforcement of the military presence in Angola. In particular, these reforms allowed the access of a greater number of Angolans to secondary education and intermediate posts in public administration as well as the changing of work relations, with the substitution of the Native Work Code by the Rural Work Code. The resorting to contract labor became more and more sporadic. This contributed towards the creation of a more modern labor market, despite the limitation derived from the racial composition of the

unskilled labor force. Because a large share of immigrant labor from Portugal reached the colony with very limited skills, the increase in the labor inflow did not improve the skill mix as much as it changed the racial mix.

D. Soldiers and Industrialization

37. The direct effects of the 1961 nationalist rebellions on productive capacity were rather small. Only the cultivation of cotton was seriously affected by the armed struggle, especially since its production area - the Cassange basin - was the scene of serious incidents in the aftermath of peasant protests. This led to a massive flight of workers, who were not replaced. In the coffee area, on the contrary, thousands of new workers were hired in the central plateau and sent north. The difference was probably due to the realization that the Angolan economy depended much more on the export of coffee than on cotton. As discussed in the following section, as a result of the events of 1961, the Lisbon authorities also abolished some laws and regulations, thus increasing the number of economic activities the colony could develop; they also improved wage conditions and created "rural markets", where the surpluses of the peasants could be sold in an organized fashion. These new policies, together with the rising Portuguese immigration and military contingent stationed in the territory, amounting to over 6000 people, created employment and increased overall purchasing power, laying the basis for the expansion of industrial activities as well as coffee production.

38. In the sixties, Angolan exports continued to be dominated by the coffee/diamond tandem. Sisal remained the third most important export product until 1968, when it was replaced by iron ore. Oil already ranked fourth in 1969 and second by 1971. In 1973, oil became the lead export, followed by coffee, diamonds and iron ore. Other products carrying weight in the export trade were sisal, cotton, sugar, manioc flour, fish products, timber, palm-oil and, after 1969, bananas. Angola's main customer in 1961 was still the US, but from the following year until 1972, it was replaced by Portugal, which bought about one third of Angola's exports, both agricultural products and minerals. Portugal was not always the final destination though, since diamonds were re-exported to the United Kingdom. In 1973, the US would again top the list of countries purchasing from Angola (with 28%), mostly due to oil and coffee exports. Portugal accounted for about one quarter of exports, followed by Canada, Japan, and major European countries.

39. From 1962 onward, the Angolan economy started to recover from the 1957-60 exchange crisis as well as from the temporary fall in the prices of its exports. A comparison of international price indices for coffee and the price of Angolan coffee shows that the years 1963/64 and 1972 were the only ones in which the international price index rose more than the Angolan index. Despite fluctuations in the relative price of Angolan coffee, export earnings grew rapidly and the balance once again recorded a surplus. This was to continue until the end of the colonial period (with the exception of

the years 1967 and 1968, as a result of a strong rise in imports of equipment and motor vehicles). The strength of the external balance is evident in the data presented in Tables 6 and 7 below.

40. Unlike the early coffee cycle, during which the structure of merchandise trade seemed to change more on the export than on the import side, a change was noticeable in the composition of imported goods after 1965. Growing imports of transport equipment, industrial and farming machinery and equipment, raw and worked iron indicated the effort to equip the light manufacturing and extractive industries as well as the creation of infrastructure, such as roads and other forms of communication. The rising military contingent may also have helped step up the importation of Portuguese food and drink products, as well as textiles.

41. Regarding the supplier countries, Portugal remained at the top of the list even though its share of Angola's imports gradually diminished from 44% in 1961 to 26% in 1973. In 1971, Portugal's share was still larger than the combined share of the next three suppliers, Germany, the US and the UK, with about 10% each. Despite the possible demand bias for Portuguese consumer goods, a pattern similar to the one which followed the protectionist regime of 1892 can be observed in the structure of trade during the sixties. Despite the increase in volume, Portugal's share was decreasing significantly.

A New Colonial Economic Policy

42. As mentioned above, after the events of February 1961, the Lisbon authorities felt the need to reinforce the Portuguese presence in the territory. To this end, the Portuguese government adopted a series of measures which stimulated export-led economic development and industrialization in Angola. This was also the policy that the Portuguese government was pursuing for the development of the mother country, in the framework of the European Free Trade Association (EFTA), of which Portugal was a founding member since 1960. At that time, Portugal's accession to the General Agreement on Tariffs and Trade (GATT) required the creation of an additional free trade area with the overseas territories, in such a way as to avoid the application of the most favored nation clause to the trade between GATT partners and the Portuguese colonies.

43. A significant step was taken by a Decree in November 1961 which abolished all barriers to the free circulation of domestic products within the various territories of the nation. As general economic conditions warranted, capital account liberalization was also to be attained. The abolition of customs duties was to be implemented progressively, in accordance with the level of imports. Existing quantitative restrictions, or the introduction of new ones were to be justified on grounds of facilitating the adaptation of economic activities to the new conditions of competition or in situations where a particular sector was experiencing

difficulties which threatened the economic situation of a region and no other measures could be taken. This Decree also took measures to promote the elimination of disparities between legal and administrative systems, which hinderedinter-regional trade, as well as the improvement of transportation. Finally, the Decree contemplated the liberalization of exchange controls between territories.

44. Even from a strictly commercial viewpoint, Portuguese economic integration had much weaker effects than the integration of the metropolitan area with Europe, including both the European Free Trade Association to which Portugal belonged and the European Community, with which it signed a free trade agreement in 1972. In the fifties, the share of the overseas territories in metropolitan Portugal's imports declined while the corresponding share increased for exports. In the sixties, however, both shares declined significantly. In 1972, the share of Europe in metropolitan Portugal's trade reached 56% for imports and 62% for exports, up from 40% in 1954, while the corresponding figures for shares of all the "overseas provinces" were 10% (down from 17% in 1954) and 15% (down from 25% in 1954). The introduction in 1961 of a free trade area with the overseas territories was therefore not as important economically as it was politically.

45. Accordingly, an exchange rate union was set up in 1963, which was maintained until 1971. The new system of payments, known as the Escudo Zone, started from the principle that there would be no shortage of foreign exchange in any of the component parts of the system.If this should occur, the Monetary Fund of the Escudo Zone would intervene, granting credit to the Exchange Fund of the colonial territory in deficit. For example, an Angolan importer who purchased merchandise from Portugal would have to pay his debt in "Angolan" escudos to the Exchange Fund which was managed by the Bank of Angola, which would then automatically effect the transfer, in Portuguese escudos, to the creditor in Portugal.

46. The improvement in the foreign exchange situation thus allowed the liberalization of payments outside Angola. The system of designating priorities for transfers, in force since 1955, was abolished. The surplus in the overseas territories' external payments contributed to the overall surplus of the "Escudo Zone" in the period. Despite the emergence of a growing trade deficit after 1964, invisible receipts allowed a surplus on the current account throughout the period. Similarly, despite a deficit on capital account between 1963 and 1968, the overseas territories contributed to the accumulation of reserves at the Bank of Portugal, a situation not unlike the Franc Zone during the same period.

47. An "Investment Code" was also enacted in April 1965 to strongly encourage the flow of foreign capital to Angola. This Code - which also coincided with a greater opening of the Portuguese economy to foreign investment from other countries in the Organization of Economic Cooperation and Development (OECD) - was seen as a signal for the start of the "race for the progress of Angola". The Lisbon authorities wanted to be able to count on the military, political and economic support of the major OECD countries. Therefore, they could no longer keep exclusive control of such widespread

natural resources; it was necessary to share them. Later in 1965 scheme of "new industrial licensing" was revoked, cancelling the previous legislation that prohibited the setting up of new industries in the colonies, especially textiles.

Coffee-Led Industrialization

48. These new policies contributed to the year 1965 being a turning point in the growth of the Angolan economy. From a level of about 17% of gross domestic product in the early sixties, the industrial sector (including extractive and construction industries as well as manufacturing proper) reached 38% of GDP in 1970. Metropolitan and foreign capital were concentrated in both the more capital-intensive extractive industries such as diamonds, oil, iron ore, petroleum derivatives, cement and the more labor-intensive activities of the agricultural sector, such as coffee, cotton, sisal, sugar, tobacco. In addition to these activities, which in one way or another used natural resources, several manufacturing activities were created in the sixties, particularly during the second half of the decade, including chemical products, paper, glass, electric cables, paints and metal containers.

49. Industry was very dependent on Portugal from where a high percentage of raw materials and semi-finished products came. The Portuguese authorities encouraged the process by exempting those materials and products from import duties. There were also tax exemptions granted by the Overseas Minister for the new industries to be created in the colony. These exemptions and tax incentives allowed the development of some industrial zones, centered in the Luanda area and to a lesser extent in the area of Lobito and Benguela. Moreover, in 1971, pressure from local industry forced Lisbon to adopt protective customs measures against competitive imports.

50. The sectors of activity that dominated local industry were: food and beverages, textiles and tobacco, contributing (in the 1966-71 period) an average of about 54% to the global value of sector output (Table 5). The food and drink industries alone accounted for 44% of total output. Overall manufacturing industry grew, between 1962 and 1967, at an average annual rate of 15%, and, from 1968 until independence, at a rate of 20%. This growth reflects the effects of economic measures such as the Investment Code, new Rules of Industrial Licensing, dismantling of Customs tariffs, tax exemptions, and investment in transport infrastructure, adopted in the mid-sixties and incorporated in the Interim Development Plan (1965-67) and the Third Development Plan (1968-73).

51. Although Angola had one of largest industrial sectors south of the Sahara, the participation of the manufacturing sector in exports from Angola was weak. As shown in Table 5, the average percentage of gross industrial production exported was about 20% during the 1966-71 period, the rest being absorbed by the domestic market. By 1973, the food and beverage industries represented about 6% of the total export value, the chemical industry about 0,4% and textiles about 6%. With respect to the textile industry, more than half of the value of these exports was accounted for by cotton wool for

metropolitan Portugal, and the remainder by fabrics and other textile articles exported to Zaire and Sao Tome and Principe, according to the Bank of Angola (1973 Report). The local textile industry (which had strong competition from Macao) concentrated basically on seed-removal or ginning and pressing of cotton, spinning, weaving and finishing of cotton, the shredding of sisal and rope-making. Malange was the main center of the cotton textile industry, with the factories of Cotonang and the city's Agricultural Cooperative.

52. In addition to the increased industrial activity, large- scale agricultural and other projects were also implemented in the sixties and early seventies. The Rural Extension Missions were created in 1971, to co-ordinate projects for the development of zones with agricultural potential,in much the same way as the settlements created in the fifties. Besides the promotion of agro-livestock activity, these projects were also intended to improve the living conditions of the peasant population. In the Lunda district, the activities of Diamang became quite significant in the late sixties, when production reached 2 million carats. About 20,000 people were employed by the company, which also had a dominant role in providing the region with infrastructure.

Colonial Finances

53. Angola had its own budget, containing all of the revenues and expenditures authorized by the Central Government. Expenditures had to be fully covered by the revenues obtained from the colony's resources. From the thirties onward, Angola's general budget always showed an overall surplus. However, after 1961, the effort required by the colonial war, which was not entirely supported by the extraordinary tax for the defense of Angola, caused the budget surplus to drop, and even required borrowing at times. The budget structure, which did not change much from 1930 through 1973, included an "ordinary budget" and an "extraordinary" budget. Ordinary expenditures included civil service and its management. Revenue sources included direct and indirect taxes, taxes on industries subject to special tax schemes as well as taxes on other activities. Until 1973, the direct taxes were the most important revenue source, but after that year the taxation of industries subject to a special scheme (e.g., oil products) took the lead because of the large increase in oil production. Taxes accounted for half of revenues and state property provided about one quarter. The extraordinary budget included development expenditures on social and economic infrastructure. Up to the end of the fifties, these expenditures were mostly borne by Angola itself in view of the large surplus available. From the sixties on, extraordinary expenditures were mostly financed by loans provided by Portugal as well as shares of Diamang profits, sales of bonds and proceeds from a tax on extraordinary rents (imposto de sobrevalorizacoes).

Money and Banking

54. The rapid growth of the Angolan economy was facilitated by the liberalized payments system. Even though the Escudo Zone seemed beneficial

to the metropolis (where most of Angolan savings were transferred through an increase of imports and over-invoicing as well as remittances from the settlers) it turned out to generate large foreign exchange payments on Angola's behalf, so that it accumulated liabilities to the Monetary Fund. Indeed, the liberalized system of payments was to be abolished again when the financial system was seriously strained by an extraordinary volume of delayed transfers. In November 1971, Lisbon once again introduced limitations with a view to "stopping the accumulation of the so-called `delayed transfers' from the province to the metropolis, and trying to create the conditions required for the regularization of those `delayed transfers' (see Table 6 on the balance of payments).

55. The general principles in the decree which re-imposed exchange restrictions were the following: a) the limitation of transfers from each of the overseas provinces abroad (including other national territories as well as foreign countries) to the extent of the cover obtained by the same province; and b) the channelling to the official market means of payment which fed the parallel foreign exchange markets, to prevent unofficial dealings in escudos or in foreign currency. Thus, the colonies were subject to prior registration of imports, exports and re-exports, as well as to "special and prior" authorization of current invisible transactions, and the import and export of capital. At the time, there was concern in Portuguese government circles about the effects of the limits imposed on imports (especially Angolan and Mozambiquan) on Portuguese exports, assuming that such limitations "of merchandise from the metropolis are reduced to the barest minimum for the realization of that objective". The list of priorities for the spending of foreign exchange favored the import of equipment and raw materials to the detriment of other current consumer goods. In other words, the exchange system which came into force in 1972 reinforced the Code of Investment of 1965, trying to turn it into a true instrument of development for Angola, based on the transformation of agricultural and mining products.

56. Accelerated growth dating from the early sixties was accompanied by a strong money supply increase (about 843% from 1960 to 1973). During that period, the share of currency fell from 28% in 1960 to 6% in 1973. The high level of banking time deposits are shown in Table 7, as an indicator of the financial development experienced by Angola. Another indicator of financial development, the income velocity of money, doubled in the ten years from 1960 to 1969. By then, the growth of money supply at a rate higher than the GDP played a role in the appearance of a parallel exchange market where the Portuguese escudo brought 10 to 20% more than the official exchange rate. Moreover, a certain inflexibility of the system of payments between the two countries in force since 1963 raised difficulties in obtaining Portuguese escudos in time to meet the growing demand due to the acceleration of economic growth.

57. Another indication of its financial development is the consider-able banking network Angola acquired. The commercial banks (including the Bank of Angola founded in 1926) were connected to the metropolis (Banco Comercial de Angola, a branch of Banco Portuges do Atlantico; Banco de Credito Comercial e Industrial, a branch of Banco Borges & Irmao; the branch of

Banco Pinto & Sotto Mayor of Lisbon) or to foreign banks (Banco Totta Standard de Angola an association of Banco Totta and Standard Bank of England; as well as Banco Inter-unido an association of Banco Espirito Santo and The First National City Bank). In addition to the commercial banks, special investment banks also operated in Angola, mostly engaged in credit operations covering real estate, industry, agriculture and cattle- breeding. These included Instituto de Credito de Angola, Banco de Fomento Nacional, and Caixa de Credito Agropecuario.

The Origins and Role of the Oil Enclave

58. Although oil only becomes the main export product of Angola during the last two years of the colonial period, drilling and searching had begun much earlier. In 1952, the Ministry of Overseas Colonies had been authorized to sign a mining concession with Companhia de Combustiveis do Lobito (Carbonang). Carbonang established the Missao de Pesquisas de Petroleo (Petrofina) which began working in a coastal region between the rivers Kwanza and Zaire. In 1955, oil was discovered in a region near Luanda called Benfica. Oil extraction began in 1958, in small quantities. Only after 1968 did oil become noticeable in the list of Angolan exports, with 0.1% of the total value of exports. In the following years, though, oil exports increased, rapidly becoming one of the key exported products. In 1973, oil overtook coffee as Angola's first export product and by 1974, oil export values were higher than the combined total of coffee, diamonds, iron, sisal, cotton, fish, fishmeal and corn. As of the end of 1973, there were four companies with a concession for search and exploration, the most important being the Cabinda Gulf Oil Company (CABGOC), a subsidiary of Gulf-Oil.

A Fragile Pattern of Growth

59. Despite the limitations of the data, the output figures reported in Table 8 show a pattern of accelerated output growth in the mid to late sixties, which becomes increasingly inflationary in the last years of the colonial period. The effect of the government budget on the one hand and external constraints on the other, on this pattern of growth are illustrated in Table 8. Throughout the period, private savings exceed private investment, the difference fluctuating from 2% to 7%. This is consistent with acceleration of growth in the mid to late sixties, when the new colonial policy began to have a positive effect on industrialization, and induced greater investment opportunities. Indeed, the decomposition of this difference between public dissaving and foreign investment confirms that growth accelerated in the late sixties, inducing an overall budget deficit of 5% of GDP in 1971, whereas in the late fifties and early sixties the deficit was less than 2%.

60. To understand Angolan development in the late colonial period, it is important to examine relative price movements, as suggested by the ratio of output deflators in Portugal and the United States and in Angola, given that the nominal effective exchange rate measured with equal shares for the two countries remained fixed until 1971, and only registered a slight

revaluation in 1971 and 1973. A real devaluation of about 6% over the second half of the fifties is evident, exactly offset by a real revaluation over the second half of the sixties, and stability of the real exchange rate in between. In the early seventies, however, there was a change in the macroeconomic balance, with the savings/investment gap disappearing in 1973, and a real revaluation of 20% developing between 1971 and 1973, and of 25% between 1973 and 1975. It is clear that the extraordinary improvement in the terms of trade may make Angola in the early seventies another example of the so-called Dutch disease, observed in many developing countries, whereby manufacturing is discouraged and loses com3petitiveness due to the export of mineral resources.

61. The real appreciation of the Angolan currency also appears to be a strong reason to doubt that the coffee-led industrialization could ever have turned colonial Angola into a newly-industrializing country, even without strong protective barriers. The income elasticity of imports was originally close to 2, but it was negative in 1972 - a consequence of the change in the payments regime - and fell below 1 in 1973. A comparison of receipts from trade taxes and imports does not suggest an increase in protection, but the elasticity remains about 1.5, suggesting that the level might be considerable in light of the free-trade objective. In any event, given the available evidence, the demise of coffee-led industrialization was due largely to oil and exchange rate appreciation rather than changes in tariffs, given that the changes in payments regime implied stricter exchange controls.

62. The oil boom thus obscured the fragility of the industrialization pattern brought about by the combination of primary product exports and a rising urban population, increasingly made up of soldiers, as well as a growing group of settlers and mixed groups, with no political allegiance to colonial rule. Put another way, the policies of 1965 and 1971 did not prevent a duality in Angolan economic development. The peasantry, and to a much lesser degree, the urban worker may have in fact suffered from perverse changes in the distribution of income during the process. Gross domestic product per capita in 1972 was about $200. While this places Angola among the highest levels in sub-Saharan Africa, it masks large discrepancies between the income of the white and "assimilado" population and the remaining 90%. Per capita income of the black population was less than 10% of average white and "assimilado" incomes (though there were significant variations in the latter category). In addition to this perverse pattern of income distribution, education and health standards did not significantly differ from the ones observed in African countries with lower incomes per head. This suggests that, whatever the effect of colonial rule in bringing Angola to the middle-income level in the early seventies, it did not bring higher social welfare at the time of independence (See Table 9 for some Angolan social indicators). Moreover, even at similar income levels, there were qualitative differences between the social services available to the African population relative to the Portuguese soldiers or even the population of Portuguese descent.

E. ECONOMY AND SOCIETY AT INDEPENDENCE

63. The revolution of April 1974 in Portugal led to a decisive political opening in all territories under Portuguese administration. Though at the time the war was not very intense in Angola, the Portuguese revolution did not put an immediate end to it. There were three cease-fire agreements, the last of which was signed about the middle of the year. Meanwhile, several incidents occurred in Luanda, giving rise to racial confrontations. The major economic consequences of these incidents were a strike explosion, especially a strike on the part of the stevedores and other port workers, and the total destruction of shops established in the African residential area ("muceque"). The port strike was important for two reasons. In view of the strategic importance of seaports in the Angolan economy, the interruption of port activities was reflected in almost all other economic activities. Secondly, the hardship involved in loading and unloading ships made the workers more aware of how low the pay had become, given the change in political environment. Another crucial link of the colonial economy with the rest of the world was cut when the banks also went on strike. There, the great majority of clerks was white or mixed; nevertheless, the strike found a virtually complete acceptance.

64. The destruction of the muceque shops also had a major economic and social impact. These shops were owned by Portuguese traders who controlled almost all the distribution of staples and other essential commodities. The muceque merchants were a symbol of colonial oppression, which was reinforced every day since the shops made evident how weak the purchasing power of black families was. Customers also found falsified products, weighing and measuring frauds as well as threatening and racist behavior. Among whites, the muceque business was seen as the result either of the lack of skill or capital to set up another commercial activity. The muceque merchants and, to a lesser extent, the traders in the bush, were led to exploit all the opportunities for quick profit at the expense of the native population, so as to get enough capital to start a more comfortable - so called "rich"-business. The resentment against these merchants made them a logical target for anti-colonial feelings among the population.

65. The bush merchants were not only devoted to sell but also to buy products from peasants and re-sell them to wholesalers. These dealers went out of business later than the muceque dealers did, and rarely as a result of direct violence upon them. Most fled when overall village safety was at stake or the threat of agitation became intense. When these two groups of merchants vanished, a source of social tension and occasional racial conflict ended but a serious problem came to the fore: the supply and distribution channels vanished and no alternative arrangements were in place. The lack of internal trade activity, together with the existing military and political conditions created an atmospher a) If the colonial economy was first hit by the deterioration of foreign trade and commercial and financial activities, the entire colonial society quickly collapsed after civil rights were restored for the whole population. People responded in a way that seemed to reflect the importance of their roots in the

country: most of the adults made plans to leave while many of their grown children born in Angola, mixed as well as white, initially chose to stay. Those plans notwithstanding, a massive exodus of the Portuguese population began.

66. Beginning in the last quarter of 1974, over-invoiced goods began to be supplied against import contracts, as a way to smuggle out foreign currency, further reducing the quantity of goods imported, since prices had also increased sharply in the wake of the oil crisis. The production stoppages also explain why machinery imports fell by a much greater percentage than imports of consumer goods. A good example is the pattern of automobile imports, which were subject to quantitative restrictions. In 1974, the overall figures fell by 50% relative to 1970, and the share of commercial vehicles dropped from 38% in 1970 to 10% during the same period. Value figures reported in the 1974 Report of the Bank of Angola show a 15% increase in 1971, no change in 1972/73 and a drop of 50% in 1974. For export trade, due to a terms of trade improvement of about 75% implied by the oil price rises, quantities were slightly reduced but values almost doubled.

67. In contrast to most of the colonial period, on the eve of independence, the financial situation of the country was excellent. However, the economy was quickly disintegrating, with the collapse of distribution networks and the subsequent fall in production in 1975. Against the background of declines of 30% in economic activity and even higher figures for exports, small industry geared to the domestic market was temporarily stimulated by wage increases in 1974. According to the booklet of official statistics for 1974, food industries increased output by 25% and textile industries increased by over 40%.

68. After the mid-1974 cease-fire agreements with the Portuguese, an intense social and political upheaval, soon to have significant military consequences, was felt throughout the country, but mostly in Luanda. At year-end, the Alvor agreement, between the three parties recognized by the colonial authority, namely the Popular Movement for the Liberation of Angola (MPLA), the National Front for the Liberation of Angola (FNLA) and the National Union for the Total Independence of Angola (UNITA) established the date of independence as November 11th, 1975 and determined the conditions for the transition government. It was formed by an equal number of Ministers from each one of the three Movements as well as from the Portuguese Government. A triumvirate performed the functions of Prime Minister according to a monthly rotation. The Portuguese Army as well as armed people attached to the three Movements formed the Mixed Armed Force of Angola.

69. Only two months after the transition government was sworn in, though, new encounters took place between the MPLA and FNLA, simultaneously with widespread armed robbery in the muceques, leading the urban population to feel more and more insecure. By the middle of 1975, when the transition government was almost paralysed, a reconciliation attempt took place in Nakuru, Kenya, resulting in a protocol signed by the three different

parties. However, this protocol did not last longer than a few weeks and was followed by open war between the liberation movements, this time involving UNITA as well. In August 1975, the Angolan territory was divided into three zones, with Luanda held by the MPLA and the Portuguese Army.

70. A short while after the transition government began, the Minister of the Economy, who had been selected by the Portuguese, submitted an Economic Programm for accelerated growth based on the existing infrastructure and on the production levels obtained before the Revolution. A reduction in foreign dependence and a better distribution of resources were other objectives included in the development policy recommended by the transition government. To follow this program, Angola had to keep growth rates equal to those of the past years and correct some of the previous distortions, especially in income distribution. This required respect for the Alvor Agreement, no resort to violence and the possibility of carrying out elections and forming a stable government. At the same time, it was necessary that most of the technical and professional labor force remain in Angola. As none of those conditions were met, the program did not begin to be implemented.

71. When shortly after the cease-fire of Nakuru, violence resumed, there was a sudden change in the attitude of the Portuguese. Very quickly, nearly all farms were abandoned not only by the farmers themselves but also by workers who had no pay and feared military attacks. The same applied to most of the small and middle-sized industries, while commercial activity in towns was mostly confined to drawing down inventories. With the interruption in supplies, and the massive flight of Portuguese owners and technicians, together with the paralysis of most banks, Angolan industry suffered a devastating blow from which it has not yet recovered. The same characteristics manifested themselves in construction activity, which was already in recession. The exodus of the Portuguese, both from public and private management and other technical activities, created an enormous vacuum, since an insignificant number of Angolans had the chance to get proper skills, and some of those who did also left the country.

72. As the colonial administration ceased to function without being replaced by any of the liberation movements, taxes were not collected and maintenance of infrastructure ceased. Large businesses (commercial, agricultural or mining) kept their local management but limited their activities as much as possible to a mere presence. For security reasons, even oil production was suspended for a few months. As far as transportation was concerned, the Luanda airport and the seaports operated under top priority of evacuating the Portuguese people and their belongings. It is estimated that Angola lost by destruction or smuggling 75% of its stock of trucks, which was about 27,000 vehicles. Finally as a result of the country's division into three warring zones, any regular long distance communications, including postal services, were suspended.

73. When Luanda was taken by the MPLA, the FNLA and UNITA ministers took cover in their own zones of influence. The first foreign troops entered the country and on November 11, 1975, which had been designated as Independence Day, the colonial period ended and all the conditions for a protracted economic and social crisis were in place.

ANNEX I

Table I.1

ANGOLA

PRINCIPAL EXPORTS (%), 1950-1973

Year	Coffee	diamonds	Oil	Sisal	Other
1950	34.0	9.0	0.0	9.0	48.0
1951	48.0	7.0	0.0	10.0	35.0
1952	41.0	11.0	0.0	10.0	38.0
1953	53.0	10.0	0.0	5.0	32.0
1954	44.0	12.0	0.0	6.0	38.0
1955	44.0	12.0	0.0	7.0	37.0
1956	47.0	10.0	0.0	6.0	37.0
1957	42.0	13.0	0.0	6.0	39.0
1958	41.0	15.0	0.0	6.0	38.0
1959	39.0	17.0	0.0	8.0	36.0
1960	35.0	14.0	0.0	11.0	40.0
1961	36.0	17.0	0.0	8.0	39.0
1962	44.0	13.0	0.0	10.0	33.0
1963	40.0	16.0	0.0	12.0	32.0
1964	49.0	13.0	0.0	8.0	30.0
1965	47.0	16.0	0.0	5.0	32.0
1966	48.0	18.0	0.0	5.0	29.0
1967	52.0	18.0	0.0	3.0	27.0
1968	45.0	17.0	1.0	3.0	34.0
1969	34.0	20.0	5.0	2.0	39.0
1970	32.0	19.0	11.0	2.0	36.0
1971	33.0	13.0	18.0	2.0	34.0
1972	28.0	11.0	25.0	2.0	34.0
1973	26.0	10.0	30.0	2.0	32.0

Source: Bank of Angola, Annual Reports

ANNEX I

Table I.2

ANGOLA

MAJOR IMPORTS, 1952 - 73

Goods	1952	1961	1968	1973
Fabrics	14	11	6	5
Wines and spirits	10	11	6	3
Vehicles and accessories	7	6	12	11
Iron works and bar	6	8	10	8
Railroad tracks and other materials	4	13	-	-
Industrial machinery and appliances	3	2	7	13
Gasoline and fuel oil	4	4	2	3
Other Imports	52	45	57	57
TOTAL	100	100	100	100

SOURCE: Estatisticas Industriais da Direccao dos Servicos de Estatisticas, Luanda 1974.

ANNEX I

Table I.3

ANGOLA

PRODUCTION OF MAJOR AGRICULTURAL PRODUCTS (1952-1973)

(thousand tons)

ITEMS	1952	1961	1968	1973
Cotton seed	21	13	41	79
Coffee (Rob./Arabica)	51	68	198	225
Manioc	-	-	-	1100
Corn (b)	70	150	142	300
Sisal	25	59	58	60
Sugar cane	-	643	69	967
Palm-oil (a)	20	_	47	48

(a) Estimates
(b) Acquisitions by "Gr]mio de Milho do Ultramar"

SOURCE: Relatôrio e Contas do Banco de Angola

ANNEX I

Table I.4

ANGOLA

POPULATION AND GDP BY TYPE OF ACTIVITY (%)

BRANCHES OF ACTIVITY	POPULATION			PRODUCTION (GDP)	
	1960 (1)	1970 (2)		1966	1970 (3)
PRIMARY SECTOR: (Agric., Forestry and Livestock)	83.0	76.0	32.0	32.0	23.0
SECONDARY SECTOR: (Mining, Manufacturing and Construction)	14.0	11.0	38.0	14.0	21.0
TERTIARY SECTOR: (Transportation, Services and Public Administration)	3.0	13.0	30.0	54.0	56.0

SOURCE: (1) Adapted from "La Guerre en Angola", Mario de Andrade and Marc Olivier, Paris: Maspero, 1971;

(2) GDP is from a sample of 80% of output reported in "Servindo o futuro de Angola", Costa Oliveira, Luanda, 1972.

(3) GDP includes non Monetary Flows (about 20%) which are all ascribed to agriculture, according to estimates in IV Plano de Fomento.

ANNEX I

Table I.5

ANGOLA

MANUFACTURING OUTPUT BY MAJOR INDUSTRY GROUP, 1966-70

(PERCENTAGES)

ITEMS	1966	1967	1968	1969	1970
Food and drinks	46	46	45	42	43
Fabrics/shoes	10	10	10	10	10
Chemical and oil products	19	15	15	16	14
Non metal mineral	8	7	7	8	7
Metallurgical products	2	2	3	3	5
Machinery and equipment	1	6	5	6	6
Others	14	14	15	15	15
Total	100	100	100	100	100
Rate of growth of Total	-	26	22	19	17
SHARE OF EXPORTS	20	22	21	21	18

SOURCE: Estatisticas Industriais e Direccao dos Servicos de Estatistica (Luanda 1974). Share of exportable production adapted from IV Plano de Fomento (1974-79), vol. II and Relatorio e Contas do Banco de Angola.

ANNEX I

Table I.6

ANGOLA

BALANCE OF PAYMENTS (1955-1973)

(million escudos)

ITEMS	1955 (c)			1960 (a)			1965 (b)			1971 (c)			1973 (c)		
	Debit	Credit	Balance	Debit	Credit	Balance	Debit	Credit	Balance	Debit	Credit	Balance	Debit	Credit	Balance
1. Current Account Bal.	2362	2662	300	3316	3089	-227	7276	7907	631	13958	12075	-1883	15904	17187	1283
a) Merchandise	1743	2539	796	2411	2884	473	4860	5065	205	11388	9166	-2222	12300	14475	2175
b) Invisible Trade				905	204	-701	2416	2842	426	2570	2909	537	3604	2712	-892
Tourism+Priv.Transfers				489	28	-461	875	81	-794	879	58	-821	1066	97	-969
Transport+Insurance ...				42	118	76	164	258	94	331	898	567	116	1274	1158
Capital Revenue	< 619	123	-496	296	-	-296	501	34	-467	210	12		783	28	-755
Others (including official) ..				84	58	-26	876	2469	1593	1150	1941	791	1639	1313	-326
2. Capital Flows..........				-	66	66	359	522	163	808	878	70	1522	540	-982
3. Official Reserves ..... (increase -)	1743	2539	-796	3316	3149	167	7635	8429	-794	14766	12953	1813	17426	17727	-301

SOURCE: (a) Cited by W. Marques in "Problemas do Desenvolvimento Económico de Angola", 1962
(b) III Plano de Fomento (1968-73)
(c) Relatório e Contas do Banco de Angola

ANNEX I

Table I.7

ANGOLA

MONETARY DEVELOPMENT, 1960-73

(PERCENTAGES)

ITEMS	1960	1965	1970	1971	1973
Time Deposits/M2	1.0	4.0	19.8	21.2	24.3
M2/GDP	30.5	35.7	50.5	59.2	56.8

Source: Adapted from "Relatorio e Contas do Banco de Angola."

ANNEX I

Table I.8

ANGOLA

GROSS DOMESTIC PRODUCTS, 1953-73

(MILLION ESCUDOS)

YEAR		CURRENT PRICES	1963 PRICES
1953	(1)	9078	9759
1961	(2)	12665	13890
1963	(2)	14820	14820
1965	(2)	19200	17167
1967	(2)	24633	19829
1969	(3)	33676	24042
1971	(4)	42078	27196
1973	(4)	58707	29391

SOURCE: (1) Adapted from "III Plano de Fomento: (1968-73):
(2) Gathered from "Estimativas Abreviadas do Rendimento Nationcal do Ultramar Portuges", MERNU, Lisboa, 1969;
(3) Gathered from "servindo o Futuro de Angola", Costa Oliveira, Luanda, 1972;
(4) Gathered from World Tables, Vol. I-Economic Data;

ANNEX I

Table I.9

ANGOLA

SELECTED SOCIAL INDICATORS, MID-1970S

POPULATION	
Total (1975; in thousand)	6,687.1
Annual Growth Rate (1970-75; percent)	2.5
Urban Share (1975; percent)	17.8
GNP per capita (1975; US$)	404.0
EDUCATION	
Adult literacy rate (1970; percent)	7.6
Primary enrollment rate (1970)	59.0
Secondary enrollment rate (1970)	7.0
Primary Pupil - Teacher Ratio (1970)	44.0
HEALTH AND NUTRITION	
Infant Mortality rate (1975; per thousand)	166.6
Life Expectancy (1975; years)	39.0
Population per physician (1970)	9130.0
Calorie Supply per capita (1975; percentage of requirements)	80.2

Source: World Bank, EDP date files

BIBLIOGRAPHY

REPORTS

Anuarios Estatisticos de Angola (1952 to 1965)

Estimativas Abreviadas do Rendimento Nacional de Angola do Ultramar Portugues, Lisbon: Missao de Estudo do Rendimento Nacional do Ultramar Portugues (MERNC), 1969

Informacao Estatistica, Instituto Nacional de Estatistica de Angola (1970 to 1974)

Planos do Fomanto de Angola (1o, 2o, 3o e 4o)

Relatorio e Contas do Banco de Angola (1953 to 1974)

Relatorios da Secretaria Provincial de Economia, 1962-68 and 1972, Direccao Provincial dos Servicos de Economia de Angola

BOOKS AND ARTICLES

Andrade, Mario and Olivier, Marc., La Guerre en Angola, Paris: Ed.F. Maspero - Cahiers libres, 1971

Bender, Gerald J., Angola Under the Portugese - The Myth and the Reality, (Berkeley: University of California Press, 1978)

Bhagavan, M.R., Angola's Political Economy 1875-85 (Uppsala, Scandinavian Institute of African Studies, 1986)

Bhagavan, M.R., Prospects for Socialist Industrialization, Uppsala, Scandianivan Institute of African Studies, 1986)

Birmingham, D., Trade and Conflict in Angola (1483-1790). Oxford: Clarendon Press, 1966

Birmingham, D. and Martin, P.M. History of Central Africa, London: Longman, 1983

Carreira, Antonio, Angola, da escravantana ao trabalho livro, Lisbon: Ed. Arcadia, 1973

Castro, Armando, O Sistema Colonial Portugues em Africa, Lisbon: Ed. Caminho, 1978

Cerqueira d'Ázevendo, Joao Maria, Subsidios para o Estado Economico de Angola nos Ultimos Com Anos, Luanda, 1950

Comte, Phillippe, L'abolition du travail force en Afrique Portugaise, policopiado, s/d

Costa Oliveira, Jose Eduardo, Servindo o Futuro de Angola, Luanda, 1972

Delgado, Ralph, Historia de Angola, Lisbon: Ed. do Banco de Angola

Dilolowa, Carlos R., Contribuicao a Historia Economica de Angola, Luanda: I.N.A., 1978

Duffy, James, A Question of Slaves, Oxford: Clarendon Press, 1966

Estermann, Carlos, Etnografia de Angola (Sudoests e Centro), Lisbon: Instituto de Investigacao Cientifica Tropical (I.I.C.T.)

Ferreira, Eduardo de Sousa, Aspectos do Colonialismo Portugues, Lisbon: Soara Nova, 1974

Founou, Bernard, Cours sur le Developpement de l'Áfrique - Amorce du Sous-developpment: La Traite Negriere, quelques donnees chiffrees, Institut Africain de Developpement Economique et de Planification (IADEP) - Dakar, March 1979

Goncalves, Antonio C. Kongo - Le Lignage contre l'Etat, I.I.C.T. e Univ. de Evora, 1985

Goncalvos, Jose, Le Developpment du Capitalisme Colonial en Angola, IADEP, Dakar, 1973

Goncalvos, Jose, Sobre a Economia Colonial de Angola, draft, Centro de Socio-Economia (CSE)/I.I.C.T., Lisbon, November 1987

Guerra, H., Angola, Estrutura Economica e Classes Sociais, Luanda, 1974

Guimaraos, A., Uma Correnie do Colonialismo Portugues, Livros Horizonte, 1984

Henderson, Lawrence W., Angola: Five Centuries of Conflict (Ithaca, Cornell University Press, 1979)

Historia de Angola, Rep. Popular de Angola, mimeo, s/d

Hodges, Tony, Angola to the 1990s: The Potential for Recovery (London, The Economist Intelligence Unit, 1987)

Kaplan, Irving (ed.), Angola: A Country Study (Washington, American University Area Handbook Series, 1979)

Kitchen, Helen (ed.), Angola, Mozambique and the West (New York, Praeger, 1987)

Klein, Herbert, "The Portugese Slave Trade from Angola in the 18th Century", Journal of Economic History, Dec. 1972

Macedo, Jorge Braga de, Notas sobre a Historia Economica de Angola, mimeo, Luanda: CCFAA, 1975

Macedo, Jorge Braga de, Colonial Development of Angola: The rise and fall of a South Atlantic link?, mimeo, Yale University, March 1978

Macedo, Jorge Braga de; Cristina Corado and Manuel Porto, the timing and sequencing of trade liberalization episodos in Portugal, draft, Country Policy Department, The World Bank

Macedo, Jorge Braga de, "Collective Pegging to a Single Currency: The West African Monetary Union" in Economic Adjustment and Exchange Rates in Developing Countries, ed. by Sebastian Edwards and Liaquat Ahamed, NBER, the University Chicago Press, 1986

Macedo, Jorge Braga de. Interpendencia Economica, Sistema Monetario Internacional e Integracao Portugeuesa, ed. Banco de Fomento Nacional, Lisbon, 1977

Macedo, Jose, Autonomia de Angola, Lisbon, 1910

Marcum, John, The Angolan Revolution: The Anatomy of an Explosion (1950-62), Cambridge, MA: MIT Press, 1969) and The Angolan Revolution: Volume Two - Exile Politics and Guerilla Warfare (1962-76), (Cambridge, MA: MIT Press, 1978)

Martin, Phyllis, M., Historical Dictionary of Angola, Metuchen, N.J., The Scarecrow Press Inc., 1980

Memoria a respeito dos escravos, Communicacao em 1973, reeditada por Cadernos "Homen e Sociedade", Porto: Pub. Escorpiao, 1977

Mendes, A., O trabalho assalariado em Angola, Lisbon: I.S.C.S.P.U., 1966

Randless, W.G.L., L'Ancien Royaume du Kongo des origines a la fin du XIX siecle, Paris: Ed. Mouton, 1968

Redianha, Jose, Distribuicao, Etuica de Angola, Luanda: Centro de Informacao e Turismo de Angola (C.I.T.A.), 1971

Santos, Fernando, B., Angola na hora dramatica da descolonizacao, Lisbon: Ed. Prolo, 1975

Smith, Cervase C., The Third Portugese Empire (1825-1975), a Study in Economic Imperialism, Manchester University, 1986

Somerville, K., Angola, Politics, Economics and Society, London: Frances Pinter; Colorado: Lynne Rienner Inc., 1968

THE ANGOLAN ECONOMY IN COMPARATIVE PERSPECTIVE

1. This Annex presents some comparisons between the social and economic conditions of Angola and those of other countries in sub-Saharan Africa. Such comparisons are based on statistical data which are of especially poor quality and should therefore be viewed cautiously. 1/ Nevertheless, they can provide a useful general portrait of Angola's economic and social development in comparative perspective.

2. Social conditions in Angola are among the lower range of those found in low-income countries, where low-income countries are defined as those with 1986 per capita gross national products of US$425 or less. In Angola, life expectancy at birth in 1986 was 44 years, compared to an average of 61 in low income countries and an average of 50 in sub-Saharan countries. Related social indicators also place Angola in the lower range of low-income countries. It is estimated that in 1985, 160 infants out of 1,000 born in Angola died before reaching one year of age. This compares with an average of 69 for low-income countries and an average of 113 for sub-Saharan Africa.

3. Indicators of health conditions also place Angola in the lower range of low-income countries. Per capita daily calorie intake in Angola was estimated to be 1,926 in 1985 which compares to an average of 2,329 for low-income countries, and 2,024 for sub-Saharan Africa. The estimated population of 15,521 per physician in Angola in 1985 compares with an average of 5,410 for low-income countries (1984 data), and 23,760 for sub-Saharan Africa (1984 data).

4. While indicators of social conditions in Angola place it in the lower range of low-income countries, on the basis of per capita GNP, Angola would be placed in the lower range of lower middle-income countries. However, it should again be emphasized that in view of the incomplete data on the Angolan economy, any GNP estimates are necessarily crude. Keeping this caveat in mind, in 1987 Angolan per capita GNP was equivalent to US$537. This compares to a 1987 average of US$290 for low-income countries, US$330 for sub-Saharan African countries, and US$1200 for lower middle-income countries.

5. The structure of production in Angola differs from the average for sub-Saharan Africa in that agriculture and fisheries contribute a significantly smaller share of output. For example, from 1980-87, 21.0% of Angolan GDP at 1980 official prices came from agriculture and fisheries, 44.7% from industry, and 34.3% from services. This compares to a 1987 average in Sub-Saharan Africa of 33% from agriculture and fisheries, 28% from industry, and 40% from services. The difference is explained mainly by the impact of the war on rural areas and by the large share of oil output in Angolan GDP.

6. The structure of aggregate demand in Angola is much more oriented toward government consumption and away from private consumption in comparison

---

1/ In the intercountry comparisons that follow, data for countries other than Angola are from the World Bank's World Development Report 1989. (Oxford University Press: 1989), and World Development Report 1987 (Oxford University Press: 1987).

with most other countries in sub-Saharan Africa. From 1982-87, government consumption in Angola averaged 30% of GDP, private consumption averaged 52%, gross domestic investment averaged 17%, and exports of goods and non factor services averaged 42%. This compares with a 1987 average for Sub-Saharan Africa of 15% for government consumption, 72% for private consumption, 16% for gross domestic investment, and 25% for exports of goods and nonfactor services. The comparatively large weight of government consumption reflects mainly the burden of war expenditures on the budget. In Angola, defense accounted for almost 44% of recurrent expenditure in 1984-87. In addition, large expenditures are incurred for military equipment. In sub-Saharan Africa, defense expenditures averaged 11.2% of total central government expenditure in 1985.

7. In the area of government finance, Angola is notable for the large proportion of government revenue that it derives from the petroleum sector. In recent years this proportion has varied between 40% and 60% since fluctuations in oil prices introduce a strong element of instability in the budget. On the other hand, non-oil taxes are relatively low, averaging 10% of non-oil GDP in 1985-87. In sub-Saharan Africa, the average ratio of taxes to GNP was 17% in 1985.

8. The Angolan budget deficit, at 8% of GNP in 1985-87, is more than twice as large as the average for sub-Saharan Africa (3.3% of GNP in 1985). The budget deficit has been a major cause of the rapid growth of the broadly defined money stock in Angola, which has averaged 17% annually from 1982 to 1988. In Angola, this growth in the money supply did not result in open inflation in the official market because of tight and pervasive price controls and the fixed exchange rate, which at present is grossly overvalued. However, strong repressed inflationary pressures are evident in Angola in the extreme scarcities of goods offered at official prices and in the very large differences between prices in the official and parallel markets (which tend to range between 1 to 20 and 1 to 60).

9. The structure of Angolan merchandise exports is very unbalanced, due to the extreme dependence on petroleum exports. In Angola, fuel and mineral exports comprise more than 90% of total exports. Diamonds account for most of the rest. The average sub-Saharan African country derived 48% of its merchandise export earnings from fuels, minerals, and metals, and 40% from other primary commodities. The only sub-Saharan African countries which share Angola's extremely unbalanced dependence on the output of one sector are Zambia and Nigeria, which derive 93% and 91% respectively of their export earnings from mineral exports (copper and oil).

10. Angola's holdings of gross international reserves are characteristic of the low levels generally maintained by low and lower-middle income countries. Angola's reserve holdings from 1985-88 covered on average about 1.2 months of imports. This compares with a 1987 average of 2.1 months coverage for sub-Saharan African countries. In the area of external debt, Angola's situation is also fairly characteristic of other sub-Saharan African countries. In 1987, Angola's external debt was about 115 percent of GNP. In 1988, its external debt was 244 percent of export earnings. Fully servicing its debt in 1988 would have required almost half of Angola's export earnings. On average, sub-Saharan African external public debt was 81 percent of GNP in 1987. Debt as a percentage of export earnings averaged 330 percent. The average ration of scheduled debt service to goods and service exports was 61 percent.

GOVERNMENT INSTITUTIONS

General Aspects

1. The Popular Movement for the Liberation of Angola, MPLA, was founded in December 1956 with the objective of liberating the country from colonial rule. The armed struggle against the Portuguese colonial regime began in February 1961. After a period of struggles with other rival liberation movements in 1975, the MPLA assumed control of the Government when Independence was proclaimed in November 1975.

2. In December 1977 the MPLA became a party, and renamed itself MPLA - Labor Party (MPLA-PT). The MPLA-PT declared itself the "leading force of the Angolan State and Society," organized and acting "according to the principles of Democratic Centralism" and having as its strategic objective the construction of socialism. Party structures are visible in all aspects of the country's social, economic and political activity. The MPLA-PT is associated in particular with all major decisions concerning the country's economic management. In addition to guiding the activities of administrative departments, enterprises and trade unions, which are the three focal points of the country's economic activity, the Party also defines basic principles and policies. The Constitutional Law reinforces the dominant position of the MPLA-PT, particularly through Article 2 which gives the Party "the economic and social leadership of the State in its efforts to construct a Socialist Society."

The Organization of the MPLA-PT

3. The MPL-PT's higher organs are:

(i) The Congress, at the national level, whose functions include electing the President of the Party, determining the orientation of internal and external policy;

(ii) the Conference, held at national, provincial, municipal and communal levels, which is responsible for orienting regional activities according to the decisions of the Congress and of other central organs of the Party;

(iii) the Assembly of Members, held at the level of base organizations, which are structured in cells and committees formed in work places, residential units, etc., and are grouped spatially within the country's administrative framework, namely communes, municipalities and provinces;

(iv) the Central Committee, which ensures the direction of the Party in the periods between the Congresses, and the Political Bureau, which directs political activity between Central Committee meetings; and

(v) the President of the MPLA-PT, who is a full member of the Central Committee and of the Political Bureau, elected by the Congress. The President of the People's Republic of Angola is the President of the MPLA-PT.

4. The MPLA-PT guides and directs the work of popular and social organizations, such as the National Union of Angolan Workers (UNTA), which is a

non-Party organization. The Party's orientations are transmitted through the influence of MPLA-PT members within this organization.

General Organizational Aspects of the State

5. Two organization charts are attached to this Annex, one showing the relations between government and party organs (Chart 1) and the other showing the main structure of the Government (Chart 2). As indicated in Chart I, each of the designated "spheres" of government is linked to a corresponding party unit. The People's Assembly is Angola's supreme organ of State power and it normally meets twice a year. Law 2/86 introduced important modifications in government structure. New changes were introduced at the beginning of 1989. The Head of State is also the Head of the government.

6. Two other organs of the State apparatus should be noted, the Council of Ministers and the Council of Defense and Security. The Council of Ministers has the traditional functions of organizing, directing and coordinating all the ministries' activities. It is also charged with preparing the National Plan and the General State Budget for discussion and approval by the People's Assembly. The Council of Defense and Security was created in 1984 and assumes the functions of the Council of Ministers in the periods between meetings of the latter. It is presided by the President and constituted by the Ministers of Defense, Interior and Security, the three Ministers of State and others. Since it is a more flexible body than the Council of Ministers, it has been particularly important in making decisions regarding economic policy.

7. Territorially, of Angola is divided for political and administrative purposes into provinces, municipalities, communes, neighborhoods and settlements. The People's Assemblies are the highest organs of State power at each level of the territorial division of the country. The executive organs of these Assemblies are the Provincial, Municipal and Communal Commisariats. The Commissariats are directed by a Commissar who is the representative of the President and of the Government at the provincial level. Law 8/81 which establishes local state institutions, has not been applied. Therefore, certain basic legal instruments for decentralizing administrative actions have not been created.

8. The lack of operating regulations is in fact, a quite common situation in Angolan economic administration. Thus, operating regulations do not exist for the National Price Directorate, for example, or for a large proportion of the National Directorates covered by the Ministries. These institutions were created, given personnel and other means for functioning, but were not given operating instructions: what and how they should do was not defined. Nor were their employees's jobs defined. Thus, a large part of public administration lacks a description of the activities it is supposed to perform.

9. An Economic Commision presided by the Head of State and including by 13 Ministers was created in 1988 to discuss all the important decisions in the area of economic policy and in particular to approve the legislation and all the more important measures required by the implementation of the SEF program. The Commission comprises three sub-committees for economic affairs, for the productive sectors and for social affairs, respectively. The Commission is supported by a technical committee, which prepares the proposals of decisions, the draft laws and the analysis of the problems submitted for discussion.

THE SYSTEM OF NATIONAL ACCOUNTS IN THE PEOPLE'S REPUBLIC OF ANGOLA

Introduction

1. This Annex has the following purposes: (a) to provide a brief presentation of the current system of national accounts and of its scope and limitations as regards national product and expenditure; and (b) to analyze the difficulties involved in establishing a unified system of national accounts. It considers the available information from each of the three approaches usually followed in compiling national accounts: factor income, production, and expenditure. Some general remarks are then made about requirements for a unified set of accounts. Finally a first effort is made to estimate GNP per capita in US dollar terms.

GDP Estimates Using the Factor Income Approach

2. The gross domestic product at factor cost (GDP fc) refers only to official transactions, and consists of total factor income, as presented in the various ministries' reports on financial execution of the National Plan. Although limited in scope, the methodology for this calculation is satisfactory. However, the quality of the calculations is constrained by the enterprises' accounting capability. In addition, the National Accounts Center does not have the direct access to the enterprises' balance sheets that would enable it to assess the quality of the data. Information by enterprise is furnished only in the reports on industry and fishing; the remaining execution reports provide only aggregates, some of these being incomplete, so that indirect estimates must be used, with varying degrees of reliability. It must also be noted that the calculations are performed by the supervisory ministries, and therefore do not correspond exactly to the standard economic classifications for output by sector. For example, sugar cane as well as sugar production is included in the industry accounts, because agroindustry enterprises are supervised by the Ministry of Industry.

3. The following paragraphs describe the scope and the quality of the calculations of value added by sector.

(a) Agriculture, Forestry and Livestock

This includes the activities of state enterprises, associations, and the output of small-scale farmers traded by the state through the Ministry of Internal Commerce. It also includes Frescangol marketing (i.e., the distribution of imported meat). It excludes on-farm consumption and sales to the parallel market. It is estimated that only 10% of output passes through the official market.

(b) Manufacturing and Mining

This includes output from state, mixed, and private enterprises, together with the production and processing of sugarcane by state enterprises in Benguela and Bengo. The calculation of value added in this sector covers approximately 80% of total activities.

(c) Fishing

This includes fishing itself (with six state enterprises, one being a joint venture with the Soviet Union, and fishermen's cooperatives); fish processing (ten state enterprises, together with the enterprise Manpesa in Benguela, which was excluded from the 1983 and 1985 figures because of delays in the provision of data); ship repair (four enterprises, three belonging to the state, and one being a joint venture with Portuguese nationals, i.e., the former Sorefame); salt extraction (accounts for the two state enterprises are included, although there are certain private enterprises that were excluded, mainly in Namibe province); and wholesale fish marketing (four enterprises, retailing being part of the commercial sector). Not included are output produced by fishermen not belonging to organizations (this being sold in the parallel market), own consumption, and the output from two salt-extracting enterprises in Namibe. In addition, the accounts exclude half the landings resulting from operating agreements with non-Angolan enterprises, although the tax on fishing rights paid by foreign fleets is included.

(d) Transportation and Communications

This includes enterprises operating road transportation (64), rail transportation (four), airlines (two, one of which is TAAG), ports (five), and communications (three). Accounts in this sector do not include transportation-related enterprises supervised by other ministries, and whose accounts are reported by those ministries, such as fishing and internal commerce. There are also some transportation-related enterprises whose accounts are not recorded anywhere (as in the case of industrial enterprises). The accounts also excluded small private freight and passenger carriers estimates.

(e) Construction

This includes state and private enterprises concerned with construction, engineering, the manufacture of construction materials, and the Angola engineering laboratory. It excludes self-construction and construction by non-Angolan enterprises operating in the oil sector (drilling activities are regarded as part of the oil sector, but the accounts for the construction of houses, buildings and other works are not recorded anywhere), and in the energy sector (i.e., Gamek in Kwanza). It is estimated that value-added calculations cover only 50% of the sector.

(f) Petroleum (and LNG)

The accounts include: indirect taxes, profits, payroll, and depreciation (Sonangol); and direct taxes from non-Angolan enterprises, and refinery profits. They exclude payroll, profits, rentals, depreciation, interest from non-Angolan enterprises, and Sonangol rentals and interest. Although Sonangol does not regularly provide balance sheets for inspection and recording in the national accounts, the statistics are reliable, and include about 70% of value added generated by the sector.

(g) Electricity1/

This includes only payroll, depreciation, profits and direct taxes relating to the five electric power enterprises in the sector. It does not include rentals and interest for electric power enterprises, or household production of charcoal and fuelwood.

(h) Commerce

This includes retailing, hotels and catering, worker's food services, and social consumption (e.g., hospitals, creches, etc.). Retail value added is calculated from the commercial fund (**fundo mercantil**)--i.e., deposits in BNA (the National Bank of Angola) by private, state and cooperative retail enterprises--and from the marketing margin (officially set at 25%), excluding administrative expenses (published in the Ministry of Commerce's execution report). This results in a value added of between 15% and 18% of GDP. The commercial fund information provided by BNA is comparable to the data in the National Plan's financial execution report, so that the statistics used are cross-checked. Not included are the parallel market, the wholesale fish market (which is included in fishing), or the supply of spare parts (which is included in the transportation subsector). Data quality is low, because calculations are based on subjective assessments.

(i) Services

This includes payrolls for central and provincial governments, education, health, culture, social services (excluding creches, which are free) and defense. The source is OGE, and data quality is good. Excluded are payments in kind to the armed forces (i.e., food, drink, tobacco, and clothing). Food baskets provided by BNA, the Ministry of Planning and the oil and energy industries are bought by government personnel, and therefore regarded for accounting purposes as part of the commercial fund. In the case of the Ministry of Planning, the baskets are bought from Angoship, a private enterprise providing supplies for vessels. The enterprise uses the resulting revenue (in Kz) to buy US Dollars from the Government at the official price.

4. For calculating gross domestic product at market prices (GDP mp), indirect taxes are added to the gross domestic product at factor cost (GDP fc), and subsidies are subtracted. Indirect taxes include those applied to the production and consumption of industrial alcohol, petroleum products, liquified gases, domestically produced beer, imported beer, and other taxes on production and consumption, together with national reconstruction stamp taxes, tax payment certifications (selo de verba), the oil industry output tax, export and import levies, taxes on services, and the people's resistance tax. The people's resistance tax is incorrectly classified as an indirect tax, because it is really a surtax applied to income taxes payable by natural and legal persons. The sources used in calculating indirect taxes are the National Plan's financial execution reports (which contain

---

1/ Water is excluded from the country.

the enterprises' own figures). These show a small statistical discrepancy with the data published by the Ministry of Finance (which indicate the figures for budget execution). Included as subsidies in the calculation of national accounts are all losses published in the National Plan's financial execution reports; i.e., total subsidies to state enterprises (UEEs) are equal to OGE transfers (i.e., losses from UEEs plus allocations of available own resources and price subsidies) plus loans to enterprises from BNA, covering the difference between total losses and resources provided by OGE. Such a classification is incorrect, because the loans are not used solely to finance the enterprises' deficits, even if interest and amortization payments are later deferred.

GDP Estimates Using the Product Approach

5. In 1986 the Angolan authorities, with the assistance of the United Nations Development Program (UNDP), began preparing preliminary estimates of GDP based on the value added production approach using 1980 official prices. While these estimates are still tentative, they represent an improvement in the estimates of subsistence agricultural production and are not as distorted by delays in delivery of the required information. The estimates have been prepared for 1980-87 using data mostly from the enterprise level, complemented by indirect estimates and ministry information to complete the available data series and to check the reliability of the aggregates. The defined sectors follow the Angolan classification of economic activities, but can easily be translated into the standard UN classification.

6. The following paragraphs describe in more detail the estimates of the valued added production of each of these sectors.

(a) Industry. This comprises extractive and manufacturing activities: energy, mining, metallurgy, metal construction, electronics, machinery, chemistry, rubber, printing, lumber, paper, construction materials, transport materials, glass ceramics, textiles, clothing, leather goods, food, beverages, coffee, sugar, tobacco and other manufacturing. Production is mostly by state, mixed, and private firms as well as foreign enterprises, which account for about 90% of the total. The remaining component comes from estimates of the output of small producers not under government supervision, which were based on previous studies of production capacity and indirect information.

(b) Construction. This includes the construction activities of state enterprises (under the Ministries of Construction, Energy, and Petroleum), foreign firms, and self-construction. It includes self-construction estimates, based on population growth, size of a standard house, cement consumption, and international indicators.

(c) Agriculture, Livestock, Forestry and Fishing. This includes farming, cattle raising, forestry, and fishing activities of state enterprises and of about 850,000 small producers working in associations or individually. It includes production for self-consumption as well as production for the market by state enterprises and small producers. It includes a self-consumption estimate, based on the size of the farming areas, average productivity, nutritional habits, and population growth.

(d) Transportation and Communication. This comprises railroads, air, coast and ocean shipping activities, including loading, unloading, and expedition services. Data on communication services were collected from the relevant enterprises under the supervision of the Ministries of Transportation and Communication. Highway transportation of passengers and freight were collected from public enterprises under the supervision of the Ministry of Transportation. These estimates are currently being revised to include missed information and add private transportation.

(e) Commerce. This includes retail and wholesale activities, rural trade, hotels and foreign trade. The commercialization margins were estimated from state enterprise sales and purchase data. Preliminary estimates of the value in the parallel market are also included. The product approach estimates of the value added in the commerce sector are an improvement over the previous factor income approach because they include the commercialization margins for trade in rural areas and foreign trade. They are also based on actual measure of commercial margins rather than the fixed official margins used in the factor approach. The commercialization margin from oil exports is not yet included, but exports of oil are included in the industrial value added at FOB prices.

(f) Services. Estimates of the value added in the service are based on the budgeted salaries in the sector.

GNP from the Expenditure Side

7. There is no official calculation of GDP from the expenditure side. Accounts for the public, financial and external sectors are incomplete, and their structure is unsuited to the preparation of national accounts. In addition, there is no coordination between the Ministry of Planning, the Ministry of Finance, and BNA in the use of data. Examples of the inadequacy of existing accounts are that the government budget makes no provision for interest payments on external debt payable by the Treasury, it does not record external debt managed by BNA, and the government accounts do not provide any means for calculating gross fixed capital formation (GDCF) by the Government and by state enterprises. Balance of payments figures for capital goods imports are not reliable. Because data on long-term loans are also incomplete, it is difficult even to estimate such imports indirectly, i.e., on the basis of capital flows.

Requirements for the Implementation of a Unified System of National Accounts

8. Developing a reliable, unified system of national accounts requires that it become a political priority. This will be done only when the government is convinced of the importance of national accounts for economic planning, monitoring, and evaluation. Once the political decision has been taken, establishment of a unified system of national accounts will depend on three factors: organization, discipline, and resource.

9. As regards organization, it is recommended that a Department of National Accounts be established, subordinate to the Director of Planning at the Ministry of Planning. This measure is justified by the need to establish a link to BNA and the Ministry of Finance. Currently, there is merely a project (under an agreement with the UNDP) for establishing a system of national accounts, in which the national project director must fulfill a number of extremely demanding functions such as those of Director Planning at the Ministry of Planning, Technical Secretary of SEF, Director of the Department of Economic and Social Affairs of the Central Committee of MPLA-PT, and National Director of the National Accounts Project. It is proposed that the Department of National Accounts should be the responsibility of the Head of the Planning Board, together with the Department of Foreign Exchange for External Trade, Planning Methodology and Control, International Finance and the Data Processing Center. An alternative would be to make INE responsible for national accounts. This possibility should be considered after the implementation and consolidation of the system of national accounts. However, during the initial phase, the preparation of national accounts should be kept separate from the compilation of basic statistics, which is INE's function. Such a separation would enable qualified experts to be deployed exclusively in the preparation of national accounts.

10. In whatever department the national accounts are prepared, it is imperative that efforts to improve the national accounting framework be closely coordinated with the work on basic statistics done in the INE. The national accounts will only be based on reliable, well-defined data when the INE fulfills its role as the central institution which specifies classifications, defines statistical concepts, develops survey methodologies, designs questionnaires, and provides a central source for the exchange and publication of national data. Currently, the INE's performance of these crucial functions is far from satisfactory. Consequently, any attempt to improve the national accounts must be combined with a major effort to upgrade the ability of the INE to provide comprehensive and accurate economic and demographic data in a timely fashion.

11. Establishing a form of discipline by which economic agents will provide the data necessary for operating the unified statistical system will be a difficult obstacle, and will require firm political will on the part of the country's leaders. An indication of the lack of discipline in this area was provided by the enterprises' response to the attempt to establish the SCOPO (the Operating Control System for the National Plan).

The main 172 enterprises in the country were to provide monthly data on 163 selected indicators. INE was to use these data to prepare a monthly report monitoring execution of the Plan. So far, only nine enterprises have complied.

12. It must be recognized that developing a national accounting system that can be used with confidence to monitor the economy, measure the impact of policy changes, and serve as a basis for national economic plans will require a substantial commitment of scarce human resources. While in the short run it is advisable for the Government to contract outside experts to aid in establishing basic statistical methodologies and procedures, it is imperative that high quality counterpart personnel are also involved to sensitize the experts to local conditions and to continue the development of the national accounts after the foreign experts have departed. Establishing technical training programs for personnel involved in data collection and analysis should also be a priority.

13. Finally, it should be noted that UNDP is currently involved in a technical assistance project (ANG/84/001) directed toward improving the national accounting system. While the project has made steps in this direction, its scale is too small to adequately address Angolan needs and it has been hampered by delays. For example, the project called for stationing in Angola two experts in fiscal accounts and the balance of payments, but this has not yet occurred because, of apparent delays in appointing Angolan counterpart personnel. Moreover, project participants spent almost the whole of 1986 preparing basic statistics to be used in the national accounts. Consequently, it is suggested that UNDP and the Angolan authorities extend this project for at least another year and broaden its scope to include upgrading the process of collecting and analyzing basic descriptive statistics.

Per Capita U.S. Dollar GNP Estimates2/

14. In deriving a first estimate of Angolan per capita GNP in U.S. dollars, it is better to rely on the data from the production approach rather than the factor approach due to the former's greater comprehensiveness and better methodological foundation. However, a major drawback of the production approach data is that calculations are reportedly based on 1980 official prices and cover a period in which there were major changes in the relative price of oil and non-oil production.

15. Since the authorities specified the 1980 value added in the oil sector by converting dollar oil sales and costs of production into kwanzas at the official exchange rate (29,918 kwanzas to the U.S. dollar), the 1980 oil sector value added in U.S. dollars was obtained by using the official exchange rate to reconvert the data into dollars. Using the authorities' estimates of oil production value added for subsequent years at 1980 prices, an index of the real value added from oil production for 1980-87

2/ Subsequent work by the World Bank, begun in late 1989, suggests that the estimates obtained at this earlier stage are on the low side.

can be constructed. This index, combined with the annual average dollar prices of Angolan oil from 1980-87, permits an estimate of the nominal value added from Angolan oil production.

16. Converting the value added from non-oil production into U.S. dollars is more problematic. From the authorities' production estimates using 1980 official prices, an index of the real quantity of non-oil production value added can be constructed. However, it would be misleading to use the official exchange rate to convert the 1980 kwanza value of non-oil production into U.S. dollars since there are strong indications that the official exchange rate was overvalued. In fact, the official exchange rate, which was established in May 1976, had by 1980 substantially appreciated in real terms. Rough estimates indicate that the 1980 purchasing power parity exchange rate for officially prices goods should be depreciated 23% relative to the official exchange rate. Using this estimate, to obtain a U.S. dollar measure of non-oil production for 1980, indicates that oil production was 29% of GDP at factor cost. Since alternative estimates have placed oil production as 30 to 35% of GDP, the resulting U.S. dollar GDP estimate for 1980 appears reasonable, but perhaps biased up slightly. Finally, assuming that the dollar price of non-oil production grows at the same rate as the U.S. GNP deflator, a nominal U.S. dollar estimate of non-oil production is obtained for 1980-87.

17. From the U.S. dollar estimates of oil and non-oil production as well as population and net foreign factor income estimates, an estimate of Angolan per capita GNP in U.S. dollars is obtained. This estimate is presented in the Appendix in Table C.3.

LEGAL FRAMEWORK OF SEF

1. The content of the SEF program is such that it requires adjustment of major areas of the law. The Government of Angola has already published new legislation on foreign exchange, economic activities in general, securities, foreign investment, and state enterprises. This annex provides an overview of the content of these various legislative initiatives. Their development at the regulation level is at an advanced stage and legislation on the banking system and procurement is also under preparation. Legislation governing enterprise management and economic planning has also been approved.

2. The following overview of the legislative measures taken so far by the Angolan Government show the commitment with which it is pursuing the implementation of the SEF program and its institutionalization. In particular, the changes made in the area of foreign investment and public enterprises are worth highlighting. Foreign investment outside the context of mixed economy enterprises is now permitted in other than import substitution activities, the approval process has been simplified, and arbitration is recognized as a means of solving investment disputes. In the field of public enterprises, the emphasis is on providing effective autonomy, on the enterprises taking responsibility, on reducing the number of supervisory bodies and delimiting more clearly their supervisory function. As stated above, there is a series of legal instruments under preparation which will develop those reviewed here and complement them. It is to be hoped that their application will be in the same spirit with which they have been or are being prepared.

Exchange Law (Law 9/88)

3. The exchange law establishes the obligation of delivering to the exchange authority (the Minister of Finance) the foreign exchange received by the residents, forbids compensation of debts and credits between residents and non-residents, and limits the ability to carry out exchange functions to the entities so authorized by the exchange authority. One of the reasons for issuing the new law is the fact that exchange legislation is very dispersed, out-of-date and unknown to the public at large. The law applies to the state enterprises (unidades economicas estatais) and to the State itself and its services or to public collective entities whose activities will be regulated separately.

4. The Central Bank is responsible for managing the foreign exchange and resolving any doubts on whether a person or entity is or is not a resident for purposes of the exchange law. Only with Central Bank authorization may residents open foreign exchange accounts or non-residents foreign exchange accounts with national credit institutions. The law has detailed provisions on monetary and jail sanctions for foreign exchange contraventions. The Central Bank has also exclusive responsibility to institute any suits for breaches of the Exchange Law.

5. The Exchange Law has been developed by three regulations approved by the Council of Ministers, Decrees No. 11/89, 12/89, 13/89 dated April 29, 1989. They cover current operations of invisibles, operations related to goods and operations related to capital:

(i) capital operations need authorization by the Central Bank and beyond a certain level by the Minister of Finance. Foreign investment will need to be authorized and registered by the Central Bank. The Central Bank is responsible for issuing the corresponding licence;

(ii) goods operations: the import, export or re-export of goods requires a licence. The licensing authority is the Ministry of Foreign Trade. The first fortnight of each month the Central Bank will inform the Ministry of the maximum amount of foreign exchange available for licences to be issued the next month. Priority in the issuance of licences is given to those which will meet the objectives of the National Plan. Overall, the distribution of licences is left with the licensing authority;

(iii) invisibles: The licensing authority is the Central Bank which may give global licences for up to 180 days when it is necessary for the activities of the beneficiary.

Law on Economic Activities (Law No.10/88)

6. This law is a basic or framework law to regulate economic activity in the country. It applies to activities related to the production or distribution of goods or the rendering of services with the objective of making a profit. The State reserves itself activities in central banking functions, military industry, distribution of water and power, basic sanitary services, telecommunications, transport, except for short range maritime transport, and port and airport administration.

7. No economic activity may be performed without previous authorization by the competent authorities. Economic activity may be developed individually or through enterprises. Enterprise activity may be performed by state enterprises, mixed enterprises, cooperatives and private enterprises. State enterprises are classified as enterprises to which the Law of State Enterprises applies, which means enterprises owned by the State but operating under commercial law. Mixed enterprises are those established by state funds or state enterprises and private capital (national or foreign).

8. The law recognizes the right of individuals to practise their own professions independently and the right of individuals and companies to associate to further their economic and professional interests. Except for central banking and military industry the Council of Ministers may, exceptionally, authorize the performance of economic activities by other private parties in the other sectors reserved to the State. Natural resources owned by the State in terms of the Constitutional Law may be explored only through concessions or other regime not involving the transfer of ownership.

9. The Law gives the Council of Ministers 60 days to define the rules for the reorganization of the public enterprise sector in order to establish sector and regional priorities and criteria of economic, technical and financial viability. The Council of Ministers is charged with revising the legislation on establishment and functioning of cooperatives, nationalization and expropriation, intervention of the State in private enterprises, and licensing of economic activity. In the meantime, any intervention of the State in private enterprises on the basis of the existing legislation requires authorization by the Council of Ministers.

Securities Law (Law No.8/88)

10. This law regulates the issuance of treasury bills with the objective of raising financing for the national budget and to balance the monetary resources distributed as salaries to the level of goods available. In addition, it was necessary to create a legal instrument to give the State the possibility of proceeding with the financial restructuring of state enterprises and to channel national savings towards the financing of investments.

11. The law provides for the following types of securities:

(a) Savings bonds described as bearer bonds with maturities ranging from 12 to 18 years. Savings bonds may be subscribed by individuals, residents in Angola, and will be denominated in kwanzas but, at maturity, the holder may receive the total or partial amount of the bond in foreign exchange.

(b) Development bonds which will be nominative, with a maturity of up to 7 years. Development bonds are intended to be subscribed by collective entities and the interest or the capital of these bonds may be paid in foreign exchange. The funds raised by the issuance of these bonds will be used exclusively to finance investments included in the general budget of the State.

(c) Restructuring bonds which will be nominative with maturities ranging from 5 to 10 years. Restructuring bonds are meant for creditors of bankrupt public enterprises and, in conditions to be determined, could be converted into development bonds.

12. The People's Assembly will determine annually the global limit of the bonds to be issued under types (a) and (b). Restructuring bond amounts will be decided by the Council of Ministers. The bonds will be exempt from taxes, may be pledged and can't be subject to expropriation or any other act of intervention by the State.

Foreign Investment Law (Law No.13/88 of June 16, 1988)

13. This law abrogated the previous law of 1979 which was never developed by the necessary regulations. It has as an objective to improve the organization, function and supervision of the Government related to foreign investments, and to simplify the process of negotiation and approval. This law expressly leaves standing the laws applicable to petroleum and mining to the extent that they don't contradict it.

14. Foreign investments will be permitted by entities of adequate technical and financial capacity provided that the investments are in accordance with the social and economic development interests of Angola. The law excludes from investment by non-residents the areas of defence, central banking, education, health, water supply and sewerage, electric power, postal services, telecommunications, social communications, administration of ports and airports, air transport, long range maritime transport. This list notwithstanding, the Council of Ministers may authorize specific investments in areas complementary to those so listed.

15. A foreign investment may consist of the actual transfer of funds, supplier's credits, equipment or rights to industrial processes. Decree No. 6/89 created the Foreign Investment Cabinet (GIE) which is responsible for the application of the law and the evaluation of investments. In the concrete case of equipment, its value will be the actual market value. The law does not provide for the basis of valuation of rights to industrial processes or suppliers' credits. The Council of Ministers is competent to determine the priority areas in which foreign investment should take place.

16. Foreign investment may take place through the following possibilities:

(a) Mixed Enterprises of a foreign company with a state enterprise. The state enterprise should have 51% of the equity unless the Council of Ministers permits a lower percentage.

(b) Joint Enterprises of a foreign investor with a non-statal national investor.

(c) Private Enterprises entirely owned by the foreign investor.

17. The law specifically provides that in the first three cases the requirements of commercial laws regarding the establishment and registration of companies apply. In the last instance, it goes further to say that the companies so established will be regulated by commercial law.

18. The law recognizes a just and equitable treatment to the investors and in particular it guarantees the repatriation of profits or of the foreign investor's share in case of liquidation or sale of the enterprise. In both instances, the prior authorization of the Minister of Finance is required. In case of expropriation, the investor will be given "just compensation".

19. Entities established under this law may be given certain incentives, such as the exemption or reduction of income taxes and customs duties on inputs or outputs. They may also benefit of other incentives available under existing legislation in cases in which they reinvest profits, develop activities of a social character, and train and use local labour and management.

20. A specific investment proposal must be presented to the GIE which will evaluate it within 90 days. After evaluation, it will make a recommendation for approval or rejection to the Minister of Planning. If the Minister accepts the recommendation of approval, the investment proposal is forwarded to the Council of Ministers for final approval. The Council of Ministers has 45 days to decide from the date of evaluation. The GIE will keep an investments register.

21. In case of disputes between the foreign and local investor which can't be solved amicably, the parties may have recourse to arbitration according to UNCITRAL rules. It should be emphasized that the disputes which may be subject of such arbitration are not those involving the State but only those between the local and foreign partners. Thus, in the case of expropriation, there would not be the possibility of submitting a dispute regarding compensation to arbitration.

22. The law leaves a number of matters to future regulation. These include areas of compensation in case of expropriation, guarantees which might be required from the investor, terms of the contract to be signed between the investors after approval of the investment, and obligation of employment of local labor.

23. In addition to future regulations of the foreign investment law, there are a number of other laws which will be of interest to investors and which will affect the assessment of whether to invest in Angola is an attractive proposition. The main ones would be the Labour Code, Tax and Exchange laws and the Portuguese Commercial Code of 1822 which is still in effect in Angola.

24. It would be very useful if as soon as the various regulations have been published, a publication for investors be issued with practical advice and guidance on all the relevant legal norms and administrative procedures applicable to foreign investment in Angola. This publication could also include information on bilateral treaties on investment protection, double taxation, or recognition of arbitral awards.

Law of State Enterprises (Law No.11/88)

25. It is the objective of this law to reinforce the autonomy of the state enterprises, to increase their efficiency and rentability, to increase their influence in the distribution and commercialization of their products, and to improve the process of constitution and organization of state enterprises.

26. State enterprises are defined as those owned by the State with separate juridical personality, and administrative, financial and patrimonial autonomy. The law states the principle of autonomy in the management of the enteprises and, except as provided by the law, no organism of the State or other third party has any right to interfere in the conduct of the enterprise business. State enterprises are expected to generate profits, to charge for their products or services and to be self-financing. Enterprises should be managed so as to increase efficiency and productivity, to make investments based on their rate of return, and assessment of risk and of period needed to recover the invested capital, and to increase the professional level and the working conditions of their workers.

27. State enterprises are responsible for the preparation of multi-year plans and budgets and annual plans and budgets. They may fix the prices of their products on the basis of current legislation and are subject to taxation. They respond of their obligations with their own patrimony. The State is not liable for their obligations.

28. At the time of their constitution, the State provides each enterprise with a "fundo de constituicao" ("establishment fund") which would be in an amount adequate for the exercise of the enterprise activity. Profits after taxes will be allocated in accordance with the following priorities: constitution of a legal reserve as required by commercial law, of an investment fund, and of a social fund. Any remaining profits will be distributed to the State as owner of the enterprise and to workers in order to recognize their individual performance.

29. The supervision of the enterprises corresponds to the Ministries responsible for the sector ("Ministro de Tutela") of the activity concerned and Finance. The sector Minister guides and supervises the activities of state enterprises by defining the development policy of the economic activity concerned, approving the multi-year plans and budgets proposed by the enterprise, evaluating the performance of the enterprise, appointing the administrators and directors and approving the enterprise accounts. In case of companies of large dimensions, the Council of Ministers may require approval by the Minister of Planning of the multi-year plans and budgets and of the investment programs of the enterprise.

30. Enterprises may only be created by the Council of Ministers by decree. They are subject to the registration requirement of commercial law.

31. The organization of the enterprises consists of a Board, the Management, a Management Council and a Fiscal Council. For the medium and small-scale enterprises these organs are reduced to a Director, Management Council and Fiscal Council.

32. The Board has responsibility for preliminary approval of the multi-year plans and budgets, investments, follow up the activities of the enterprise, approve the internal regulations, present the proposals for the appointment of director general and evaluate his performance, and approve price proposals. The members of the Board consist of a President appointed by the Council of Ministers or the "Ministro de Tutela" depending on the size of the enterprise, one Board member each by the "Ministro de Tutela" and the Minister of Finance, one member elected by the workers, and the Director General. If the Board consists of only three members, the President is the Director General appointed by the Ministro de Tutela. The other two members are appointed by the Minister of Finance and the workers. The Board meets every three months and decides by majority of its members.

33. The Management consists of the Director, Deputy Director and those responsible for various areas of the enterprise (area managers). In the case of large enterprises, the Director is appointed by the Ministro de Tutela as proposed by the Board, or by the Ministro de Tutela without any further intervention of other parties in the case of smaller enterprises.

34. The Management Council is a consultative organ which the Director needs to consult on the draft plans of the enterprise, accounts, report on the execution of the plan, sales of fixed assets, investment programs, classification and training of workers, management appointments and criteria to give premia to compensate good performance. This Council is composed of the Director, area managers, two party representatives, and one representative of the trade union.

35. The Fiscal Council is basically responsible for checking compliance with the laws by the enterprise and giving its opinion on the accounts. It consists of a president and two members. The President and one member are appointed by the Minister of Finance and one member by the Ministro de Tutela. In small enterprises, the function of this Council may be

performed by one person appointed by the Minister of Finance. All members of the Fiscal Council will need to be registered accountants and not be staff of the enterprise.

36. The statute of manager of public enterprises has been regulated by Decree No.6/89 of March 13, 1989 providing for a definition of the technical requirements, duration of the mandate, cases in which they may be removed and accountability.

37. In addition to the participation of workers in the Board and in the Management Council, the law provides for Workers Assemblies which will "analyze" the drafts of the plan and budget of the enterprise, degree of execution of the plan, productivity level, working conditions and compliance by the enterprise with the labour legislation.

38. The extinction or dissolution of a state enterprise is the responsibility of the organ which created it. The commercial laws of bankruptcy or dissolution of companies do not apply to state enterprises. Consequently, the law provides for a special liquidation commission which will dispose of the assets of the bankrupt or dissolved enterprise and settle the claims. The State will pay out of the budget any claims accepted by this commission which the assets of the enterprise are not sufficient to cover.

39. The new law will be applied to existing enterprises as determined by the Council of Ministers on a case-by-case basis and as part of the process of financial restructuring of the public sector. Decree No.36/89 of July 22, 1989 established the Enterprise Restructuring Cabinet ("GARE") for these purposes. The success of the new law will depend on how effectively it is applied in terms of non-interference, accountability and how effectively prices and salaries are also liberalized.

THE TAX SYSTEM OF ANGOLA

1. Tax revenue in Angola is derived from four main sources: taxes from the exploitation of petroleum, taxes on income, taxes on production and consumption, and taxes on international trade.

Taxes on Petroleum

2. The government receives revenue from exploitation of Angola's oil reserves in the form of royalties, taxes on profits and a share in the profits of Sonangol, the state-owned oil company. Two types of agreement govern the relations between the government and the operating companies. The tax regimes applied by these agreements differ in their impact on government revenue. The joint venture agreement between Sonangol and the foreign partners is the oldest type. Under this agreement, Sonangol, the sole concessionaire for oil exploration and production, shares the investment with foreign companies. The joint venture pays three kinds of taxes: (a) a royalty, currently 20% of crude oil sales; (b) a tax on profits of 65.75%; and (c) a tax on excess profits (transaction tax) of 70%.

3. Under the more recent production sharing agreements, Sonangol subcontracts with foreign companies to undertake the exploration and production operations in return for a share in the output. The foreign company retains part of the output (maximum 50%) to cover its costs ('cost oil'), and pays a 50% income tax on its share of the remainder of the output ('profit oil'). In addition, the government receives a share in Sonangol's profits. The principal difference in fiscal impact between the two agreements lies in the tax yield over time. Compared to a joint venture, the production sharing agreement yields less revenue in the early years when high initial costs result in retaining the full 50% 'cost oil' allowance. Furthermore, it tends to provide Sonangol, rather than the treasury, with the largest part of Angola's share, while in joint ventures the bulk of the revenue accrues directly to the government in the form of taxes. In 1986, joint ventures accounted for approximately 80% of government revenue from oil. Table VI.1 shows a breakdown of government revenue from oil.

Table VI.1: PETROLEUM TAXATION, 1980-88
(Kz. billion)

	1980	1981	1982	1983	1984	1985	1986	1987	1988
Royalty	6.4	9.1	6.8	7.0	11.2	10.2	6.4	8.7	9.0
Income tax	17.6	26.6	10.7	14.6	14.0	11.8	7.9	12.5	9.4
Transaction tax	8.3	8.4	3.5	5.0	17.0	19.7	6.7	11.7	13.7
Transfers from Sonangol	1.6	1.1	0.1	-	-	-	9.0	2.9	3.8
TOTAL	33.9	45.2	21.0	26.7	42.3	41.7	30.1	35.8	35.8

Source: Appendix table D.1

4. Since 1980, price and output of oil have moved in opposite directions (see table VI.2). A strong rise in production followed a slump during 1972-82. The latter resulted from a lack of exploration and development during the few years after independence. Output then doubled between 1982 and 1986, which cushioned the effect of the fall in the oil price, and contributed to the recovery from 1982 to 1985. However, changes in price and output differ in their impact on revenue due to the nature of the tax regime. Since profits from oil operations are the primary source of oil taxes, and excess profits are highly taxed, government income from oil reacts more sharply to variations in price than in production. Another factor that prevented the full revenue impact of the price decline in 1986 from being felt was the large transfer of profits from Sonangol in that year (Kz 9 billion), which included arrears for 1983-85 when no transfers were made.

Table VI.2: CHANGES IN PRICE AND OUTPUT OF CRUDE OIL, 1980-86
(1980 = 100)

	Price	Output
1980	100	100
1981	110	95
1982	86	96
1983	87	132
1984	86	151
1985	81	171
1986	45	208

Source: IBRD: Angola, Energy Assessment.

Taxes on Income

5. This category includes four types of taxes: transfers from public enterprises, corporate income tax, personal income tax, and a tax on income from capital. Together they are the principal source of non-oil taxes, accounting for between half and two-thirds of the total. Income taxes on the whole have not performed well, judging by their average nominal growth of 2-1/2% a year since 1980. This has been largely due to a lack of growth in the transfers from public enterprises which account for the bulk of these taxes. However, the other tax components show a more encouraging trend.

6. Transfers from public enterprises. Public enterprises have to remit part of their profits to the state. Until recently this share was: 90% for firms in the productive sectors, 97% for those in the petroleum sector, and 98% for service industries. With effect from 1986, the transferable portion has been reduced to a flat 50%. The share of these transfers in total taxes on income declined from around 80% in the early 1980s to 67% in 1985 and 62% in 1986. As most enterprises have greatdifficulty in preparing timely accounts, the transfer to the State is calculated on the basis of the planned

financial results for the year as agreed by the management and the Ministry of Planning. It is payable in quarterly installments. When actual data become available, adjustments are made.

7. In 1986, the financial sector accounted for the largest share of profit transfers (23%), followed by internal trade (19%) and fisheries (17%) (see Appendix table D.2). Of the 137 enterprises (excluding Sonangol) that made transfers that year, 3 firms account for 30% of total transfers (BNA, Cafangol and the National Lotteries), and the 10 largest contributors for 57% of the total. However, the profits on which they are based do not always represent genuine operating results of these companies. E.g., the profits of Cafangol include increases in the value of large state-held stocks of coffee, and the results of fishing enterprises include part of the fish catch of foreign operators.

Table VI.3: TRANSFERS TO GOVERNMENT FROM SELECTED PUBLIC ENTERPRISES, 1984-86, (PERCENTAGES)

	1984	1985	1986
BNA	30	11	12
National Lotteries	11	8	10
Cafangol	2	15	10
Edipesca (Namibe)	5	5	7
Edipesca (Luanda)	5	5	1
Expedicao conjunta	--	3	5
Emprotel	--	6	--
Frescangol	--	--	4
Other	47	47	51
TOTAL	100	100	100

Source: Ministry of Finance

8. Corporate income tax. A basic rate of 35% is levied on the income of enterprises in the private sector, including so-called mixed enterprises in which the state has a share (imposto industrial). In addition, there is a progressive surtax ranging from 2 to 30% imposed on the same income (imposto de resistencia popular). While the maximum tax rate on enterprise profits is, thus, 65%, the average is around 50%, which equals the current share of profits transferred by state enterprises. The share of corporate income tax in total tax on incomes rose from 14% in 1980 to 28% in 1986. The government intends to merge the basic tax and surtax, and impose a single tax on profits of all enterprises, public and private.

9. Personal Income Tax. Income tax rates range from 1% to 40% for wage and salary earners, deducted at source, and from 3% to 60% for those independently employed. The system is quite complex, and collection problems are severe, although there has been a considerable improvement in tax yield in recent

years. Nevertheless, total tax collected, including from those independently employed, represented only 3% of the total government wage and salary bill in 1986, and less than 6% of non-petroleum taxation.

Taxes on Production and Consumption

10. These indirect taxes include duties on petroleum products consumed locally, on production and consumption of beer and about a hundred other products whether produced locally or imported, stamp duties, and royalty on diamonds. Together they accounted for 22% of non-oil taxes in 1986. After stamp duty, the most important source of these taxes is the duty on beer. However, beer production, and thus the tax yield, is sensitive to the availability of imported inputs, which accounts for the fall in revenue in 1986, when foreign exchange allocations to industry were reduced. Moreover, theft and payment-in-kind of workers is widespread in industry and further reduces the indirect tax base.

Taxes on International Trade

11. Given Angola's relatively high level of imports, taxes on imports could be a significant source of budgetary revenue. However, in 1985 the effective duty on (recorded) merchandise imports was only 9.4%, having dropped from 15.5% in 1982. These import duties have been contributing between 15 and 25% of non-oil taxes. An outdated import tariff, serious collection problems, and a shrinking tax base account for the low yield of these taxes. The tariff, which dates from 1953 and contains many specific duties, has never been brought up to date. As a result, many imports carry low duties. Moreover, the tariff structure is complex and hinders implementation.

12. The collection problem has several causes: the import tariff is complex, which makes proper application difficult; the Customs service operates with about a third of its estimated personnel requirement, and staff lack necessary qualifications; 1/ available transport, communications and office equipment are totally inadequate; and due to the war, the surveillance of borders is hazardous and communication is difficult. Tax collection is further affected by the decline in the volume of imports on which duty is paid. Many imports are covered by exemptions issued by various authorities, and tax evasion is widespread. The latter is made easier by the lack of authority customs staff have in the port. Army, police, port security staff and others interfere with the customs operations. Many take advantage of the lax application of procedures governing importation and clearance of goods; unauthorized imports are a major source of supply of the parallel market. 2/

1/ According to one estimate, the Customs service requires a total of 2,800 staff. Its actual strength is only 832.

2/ More than 50% of imports are said to enter Angola without an import license.

AGRICULTURE

A. Agricultural Performance, Policy and Production Response

1. Agricultural Performance. Seventy to eighty percent of the population derive a living from agriculture, which generates about 20 percent of official GNP. 1/ With an area of 1,246,000 km^3 (481.3 thousand square miles) and diversified ecological setting, Angola can grow a large variety of tropical and semi-tropical crops. Extensive areas are suitable for grazing with the Southern regions free from the tsé-tsé fly. Arable land is plentiful with estimates ranging from five to eight million hectares. There is potential for significant production of a broad variety of agricultural, livestock and fishery products, including, corn, cassava, beans, sorgum, sunflower, millet, potatoes, coffee, citrus, cotton, sugar, tobacco, bananas, palm oil, sisal, beef, pork, poultry, forestry and fish products. This range of crops can adapt to most soils and climatic conditions, ranging from cereals grown under irrigation in the cold season in the plateau region, to other cereals suited to the hot, rainy season; from robusta coffee in the forests (matas) of the Northeast to arabica coffee in the central plateaus; or from oil palm in Cabinda and Zaire Province to olive trees and vines in the Bero and Giraul lowlands, in addition to the country's forestry, livestock and fisheries potential. In the Maiombe and Dembos massifs, valuable forestry species abound such as African mahogany. Forests in the East and Southeast contain sizable stands of other worthwhile tree species. Eucalyptus and pine, of proven economic value, perform well in commercial plantations, especially above the 1,200 - 1,300 meter line.

2. Agricultural production, including livestock and fishery products, grew steadily until the disruption by the anti-colonial war. Angola was self-sufficient in all major food crops. The production of maize, the basis of the diet in the heavily populated central zone, had reached 710,000 tons in 1971, sufficient to permit significant exports (112,000 tons). Surpluses of other food crops, notably bananas, rice, sugar and palm oil, were also exported. Angola produced enough tobacco to satisfy its own needs and, in addition to being the fourth largest exporter of coffee, it was also one of the world's major producers of sisal. Exports of forestry products were considerable and livestock resources were abundant. According to the 1971 census, the last census available, there were more than 2 million heads of cattle and nearly a million goats. Moreover, Angola's long shore line (1,600 km) and Benguela's sea current provide rich potential for fishing along the Southern seaboard. In the early seventies, fish harvest reached 700 thousand tons.

3. Since independence, agricultural output has experienced a dramatic decline which has affected virtually all products. The sudden departure of the Portuguese resulted in the abandonment of most of the Portuguese-owned

---

1/ Represents only agricultural production marketed through official channels, estimated to be 10 to 15% of total production.

and managed farms, and created a manpower vacuum in many areas that are crucial to the effectiveness of agricultural operations, such as agricultural marketing, transport, input supply and research. Another major cause of the poor agricultural performance since independence is the war. The limited access to the rural areas, the destruction of infrastructure, the disruption of families and communities, and the budgetary demands of the war have had an immense impact on agricultural activity. Finally, an equally important contributory factor has been the failure of agricultural policy and government intervention to provide producers with adequate incentives and the necessary support services.

4. The current situation in the sector is in stark contrast to both pre-independence production levels and to Angola's agricultural potential. Appendix Table F.1 presents estimates of current output levels for a range of agricultural products compared to pre-1975 figures. Production of the principal staple foods (maize, cassava, sorghum, millet) is estimated at 25-35% of the maximum output achieved just before independence. Production of many other crops (tobacco, sisal, cotton, palm oil, groundnuts) does not even reach 10% of earlier levels. While the number of cattle declined by only about 20%, and the goat population actually grew by around 50%, the number of swine as well as beef production were well below previous levels. The fish catch had dropped to a fourth of the 1972 catch as the Portuguese exodus deprived Angola of its fishing fleet and expertise.

5. Angola has been transformed from a country self-sufficient in food to one dependent on increasing food imports, including food aid, and on the verge of famine. Food aid requested for 1987/88 amounted to 200,000 tons of cereals, three times morer than the 68,000 tons requested in 1983/84. The ability of government to finance commercial food imports diminished from 238,000 tons in 1983/84 to 94,700 tons in 1986/87. In addition, 18,000 tons of meat were imported in 1987.

6. Agricultural exports have virtually dried up. Production of coffee, until 1973 the principal foreign exchange earner, had fallen to 13,500 tons in 1987 as compared to 240,000 in 1974. Timber exports in 1985 were only 14% of the volume exported in 1973. A number of products that were previously exported are now imported (e.g., sugar, palm oil, beans).

7. Agricultural Policy. The massive abandonment of the Portuguese-owned and managed farms at independence created a vacuum with which the new government had to deal. With commercial private sector agriculture disintegrating, a centralized organizational set-up was introduced in an attempt to quickly fill the gap and establish a state controlled agricultural model. The central government institutions dealing with agriculture, have since formally administered prices, production, investment, marketing, distribution, exports, imports and all other aspects of the sector. They have attempted this in the face of severe technical, human resource, and administrative deficiencies. Central planning, price controls and other macro-economic distortions, together with the neglect of the peasant sector, which was the major producer of food, eliminated incentives to

produce and market output. Prices at all levels have been centrally determined and rarely changed and consumer goods have become increasingly scarce in the countryside.

8. A plethora of agricultural agencies has been established in spite of severe deficiencies in qualified staff. Only 1 percent of the labor force under the jurisdiction of the Ministry of Agriculture is classified as technical and most agricultural schools are closed. Under the Ministry of Agriculture alone, there are more than one hundred public enterprises and agencies. They include state farms and integrated agrarian complexes, as well as specialized forestry enterprises, service companies, etc. Under yet different bureaucratic jurisdictions, other public entities are responsible for agro-industries such as sugar cane, the production of agricultural implements and materials. In summary, Angola's initial experiment with centralization and administrative controls is understandable, in view of the post-independence disruption and insecurity and is to a large extent a reaction to the harshness of the Portuguese system of private sector exploitation and the subsequent the disarray following the massive exodus of Portuguese farmers and traders. Nevertheless, the maintenance of these policies despite the obvious constraints and failures is now recognized by many Angolan policy-makers as a mistake and especially by those at the Ministry of Agriculture.

9. In addition to the problems of security and inadequate policies, investment in agriculture has been limited and poorly planned and implemented. In 1986, for instance, of the US$12.6 million in foreign exchange equivalent originally approved for investment, only US$2 million was made available, in view of the severe balance of payments constraints and the central control and allocation of foreign exchange. Moreover, while a cursory review of the 1986 investment performance shows a level of implementation exceeding 100 percent, it appears that 69 percent of the total investment for agriculture went to build 900 residences in Kuanza-Bengo, a questionable project not contemplated originally in the Ministry of Agriculture's plan. In contrast, only 47 percent of the planned investment for training and support services took place.

10. Production Response. Because of the internal conflict and the uncertainty as to how and when it will end, two different situations of geographic response are examined. (a) secure areas; the part of the country under government control where agriculture can be carried out consists primarily of the western coastal strip and amounts to about 20% of Angola's land area. The supply of agricultural products from these areas is of considerable importance. Three million inhabitants, or 38% of the population, live there, the majority concentrated in the urban centers of Luanda, Lobito, Benguela, Lubango and Namibe. And (b) insecure areas; the rest of the country's territory is subject to considerable security constraints and limitations of movement.

11. The secure area where agricultural supply response to policy reform is now possible can be divided into two zones: (a) the South-Southwest Zone(S-SW); this extends from Lobito-Benguela to the Cunene and consists

largely of the territory of the Fifth Military Region (provinces of Namibe, Huila and Cunene). Areas of greatest potential are the Huila Uplands, the mid-Cunene Valley and the plateau strip from Lubango to Matala/Capelongo; and (b) the North-Northwest Zone(N-NW); this consists of the coastal strip from Cabinda to Sumbe (formerly Novo Redondo), of varying width but widest in the Soyo and Luanda-Dondo areas, coinciding with Baixo Cuanza.

12. In the South-Southwest Zone(S-SW) zone, the Huila Uplands and the strip extending eastward to the Cunene (Matala-Capelongo) have high agricultural production potential, especially for maize growing. Within a short period (two to four years), Huila could probably supply the entire S-SW region's market grain needs, estimated at 90,000, t/a in addition to the farmers' own consumption of about 70,000 t/a. Infrastructure is mostly in place in this area. The traditional sector plus a number of medium-size commercial farms in the plateau area are expected to respond quickly to incentives. About 25,000 tons of maize were marketed in the course of the current farm year (1986-87), compared with 8,000 tons in the previous year following an improvement in incentives for farmers. Huila could also contribute substantially toward meeting the region's demand for beans, potatoes, sweet potatoes and various fruits (pears, apples, citrus and plums). Livestock potential is considerable in the S-SW region, particularly for cattle. Sufficient surpluses to meet the regional requirements, estimated at 8,000/10,000 tons of beef per year, are possible in the short run. Potential exists to meet the needs of the N-NW region as well, which includes the densely populated Luanda area. The region also has considerable potential for export crops of which cotton and tobacco are the most promising. Processing facilities for these crops exist in Benguela. The alluvial plains of the Benguela and Namibe areas in the S-SW offer high potential for irrigated agriculture. The supply of horticultural products and tropical fruit (bananas, papayas, mangoes, avocados) could easily be assured from the truck-farming area of the Cavaco in the Lobito-Benguela area and those in Bero-Giraul in the Namibe area. Fruit canning plants in Lubango and Lobito can be reactivated.

13. The North-Northwest Zone(N-NW) includes the city of Luanda. Improving agriculture in this region is essential. Shipments of food from Huila, in addition to what is already brought in by air, are problematic because of the long distances involved and the lack of security. Cultivation of the basic food staple, Cassava, is best suited to the N-NW area. Cultivation of this crop has already been considerably expanded in the areas around the capital. Cassava is now grown on many thousands of hectares of "musseque"-type soils on the Luanda plateau. Its expansion into the interior of the strip has been continuing steadily, despite the fact that unit yields have fallen sharply as a result of viral diseases. Another major crop is sweet potatoes which is grown in the wet lowlands. Various forms of peas and beans such as the cowpea, the pigeonpea or Angola bean and the hyacinth bean are also grown, while maize is also becoming quite popular. Fruit and vegetable growing in the Luanda surroundings are carried on by large numbers of family-type operations. This source

constitutes the main supply of fresh produce for the capital. A wide variety of horticultural products are grown in the dry season and tropical fruit the year round.

14. Development should focus on rainfed crops since they will contribute most decisively toward resolving the regional food problem. Nevertheless, because of rapid population growth and land scarcity arising from a lack of security, irrigated agriculture should also be considered. From a technical point of view, prospects for irrigated agriculture in the N-NW strip are good. Land suitable for irrigated crops in the Lucala-Mucoso zone have been identified. Development of 30,000 ha based on gravity-type irrigation would be feasible through diversion of the Lucala river. Until such time as this area comes under irrigation, efforts in the river plain will be limited to the areas that are least affected by flooding. A wide variety of crops is raised in this area (bananas, oil palm, mangoes, papayas and citrus) together with a range of horticultural products. A substantial proportion of the agricultural products sold in the Luanda markets today comes from this region.

15. The N-NW strip is also suitable for cotton. It used to be grown in large parts of Bengo and Cuanza Sul provinces and especially in the Catete, Dondo, Porto Amboim and Sumbe areas where industrial-scale cotton ginneries are still to be found. Peasant farmers are familiar with the crop and the traditional system of cultivation practices. They should readily respond to policies and incentives aimed at reactivating cotton production. Livestock potential in the secure areas is especially promising in the coastal area south of the Longa river down to the Balombo Falls, with tens of thousands of hectares of prairie land on the Porto Amboim and Sumbe plateaus. This used to be an extensive commercial ranching zone with some tens of thousands head of improved cattle, while the raising of Karakul sheep was becoming a significant activity. Reactivation of stock raising in this zone should not present major difficulties. The forestry sector is also of significance in the N-NW region with a considerable production potential in the Maiombe forests in Cabinda and the Dembos in the interior of Luanda-Ambriz. Forestry development should focus on Cabinda province for a number of reasons including the proximity of the forests to the ports of shipment and the existence in the area of infrastructure facilities, most of which are still usable or can be rehabilitated.

B. Major Agricultural Products

16. This section presents in some detail the characteristics of the major agricultural products most of which will respond significantly to structural adjustment and reform. The areas referred to are the 36 agricultural zones (AZs), identified in Map 1 attached to this Annex. They were delineated by the Angola Agriculture Study Mission, 1970-71 (Missâo de Inqueritos Agricolas de Angola). They represent homogeneous units on the basis of soil, economic and environmental characteristics.

(1) **Crops and Forestry**

17. Cotton was for decades confined to the semi-arid coastal strip (AZ 7/8 and 15) where production fluctuated because of low and irregular rainfall. Cotton growing in the Cassange Basin (AZ 9) was more satisfactory due to more and regular rainfall. In the coastal zone cotton is grown on heavy soils (vertisols) known locally as the "black Catete soils" (terras negras de Catete) which retain water well. Starting in the mid-sixties cotton spread to other regions, covering large areas in the Cubal and Quilengues regions (AZ 23 and 27) where rainfall patterns are much more favorable than along the coast; also to the Malange plateau, especially in the Cacuso and Cota regions (AZ 13/14). Cotton-growing potential also focused in other areas, notably the alluvial fringes of major rivers in the semi-arid South and Southwest, more particularly the extensive Cunene lowlands and adjacent areas. Total production of 86,000 tons, of which 25% (19,992 tons) from peasant holdings and 75% (62,795 tons) from the commercial sector, was reported in the 1970/71 crop year. At present cotton production is down to about 300 tons. Peanuts (Ground Nuts) are a traditional food in northern and eastern Angola. In the traditional growing areas, peanuts do well on recently cleared light soils. Peanuts are a traditional smallholder crop grown for both on-farm consumption and for sale, promising quick response to production incentives. Production in 1970/71 amounted to 26,936 tons, mostly from the smallholders, although commercial production was rising sharply at the time, notably in the Cubal-Ganda region (AZ 23). Present production is only, about 1,700 tons.

18. Rice is an important crop in the areas of the Cuquema and Songo Rivers. Smallholder rice growing takes advantage of the temporary flooding during the rainy season which coincides with the growing cycle. Yields vary depending on fluctuations in water levels. Rice is grown commercially in regions such as the Quibala (AZ 17), where the flooding of river bottom lands can be controlled, and on higher elevations in northeastern Lunda (AZ 10), where upland rice is grown. The semi-arid belt in southern Angola, particularly the vast river plains of the Cunene and Cubango, should also be able to produce high rice yields. In 1971/72 paddy (unhulled rice) production amounted to 57,604 tons. Smallholder production was approximately 52% of the total. At present rice production is estimated at about 800 tons. Bananas grow throughout much of the country and are an important element in the local diet. Areas of greatest potential are limited, however, to the littoral and sublittoral zones north of the Coporolo, extending from the shoreline to 400 m elevation (AZ 2,4,7/8 15 and the northern portion of 22/29). Because this section of the country is prone to drought, irrigation is needed, and deep, fertile soils with the correct characteristics are required. Best conditions are found in the lower reaches of the main watercourses. These river valleys offer the most favorable climatic conditions: high mean annual temperatures (above 23-24 degrees C), stable temperature and weather conditions. Commercial banana growing started early in the sixties in the Cavaco Valley (Benguela),

spreading to favorable areas in the Cuanza, Dande, Lifune, Cubal and Cuvo Valleys. Exports totaled 75,000 tons a year in 1974 and 1975. About 25,000 tons are produced at present.

19. Potatoes. Potato cultivation spread considerably during the sixties. Growing was initially confined to higher elevations (above 1,600-1,700m) in the Central Plateau, in the mountainous region of Vila Flor - Quipeio. The cultivation soon extended beyond to the Central Plateau (AZ 24) and in surrounding transitional zones (AZ 17 and 31). The Cela region became particularly important for commercial growing, in the early sixties, as the main supplier of potatoes for the Luanda market. Outside the plateau region, potatoes can be grown during the cooler season, where the lower the temperature, the better the results. Potential also exists in the alluvial bottom lands along the coast south of the Rio Catumbela, particularly the valleys of the Cavaco (Benguela) and the Bero and Giraul (Namibe). In 1971/72 production amounted to 138,757 tons with 54 percent from the commercial sector, and 46 percent from the smallholder. Production has since declined to about 8,000 tons. Sweet Potatooes are an important local food staple, following cassava and maize in importance. They are grown widely throughout the country, on land adjacent to river bottoms. They require relatively fertile soils, either dry (or not very susceptible to flooding) or growing on higher ground or hillsides in rainier areas. They are usually associated with other crops (intercropping). Yields are best in the humid and subhumid areas with higher mean temperatures; they do less well below latitude of 14 degree S. Estimated production was about 250,000 tons in 1973. Present production is estimated at about 100,000 tons.

20. Robusta Coffee is grown over a wide area, ranging from the northern and northwestern frontier zones to latitude 12 degree S along the mountain relief between the sublitoral zone and the subplateau region in the interior. This area benefits from ocean moisture which helps form on-shore fogs of considerable duration in the dry season, offsetting the lack of rainfall. This sustains the dense semideciduous type forest where robusta coffee (coffea canephora) is a subforest shrub. Growing is largely confined to Dembos-Uite (AZ 3) and Libolo-Amboim (AZ 16), occupying only a fraction of the potentially suitable area, particularly in the case of Dembos-Uige, where plantations can be established under the cover of the natural forest. Certain savanna areas (AZ 17) bordering the forest and enjoying similar climatic and soil conditions (paraferralitic soils and ferrisols), are also favorable for coffee plantations under forest cover. Arabica Coffee: Favorable conditions for arabica coffee are found in the central region above elevations of 1,400 - 1,500 meters where mean temperatures fluctuate in the 18-19 degree C range and mean annual rainfall is in excess of 1,300 mm. These areas are associated with a particular type of paraferralitic soils (thick, agrillaceous and well structured), with capacity to retain and store water for the 5-6 month dry period. Serra da Chicuma, where commercial growing predominates, and Andulo-Nhareia, where smallholder production prevails, are traditional arabica growing areas. (AZ 24). Output of arabica coffee is small, representing

not more than 4-5% of the total quantity of coffee traded. Total coffee production (robusta and arabica) reached 240,000 tons in 1974 but has declined to 13,500 tons since then.

21. Sugar Cane is grown over a vast expanse of Angolan territory (AZ 7/8, 17, 22/29, 23, 27, 33, 34, 35 and 36). Production scale requirements and high costs of sugar mills limit the potential areas. Irregular rainfall in areas otherwise suitable make irrigation necessary. Consequently sugar mills were all established on the coastal belt and on the margins of large rivers, where - in addition to large tracts of suitable alluvial soils - they found a convenient and assured source of irrigation water. This low-lying littoral and sublitoral zone, particularly the alluvial lowlands of the Cuanza, Lucala, Longa, Queve and Coporolo, represent the country's potential sugar-growing reserve. The Lower Cunene region (AZ 34) with its favorable climate holds high potential for industrial-scale production. Now that the flow of the Cunene has largely been regulated (Gove reservoir), water could be made available to irrigate land suited to growing cane. In 1970/71 sugar production was 75,864 tons. By 1974/75 it had risen to 80,000 tons. Thereafter production declined sharply, and is now at less than 15,000 tons a year; one of the four refineries (the Açucareira do Bom Jesus) has in the interim suspended operations.

22. Beans. Various types of beans are consumed by the population. Important are the different varieties of kidney bean (Phaseolus vulgaris) and cowpea (Vigna unguiculata) which grows just about everywhere, frequently in association with other crops, mostly in the plateau areas of central Angola (AZ 17, 23, 24, 25 and 31). Beans are a standard item in the popular diet, a good source of protein consumed daily when available. Yields fluctuate with soil fertility and cultivation practices. Other types of "pea" and "bean" are Angola, Congo or pigeon peas (Cajanus cajan) and hyacinth beans (Lablab vigor), characterized by their hardiness and adaptability; the former are of particular interest for northern Angola, especially the drought-prone areas (AZ 2 and 7/8). Production in 1970/71 amounted to 65,479 tons, with the peasant sector accounting for much of the total. Commercial growers contributed less than 4 percent. Production has declined significantly since then to 2.5 thousand tons.

23. Fruit. Economically significant fruit growing for which conditions are favorable include pineapples, mangoes, papayas, passionfruit (maracujâ), guavas, avocados and various types of citrus. Pineapples adapt readily to medium-elevation subplateau conditions with well-drained ferralitic soils of medium to light texture, conditions found in large parts of AZ 4, 5, 13/14, 17 and 23. Mangoes and papayas are widely distributed but they do best in hot, humid regions without major temperature fluctuations, and deep, well-drained, fertile soils. This explains the preference for low- to medium-elevation areas in the northern half of the country, more particularly AZ 2, 4, 7/8, 13/14, and 17. Passionfruit, guavas and avocados grow readily in large parts of the country, and do best at medium elevations in the subplateau and plateau regions. Citrus fruit, including oranges, tangerines, lemons and

grapefruit, adapt well to ecological conditions found in Angola, provided suitable soils are chosen and irrigation offsets lack of water during the dry season. Certain areas lend themselves to large-scale expansion of citrus growing for juice concentrates. These areas are in the southern half of the country (AZ 31, 33, and 34).

24. Sunflower became an important crop in the provinces of Malange, Cuanza-Sul and Benguela. Seeds were processed locally for oils and fats. As a commercial crop, it would be of potential interest in the South and Southwest, largely between latitudes 12 degrees S and 15 degrees S (AZ 23, 27, and 31) where there are large areas suitable for sunflower cultivation. With proper cultivation techniques, fairly high yields should be possible, making sunflower growing an attractive proposition for Angola. From a start in the early sixties, production rose steadily to almost 20,000 tons a year (17,930 tons in 1970/71). Present production is negligible. Cassava is the most widely consumed food of the local diet. It is a traditional crop in the northern half of Angola, (AZ 1, 2, 3, 4, 5, 6, 9, 11, 13/14, 19, and 21). Climate and soils are very favorable for cassava: 6-7 month rainy season followed by a dry season, rainfall ranging between 700 mm and 1,400 mm, mean annual temperature from 21 degrees C to 26 degrees C, and relative humidity averaging 65% over the year. Cassava is eminently a peasant crop. Production amounted to 1,134,262 tons in 1970/71, exclusively from the smallholder sector. It is presently down to 250,000, though this estimate is very tentative.

25. Sorghum (known locally as massambala) is a cereal characteristic of hot, dry climatic zones, found particularly in the semi-arid band occupying the South and Southwestern parts of the country (AZ 27, 30, 31 (southern portion), 33, and 34). Sorghum, and also millet, another cereal resistant to drought, are closely linked with the traditional practices of pastoral peoples who engage in subsistence farming and cattle raising. Sorghum is relatively undemanding in terms of soils and cultural practices, and it adapts well to heat and drought. It provides a good dietary complement to the milk and dairy products which are the mainstay of the local population. Production estimates are difficult to make. Millet (known locally as massango) is grown in the broad stretch of southern Angola that extends from the Cunene to the Cuando, (AZ 32, 33, 34, 35, and 36). Millet is characterized by its hardiness, and is more drought resistant than sorghum. It is well adapted to the poor sandy soils of the South and Southeast. Like sorghum, it is typical of the subsistence agriculture of pastoral peoples, who frequently establish their plots (lavras) in areas that have been manured by their cattle.

26. Maize is the basis of the diet in the densely populated central region of Angola. It is grown over a wide area. Essentially a rainfed crop, it is the cornerstone of smallholder farming (AZ 17, 18, 24, 25, 30 and 31). Most favorable conditions are found between latitudes 14 degrees S and 15 degrees S, with precipitation in the 800-1000 mm range concentrated in a relatively short period of 4-5 months. This characteristic rainfall pattern changes from S to N, with the rainy season growing longer and having a brief dry period (known as the pequeno cacimbo)

separating two periods of heavy rainfall. Well-structured argillaceous soils are well suited to this crop, particularly those with vertic characteristics and even tropical fersialitic and parferralitic soils. Until the mid 1970s, Angola produced sizable maize surpluses. Output in 1970/71 amounted to approximately 709,750 tons, of which almost all came from the peasant sector. We estimate present production to be about 250 to 300 thousand tons a year, mostly for home consumption.

27. Oil Palm (elaeis guineensis) grows in a band of territory in the N and NW up to an elevation of 500-600 m. Oil palm trees are found in the hot, humid valleys (AZ 1, 2, 3, 4, 6, 7/8, and 15), where dry-season water requirements are met by groundwater close to the surface. Palm oil plays a major role in the local diet, extending far beyond the tree growing areas. Smallholder cultivation would be of considerable interest along the banks of the major watercourses. Oil production was in the 20,000 ton range in the early 1970s with the smallholder sector accounting for about 10 percent of the total. Production has since declined to negligible levels, about 600 tons in 1986. Sisal: Angola was one of the world's major sisal producers. This fiber was grown in two main regions: north of the Cuanza, in the subplateau region of Lucala-Cacuso (AZ 13/14), and South, in the Bocoio-Cubal region and subplateau region (AZ 23). In addition to these areas with favorable transportation infrastructure (with the southern area also benefitting from proximity to the port of Lobito), sisal plantations were also found in other parts of the country, notably the interior plateau in Kuanza-Sul. Yields were generally high. The Lucala-Cacuso subplateau zone can be identified as the most favorable area for this crop. (AZ 17,23 27). The region generally has a subhumid climate with a relatively hot six-month dry season followed by a rainy season with precipitation averaging 800 - 1,100 mm. and good soils. Sisal cultivation has virtually ceased today. Production was around 48,000 tons a year in 1970/71.

28. Tobacco is an important smallholder crop especially in the Cacuso-Cota area (AZ 13/14) and a significant commercial crop in the Southwest, particularly in the Quilengues-Chongoroi area (AZ 27). Smallholder production is in small plots using simple technology to produce a dark air-dried tobacco with ready local market. Commercial growing is practiced on the moderately fertile light or medium-textured soils found along the banks of the major rivers of the Southwest, yielding high quality flue-dried yellow tobacco. In addition to the traditional tobacco-growing areas listed above, other regions also lend themselves to this crop, notably AZ 25, 31 and 34. Tobacco production satisfied the needs of the Angolan market. Three processing plants (two in Luanda and one in Benguela) were fully employed. In 1973, 4,800 tons of Virginia and Burley type tobacco were produced, including a few hundred tons of dark tobacco produced by the smallholder. Today production is negligible. Wheat growing was widespread in the higher-elevation areas of the planalto, particularly in the Central Plateau (AZ 24) and the Huila Highlands (AZ 30), where it is cooler during the rainy season. Cooler conditions coincide with the crop's vegetative cycle, making it rather susceptible to rust and causing considerable fluctuations in output. Thus, whereas production in the fifties was in the region of 30,000 tons, the 1970/71

harvest amounted to only 22,566 tons. The smallholder sector contributed 43% of the total. Trials at the Cunene Experimental Station for Irrigated Crops (AZ 34) with irrigated wheat, produced excellent results, effectively controlling the rust problem.

29. Forestry Resources: Angola's forestry resources and potential are considerable. In 1973, 182.0 thousand tons of forestry products were exported. In 1985 wood exports were 24.9 tons, up from 1.2 thousand tons in 1980 (Appendix table F.6). Maiombe in Cabinda (AZ 1) and Dembos (AZ 3) regions have the main forestry potential. Dense humid forests are the centers for the production of such valuable species as mahogany, mulberry, tola and limba. Worthy of mention are other stands of forest in other parts of the North and Northeast, (AZ 6), containing noble species (panga-panga), (AZ 4). In the East and Southeast of Angola, (AZ 26/28, 32 and 35), the dry forest or open forest stands growing in the vast territory covered by Kalahari sand also include a variety of species of economic value such as girassonde and mussibi. The potential for exotic species of trees such as eucalyptus and pine is considerable. Eucalyptus grandis and E. saligna adapt well, particularly at elevations above 1,200-1,300 meters. A number of pine species do well, notably pinus patula, found in extensive areas at higher elevations. The eucalyptus area exceeded 150,000 ha in the early 1970s, with the wood produced going to the Alto Catumbela pulp mill and the Benguela Railroad. A second pulp mill was under construction in the mid seventies but was never completed. The Alto Catumbela pulp mill has been out of operation for several years.

(2) Livestock

30. Livestock potential is significant though production faces similar difficulties as the rest of agriculture. Water has become a major problem. Livestock acquires special importance in the immediate future considering that about 45 percent of livestock is found in relatively secure areas. Native livestock herders, pastoralists, raised cattle as a way of life long before the arrival of the Portuguese colonizers in the 1500s. In the early colonial period Portuguese merchants exchanged goods for animals with the pastoralists. As the colonial rule became more established, merchants turned farmers and cattle raisers while continuing to trade with the native people. Later, large scale ranches were established with improved animal stock and increased commercialization. The pastoralists travel from place to place as a way of life, searching for water and grass, trying to escape from tripanosomiasis transmitted by tsé-tsé fly. For them cattle are the main source of food, beef and milk, which is bartered for goods. They are also the peasant's status symbol. Cattle raising, due to its economic, social, religious, and cultural characteristics, is the center of a peasant's life in these regions, the standard of value, and cattle are part of the festivities of birth, puberty, and wedding. Though pastoralism and ranching are different systems of cattle raising, the two became interdependent. The ranchers were the main source of meat, the pastoralists were an alternative source, with the stock they maintained as their security and savings. The disruption of ranching at independence and the neglect of the pastoralists, compounded by security

problems and lack of goods for exchange, reduced beef production from 24.5 thousand tons a year in the early seventies to 3.5 thousand tons at present. Having been a meat exporter in the early 1970s, Angola is now a meat importer, importing about 20.0 thousand tons of meat yearly.

31. Beef Cattle raising in the South and Southeast is dependent on the availability of water. Water tends to limit, even more than pasture, the reproduction rate and herd size. In the traditional pastoral zones (AZ 22/29, 23, 27, 30, 31, 33, 35 and 36), cattle numbers reflected the limitations imposed by the environment. Numbers would decline sharply at the height of the dry season, when the animals are obliged to crowd around the few sources of water. Many would die from lack of food brought on by overgrazing. Action was taken in the mid-fifties to break the boom-and-bust cattle cycle of abundance followed by drought. These measures took the form of providing, throughout the region (AZ 22/29, 33, 34 and 35), a series of livestock watering facilities by tapping underground water resources and constructing reservoirs. The results of these measures were spectacular. Instead of the old pattern of disastrous concentrations of animals around the few permanent water sources and on the banks of the Cunene during periods of crisis, the herds remained uniformly distributed across the territory, allowing a significant increase. In the course of some two decades, this expansion in grazing areas in the South resulted in an increase of one million head of animals (from 1.8 million in the mid fifties to approximately 2.8 million in 1974/75). The commercial sector increased significantly, with grazing areas ranging in size from 5,000 ha to 20,000. The period saw the establishment of several dozen large cattle ranches. Meanwhile beef cattle raising spread outside the traditional pastoral areas of the South into the plateau region (AZ 13/14, 17, 24 and 25) where oxen had hitherto been associated with farming only as work animals (for plowing and animal traction). The harshness and difficulties of the environment (poor natural pasture and inadequate health conditions) were overcome through proper disease and pasture control. The central region became a favorable area for stock raising, and in some respects more promising than the traditional areas in the South, as it was possible to raise a higher number of animals per unit of land without water availability problems. A large industrial abattoir was established in the city of Huambo, processing several hundred head of cattle a day. Cattle raising in Southern Angola is becoming increasingly difficult. South-African troops have systematically destroyed the water spots (artesian wells, small dams and water pools), most of which are now unusable. In consequence of the water problem, security and policy conditions, several areas where cattle were previously raised are now almost deserted.

32. Dairy Cattle. To judge by the success achieved in Cela where output reached 120,000 liters of milk a day after just a decade of operation, Angola's dairy potential is considerable. In many other parts of the country, particularly in the higher-elevation plateau regions, potential is as good. At independence, Angola had three main dairy production centers. The largest of these was the Cela-Catofe dairy with some 60,000 cows producing 120,000 liters a day, followed by Huambo (30,000 liters/day) and

Matala/Capelongo (15,000 liters/day). Apart from these modern well-equipped creameries (pasteurized and sterilized milk, cheese and butter), there were also smaller production facilities near the towns of Lubango, Benguela and Luanda. Goats represent a major source of animal protein for the local population and are resistant to drought. Like pigs, goats are found throughout the country. Their concentration was highest where a system of markets existed, geared to the consumer market in Luanda.

33. Herd Estimate. The likely distribution of cattle and goats in Southern Angola is shown in Table VII.1.

TABLE VII.1 Distribution of Cattle and Goats in Southern Angola

Province	Cattle	Goats
Huila	45%	63%
Cuneme	30%	14%
Namibe	10%	9%

Source: Ministry of Agriculture and Mission estimates.

According to the 1971 census, the last census available, there were 2,244,000 cattle and 872,000 goats. The Ministry of Agriculture estimated that in 1984 there were 5,408,000 cattle and 2, 101,000 goats. For these estimates, it was assumed that the annual net growth rates remained the same since independence as in the colonial period, i.e. an average growth rate of 7% per year for cattle and goats. A 7% growth rate, however, is excessive for the conditions prevailing in Angola since independence. The Mission estimates that cattle and goats have had a more modest rates of increase: 5% from 1971 to 1975, 2% from 1976 to 1981; 1% from 1982 to 1987. Thus in 1987 the cattle stock of Angola should be closer to 3,420,000, and the goats to 1,300,000 animals (Appendix Table F.1).

(3) Fisheries

34. Angola has a rich 1,600 km long shore for fishing. The Benguela's sea current improves the potential for catch along the Southern seaboard. The 1972 fish harvest reached 600 thousand tons. The Portuguese exodus in 1975 depleted Angola of its fishing fleet and expertise and the catch declined to as low as 76 tons in 1983. Present estimates are around 200,000 tons. The increase is due to the agreements the Angolan government reached with foreign companies to fish Angolan waters. These contracts helped to increase the catch, of which Angola receives 15 to 20%. The problem with these arrangements is that Angola does not have the means to independently verify the catch. Thus, although it is estimated that in 1985, 470,000 tons of fish were caught, reported amounts were only 195,000 tons. The technologies used by some foreign fishing fleets are endangering future

potential. It is suspected that some use sucking techniques, which cause irreparable damage to seashore plankton. There have been reports of deterioration in fishing locations.

C. Rural Structure

35. Producer Organization. Policies regarding the organization of agriculture since independence have emphasized state or collective ownership. In the words of Agostino Neto, Angola's founding president, soon after independence, "Thousands of Angolans are owners of the means of production. We know very well how difficult it is in rural areas to transform these small-holdings into cooperatives or state farms. . .". 2/ However, some private commercial farms continued to exist and the present S.E.F. program encourages the expansion of private commercial farming and gives greater attention to the individual peasant producer. 3/ Two main forms of production organization were established:

1. The AUPs (Agrupamentos de Unidades de Produçâo) or State Farms. Abandoned commercial farms were combined into state-owned production units with managers and workers as public employees. In the case of coffee they are known as " empresas territoriais de café " (ETC). AUPs depend on the Government for financial support and almost without exception, they have incurred substantial losses. In 1986 the reported losses of state agricultural enterprises were 1,815 million Kwanzas, or U.S. $61.3 million at the official rate of exchange (Table VII.2). The AUPs reported a loss of 477 million Kwanzas, or 26% of the reported financial loss of the enterprises under the Ministry of Agriculture.

Table VII.2: Losses of State-owned Agricultural Enterprises
('000 Kwanzas)

	1983	1984	1985	1986
AUPs (State Farms)	1,259,957	714,800	399,073	476,590
Comp. Agrâr. e Empresas Locais	849,084	738,100	456,843	449,816
Emp. Territ. Café	396,537	725,600	1,178,771	951,519
Emp. de Serviços	923,867	245,700	47,768	379,737
Emp. Sect. Florest	-	-	52,394	261,512
EDAs	-	-	-	54,825
TOTAL DEFICIT	**1,581,711**	**2,424,200**	**2,134,849**	**1,814,525**

Source: Relatorio Sobre a Actividade do Sector Agrario em 1986, Ministry of Agriculture, 1987. This table does not include ENCODIPA which comes under the Ministry of Commerce. Its deficit was reported to be at about 100 million Kz in 1986.

2/ As reported in M. Wolfers, and J. Bergerol, Angola in the Front Line, Zed Press, 1983 p. 140.

3/ The Angolan constitution allows private ownership: "private activities and property, even those of foreigners, so long as they are useful to the country's economy and to the interests of the Angolan people"

2. Peasant Associations. Intended originally to be collectives, some as cooperatives, they have become agglomerations of peasant households making their own production decisions. Their presumed advantage is priority access to government services and inputs. Unlike state farms, peasant associations do not collectivize production.

36. Despite the effort to change the rural structure to conform to ideological considerations, the underlying peasant organization remains the same as it was before independence. Today the rural structure consists of three major groupings: (a) declining large-scale state farms; (b) relatively small numbers of Portuguese farmers known as "cooperantes," producing mainly fruit and vegetables; and (c) a large and dominant sector of peasant (small holder) agriculture. Various types of producers make up peasant agriculture. They include pastoralists herding in the Southern regions; small scale farmers producing maize, sorgum and cattle in the transitional zones of the pastoral areas of the South; small farmers of the fertile and densely populated central plateau; small farmers in the coffee areas; small farmers growing cassava as their main staple in the Northern and North Eastern regions and in the tropical forest; and a small number of hunters in the far South. The typical peasant family cultivates 1.5 to 2.5 ha with subsistence crops. Rotation and intercropping is the usual practice. Tools are rudimentary with the hoe most common. Animal traction is used in some areas as in the fertile areas of Huila province. We estimate that there are about 800,000 peasant family units.

37. Whereas peasant agriculture remained essentially unchanged since independence, commercial farming which flourished in colonial times, has almost disappeared. The Portuguese colonial policy supported settlers from Portugal with land grants and financial incentives (coffee, cotton, citrus, tobacco, beef, poultry, etc.) Substantial investments were made in infrastructure such as irrigation and transport in support of commercial farming. Efficiency varied, with highly productive farms in the minority, many of which belonged to urban-based industrialists and businessmen. Farm size varied, with some farms as large as several thousand hectares. Commercial livestock production is estimated to have been as high as 40% of the total. The commercial sector was supported by agro industries, marketing and processing infrastructure. Animal feed mills catered to the dairy, swine, and poultry industries. Other industries included flour mills, slaughter houses, fruit canning, vegetable processing, tobacco, and cotton processing.

38. Marketing. The Ministry of Internal Commerce (MIC) is responsible for the supply and distribution of goods in both rural and urban areas. In rural areas MIC is expected to supply consumption goods in exchange for agricultural products. However, the distribution of meat comes under the Ministry of Agriculture. Between twenty and thirty thousand merchants performed the rural marketing function before independence. Most combined trading with farming and cattle raising. The variety and flexibility of the large number of private traders and entrepreneurs responded to the local conditions in ways which the present centralized national trading system is not able to do. The availability of consumer goods and access to

them by the peasantry determine the amount of rural surplus available for exchange. The present system is failing to provide these needed goods, both consumer goods and agricultural inputs. As a result, the peasant is no longer producing for the market but only to meet his family's needs. In response to this situation, a sizable parallel market developed with prices that range from 20 to 60 times official price. With such major markets distortions, government stores have few goods to offer. It is estimated that up to 90% of family income in Luanda is consumed in the parallel market. Imports and food aid are increasing dramatically to close the food gap. As most peasants have sufficient cereals, imported food goes to meet urban demand, the needs of the armed forces, and the displaced.

39. It is difficult to estimate how much of the domestic agricultural production moves through official channels, although it could not exceed 10 to 15% of production. For instance, in 1986, maize production through official channels was 18.6 thousand tons. In contrast, total maize production is estimated to be about 300 to 350 thousand tons, having been as high as 700,000 tons in 1971. Consumer goods, when available in rural areas, can be purchased up to the value of the produce the peasant supplied the store at official prices. The shelves of these stores, however, are empty and what goods become available move quickly to the parallel markets. Greater reliance on market forces is needed, not because such reform is in itself sufficient to encourage agricultural development but because the flexibility which markets allow is a prerequisite for other requirements of long-term agricultural development.

D. Agricultural Support Services

40. The Ministry of Agriculture is responsible for most agencies and organizations that provide services to agriculture. Their effectiveness is seriously compromised by excessive centralization and a shortage of qualified staff. In the provinces, the Ministry of Agriculture is represented by the Delegation (Delegaçâo) with "directorates" supporting peasant associations, livestock, conservation, and other corresponding services from the national level. The emerging attention to the neglected peasantry is mistakenly perceived as requiring the creation of another layer of costly official institutions. The recently introduced agricultural development stations (EDAs), for instance, are already burdened with Departments of Planning, Finance, Human Resources, Technology, Supply, etc., another cumbersome bureaucracy. Agricultural policy should move in the opposite direction and should rely less on the public sector because of the latter's severe human, financial and organizational constraints. Some of the agricultural support service institutions are described below.

41. Mechanization: ENAMA (Empresa Nacional de Mecanizaçâo Agricola) provides mechanical services to agriculture. It is involved in ground clearing, leveling, and construction of earthworks for reservoirs. ENAMA's work is presently concentrated in the most secure areas in the south and in large scale state farms. In the absence of precise data it is difficult to assess the performance of the ENAMA. It is unlikely, however, that tractor

cultivation, with some exceptions, is economic in the conditions prevailing in Angola. Scarcity of technical and material resources have severely affected the work of ENAMA as well as the rest of agricultural services. In 1986 less than 2% of the work force of ENAMA was classified as technical. More than 70% of its tractor fleet was inoperative due to lack of spare parts and maintenance problems. The parts problem is complicated by a lack of uniformity in makes of equipment, a problem that is aggravated by individual donors promoting their own brands of equipment.

42. Fertilizer and Implements: DINAMA (Distribuidora Nacional de Materiais Agricolas) is responsible for the procurement and distribution of implements, fertilizer and insecticides. It distributes these materials on the basis of a national master plan for the agricultural sector as elaborated by the Ministry of Agriculture and approved by the Ministry of the Plan. DINAMA is heavily dependent on imports (Appendix Table F.4). There exists some Luanda-based capacity to manufacture small equipment such as machetes, hoes, and plows. Domestic production of implements is at a standstill, however, because of a lack of raw materials. All chemical fertilizers are imported. DINAMA has warehouses in Luanda and in the provincial capitals with outlets in some localities, which sell directly to the public and act as distribution points for delivery to state farms, peasant associations, etc. However, even when fertilizer and other inputs are available, transportation is a major constraint. The transport fleet of DINAMA cannot meet the demand for transport of large volumes of materials over long distances on poor quality roads. The problem is exacerbated by the high percentage of equipment out of commission, estimated at about 70% of the fleet. The security situation further hinders distribution.

43. Seeds. AGROSEMENTES is responsible for the purchase and distribution of seeds. Agrosementes was formed under the Ministry of Agriculture in 1983. Until then ENCOPIDA was responsible for this service. Seed distribution is given high priority by the Ministry of Agriculture. The amounts of seed distributed have been increasing in recent years. The distribution of maize seed increased from 773 tons in 1984, to 1,668 tons in 1985, and 1,994 tons in 1986. There has been some improved seed production under Yugoslavian supervision. There are plans for seed development in multiplication centers in a number of areas. Even when seeds are timely distributed the productivity of hybrid seeds is dependent on the timely availability of fertilizers (supplied by DINAMA). The coordination of complementary inputs has not worked well. AGROSEMENTES emphasis upon hybrid maize appears to be of limited relevance to the mass of peasants for whom the supply of proven local varieties might well be more beneficial.

44. Marketing and Distribution of Goods: ENCODIPA (Empresa Nacional de Comercializaçâo e Distribuiçâo de Produtos Agricolas). ENCODIPA provides consumer goods to rural areas in exchange for agricultural products. Until 1981 ENCODIPA was in the Ministry of Agriculture. Since then it has been under the Ministry of Internal Commerce. It operates through commercial outlets in urban and rural areas. The amounts of goods

procured and distributed by the Ministry of Internal Commerce are determined by the central government, as are the distribution among provinces and between cities and the countryside. The goods available through ENCODIPA fall far short of need and the system as presently functioning does not provide adequate incentive for production and exchange. Extension Services: The "dinamizadores rurais" (rural mobilizers) can be considered a type of rural extension agents. Approximately 1,000 dinamizadores have been trained since independence. Attrition has been around 30%. Their preparation is poor with only about one-third receiving any training in agriculture. Many receive only six months of training in total, some only three months. There does not seem to be any linkage between the work of the dinamizadores and the other services to agriculture.

45. Agricultural Development Stations (Estaçoes de Desenvolvimento Agricola - EDAs) are a recent introduction and a response to the failures of other institutions. EDAs aim to support peasant associations by helping with organization, technical, financial, and marketing services. The intention is to transform the state farms into peasant associations. Unlike state farms peasant associations do not collectivize production. The EDAs were designed to fill the gap between DINAMA and AGROSEMENTES and the peasant. They are to receive supplies and deliver them to the peasant associations through lower level Centros de Desenvolvimento Agricola (CDAs). The CDAs in turn direct the activities of the dinamizadores rurais (extension). EDAs are flawed by the same structural and strategic inadequacies found in the overall agricultural structure and policy. They face the same problems as all institutions set up to serve agriculture, notably a lack of training, an excessive centralization, a lack of resources and economic policies adverse to agriculture and the peasantry.

46. Agricultural Education and Research. (a) Agricultural Education. The institutions which serve agriculture, whether private or public, depend upon skilled people. The scarcity of trained people at all levels is enormous. The colonial regime provided little training to Angolan nationals. Decolonization and the withdrawal of trained persons depleted all sectors of the skills needed to manage agriculture from the most basic level. The situation of the agricultural schools described below shows the poor state of agricultural training facilities.

47. The Agricultural School at Huambo began graduating Eng. Agronomos (general agricultural degree) in 1983. It expects eight to ten graduates a year in agriculture plus four to five in veterinary science. Of about 80 students admitted, 75% dropped out the first year. Staff, materials and general infrastructure are very deficient, and lack of food is a main reason for the high drop-out rate. Of the elementary and secondary level agricultural training schools in Angola, none is fully operational, due mainly to the security situation. They include:

(1) Escola de N'Gangassol; Situated in the province of Malange, it was inaugurated in 1979 to offer training in basic agriculture, livestock, cooperative development, accounting and agricultural mechanization. The

plan was to have 300 students. Because construction was not completed, the maximum capacity is 80 students. As of August 1983 this school has been closed due to the gravity of the military situation.

(2) Escola de Mecanizaçâo de Sumbe; this school is located in the province of Kuanza-Sul. It was inaugurated in 1979. Its objective is training in agricultural mechanization at the regional level. Its planned capacity was 200 students, but construction was never completed. Though enrollment reached 59 students, the facilities proved inadequate. The deterioration of the military situation in the area forced the school's closing in March of 1984.

(3) Escola de Mecanizaçao de Huila; this school is situated in the city of Lubango. It was inaugurated in 1978 as an agricultural mechanization training school to serve the needs of the provinces of Huila, Namibe, Kunene and Kuando Kubango. The school has a maximum capacity of 120 students, and being located in a secure city continues to be in operation.

(4) Escola Agraria do Café da Gabela; this school is in Gabela in the province of Kuanza-Sul. In 1978, 127 students studied courses in sanitation. Its present state is not clear, but it is probably closed.

(5) Centro Comandante N'zage (Huila). Closed. Offering only occasional seminars.

(6) Centro de Formaçâo de Dinamizadores Rurais para o Cafe do Kilombo (Kuanza-Norte) has been closed since May 1982 because it has no eating facilities. There is lack of water, light and food.

(7) Centro de Formaçâo de Quadros do Huambo; has been closed since 1982 for regular courses. A few training courses are given intermittently in the province.

48. With such limitations in training facilities and the exodus of qualified personnel at independence, human resources for agriculture are practically non-existent. The human resource deficiencies and the long time needed to reach even a minimum critical manpower level call for alternative less human-resource intensive paths. Even when institutions such as those for extension and research are considered immediate prerequisites to agricultural development, simple and very selective forms should be encouraged rather than the wholesale transplant of institutions from environments with ample human resources. A better understanding of already existing peasant systems and their improvement might be a better approach to rural development in these circumstances.

49. (b) Agricultural Research: The Instituto de Investigaçâo Agronomica has a staff of six agronomists, five of whom studied at Huambo. The institute is the entity responsible for agricultural research in Angola. It is located at Chianga, 25 km from Huambo. Before independence the institute had 60 professionals, some with graduate training. With the Portuguese exodus only one remained. The lack of trained people and the

dismantling of the limited agricultural research at independence, left Angola with no research capability. Some sporadic contacts with international research centers take place (CIMMYT, ICRISAT, INTSORMILL) 4/ and national programs, such as with EMBRAPA in Brazil. Such linkages, when systematic and over the long term are vital to Angola's needs for agricultural development. For this to happen, however, a minimum of human resource development must take place. More interaction with international research efforts is of benefit to Angola and must be encouraged. The necessary two way scientific communication, however, can take place effectively only when national professionals with minimum scientific and research method training are available. Without Angolan professionals agricultural research will remain dependent on external human resources and Angola will not acquire the capability for adaptation and continuity.

E. Agricultural Policy Adjustment and Reform

50. Policy Adjustment and Response. The memory of colonial exploitation and the identification of that period with a liberal market-based agricultural policy, should not prevent the return to greater market reliance. The objectives of SEF are an indication that Angolan economic policy is beginning to make this distinction. The distribution of power and land ownership are now different from that in the colonial period. The possible adverse effects of market-based agricultural policy can be dealt with through corrective measures and selective controls. The balance between social and economic objectives in agriculture does not have to preclude incentives for individual production, especially from the peasantry.

51. The Government authorities consulted by the Mission were unanimous about the need for urgent reform of agricultural policy. Policy reform is prerequisite to the neened technical assistance, institution building and agricultural investment for the country's long-term agricultural development. Present production levels are so distant from production possibilities and past performance, that an initial positive response is assured. A program of agricultural policy adjustment should draw from experience elsewhere in Africa and should include: (a) production incentives through remunerative prices and the availability of consumer goods and inputs in the country-side; (b) institutional reform encouraging local intermediaries and private transport for marketing and distribution; (c) investment for rehabilitation of storage and transport; and (d) coordinated and focussed technical assistance and training to strengthen selective support services for agriculture, especially agriculture research.

4/ CIMMYT - International Center for Wheat and Maize, Mexico
ICRISAT - International Center for Semi-arid Tropics, India
INTSORMILL - International Project for Sorghum and Millet, Nebraska
EMBRAPA - Brazilian Agricultural Research Company

52. Agricultural supply response to price incentive is shown to be positive throughout Africa, and Angolan agriculture should not be an exception. A recent experience in Angola illustrates this. Improved availability of goods in the countryside of the Huila Province has brought about significant increase in marketable supply. The total production of maize moving through official channels reached 17.5 thousand toons in 1986, of which 1/3 was produced in Huila. Though this performance reflects better security conditions in this province, it is also an indication of peasant response to incentives. This production increase is modest when considering that in 1970 Huila marketed 50.0 thousand tons of maize.

53. Marketing Policy should focus on improving domestic and international marketing of agricultural products. The marketing structure for agriculture should follow the guidelines of S.E.F. for decentralization and reducing public sector dominance of the economy. Retail outlets should be transferred to the private sector. The Ministry of Internal Commerce (MIC) should become a regulating and monitoring agency instead of being directly involved in the marketing function as at present. Public sector marketing, to the extent that it remains, should have to compete with the private sector with respect to imports and wholesale trade. Measures to improve marketing include: (a) legalization of the "Candongueiro" (private intermediary) and development of a system of support for marketing such as credit for transport; (b) transfer to the private sector of the retail outlets of the Ministry of Internal Commerce; (c) concession to private traders of a major share of foreign exchange earnings from exports; and (d) review of the operations of the more than one hundred public enterprises under the Ministry of Agriculture with a view to divesting or eliminating them, with exception of those providing technical assistance, training, and research services.

54. The projected supply response outlined in Appendix table F.7 is thought to be attainable with resources already available. Maize yields are presently about 500 kg/ha. At present average yields, 1.6 ha per family is needed to meet subsistence needs; without land productivity gains a family can increase cultivation to 2.5 ha. with their available labor and land. Even though short term production response can come from the available labor and land, the long term development of Angolan agriculture will require improved practices, inputs and trained people. Increasing the financial and human resources, and improving the institutional set-up and organization necessary for such development is a long-term process. Use of improved seeds, fertilizer, insecticides and animal traction will raise yields significantly. The project "Le Developpement des Cultures Vivrieres dans la Province de Huila" with support from Caisse Centrale de Cooperation Economique of France, expects yields of 1.5 tons for maize per ha by the participating 15,000 target farms. The average yield of maize reported by the pilot survey at Hogue was 1,216 kg/ha.

55. Increasing agricultral production will require <u>institutional reform</u> to reduce central state control and provide for more reliance on markets and the peasantry. Such a reform is not as radical as it might appear since, in practice, production and distribution of the bulk of the

agricultural output already takes place outside the formal institutions and controls. This is also the case with institutional policy, i.e., the gap between the official, controlled and planned actions and what actually happens, is considerable.

56. The political economy of adjustment. A broad liberalization of agricultural production, marketing and distribution for all agricultural and food products within the context of a liberal macroeconomic policy as expounded in the objectives of S.E.F., is a preriquisite to reversing the dangerously declining food situation in Angola and to start re-energizing the country's agricultural potential. The major part of the economy already operates in the parallel informal sector. As the contribution of agriculture to Government revenue is marginal, with the exception of coffee, the liberalization of agricultural policy will have no adverse effect on current public finance. Rather, with appropriate policies, the increase in agricultural production should improve agriculture's contribution to public revenue.

57. The short-term effect of price liberalization will be adverse for those who presently benefit from access to agricultural products through channels at controlled prices. But only a small share of the population has access to this limited supply and the percentage of income spent on price controlled goods is small. A senior level public servant family in Luanda, with two members working, consumes about five percent of its monthly incomeon "the circuito official" --Goverment stores at official prices. What the agricultural policy reforms will accomplish is to formalize/legitimize what is now the parallel economy. An indirect benefit of more reliance on the market, would be the reduction of corruption which the large discrepancies between official and parallel market prices is fomenting.

58. In conclusion, there are secure areas in Angola for an immediate agricultural production response to policy adjustment. The gap between present levels of production and potential is so great, that initial response should be significant. For this to happen the system of state control must move toward much more reliance on markets and private initiative than at present. The social costs of such adjustment are small as the bulk of the agricultural economy is already operating outside the formal channels. Policy incentives and institutional reforms should be followed by investments for long-term development of human resources, infrastructure and services to improve productivity. Agriculture is therefore, a key sector in the on-going transition of Angola from a most suffering and centrally controlled economy, to a country of peace and a market enabling system. Agriculture, especially the food producing peasantry, will be a beneficiary of such a change and also a major contributor to its success.

TRANSPORT AND COMMUNICATIONS

A. Sector Overview and Organizations

1. Sector Overview. Angola's basic infrastructure reflects strong colonial antecedents and its present configuration, though not its condition, is essentially unchanged since Independence (see map 1). In 1975, the system had an enviable modal mix for a developing nation - rail, highway, air, cabotage and shipping - which provided an excellent opportunity for potential transit facilities to match any coherent economic development planning. It possessed a distinctive lateral three rail-port corridor symmetry (north, central and southern), supported by feeder road networks. Additional highways provided very basic north-south provincial links, as well as access to national borders. The air sector linked all key provincial cities and has subsequently grown to become the only dependable means of passenger and light freight transit over much of the country.

2. In general, Angola has a sparse provincial transport coverage which reflects the export corridor orientation inherited by the Government and the subsequent inability to modify this in the immediate post-colonial period. The air sector has grown significantly in terms of traffic, stock and revenues during this same period, though its infrastructure remains weak and under-invested. Ports are struggling to adjust to bi-directional traffic flows, new technologies and a cumbersome, inefficient labor system. Cabotage and international shipping services languish for lack of investment, poor organization and elderly, obsolete ships.

3. In 1987, Angola's transport infrastructure comprised 72,000 km of roads, 2,500 km 1/ of railways, 3 international and 3 cabotage ports, and a hierarchy of 31 airports. An estimated 12,000 non-military trucks and 400 buses, 40 locomotives, 11 long distance ships, 10 cabotage vessels, and 21 aircraft operated infrequent modal services at low levels of efficiency. Rail and port systems form specific corridors, which in 1975 ran eastward from Luanda to Malange (a distance of 430 km) in the north, Lobito to Luau (1,350 km) in the central heartland and Namibe to Menongue (750 km) in the south. Regions are linked to these corridors by 7,700 km of paved highway and 64,000 km of secondary and feeder roads, which together with the air services provide the main means of north-south travel. Cabotage currently accounts for 180,000 tons of freight between the four main ports and has potential for substantial growth. The Cabinda enclave is dominated by the oil industry and the non-petroleum infrastructure is small.

4. Output in 1985 and 1986 for the system under the Ministry of Transport and Communications (MINTEC) control is given in Table VIII.1. Total freight

---

1/ The figure of 2,500 km for the rail network is "operational or quasi-operational". For example, it includes the whole Benguela corridor kilometrage, incorporating that portion not used due to the security difficulties. The figure of 3,069 km cited in Vol. 1, Chapter 1, page 2, probably represents the total registered network, including abandoned sections.

traffic for 1986, at around 4 million tons, is about the same for 1985, the road and maritime sectors more than compensating for the continuing slide in rail traffic. In 1986 the number of passengers carried fell to below 30 million, following a decline in bus services, despite improvements in rail and air transit. The importance of the sector in terms of the national social product can be seen in Table VIII.2, where the performance of the transport sector under MINTEC control for selected post-Independence years in the 1980's is compared with the final year of colonial rule. The data for the first half of the 1980's show a significant decline in road revenues, rail and maritime holding constant, ports output slightly rising while communications and air travel have both shown strong growth. It is sobering to note, however, that the total sector value in 1985 was less than half that achieved in 1974.

Table VIII.1. OUTPUT OF MINTEC CONTROLLED TRANSPORT SERVICES, 1985-86.

	Freight [1]		Passengers [2]	
	1985	1986	1985	1986
Road	996.6	1,309.2	29,475.0	19,546.0
Rail	520.6	465.5	7,200.7	7,980.2
Maritime	511.9	598.1	-	-
Air	43.0	34.7	926.7	1,097.7
Ports	1,739.0	1,551.0	-	-
Total	3,811.1	3,958.5	37,602.4	28,623.9

Notes: 1. Thousands of tons
2. Thousands of passengers

Source: MINTEC, 1987.

Table VIII.2. OUTPUT OF TRANSPORT AND COMMUNICATIONS SECTOR 1/

Sector	1974	1984	1985	1986	1987
Transport:					
Road	10,432	2,164	3,457	6,277	5,261
Rail	7,393	807	864	820	910
Maritime	1,041	1,617	1,828	2,084	2,613
Air	1,411	5,371	6,905	5,397	5,212
Ports	13,708	1,793	2,112	2,130	1,716
Communications	958	1,712	1,916	2,172	1,919
Total	34,945	13,464	17,082	18,880	17,631

Note: 1. Gross output, in nominal values.

Source: MINTEC, 1988

5. The sector has significant real potential as an earner of foreign exchange which should be recognized in future national planning decisions. Foreign exchange revenues from international air links, foreign shipping and potential mineral shipments by rail could be considerable. The dramatic decline of the rail, port and shipping sectors as foreign exchange earners, however, cannot be easily reversed, especially given the present security situation. The importance of transportation to the Angolan economy and its central role in national recovery should be explicitly recognized in assistance programs. Transport services should be organized to provide agriculture with essential inputs, as well as moving produce to marketing and export centers, and providing the population with personal mobility.

6. Role of the Ministry of Transport and Communications. Before 1975, most transport policy issues were the responsibility of the Ministry of Public Works, Highways and Transport. The new Angolan government, despite a desire for centralized planning, did not continue this apex function, possibly due to the chaotic nature of post- Independence provision of transport services and the need to separate those transport activities of a strategic nature from those with economic or social impacts. The well documented destruction and exportation of all types of vehicles, as a result of armed hostilities and repatriation respectively, devastated the Angolan stock and the supply of vehicular services abruptly ceased in many regions.

7. The Ministry of Transport and Communications - MINTEC - was formed during 1976 and 1977 with the objective of providing public freight and passenger transport services to major markets and users throughout the provinces. It was given powers to fix tariffs, routes and service frequencies, as well as regulating the inflow of spare parts for vehicles through avice frequencies, as well as regulating the inflow of spare parts for vehicles through a material supply organization (ABAMAT) and another for vehicle maintenance (MANAUTO). MINTEC's responsibility extended to all major

modes although its power was in practice limited to assisting the formulation of policy and monitoring annual performance data. In an operational sense, the entities providing air, maritime, cabotage and rail services under the MINTEC umbrella can be regarded as autonomous. Investment programs are probably the main collaborative area but there is no clear evidence that the National Bank responds to well argued foreign exchange investment requests any more effectively or rapidly because of that association. MINTEC is not a major ministry either politically or financially, although the newly formed planning unit may do much to correct this in the future.

8. MINTEC data on transport service flows, levels and efficiencies, together with output and financial information only relate to entities under its control. However, road transport is the only mode seriously affected by this constraint since highway traffic data exclude those trucks and buses operated by parastatal enterprises under other ministries, notably the Ministries of Construction, Agriculture, Fishing, Interior, and Mines and Energy. Data collection for private sector vehicles, for example, is presently the responsibility of the Ministry of the Interior. In general, a number of government officials expressed a desire to return to an apex ministerial department with sole responsibility for all transport data collection and policy planning. In the absence of such an organization, the mission had difficulty in getting some vehicle data, frequently for understandable security reasons. The considerable fleet of Angolan military vehicles is therefore excluded from this report though they do at times provide transport services in sensitive areas. It should be recognized that MINTEC data under-record the numbers of active vehicles in Angola and this should be taken into account when considering road transport data in this report.

9. Security. Any review of the Angolan transport and communications sector must be prefaced with details about the security problem. Angolan independence was born out of armed hostilities and these have persisted, with varying degrees of intensity, up to the present time. The security problem has disrupted all transport modes and severely constrained corridor dimensions. Services have been cut, capital and equipment investment programs cancelled and domestic transit efficiency has been lowered. Destruction of at least 45 bridges and key sections of track has virtually paralyzed regional rail movement and only 20 percent of the system can be operated normally. Mineral shipments have ceased and port activities, 1.7 million tons in 1986, are concentrated on handling import commodities for urban consumption, especially food, for which rail transit is not well suited. Road transport to autarchic regional centers is only possible with armed convoys, operating irregularly and at great cost. The road system has not been systematically maintained since Independence, in part due to guerilla attacks, and 4600 km (60%) of paved surfaces need rehabilitation or reconstruction. An unfortunate consequence of these severe constraints is to attribute many transport modal inefficiencies to the war and not to managerial incompetence, lack of trained staff, inadequate spare ports, subsidies and state monopolies and other constraints present in the sector. MINTEC are recognizing this in their planning, and the intent of this report is to achieve a balance between the

real and sometimes intractable problems caused by the lack of security, and those unrelated and independent issues where improvements would increase modal effectiveness.

B The Highway System

10. Characteristics. The current road network classified by type and length is given in Table VIII.3. The paved part of the system - about 7500 km or 10 percent - accords with other African countries and represents basic economic and strategic links between key provincial cities and towns. Little or no maintenance has been given to these highways and more than half the length now requires rehabilitation or reconstruction. Pavement wear over time in the absence of maintenance is exponential and unless this problem is rapidly addressed, most of the paved network will soon show severe deterioration. Although gravel material provides an excellent running surface at low cost for the traffic levels typically observed in most provinces, it represents only 3 percent of the Angolan network. Since such roads are sensitive to lack of routine and periodic maintenance, it can be assumed that such roads are now in a very poor condition. The mission travelled gravel highways near Benguela and interviewed truck operators in other regions, and both confirmed the high levels of roughness that attends lack of gravel road maintenance.

Table VIII.3. ROAD NETWORK BY TYPE AND LENGTH, 1985.

Region	Paved	Gravel [1]	Earth	Penetration
North	2,064	401	7,270	3,011
West	1,756	708	8,074	9,776
Central	2,008	413	9,385	6,159
South	1,738	440	8,917	9,760
Total	7,566	1,962	33,646	28,706
Network Total [2]	71,880			

Notes: 1. Includes other local materials
2. Excludes 443 km. of unclassified types

Source: MINTEC Annuario Estatistico, 1986

11. Almost 90 percent of the Angolan road network is either termed earth or penetration. The former has some basic engineering design standards and the latter is purely judgmental in alignment, while both rely on the qualities of local soils. Here, maintaining good drainage and appropriate grading frequencies are the key elements in ensuring reasonable vehicular passage over their surfaces. These road types, however, are very vulnerable

to lack of maintenance since they are inherently weaker than the other, more expensive, categories. Operators stated that some sections of these roads had deteriorated to the point where they were barely passable and travel speeds had fallen to under 20 percent of normal operations. The main result of such road conditions is to raise rates to compensate for high operating costs and low productivity in precisely those areas where economic development is most vulnerable to high transit costs. To summarize, the highway system is in poor condition and needs modest funding for improvements which can be expected to have high rates of return on investment levels.

12. The 1987 truck population is estimated at 30,000 units but many of these are not operational or are severely underutilized. For example, in 1986, only 34% of the heavy vehicles controlled by MINTEC were operational and averaged around 11,500 km a year. Only the State trucking sector may presently import vehicles (though there are plans to change this) and this is reflected in a fleet profile which is technically sophisticated and young in age. A representative vehicle is the Volvo N 10, either in three axle rigid form or as the tractive unit of a 40 ton unit. The private sector, in comparison, operates vehicles generally at least 10 years old and of simple, robust design. Fortunately, they are well suited to current Angolan conditions where journeys are rarely longer then 50 km and vehicle trip speeds are low. The representative truck for this category is a Scania 75 or Mercedes-Benz two axle 13 ton unit.

13. Road Passenger Transport. All transport modes in Angola are capable of providing passenger transit. At Independence, however, it was the road system which offered the best prospects for efficient movements within urban areas, between cities and for the majority of inter-provincial north-south flows. The basic highway network was sound, bus operations neither required high levels of technical assistance nor large investment plans. Tariffs, if properly structured, would have generated funds for maintenance, fleet growth and improvements in transit infrastructure, such as bases, terminals and collector stations. A study by French consultants for Luanda mass transit had been commissioned, and the sub-sector looked to have a healthy future.

14. The scale and ferocity of the struggle and disruption of the mid-1970s altered all these parameters. Most of the vehicular stock comprising over 250,000 units was destroyed, exported or abandoned without the prospect of adequate maintenance. This and the exodus of managerial staff resulted in a dramatic decline in the supply of passenger services. As noted earlier, a principal reason for the creation of MINTEC was to correct these deficiencies through the provision of public transport services, at both provincial and city levels. In spite of some early success, principally in the Luanda conurbanation, public services have failed to match demand and are currently in a state of total collapse. The war situation has contributed significantly to the decline by diverting potential investment funds, restricting non-urban flows through destruction of infrastructure and vehicles, and finally creating an impetus for rapid, unplanned urbanization.

Table VIII.4. MINTEC BUS UTILIZATION DATA, AVERAGED BY PROVINCES, 1985.

Category and Provinces	Fleet Size	Bus Availability [1]	Active Buses
1 Bie, Kuene, Kwanza N, Kuando Kubango, Moxico, Zaire.	1 - 20	3.3	1.4
2 Cabinda, Huambo, Luanda N, Luanda S, Namibe, Malanje, Uige.	21 - 50	6.5	4.6
3 Beguela, Huila, Kuanza Sul.	51 - 100	10.3	9.3
4 Luanda	236	62.0	53.0
Totals (units)	728	165 [2]	121 [2]

Notes: 1. Those available for service. Active units are those in use.
2. Availability is 23% and Active 17%, of Luanda's total fleet.

Source: MINTEC, ETP, 1986.

Table VIII.4 gives bus passenger and utilization data for the latest available years. The MINTEC controlled bus fleet has fallen consistently through the 1980's to around 700 units in 1985, but more importantly only 17% on average are actually operating. This is one of the lowest rates encountered among developing countries 2/ and confirms the failure to meet even a small proportion of potential demand levels. Passenger traffic levels have fallen for all categories of trip - urban, provincial and inter-provincial and Table VIII.4 shows that bus availability has virtually ceased throughout many provinces. Table VIII.5 takes 1981 as a base to give indices for selected performance criteria for the Luanda public transport bus fleet for 1985 to 1987, which shows the dramatic contraction of service levels for the same years. It should be remembered that this persistent decline occurred at the time Luanda experienced one of its largest growth rates with the influx of war refugees.

2/ In the World Bank Technical Paper No. 68 "Bus Services - Reducing Costs, Raising Standards", only Accra (24%) and Lagos (20%) have companies that come close to the Luanda figures.

Table VIII.5. ETP URBAN BUS PERFORMANCE INDICES, 1985-1987 (1981=100).

	1985	1986	1987
Active Units	34	27	23
Trips	30	21	18
Passengers handled	29	19	13
Passengers per trip	96	89	74
Route Kilometers	30	21	19

Source: ETP, MINTEC; 1987

15. How then do people maintain mobility if public transport is not available? In Luanda there is some use of local trains. However, in most cases they simply walk, unless they are prepared to pay for private services. At times, the flow of pedestrians in Luanda is so great that it impedes bus speeds and so contributes to lowering efficiency. The average new trip fare for public transit in Luanda is around 12 Kz. while sharing a private taxi or pick-up costs 500 Kz. This average private fare or "processo quinhentos" is universal and governs all destinations within Luanda city boundaries for passengers, excluding large baggage which is extra. Since the average monthly salary is in the region of 12,000 Kz. simple arithmetic dictates that regular use of private services is not a valid option for most travellers. Accordingly, private companies and parastatals have taken to providing buses to collect their workers, in an effort to compensate for lack of public transport and assure timely attendance at work. Such arrangements are not socially efficient, however, since these buses operate a limited schedule at less than capacity along routes where lines of prospective public passengers wait at stops.

16. Inter-provincial traffic has all but ceased, and is unlikely to pick up until after the security situation improves, although MINTEC has plans for improving mobility in safe areas. Efforts are therefore being concentrated on urban operations in general, and the Luanda conurbation in particular, to effect short term corrective actions. These will be discussed in a later section of this report.

17. Road Transport and the Security Problem. Persistent lack of security throughout much of Angola has had a dramatic impact on road use, vehicle operating costs, tariffs and highway maintenance. The typical scenario over the past decade demonstrates the pernicious effect of regional instability on highway efficiency. First, attacks on farms and marketing centers interrupt the demand for road transport services while the supply of such services is affected by armed attacks on vehicles and personnel. Rates have to increase to compensate for reduced payloads and the risk of severe vehicular damage. Road maintenance activities become vulnerable to guerilla activities and cease in sensitive areas. Pavement damage, especially to the running surface, is not corrected and the resulting roughness causes additional vehicle damage and

higher operating costs. Tariffs then become so high that many products cannot be taken to market and sold at prices that cover production and transport costs. If vehicle attacks become severe, regional authorities may institute a convoy system where 20 or more vehicles are escorted by armed military patrols. This further reduces vehicle productivity since it may take days to assemble all trucks, speed of travel is set by the slowest vehicle (typically under 20 kph) and the convoy must stop for any breakdowns. Ultimately, as in 1987, the level of service is characterized by high costs, low speed, infrequent schedules and inadequate capacity.

18. These effects can be measured in at least two ways, by surveying Angolan operators and by simulating the major cost impacts. Data collected from ETP during the mission suggests that annual vehicle utilization is now 20% of the level before Independence. Cross-checking with private operators brought a similar response. Trips that were accomplished in a week (e.g. Luanda-Andrada-Luanda) prior to guerilla activities now take a month on average and have been as long as 53 days, principally because of convoy operations. Another group of constraints identified by operators are those resulting from a lack of any vehicle servicing infrastructure over most of Angola. Vehicles therefore travel with extra fuel, oil, water, spares and food for the crew which combine to raise costs and drive up rates. Tariffs in the public sector have not changed since Independence, but few vehicles are available at these prices and their route structure is limited. Private sector vehicles are more numerous (though older in age) and owners base their prices on real resource costs.

19. Vehicle operating cost (VOCs) impacts were simulated by using the VOCs sub-routine (Brazil equations) from the 1986 Highway Design and Maintenance model (HDM III), with input data supplied by ETP Luanda. Surface roughness is measured in terms of international roughness index (IRI) units which record meters of vehicle suspension displacement per kilometer of travel. These values are therefore in nominal terms where imported items are converted at the exchange rate 30 Kz to 1 US dollar. This should not affect the thrust of the arguments, however, since it is the cost differentials not the levels that are of interest. Some of the results selected to demonstrate the security impact on vehicle operations and road maintenance are presented in the statistical Appendix Table I.3. Two average operating conditions were calculated from Angolan vehicle records; <u>normal</u>: where annual vehicle utilization is 50,000 km and the vehicle travels fully loaded in each direction of travel; and <u>current</u>: where vehicle utilization has fallen to 15,000 km per year and no return loads are available. The drop in annual utilization affects lifetime usage. In the absence of road maintenance, the ton/km cost under normal operating conditions would be about a third of the cost under current conditions.

20. ETP staff confirmed that their vehicle utilization had fallen by at least these amounts, though they were unable to measure the effect on their rate structure, which had remained unchanged. Using HDM III to quantify the impact of current low levels of use, the ton/km cost is predicted to rise by over 300 percent compared to normal operations, assuming that road maintenance is carried out. However, it has already been noted that road maintenance has

virtually ceased and if this is modeled by deteriorating the pavement to 12 IRI - as is the case over much of the country - the ton/km cost rises by over 420 percent from normal levels, and this excludes any war damage premiums. The cost differentials resulting from the security problem in Angola as modeled in Appendix Table I.3 would make most agricultural products impossible to market, thus affecting both regional development and urban food supplies.

21. Road Accidents and Safety. It is not surprising that the combination of rapid urbanization, poor highway maintenance, disregard for safety and speed restrictions, heavy pedestrian flows and the growing urban mix of light and heavy (including military types) vehicles has resulted in high levels in vehicular accidents, personal injuries and property damage. In the first six months of 1987, 2,549 accidents were reported, resulting in 475 deaths and estimated damage values exceeding Kz 30 million. Urban Luanda accounted for 75 percent of reported accidents involving over 3,800 vehicles. In comparison with the corresponding period in 1986, deaths have increased by 15 percent and accidents by more than 80 percent. Outside Luanda, Huila and Huambo provinces registered increased accident rates, although the deteriorating security situation has prevented many regional authorities from reporting any data. The figures are, therefore, incomplete and almost certainly under-reported, but at this stage of the review such precision is unnecessary. What is important for the planning process is to note that the pain, suffering and financial penalties associated with traffic accidents in Angola are on the increase and contribute to the decreased efficiency and increased costs of the road transport system.

C. Rail Transport

22. Background. The rail system was principally designed to transport minerals and other goods across export corridors to key Angolan port complexes for maritime trans-shipment. Passengers were also carried but the relatively small number of carriages in the rolling stock shows it was not the main business activity. The security situation since 1975 has hit railways particularly hard and the figures in Table VIII.2 demonstrate that by 1985 the value of Angolan railway systems had fallen to 12 percent of the 1974 figure. Rail output fell even more from 1985 to 86 for freight but not for passengers. This indicates that latent passenger demand should be a feature of a short term recovery program.

23. The financial consequences of rail's continuing inability to supply those services for which it was designed is shown in Table VIII.6 which gives the simple income and expenditure accounts of the three main rail companies in 1985 and 1986. Only Mocamedes (CFM) made money and in both years it was only enough to offset the losses of Luanda (CFL), leaving the massive annual deficits of Benguela (CFB) to accumulate into very significant amounts, sustainable only through National Bank support.

24. In all three railway systems, a variety of serious problems plague operating efficiency. The rail infrastructure is in poor shape, guerrilla activity has damaged bridges on all three systems and in some regions the track has been mined. Lack of maintenance has resulted in loss of rail

ballast and the track consequently cannot support the weight or travel speed for which it was originally designed. Rails themselves need to be made consistent in specification and renewed over selected sections. Locomotives have been under-utilized and frequently committed to premature scrapping through lack of skilled manpower and spare parts for their maintenance. The passenger and freight traffic data for the three systems over a selected period (including 1973 to show pre-Independence) given in Table VIII.6 demonstrate the serious disruptions in service schedules. Locomotives and stock availability and activity for 1985 and 1986 is given in Table VIII.7, together with a breakdown of active units by company in 1986. Yet the railway companies continue to employ the largest number of workers of any mode, nearly 8,000 individuals. The implications of these data for each of the main rail companies, together with a description of current activities is now given.

Table VIII.6. RAIL TRANSPORT, PASSENGERS AND CARGO[1], 1973-85

	1973	1978	1980	1982	1984	1985
Luanda						
Passengers ('000)	946	2,012	4,058	3,047	1,585	1,291
Cargo (1,000 tons)	301	155	129	102	84	63
Benguela						
Passengers	1,591	1,930	2,470	3,925	3,617	3,871
Cargo	3,279	379	344	296	199	263
Namibe						
Passengers	394	1,249	1,108	1,398	1,848	2,040
Cargo	6,409	144	-	251	171	196

Notes: 1. Excluding traffic at Amboim

Source: Annuario Estatistico, MINTEC 1986

25. Luanda System. Luanda (CFL) is the neglected rail corridor of Angola. It may have the best potential for making a strong short-term impact in the transport sector; since it has both links to the port of Luanda and lines through the largest conurbation, possesses excellently located (if somewhat dilapidated) secure maintenance and marshalling yards, and is regionally linked to Dondo and Malange, both of strategic and economic importance. At the moment, however, it is in a very weak and neglected condition.

26. In 1986 it employed around 1,400 and carried 1.7 million passengers, about 40 percent of its 1978 figure, and 21,000 tons of cargo, well down from the 1985 figure of 63,000 tons. Its port activities are virtually non-existent, thus contributing to downtown vehicular congestion, the service to Dondo (210 km) is down to once a day and the line to Melange is cut, with 10 bridges destroyed. The potential for providing urban passenger transit to Luanda is under-exploited and there is no interaction with bus services.

There is an urgent need to provide additional locomotives, renovated passenger carriages and other rolling stock to increase service schedules, first within Luanda province and subsequently in other regions. A proposal to improve this system is discussed in a later section.

27. Benguela System. The Benguela railway (CFB) is the best known Angolan transport facility. Running a total length of 1,350 km from the port of Lobito to Benguela, then eastward via Huambo where the engine sheds are located, to Luau on the Zambian border, it represents a social, economic and political link that both government and foreign nations have found difficult to ignore. It is by far the largest rail company, employing over 4,500 staff. A number of difficult problems would have to be resolved before the corridor could resume normal operations, including the most serious one of all, that of security and regional political stability. There are also big financial and technical difficulties to be addressed - the likely cost of renewing all corridor components is in excess of US $600 million, at 1985 prices - but these issues are secondary, and should the political issues be removed there is no doubt that international investment funding would be made available. These, however, have to be regarded as long-term planning components given the worsening war situation in the south.

Table VIII.7. RAILWAY LOCOMOTIVE AND ROLLING STOCK DATA, 1985-1986

	1985	1986	Company		
			Luanda	Benguela	Mocamedes
Locomotives [1]					
Existing	196	165			
Available	53	42			
Active	51	37	5	22	10
Carriages					
Existing	184	198			
Available	94	99			
Active	63	66	22	26	18
Wagons					
Existing	3,834	3,830			
Available	3,114	2,290			
Active	2,234	2,124	323	1,528	273

Note: 1. Excludes steam engines.

Source: MINTEC, 1986; Lobito Port Transport System, SATCC, 1987; Reconstruction Program for the Provinces of Huila, Namibe and Cunene, Dar Al-Handasah Consultants for UNDP and Ministry of Planning, 1986.

28. Currently, CFB reports that 24 of its locomotives are now out of service or sabotaged and despite five extra transferred from Mocamedes in 1984, the total of operational tractive units now numbers around 18. It has standardized on the General Electric type U-20-C, even though the 15.4 ton

axle load when laden makes it heavy for the 60 lb/yd rails used over some sections of the track east of Huambo. Diesel locomotives are used on the Lobito-Benguela link, and from the coast up to Huambo but CFB have the intention of extending diesel use over all its network given track renewal and availability of locomotives. There are sufficient wagons available but passenger coaches are in short supply, and the 26 units are totally inadequate for the existing demand. The Huambo workshops with its apprentice training school is equipped for all types of repair and maintenance work, although the new diesel repair shop is unfinished. The security problem has closed down the lucrative international mineral business and national freight traffic is confined to the Benguela province (175,000 tons) and between Lobito and the provinces of Bie and Huambo (70,000 tons). Passenger traffic has steadily grown and should be a source of future growth and income.

29. In the shorter term, there are alternative investment options that can be considered for CFB. The Lobito-Benguela-Huambo section of the system has been carrying increased passenger traffic in the 1980's and additional carriages and locomotives could significantly increase future flows. Freight traffic is very modest but if some regional agricultural development can be directed into the secure area of the central zone, demand for agricultural inputs and exports of produce should create higher levels of rail demand. Even with this program, however, significant problems remain. Like all other railway companies in Angola, CFB lacks trained operational and management staff and such shortages cannot easily be resolved. In the short run, therefore, the situation for CFB looks bleak. There is little prospect of increasing its business to the point where income and expenditures might broadly balance, and the accumulated deficit looks set to grow larger. More than any other transport entity in Angola, the future of CFB is firmly in the hands of politicians and the military, not only of Angola but those of their neighbors and the super-powers.

30. Mocamedes Railway. The Mocamedes railway (CFM) contains 756 km of track, most running between Namibe and Menongue in the Cuando-Cubango province. There are two branches; Lubango-Chibia-Chiange (120 km) now completely abandoned and Dongo-Cassinga (110 km) also closed since the iron ore mines ceased operations in 1975. Currently, traffic is operating normally between Namibe and Matala (430 km) and armed military convoys are necessary for travel beyond Matala to Dongo. The war situation makes it difficult to schedule any services beyond Matala, and the proximity to Namibia makes the system vulnerable to sabotage. Nevertheless, CFM has managed to achieve a steady growth in passenger traffic, comprising urban services in Lubango (1.02 million, 1985) and long distance between Namibe and Lubango (1.07 million, 1985). The latter trip takes around seven hours (around 30 kph) for both passenger and freight services. Costs for cargo are about one third the road ton/km rate which indicates that any regional agricultural planning will use the rail corridor as a central transit link to the coast.

31. CFM employs around 1700 staff although there is a distinct lack of trained personnel in all professional categories. The railway needs additional locomotives and rolling stock, particularly passenger coaches. Of the 10 engine units now operational, half are over 20 years old and are

considered to be in poor condition. The long distance passenger schedule is modest and runs every other day. Passenger demand is high due to the cost and irregular service of alternative modes (principally road) which results in coaches being overcrowded and comfort levels minimal. CFM believes that there is sufficient demand to run a train a day, in both directions. Freight trains are full running eastwards and empty from Lubango to Namibe, although regional agricultural planning could bring about a more equitable balance in the future.

32. To summarize, there are similar constraints within the three systems. First the security situation makes rail networks particularly vulnerable to attack and sabotage. Large sections of the network are now unusable due to damaged bridges and mined track. Second, technical assistance is urgently required to help maintain locomotives, upgrade rolling stock and check electrical equipment. Thirdly, there is lack of spare parts and special supplies like lubricants which has resulted in low utilization patterns, as equipment awaits repair, and the premature scrapping of locomotives and rolling stock. Finally, track infrastructure is weak and many stations and supply points have been abandoned. Short term investment programs can be devised for all systems, though they are challenging because they are multi-faceted. Even modest programs require engineering, management, technical and planning inputs which need careful coordination and synthesis. These will be considered in later sections.

D. The Air Sector

33. Angolan Airlines - TAAG. The domestic air system was established in 1940, when 6 seater Rapides operated services between Luanda and the cities of Lobito, Huambo and Mocamedes. It grew steadily during the colonial period and has been the only mode to show continued growth since Independence. It was reformed in 1977 as Angolan Airlines (TAAG) and by 1980 had taken over the duties of other companies confiscated or made redundant after 1975. During the period 1980 to 1986, passenger traffic has increased at an annual rate of 15 percent, while freight and mail traffic has been closer to 20 percent. Table VIII.1 shows that in 1986 over a million passengers flew TAAG and 35,000 tons of cargo was carried on company planes. The value to the Angolan economy is considerable, and Table VIII.2 shows that 45 percent of the total transport and communications sector value in 1985 was attributable to TAAG operations. It is clearly an extremely important mode in the sector and its continued prosperity and efficiency is critical to economic growth.

34. TAAG has the direct responsibility for carrying out a wide variety of activities, ranging from the usual marketing/ticketing through to cleaning and catering, the latter currently sub-contracted by the most efficient world airlines. This broad responsibility results in a cumbersome structure with a large and inefficient workforce which is difficult to manage. TAAG in early 1986 employed around 5,400 staff but most had little technical skills or managerial experience. In terms of marketing, TAAG divides its domestic operations into four regions of approximately equal importance, while international flights are grouped by continent - Europe, South America and Africa. Scheduling performance is not good and only 87 percent of TAAG's

scheduled flights in 1986 were actually operated. Timing is also poor and only 32 percent of international flights and 56 percent of domestic flights were considered on time. 1986 operations grouped by geographic markets are given in Table VIII.8.

Table VIII.8. TAAG OPERATIONS BY MARKET, 1986

Domestic	Zone			
	North	East	Central-South	Litoral-South
Passenger (%)	25	25	21	29
Freight (%)	16	16	14	54

International	Continent		
	Europe	South America	Africa
Passenger (%)	64	7	29
Freight (%)	79	13	8

Source: TAAG, 1987.

35. A balance in domestic passengers and freight is noted, with the exception of the coastal routes south of Luanda (especially the key Luanda-Benguela route) where there is a strong demand for cargo services. Internationally, Europe continues to dominate the market and more especially the Luanda-Lisbon route within the European network, which accounted for 36 percent of total passenger movement and 42 percent of cargo flows. Luanda-Brazil is the only South American route and is growing fast as trade links develop and the Kapanda dam project is implemented.

36. Details of the 1986 TAAG civil aircraft fleet are given in Appendix Table I.5. The fleet comprises 6 Boeing 707's for international routes, 5 Boeing 737's for African and domestic flights, 5 Fokker F27-600's for domestic flights to the smaller airports and 2 Yak 40's to complement the Fokkers. TAAG also operates a fleet of 10 light aircraft. The age in flight hours and years of the long range Boeing's is of interest, indicating that they will soon require replacement. The Boeing 737 is the workhorse of the fleet, and will continue this role despite the relatively high number of annual landings and a steady loss due to accidents (3 aircraft lost). The Fokkers have also provided excellent service and seem ideal for the smaller airports. The Russian Yak aircraft are not well liked and their use is infrequent, with a number waiting repair at Luanda.

37. Flight crews are highly regarded by TAAG management and the company are confident about the pure operational element of their business. Indeed, three months ago they began separate charter operations. It is the joint problems associated with general management and back-up services that create most problems. Scheduling, management, ticketing, spares and inventory control,

support services and airport management are identified by TAAG as constituting constraints to growth and efficiency. Scheduling is a serious problem, particularly on domestic services where Luanda is the hub airport. Lack of basic services at regional airports - fueling, storage, simple maintenance, cleaning and safety features - make it a general rule that aircraft return to Luanda for overnight parking. Overnight bases in addition to Luanda would permit a more efficient route network to be operated leading to higher productivity. Management of the TAAG umbrella organization is complex and inefficient in Angola's present condition where staff with technical and middle management experience are difficult to hire. A simpler structure with the timely privatization of activities like cleaning and catering would be extremely beneficial.

38. Ticketing is a particular problem given the existence of the informal market in goods and services, and the consequent variations between official and parallel prices. TAAG ticket tariffs were last changed in 1982 and remain priced at the official exchange rate. A case of beer (24 cans) sold on the informal market at Kz 1,500 per can would raise Kz 36,000 and this is sufficient to buy a US$1,200 airticket at a TAAG booking office. There are some safeguards against arbitrage - permission has to be sought before flying on international routes, for example - but there are no such hindrances on domestic flights. Accordingly, most domestic flights are heavily overbooked, creating unpleasant airport control problems, full flights and many disappointed travellers. In fact, TAAG records show capacity and load figures in excess of 100 percent on a number of internal routes. The company is conscious that it is not offering good services and attracting foreign customers who have a choice, and currently only 20 percent of TAAG's international passengers pay in foreign exchange. This could be an important growth segment of the market once TAAG becomes more competitive.

39. Regarding the problem with spares, there is a clear need to drastically cut the TAAG inventory cycle. In addition, improvements to foreign exchange access at the National Bank would enable costly items to be purchased on demand, rather than kept in stock. Almost 90 percent of the parts and materials are purchased from the United States and these can now be supplied in hours given suitable credit arrangements. TAAG has installed computer programs to track the parts inventory so use patterns can be established for more effective forecasting. It may soon be appropriate to decentralize some maintenance activities, leading to improvements at airports like Benguela and therefore making domestic scheduling more efficient.

40. Airports and Air Navigation - ENANA. Support services need drastic improvement, especially cabin cleaning and catering. The major problem is a managerial one, although lack of materials like food and cleaning items contributes to a poor service. There is a need to strengthen the technical side of the maintenance work and this should be the main focus of concern for TAAG's management. Efforts also need to be made to improve the operation of Angola's airports, most of which were built in the colonial era for light aircraft. Airports and control of airspace is the responsibility of the national airport and air navigation development company (ENANA), formed in

1980. The entity has not effectively met the basic objective of improving airport efficiency for which it was formed and its reorganization is currently under review.

41. ENANA's basic activities are to ensure an adequate network of airports and to provide and operate the basic facilities at each airport site. It is also responsible for the provision of airport safety services needed by TAAG, especially radio beacons and navigational assistance. Finally, it must maintain adequate good traffic control over Angolan airspace. The airports under its control are shown in Table VIII.9, grouped by available facilities.

Table VIII.9. ENANA AIRPORT NETWORK 1, 1987.

Category	Number	Location
I	1	Luanda
II	11	Benguela, Cabinda, Huambo, Kuito, Lubango, Luena, Malange, Menongue, Namibe, Sumbe, Uige.
III	4	Soyo, Amboim, Soyo, Wako Kungo
IV	8	Ambriz, Andulo, Damba, Jamba, Luau, Kamgamba, Nzeto, M'Banza Congo

Note: 1. Excluding numerous municipal landing strips, technically under ENANA control.

Source: ENANA-U.E.E., 1987

42. ENANA employs over 700 workers, 240 associated with air traffic control, around 170 at the Luanda international airport and over 200 at regional airports. Category II airports typically employ between 10 to 20 ENANA staff, while other categories have frequently less than five personnel. Over half the staff are engaged in various cleaning activities and turnover in this category is high, in spite of the prevailing low Angolan employment rates. In common with other companies, ENANA has introduced food subsidies and the provision of transport to work to counter this loss. A critical labor problem relates to a failure to hire technically trained personnel and is exacerbated by losing staff who have become experienced through on-the-job training within the company. Air traffic control, safety and radio communication effectiveness is vulnerable to these persistent staff shortages and partly explains the totally inadequate support services that affect TAAG's operating efficiency. The financial situation is not particularly healthy, even though the company earns a significant amount of foreign exchange from international carriers. The receipts from these services are held at the National Bank and

in 1986 totaled about US$3 million, which the company apparently had never been allowed to access. This has clearly complicated the purchase, servicing and replacement of most ENANA equipment needs.

43. With the exception of Luanda, most airports were built in the 1960's to meet the modest aviation needs of that decade. Aircraft were slow and of medium size, the Douglas DC3 being a representative type. Since Independence, the rapid and persistent growth in demand for aviation has not been accompanied by matching investment in air infrastructure. Currently there is almost total disequilbrium between demand and supply of airport services. Inadequate runways constrain airport capacities; they are too short, have poor geometry for modern craft, possess rough surfaces and weak sub-bases. Accordingly, Boeing 737's cannot operate over the full network and cannot use high pressure tires for risk of runway damage through impact loadings. The more expensive low pressure tires wear more rapidly on rough runway surfaces and consequently have shorter lives, leading to higher operating costs.

44. Facilities at airport sites are also generally weak and inadequate. Lack of refueling systems results in additional flight fuel loads, thus reducing payloads. In addition, few airports control cargo weight adequately (lack of scales, trained personnel) which can result in overloaded, dangerous takeoffs and landings. Passenger facilities of every type are poor and levels of comfort and security minimal. In 1985, ENANA recommended a regional investment program for the renovation of 12 provincial airports where operating conditions had severely deteriorated, but no decision has been reached on its funding.

45. The colonial radio navigation and communication system, with dual civil and military functions, was strengthened in 1974 by improvements recommended by Boeing Aerosystems International and implanted by 1980. However, the much needed support did not materialize due to sabotage and unforeseen air traffic growth rates. Currently, the Boeing system is virtually totally inoperative due to an inflexible system design, obsolete equipment, high cost of spares, lack of energy at many airports, armed attacks and lack of trained maintenance personnel. A consequence of these factors is an inability to navigate at night and the daily shut-down of most airports at 16.30 hours. This chronicle of constraints also affects inter-airport communication and services like meteorology, aviation information and statistics, as well as links with neighboring countries.

46. The Luanda international airport complex - February 4 - was established in the 1950s, improved 20 years later and rapidly became congested after Independence. In 1985 a new extension for domestic and international flights was completed but for security and congestion reasons, domestic flights were transferred to a nearby inferior remodeled hanger. A number of features remain to be completed at the new terminal to enable it to function as designed, although it already appears to be operating at capacity. The domestic arrangements need a total overhaul and ENANA are presently waiting for a decision on funding proposals to improve facilities. Other airport buildings are deteriorating, the parking areas and taxiing paths need maintenance and rehabilitation work, and the mix of aircraft types (civil,

military, passenger, cargo) and variations in size complicates ground control. Paris airport staff have helped develop improved facilities at the February 4 site and TAP airlines have provided technical assistance in improving air traffic control. The latter is the crucial obstacle to short term improvements in productivity and airport facilities throughout Angola must start to receive investment to improve traffic control, navigation and safety if the sub-sector is to maintain growth and competitiveness.

E. Maritime and Port Sector

47. Background. At Independence, Angola's 1,650 km of coastline, good network of ports, excellent export corridors and potential for regional growth focussed government attention on port and shipping activities. State companies were formed from nationalized entities, and joint ventures emerged where Angolan experience and investment potential was found to be weak. The sectors have been through several crises but now appear to be showing signs of recovery. Table 1 shows that the 1986 Angolan maritime sector output rose about 17 percent from its 1985 level of 512,000 tons, while total output of all ports dropped 11 percent to 1,551,000 tons over the same period. In terms of value, Table 2 shows that in the last available year, 1985, maritime value rose 13 percent from its 1984 level of Kz 1,617 million while ports rose 18 percent to Kz 2,112 million.

48. Interim figures confirm that port income decreased in 1986, reflecting the joint consequences of lower oil revenues and the escalating cost of the war. Ports and shipping represent about a quarter of the total MINTEC transport and communications sector value, and are also important for security reasons. These modes are not easily attacked and are the importing channel for defense supplies, primary goods, spare parts and food aid. They also represent a considerable opportunity for regional growth through the neglected cabotage sub-sector, and this will be considered in section 8.

49. Maritime and port activities are technically managed through the merchant marine and port national council (DNMMP), linked to MINTEC's planning division. DNMMP has three departments; merchant marine and ports, planning and finally marine security. The Angolan coast is divided into five sectors based on the main regional ports - Cabinda, Soyo, Luanda, Lobito and Namibe - for security purposes. The joint modes provide direct employment for over 10,000 staff, which exceeds all other entities in the transport and communications sector.

50. The entire maritime sector went through a major crisis in the early 1980s. Increases in oil revenues brought about a rapid growth in imports transported by sea. Angonave entered into charter contracts for much of this business but port and trans-shipment facilities proved inadequate to meet the demand. The combination of inefficient shipping operations, ineffective port management practices, weak infrastructure and an overloaded import license bureaucracy resulted in a total paralysis of Angolan ports in 1981. Most ships had to wait over 90 days, and some chartered ships anchored over 12 months outside Luanda port. It is calculated that demurrage and other associated costs totalled around US$48 million, mostly met by the state. This

lead to the whole sector being financially restructured and the period 1983 to 1986 has been one of slow recovery, limited by a persistent failure to invest in new equipment, ships and physical distribution systems and to analyze total transportation system costs, rather than specific modal cost structures. This may change with formation of the MINTEC planning cabinet, who have already made a number of substantial and far-reaching system type recommendations.

51. Maritime Activities. Currently, long distance shipping services are principally provided by Angonave-UEE and Secil Maritime, the latter linked to Africa Service (AFSER) of Copenhagen, while cabotage is provided by Cabotang-UEE. Table VIII.10 gives details of their fleet sizes in 1985 and 1986. Imported goods traffic fell significantly in 1986, and this is reflected in the fall in chartered long distance vessels. The modest fleet size contains old, inefficient and fully depreciated units that need urgent replacement. Necessity dictated that when shipping operations were restructured in the 1970s, chartered vessels would be used until Angolan ships could be profitably operated. Unfortunately, all Angolan vessels were purchased second-hand when many units were already old. Currently the fleet is unable to compete effectively for a larger share of the imported goods shipped to Angola. Export transit, where some comparative advantage should exist, remains weak and little opportunity for growth is offered. As a consequence, the fleet is underutilized.

Table VIII.10. SIZE AND OUTPUT [1] OF ANGONAVE, CABOTANG AND SECIL MARITIME FLEETS,[2] 1985 and 1986.

	1985	1986	
	Fleet	Fleet	Output
ANGONAVE:			
Company	7	7	
Hire/Lease	7	3	
Output			206,000
CABOTANG:			
Company	11	11	
Hire/Lease	0	0	
Output			120,000
SECIL MARITIME:			
Company	3	3	
Hire/Lease	14	7	
Output			210,000
TOTALS:			
Company	21	21	
Hire/Lease	21	10	
Output (2)			536,000

Note: 1. Traffic for 1986 only, in tons. Angonave data slightly larger than company report, due to reporting period.
2. Total MINTEC 1986 output is 598,000 tons.

Source: MINTEC, 1987.

52. Angonave, which is not a member of any shipping conference, was formed in 1978 to provide long distance marine cargo services through acquiring its own fleet, supplemented with chartered ships on short contracts. It was hoped that Angolan flagged vessels would take 40% of total traffic although in 1986 the company claimed just 20%. Vessels were purchased second-hand and by 1983 fleet deadweight had increased from 7,000 to 95,000 tons, which fell in 1985 with the loss of a large ship. In the crisis of 1981, Angonave lost control of their operations and became financially insolvent; facing judicial actions, millions of dollars debt, their fleet immobilized, and a ruined commercial reputation. The company has recovered slowly from that trauma but remains under-managed and under-invested. With its charter arrangements, the company currently claims a capacity of 102,000 tons. It has correctly concentrated on improving internal management controls and staff training, but still lacks the financial flexibility required to stay competitive in the transport services sector.

53. Table VIII.11 categorizes the main commodities carried by Angonave in 1986. Government food purchases make this category the most significant, about 55% of total traffic. The cargo was carried by ships in the national fleet making 26 voyages, and 51% of the traffic was in sacks, 40% general cargo (crates and bulk) and 9% in containers. The lack of silo storage of bulk commodities, especially at Luanda, is one reason for the high level of sack use. The inability to handle, store and process containers - which reached its zenith in 1981/82 when 12,000 clogged Luanda port - is shown in the low usage of this method of shipment. In fairness, it also reflects a fall in the importation of equipment, machinery and spares which are almost always sent in containers. All shipping companies complain about port efficiency levels and possible improvements that would increase marine productivity. These will be considered in a later part of this section.

Table VIII.11. ANGONAVE CARGO BY CATEGORY, 1986 (tons)

Category	Tonnage
Food	121,100
Alcoholic drinks	7,050
Equipment and vehicles	6,800
Chemicals	31,874
Other products	28,508
Containers (2,335 empty)	5,400
TOTAL	200,732

Source: Statistical Appendix Table I.6.

54. Secil Maritime offer both long distance and cabotage services, and are both smaller and more tightly organized than Angonave, despite carrying more traffic. They played a crucial role after the 1981 crisis when Angonave contracts could not be honored and few foreign shippers would deal with the

company. Secil Maritime substituted for Angonave and chartered sufficient vessels to maintain traffic flows. With the recent return to financial health of Angonave this role has considerably diminished and the company has sought traffic through tramping operations coordinated through its Copenhagen offices. The need for integrated investment programs in the sector and the lack of government recognition in this regard has made the company cautious. Accordingly, the company is not presently investing even though its fleet is between 16 and 23 years in age, and virtually obsolete.

55. Table VIII.12 shows the productivity of Secil Maritime's fleet in 1986 and demonstrates two key problems facing Angolan ship operators. First, there is the general task of finding work for the ships and secondly, there is the difficulty of unloading at Angolan ports. The latter is highlighted by the cabotage figures in Table VIII.12, and to show that this is not a special case, some Angonave data for 1985 are presented. To unload 85,000 tons of general cargo and 114,400 tons of containers (7,629 units), the 14 ship fleet spent 1,068 days in port, 25 percent at anchor and 75 percent berthed, waiting to be unloaded. The reasons for this are considered when ports operations are described, but the consequences are to raise total shipping costs either through higher operating costs or demurrage charges.

Table VIII.12: SECIL MARITIME FLEET; SELECTED DATA, 1986.

Ship	Type 1/	Trips	Days Spent: 2/			
			Port	Sailing	Cargo	Empty
Brasil	C	6	229	136		
Bengo	C	32	326	39		
Mar	C	18	315	26		
		Tonnage				
Japan	T	34,318	57	96	70	26
Angola	T	26,294	74	163	122	41
Dinamarca	T	43,067	130	162	98	64
Franca	T	19,385	38	87	59	28
Congo	T	31,162	61	118	48	70
Argentina	T	33,191	149	113	72	41

Notes: 1/ C is Cabotage, T is Tramping.
2/ Days spent in port, sailing, sailing with cargo and empty.

Source: Secil Maritime, 1987.

56. Cabotang was established as a state company in 1978 to provide cabotage services and is arguably the most neglected Angolan shipping enterprise. This is paradoxical, given the strategic importance of the coast and the ability to provide safe, reliable yet cheap passenger and freight movements between regional corridor coastal sites. It employs 320 staff,

including Yugoslavian, Cuban and Portuguese captains, and in 1986 reported a small profit of Kz 61 million. Currently, it has between 11 or 13 ships (figures disagree) totalling about 8,000 tons deadweight. Ships are old - five exceed 20 years in age - and do not have the design features to compete with other modes for specialized, profitable traffic. The heterogeneous nature of cabotage traffic, weak marketing arrangements, poor operational management (exacerbated by control problems) and inferior transshipment facilities at port complexes combine to prevent cabotage making a high impact on ameliorating transport problems in Angola's littoral regions. Tariffs have only been raised once, by 30 percent, since 1978 and a new scale of charges has been sent to the Ministry of Planning for approval. In 1987, it took delivery of a Dutch built, fast ferry boat capable of carrying 310 passengers and 440 cubic meters of cargo for use on the Luanada-Lobito route from January, 1988 onwards. A sister ship will soon join it and a network of schedules built up, including links with Namibe, Cabinda and Soyo. The potential benefits from efficient cabotage operations are at last being recognized within MINTEC and complementary port improvements should be important short term investment goals.

57. There are a number of maritime agencies handling shipping arrangements and problems associated with Angolan maritime jurisdiction. Agenang-UEE is based in Luanda, while Manubito is a mixed enterprize using capital from Agenang, Sonangol and Leopold Walford Holdings-UK. There are also smaller entities, entirely privately owned, notably Hull-Blyth (UK) and AMI (Belgium). These companies seem well organized although they all complained of poor telecommunications, bureaucratic difficulties and the appalling productivity of all Angolan ports. Business reflects the trade balance and after a stable period, seems to be on the decline. In 1985, Agenang handled 1,773 ships (951 Angolan, 822 Foreign) while in 1986 the total stood at 1,773 vessels (935 Angolan, 849 Foreign). The first six months of 1987 totalled 796 ships (338 Angolan, 458 Foreign) indicating a lower final figure for the year. Also the number of Angolan voyages are falling, reflecting falling disposable oil revenues. Maritime agencies should be recognized as providing important services to shippers, as earners of foreign exchange and an integral part of the maritime transport system, when improvements are considered.

58. Port Activities. As previously noted, Angolan ports are crucial to the effectiveness of the national transport system. Practically all freight imports arrive by ship and the coastal routes have now become the safest links throughout the littoral region. Unfortunately, port facilities have changed little since Independence and possess the characteristic of being designed for the efficient export of commodities in general and minerals in particular. The current need is the inverse; to accommodate the large import needs of the nation, particularly food products which must be stored after unloading to avoid spoiling. Only Lobito has good silo storage and the capacity of that facility now needs to be increased. Port productivity is low, at around 50 tons per ship/day compared with 250 tons per ship/day for an efficient operation. Part of the reason is equipment, with crane and forklift productivity affected by a combined lack of spares, maintenance and technical assistance. In 1985, utilization rates of 35 percent for Luanda and 26 percent for Lobito were recorded for these equipment categories. The port

sector employed 8,500 personnel in 1986, the majority being stevedores on low rates of pay. They are not well managed, with the possible exception of Lobito, and this leads to widespread corruption and absenteeism. Port officials admit their inability to control the situation, particularly at Luanda, and the "privatization" of some berths and facilities is being considered.

59. Table VIII.1 shows that Angolan port traffic fell from 1,739,000 tons in 1985 to 1,551,000 in 1986, an 11% decline. Value, however, as seen in Table VIII.2 rose 18% to Kz 2,112 million. The impact of the closure of mineral shipments at both Lobito and Sacomar at Namibe, can be realized by noting that the 1986 value is still only 15% of its 1974 figure. Table VIII.13 shows 1985 and 1986 main port throughput, and it is noted that in 1986 all ports with the exception of Cabinda registered falls in volume, consistent with the shipping and agency traffic data. Figures exclude war material and supplies, however, which were considerable during both years. Notable also is the small export volume (11% of total), which at ports other than Luanda includes cabotage data. In the two years, over 23,700 containers were shipped from Luanda compared to less than 6,000 arrivals. Low container arrival figures for 1986 (1,456) confirm both the fall in trade and shippers lack of confidence in the Luanda facility. Inadequate dockside storage can be seen from figures for the movement of cargo from port areas.

Table VIII.13. ANGOLA: MAIN PORT FREIGHT THROUGHOUT, 1985 - 1986
(thousand tons)

	1985	1986
Luanda		
All Freight:		
Import	801	639
Export	57	75
Cabotage	85	108
Total	942	821
Containers1 (In)	4,398	1,456
(Out)	11,392	12,387
Freight (Out)[2]	824	784
Freight (Warehouse)	109	45
Lobito		
Total Freight:	522	473
Import	466	419
Export	56	54
Freight (Out)[2]	493	488
Namibe		
Total Freight:	180	156
Import	165	136
Export	15	20
Freight (Out)[2]	142	106
Cabinda		
Total Freight:	95	101
Import	81	85
Export	14	16
Freight (Out)[2]	95	101

Notes: 1. Units.
2. Freight tonnage leaving port facility

Source: Annuario Estatistico, MINTEC 1986

60. Cabotage traffic data are given in Table VIII.14 for the ports of Cabinda, Soyo, Luanda, Lobito and Namibe. There are a number of small fishing ports like Tombwa and Ambiom, but data from these are not included. Distinct patterns of trade can be noted, which are a result of imports being channeled to the three major ports, prior to further transit. There is little doubt that cabotage can be improved by planning and operating facilities designed specifically for its traffic and shipping needs. Historically, cabotage has been given a low priority which is reflected in lack of security for cargo, poor transshipment and passenger facilities, and bad sitting within the port

complexes. The acquisition of a new passenger boat has not been accompanied by any related investment in port infrastructure to take advantage of the new service. As a consequence, its efficiency and commercial impact is weakened unnecessarily.

Table VIII.14. ANGOLA: CABOTAGE TRAFFIC,[1] 1985

	Cabinda	Soyo	Luanda	Lobito	Namibe	Totals
Cabinda	-	700	21,889	3,210	50	25,849
Soyo	260	-	6,791	-	-	7,051
Luanda	14,412	72	-	15,204	9,344	39,032
Amboim	-	-	-	3,406	-	3,406
Lobito	3,549	-	11,644	-	1,816	17,009
Namibe	2,030	-	24,305	6,850	-	33,185
Totals	20,251	772	64,629	28,670	11,210	125,532

Note: 1. MINTEC and private shipping, tons.

Source: Annuario Estatistico, MINTEC 1986

61. Delays in port have been a persistent characteristic of Angolan operations, reaching a crisis point in 1981 when at one time 90 vessels were waiting to be unloaded at Luanda. The sector had been expanded too quickly given its physical and management capacities; chartered ships were arriving with small quantities of cargo and shipowners content to wait and claim demurrage, given the slump in world shipping. A planned annual capacity of 7,000 containers bore little resemblance to the actual capacity based on equipment, storage facilities and, most importantly, the ability of the shippers to deal with the complicated, slow moving importation bureaucracy. The exercise was a total fiasco, goods remained in their containers for years and many importers simply abandoned them at the ports. Again, containers are rented and this resulted in large claims against Angolan shippers, agencies and ultimately the government. The 1985-86 range of between 1,600 to 2,500 containers probably represents the safe capacity of the port at the moment.

62. MINTEC data show recent improvements in turnaround times. In 1985, 327 long distance ships, carrying an average cargo of around 2,700 tons, were handled by Luanda. Each on average spent a total of 18 days, comprising 5 waiting and 13 berthed. It should be stated that any recent improvement in delay times is more likely to be a consequence of a trade decline rather than improvements in productivity. In addition, Angonave data show that their average wait in 1985 was 37 days, twice the average. This seems to confirm an impression that foreign flagged ships were being treated preferentially. The central reasons for the 1981 collapse still remain; poor management, inadequate equipment, badly organized and motivated labor, lack of storage, lack of transport, poor communications and little planning. Examples of serious delays can still be found: at the time the mission was in Luanda, a ship left having taken 73 days (39 at anchor and 34 days berthed) to unload a

frozen meat consignment of 2,000 tons. Lack of available storage space played a major role in this delay but the demurrage costs of over US$150,000 have to be met somewhere in the distribution chain, and ultimately the final price. This indicates the impact transport costs can have on commodity prices is non-trivial.

63. All ports require restructuring and Luanda has the most critical need both because of its strategic and political importance, and the growing urban market outside the city perimeter. Lobito is smaller, better organized and possesses improved facilities for long distance berths, including crainage and quayside rail services. Namibe, like Luanda, has received little investment while its neighbor Sacomar is paralyzed due to the cessation of mineral shipments from the Cassinga mines in Huila province. Unfortunately, traffic cannot presently be diverted from Namibe to this modern facility because of its proximity to a fuel shipment and storage complex. There is not much to choose between port efficiencies. In 1985, Luanda annual output per employee was 190 tons and Lobito's was 209 tons. Ships are turned around faster at Lobito; productivity in 1985 was 48 tons per ship/day (6.6 tons per ship/hour) at Luanda, compared with 73 tons per ship/day (9.1 tons per ship/hour) at Lobito. However, this may simply reflect the better equipment (cranes, silos, stores) and any comparisons need to be made with circumspection. Cabotage productivity appears to show little variation between ports. Cabotang stated that 1986 comparative daily output tonnage were Luanda 39, Cabinda 42, Lobito 40 and Soyo 65.

64. The current problems of the maritime sector stem from a lack of planning which affects financial, operational, manpower needs and management at all levels, plus an inability to synthesize these elements into a coherent strategy and policy. Low discharging rates need not drastically affect overall productivity if the other stages in the transit system work well. The total transport system cost, in financial or time terms, is crucial to efficiency levels. It is when all stages start to fail, become inefficient or are not synchronous that the cost implications become critical. There is no evidence that a macro-analysis of this type, capturing the full physical distribution costs, has been recognized in any of the government decisions concerning the shipping and maritime sectors. The sector urgently needs trained staff at all levels to motivate workers, identify and correct deficiencies (frequently of a simple nature) and to operate and maintain key equipment. It requires a radical operational re- structuring which includes both short and long term investments. A number of modes have been brought close to collapse in Angola during this decade but the maritime sector is vital to the survival and economic recovery of the nation. Therefore, it must have a key role in any investment program.

F. Mail and Telecommunications

65. In common with many Angolan sectors, the years following Independence for Telecommunications were characterized by nationalization and reorganization, with the operating needs focussed on maintaining existing service levels

in a difficult commercial environment. In 1980, the performance had deteriorated to a point where further restructuring was necessary. The existing mail and telecommunications directorate (DSCT) was disbanded and a tripartite form adopted which comprised:

- a national telecommunications enterprise ENATEL-UEE, responsible for domestic telecommunications,

- the Angolan mail service CDA-UEE, to provide national and international mail and telegraph services, and

- an international and maritime telecommunications enterprise, EPTEL- UEE, to complement ENATEL.

These entities combine with a number of small private companies (Standard Electric, Tecnidata, Teletra etc.) to make up the current communications sector. The national council for mail and telecommunications (DNCT) is responsible for coordinating activities and is linked to MINTEC's planning department in a similar manner to the maritime sector.

66. Mail Services. Mail services are clearly vulnerable to the provincial security problems in general, and the difficulties with transport in particular. Table VIII.15 shows Angolan mail service (CDA) throughput for 1986 and it can be seen that the mail system is still managing to offer a full range of services, at both domestic and international levels. Compared to 1985, packages are up by 153% while the rest are relatively constant, although telegrams are in decline as they are replaced by telex and direct dial telephone lines. Currently, the mail network is incomplete and irregular, due to the security problem. Roads cannot be used for most inter-provincial links and mail consequently depends on the air sector. Problems of limited cargo space on some planes and the inability of CDA to get designated transport priority on most modes contributes to delays in distribution. TAAG cannot meet over 13% of their domestic schedules and this adversely affects mail distribution. CDA lack a dedicated vehicle distribution fleet and the private truck sector cannot offer suitable services because of its structure and paucity of appropriate vehicle types. CDA also lacks simpler forms of delivery modes like bicycles, and this adds to their distribution problems.

Table VIII.15. THROUGHPUT[1] OF ANGOLAN MAIL OFFICE, CDA, 1986.
(thousands of units)

		In	Out
Registered Letters:			
	National	6,037	6,010
	International	3,177	3,057
Money orders:			
	National	3	3
	International	6	5
Packages:			
	National	4	4
	International	15	15
Telegrams:			
	National	125	125
	International	63	64
Sacks of Mail:			
	National	53	53
	International	30	27

Source: Annuario Estatistico, MINTEC 1986.

67. While it may be possible to augment the vehicle fleet through new investment and speed up delivery schedules by improving operational efficiencies, air travel will remain the key domestic mode as long as the present security situation exists. If tariffs could be increased, CDA might be able to pay for preferential treatment on air and other modes. The planned high speed coastal ferry network will offer a complementary form of mail transit which merits consideration in CDA's short-term planning. Management and motivation in CDA, like many other UEEs is low, adding to the problems associated with improving overall efficiency levels. The average salary is Kz 13,000 per month and there is little opportunity for making more on the job, so absenteeism is high. Government reforms targeted on raising mail service productivity seems to be the relevant action, and only after such changes should external funding agencies consider supportive investment programs.

68. Telecommunications. At Independence, Angola was served by a short wave telegram network supplemented by automatic telephone systems in five cities, a nine-city telex link and an earth satellite station at Cacuaco. Domestic equipment comprised 52 telephone exchanges containing 49,000 lines and 9 telex centers with 470 machines, representing about 60% of capacity. The new state companies for mail and domestic telecommunications were formed from existing colonial monopolies, while EPTEL was based on a nationalized private company -

Marconi - who were contracted to provide additional technical training and to supply both spares and equipment. EPTEL was also given the responsibility for maritime communications, in addition to international telecommunication services.

69. The period 1975 to 1980 was characterized by guerilla attacks, poor management, lack of technically skilled personnel and the need to continually maintain a system that was partly obsolete and operating under heavy loads. Telegraph use dropped dramatically, many local city telephone networks encountered severe operating problems that lowered service quality and telex use encountered difficulties as the network faced high demand. By 1980, telex capacity had fallen from 810 lines to 720, although the number of users rose to 587. Telex data are useful indicators of transport activity, since businesses in a number of modes (particularly shipping) recognize telexes as legal documentation. Inter-urban telephone, telex and telegraph use fell as the network deteriorated, as shown in Table 16 which compares the 1975 and 1980 networks.

Table VIII.16. INTER-URBAN NETWORK, 1975 AND 1980.

	1975		1980	
System	Stations	Localities[1]	Stations	Localities
VHF- 48 channels	28	12	15	6
UHF- 24 channels	8	6	3	2
VHF- 6 channels	6	4	3	3
VHF- 1 channel	22	20	3	3
Other	2	2	-	-

Note: 1. Communications relayed between stations to exchanges and users in various localities.

Source: MINTEC, 1987.

70. The 1980 sector restructuring was followed by five years of commercial problems characterized by increasing difficulties in maintaining inter-urban systems, a consequence of the security situation and heavy demand. However, planning and investment was at least being taken seriously at all levels and the African Development Bank provided investment funds in 1985 to improve international links and efficiency. A system of micro-wave and troposcatter stations now provide links over about 65 percent of the country, a result of the investments planned during this period. Security still affects service provision and in 1983 two troposcatter stations were damaged and the link between Malange and Saurimo destroyed. Luanda's central telephone exchange has been reconditioned and the cable network renovated. Some characteristics of the telephone system for the years 1980 and 1985 are given in Appendix Table I.7. The telex remains susceptible to lengthy breakdowns which has drawn complaints from transport agencies. In 1985, work began on developing

an overall plan for the sector, using funds given by the African Development Bank. Finally, a telecommunications institute was created which, though in its infancy, recognizes the urgent need for improved technical and managerial manpower capabilities.

71. In 1987, service levels in the sector were still variable and prone to breakdown. The inter-urban network is incomplete and likely to remain so while the severe security and transport problems remain across most provinces. New investment in automatic exchanges should result in better local and inter-urban services, and higher ENATEL revenue. Table VIII.17 gives some selected operating data for ENATEL and EPTEL covering 1985 and 1986. The impact of automatic dialing can be seen in the 1986 fall in manual services, combined with the huge rise in automatic use to more than double the demand projected by ENATEL. International telephone use in 1986 was affected by government restrictions and undervalues the actual demand levels. If the international systems can be improved, it is believed that a similar surge in demand to the domestic market will take place, especially as the current program to improve international links, funded by the African Development Bank, should improve both capacities and the number of foreign countries with which Angola has direct links. Much of this traffic will be automatic, thus improving speed and cost-effectiveness. Telex use continues to play an important role in Angolan telecommunications, and the growth of the industry in very difficult circumstances is shown in its 1986 output value rising by 11% over the previous year.

Table VIII.17. ENATEL AND EPTEL, SELECTED DATA (1985-86).

		1985	1986
Telephone Manual [1]			
Inter-urban		2,509	748
International	(In)	2,250	2,120
	(Out)	7,753	5,741
Automatic [2]		82,000	215,680
Telex[1]			
National		444	623
International	(In)	1,715	1,640
	(Out)	2,396	2,769
Value [3]		1,297,101	1,435,035

Notes: 1. Thousands of minutes.
2. Thousands of impulses.
3. Thousands of Kwanza.

Source: Annuario Estatistico, MINTEC 1987

72. ENATEL admit that the policy of concentrating investment into high technological areas, to the detriment of assets such as buildings and general infrastructure carries risks. Complementary investments for smaller

exchanges, local cable networks and non-urgent maintenance have also generally been sacrificed in the sharp cut-back of government funding. Such a policy is only sustainable in the short to medium term, and must be corrected in any future planning for the sector. Financial cut-backs by the government have affected the largest project since Independence - Angosat - which would provide national telecommunication and television coverage using satellite links. Though it has admirable qualities, and should generate good revenue making it extremely profitable, it was a casualty of the 1986 budget cuts.

73. It may now be more appropriate for management in the telecommunications sector to concentrate on routine and preventative maintenance of all assets, and complete all current investment programs as rapidly as possible. Attention now must be paid to the persistent manpower resource problem that has plagued Angola since Independence. Telecommunications is capital-intensive and skilled technicians of all types are needed to maintain the various systems at their designed levels of productivity. Unfortunately, ENATEL and EPTEL cannot apparently either attract or retain sufficient numbers of trained personnel. Government actions to correct the salary imbalances should accompany an apprentice training program to address the manpower shortages. Since 1975, there are 30% more telephone subscribers, three times more inter-urban lines, four times the international lines and automatic dialing has produced higher use and profits in the domestic market. However, all this progress is prejudiced by the failure to recruit educated and trained technicians and managers.

G. Availability of Modal Spare Parts

74. Mission visits to different modal operations noted that efficiency levels were seriously affected by chronic spare parts supply problems. In theory, public and parastatal organizations are required to put spare parts provision in their prospective budgets or "plafonds" which need ministerial approval. Spare parts for most modal equipment requires foreign exchange. Although some entities have authorization to spend up to a pre-determined level, such as $9,000 for Angolan Airlines (TAAG), generally National Bank approval is required. This may be given part, in full or not at all. It makes no difference if the enterprise earns foreign exchange or lack of the parts may damage utilization, revenues and profitability. TAAG have had "hush kit" purchase requests for Boeing 707's waiting approval for four years, even though lack of such noise control devices will ban those aircraft from using most Common Market (EEC) airports from January 1988.

75. The rules governing the supply of spare parts are basically simple. Public or parastatal enterprises need to estimate their needs 12 months ahead and include the estimated spare parts need and costs in their annual budget for approval. Mixed companies have greater flexibility since the private partner can generally provide the foreign exchange and companies have such agreements sanctioned in the legal establishment contract approved by the government. A good example of the different cost impact this can produce is given by considering that ETP truck operations at Base Bungo, Luanda have had items on order for over 12 months. Also TAAG carries a US$18

million spare part inventory to meet contingencies given their normal eight-month waiting period for parts. In comparison, Intertransportes, a joint venture trucking firm with a road freight contract for the Kapanda dam project, receives a monthly ISO 40 foot container from Italy into which telexed spares requirements can be shipped. This allows all spares to be placed on a 28-day cycle. Good cost control makes an important contribution to efficiency and profitability.

76. If enterprises are very large and important they may be allowed to deal direct with suppliers but the majority of transport operations must deal through the government importing agencies IMPORTANG or ABAMAT. The heterogeneous mix of transport types, makes and models in Angola, all obtained from a wide range of suppliers and nations, presents huge problems for any single importing agency. The problem of heterogeneity is particularly acute in road transport and MINTEC set up maintenance centers for specific vehicle makes - MANAUTO's - in the late 1970s to meet selected repair needs. Private vehicle owners are permitted to take their vehicles to these centers but generally choose not to do so. The inability of the official vehicle maintenance system to cope with demand in an efficient manner has predictably resulted in alternative private informal arrangements taking over. There is strong evidence that supplies destined for the public sector find their way into the informal markets and a new Volvo N10 fuel injection pump was noted on offer in the parallel market at Kz. 110,000 even though ETP were waiting delivery for such units. The problem has now become so serious that MINTEC have proposed an entirely new joint enterprise distribution system to ensure the regular supply of spares and materials for motor vehicles. TAAG has also made some recommendations to keep inventory costs down and both these schemes will be discussed in later sections.

77. Rail is critically affected by lack of trained personnel and spare parts for the maintenance of locomotives and rolling stock. A total of 165 locomotives, 198 passenger carriages and over 3,800 wagons (most over 15 years in age) need constant attention for a variety of skilled and semi- skilled maintenance tasks. The maintenance and repair facilities of the various railway companies are extremely underutilized and many machine tools have not worked since Independence. This accounts for the dramatic decline in registered fleet numbers and those units and stock actually working, as described in the rail mode section of this report. All rail repair facilities are in secure areas of the country and could be used as centers for carrying out and training a whole variety of engineering tasks, not necessarily confined to rail transportation. The crucial need here is trained personnel and it may be more efficient to select potential personnel for training at other African rail centers, as well as bringing in foreign specialists to assist on technical programs at the main Angolan rail centers with assigned counterpart staff.

78. All transport and communications entities have problems organizing their spare parts requirements through the exisiting government arrangements. Maritime stock seem to cope reasonably well within the current system, helped in part by the surplus capacity in the sector which means that lower utilization and efficiency levels due to lengthy waiting for parts is not

critical. In addition, ships can get serviced in foreign shipyards should it be necessary on a voyage, and this allows for particular categories of repair and maintenance to be treated effectively. Cabotage does not have these maintenance alternatives and is reliant on Angolan yards. Cabotage vessels are elderly and require frequent attention so a real problem exists if cabotage is to grow in the manner desired by MINTEC planners. However, this could be turned to national advantage by developing the well located shipyard of Estalnave to the point where it can quickly schedule and service all cabotage vessels. This would result in a southern Atlantic yard for small vessels which could be used by other African cabotage vessels and foreign fishing boats which are currently so numerous. This represents a very valuable potential source of foreign exchange.

H. MINTEC Analysis and Planning

79. Evaluation. The shortcomings and difficulties within the transport sector and their adverse effects on economic efficiency and growth lead the Second Congress of the MPLA-PT in 1986 to redefine basic objectives and to require MINTEC to develop new plans for their implementation. These objectives were to make road transport the basic national mode, complemented by rail and cabotage, and supplemented by the air sector. On the international market, air would remain the passenger mode and maritime the long distance freight mode, although both would be expected to improve service levels, competitive performance and profitability. It was hoped that a program of short term measures could be identified that would lead to rapid improvements in selected modal services. MINTEC set up a small planning unit to diagnose the central issues and make recommendations for improvement. The unit decided to examine the key areas of infrastructure, running stock and equipment, personnel and training, finance and service levels for each main mode. Their findings were released late in 1987 for consideration by the Minister, prior to submission to higher ministries.

80. Analysis. The analysis of the period 1975 to date is reasonably accurate in terms of performance, output and modal value data but the key role of central planning in this period and its total inability to forecast, organize and operate transport services is understandably ignored. Perversely, the failure in many sectors is blamed on insufficient regulation or the wrong type of planning. Their main findings, by mode, are:

(i) Good growth prospects exist for cabotage operations, both freight and passenger, given port infrastructural improvements. Though it is considered to have little flexibility and requires modest investment, its low cost per kilometer of travel over similar congested air routes and security make it extremely attractive.

(ii) Rail corridors should be treated separately. CFL is operating in most secure corridors and merits evaluation for investment. CFB is most affected by the military-political struggles and its short term prospects are limited to the Lobito-Benguela-Huambo section of the corridor. CFM has good prospects on the link Namibe-Huila, but no investments are presently worthwhile from Huila to Menongue. Rail's low cost per ton or passenger kilometer is more than offset by the vulnerability of the infrastructure, large investment needs and fixed corridor route systems.

(iii) Highway infrastructure and use have been affected by loss of security and vehicle operations by loss of authority by MINTEC. Roads require modest investment, have great flexibility, can easily be extended to new regions and allow goods and passenger movements at affordable prices. MINTEC claim that one ton of air cargo is equivalent to 5 tons by truck, 15 tons by train and 20 tons by sea.

It is proposed to reintroduce an effective road transport freight and passenger service, reactivate railways only in secure areas, invest in cabotage operations to take pressure off passenger demand for air services and to expand inter-provincial road trade links, thus allowing air to develop a strategy best suited to its operating characteristics.

81. Technology needs are addressed by focusing on the utility of renovating the existing vehicle fleet and modernizing other modes like rail, coastal vessels, some aircraft and all modal infrastructure, using the latest technology where possible. This raises the need for trained staff to install and maintain such technology, and conflicts with the desire to reduce dependence on foreign assistance. Finally, the choice of technology, equipment suppliers, spare part needs, technical training and financing have also to be considered. In 1986, the sector employed about 36,000 personnel of which 91% were unskilled workers, 7.5% administrative personnel and only 1.5% technicians. It makes no sense to increase investment in high technology without matching it with funding for technical training, since all modes currently have difficulties finding staff at existing levels of technology.

82. Strategies. MINTEC's planning unit considered three elements of the transportation problem; markets, modes and ownership. Markets were grouped into international, inter-provincial (national) and provincial for both freight and passenger traffic. The modes were treated as single entities (ignoring multi-modal systems) and ownership was defined as either state, mixed, private national and private foreign. The latter still causes much unease in Angolan planning circles and is only seriously considered in the air sector, as counterpart suppliers of international services. Matrices were drawn up representing acceptable combinations of mode and ownership forms, and MINTEC action for each combination identified six categories; develop, reorganize, negotiate, regulate, reduce and not allowed. Broad types of action, appropriate for short-term impacts, were developed from this exercise and are summarized in Table VIII.18.

83. MINTEC's planning unit is extremely well organized. Inter--provincial links that meet the criteria developed by the MINTEC unit, together with project flow rates, are shown in Figure 1 for freight and Figure 2 for passengers. Table VIII.19 summarizes the flows by modal category. Annually, about 1 million tons and 26 million passengers movements are predicted to

complement existing flows. It is difficult to give a comparison between predicted and current values, since cabotage passenger and inter-provincial road freight and passenger movements are not currently recorded. However, within the projected provincial passenger data, Luanda-Luanda accounts for 15 million passengers compared with 1.2 million current passengers. Generally, the figures represent modest projections and should well coordinated transport systems be implemented and operated efficiently, the actual demand data are likely to be much higher.

84. Short-term measures are given in Table VIII.20 although no costs were available at the time of the mission. Timing is fortuitous, however, since assistance and guidance on cost-benefit and economic/financial evaluations can now be given to allow a more detailed analysis of the proposals developed from initial proposal screening. At that time, when choices have to be made with limited funds available, the arguments for less regulation and a reduction in state or quasi-state intervention can be considered.

85. MINTEC has also made proposals for telecommunication investment but most center on completing projects underway, particularly the micro-wave system (not yet 50% installed) and the seriously delayed cable network in Luanda.

Table VIII.18. MINTEC SHORT TERM STRATEGIES (1987)

Sector	Freight
International:	Improve Angonave and Secil Maritime productivity, profitability, aim for greater market share. Re-organize CFB in Lobito corridor. Re-organize docks. Set up container company.
National:	Diminish air cargo. Regulate road transport. Coordinate needs with National Council of Carriers. Improve cabotage facilities at ports for north-south links. Organize road transport into zones, consistent with rail corridors. Regulate road transport.
Provincial:	Reorganize road transport, set prices and control supply of services. Set up road transshipment terminals.
	Passengers
International:	TAAG; better service, improved competitive image, better negotiated commercial contracts. No foreign operations without joint agreements.
National :	Develop inter-provincial links, using rail corridors where possible. Provide a cabotage service to relieve overcrowding on littoral routes. Reorganize and regulate the private bus operators, no foreign companies.
Provincial:	Organize provincial transport sector. Allow regulated private operations. Regulation through licenses and user charges.

Source: Esquema Director do Sistema de Transportacao na RPA, MINTEC 1987.

MINTEC PLANS FOR INTER-PROVINCIAL FREIGHT FLOWS

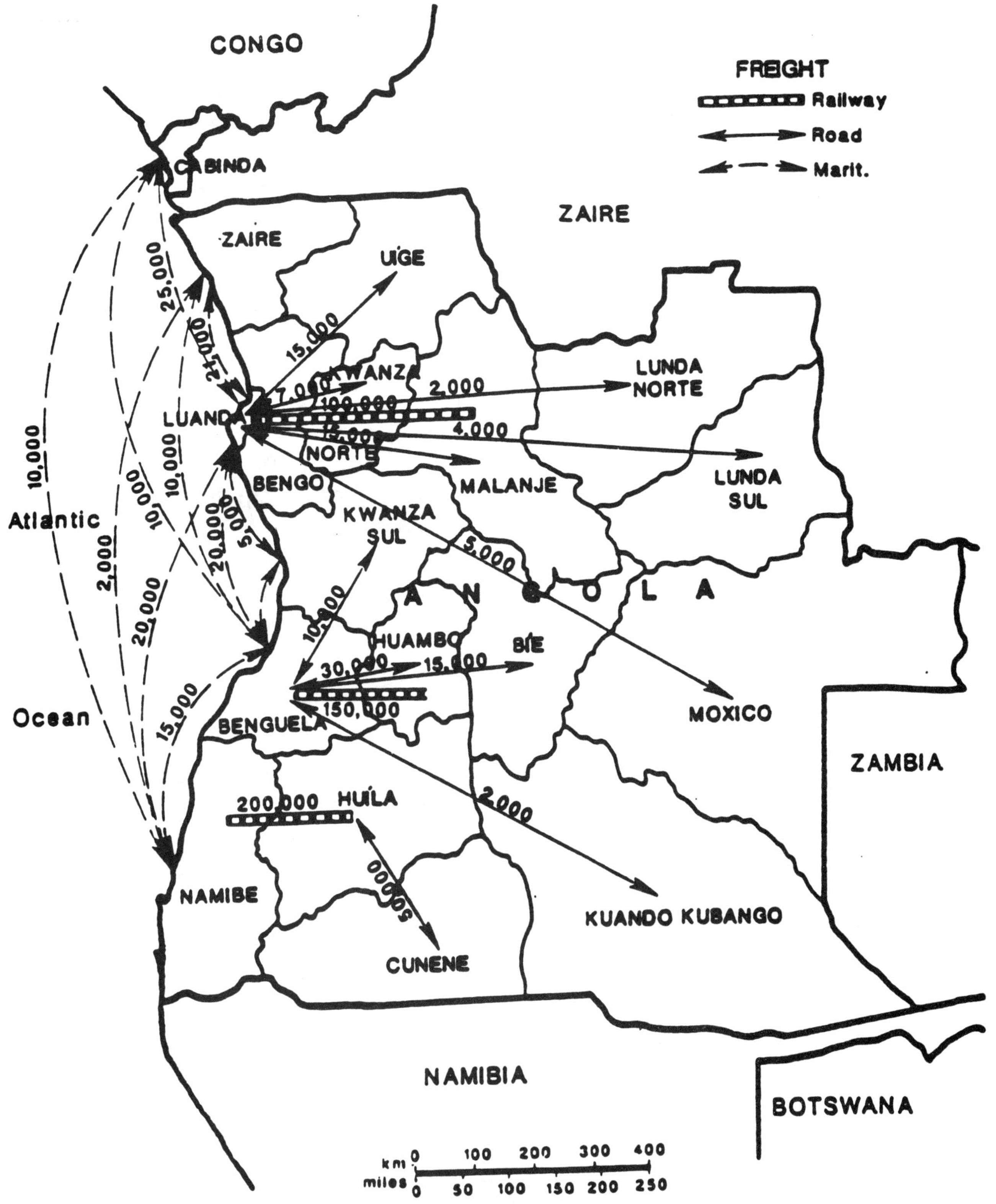

Figure 1

MINTEC PLANS FOR INTER-PROVINCIAL PASSENGER FLOWS

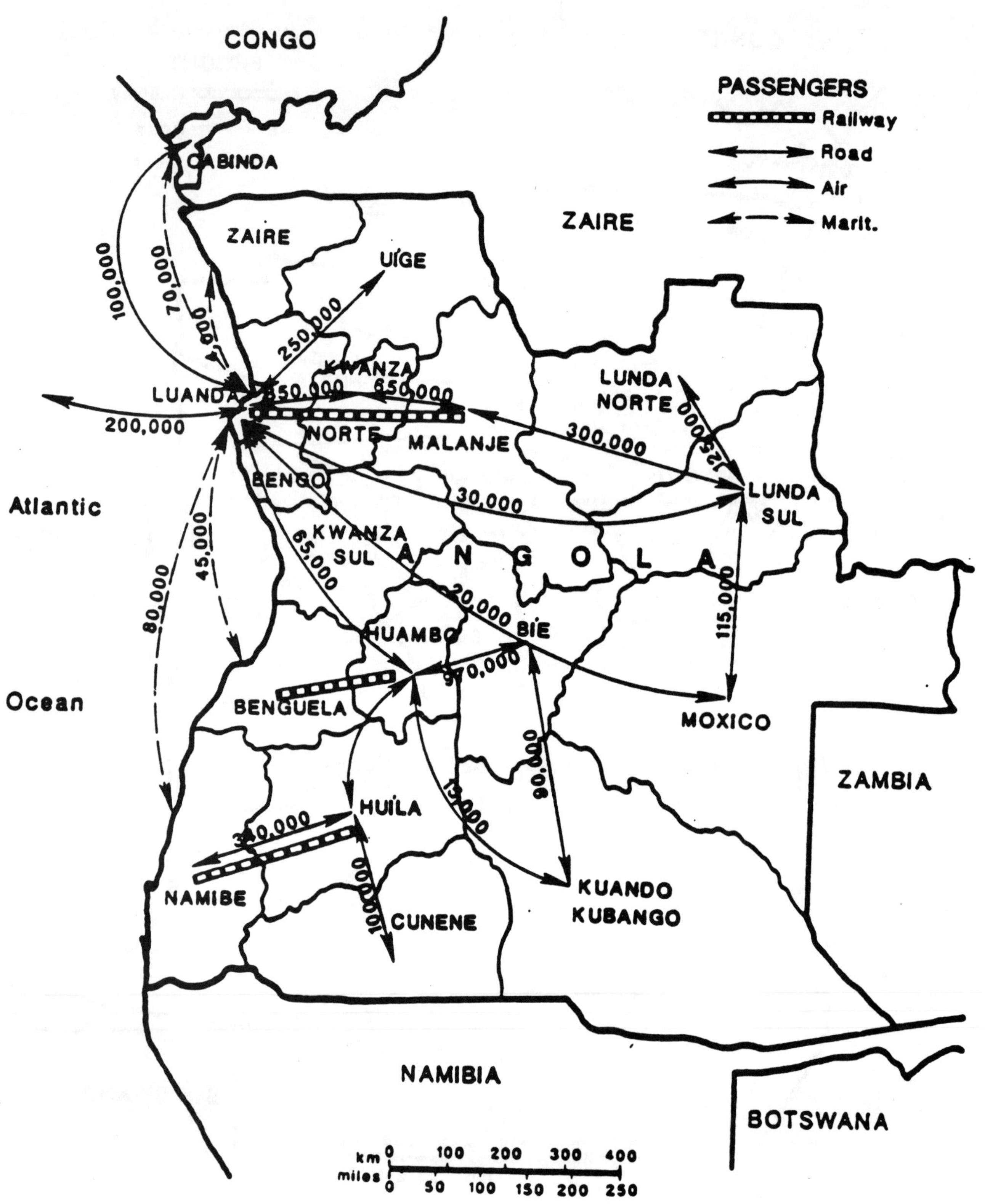

Figure 2

Table VIII.19 PROJECTED FREIGHT AND PASSENGER MOVEMENTS[1]

Mode	Freight (tons)	Passengers
Road:		
Inter-provincial	155,000	4,240,000
Rail:		
Inter-provincial	450,000	3,280,000
Provincial	250,000	18,000,000
Cabotage	148,000	210,000
Total	1,003,000	25,730,000

Note: 1. Projected data, based on MINTEC 1987 proposals.
Source: Esquema Director, MINTEC 1987.

Table VIII.20 MINTEC PROPOSED PROGRAM, 1987

Mode	Action
Road:	
Urban	Reorganize Urban Bus Transit System
Inter-provincial	Rebuild links and provide freight and passenger services: Luanda - Malange, Luanda - Uige, Huambo - Huila, Huambo - Benguela, Huila - Malange.
Rail:	
Urban	Develop: Luanda - Luanda,
Inter-provincial	Re-open: Luanda - Malange, Huila - Namibe.
Cabotage	Create regular, efficient services between: Luanda - Cabinda Luanda - Lobito Luanda - Namibe
Air	Operate a reduced schedule profitably and navigation.

Source: Adapted from Esquema Director, MINTEC 1987.

The desires to improve service, strengthen public confidence and employee morale, improve maintenance and increase training programs have not yet been translated into firm proposals. MINTEC has given the problem of spare part provision much thought, and have developed an entirely new distribution system for the road sector. This is absolutely necessary if the stated MINTEC desire to develop bus and trucking operations is to have any hope of success. The cumbersome, inefficient central importing agencies would be replaced by single manufacturer parts distribution systems reflecting the importance of makes in the vehicle fleet composition. It is proposed to have two levels, the first representing key manufacturers like Scania, Mercedes, Volvo and IFA where the supply of parts is absolutely crucial to national productivity and a second tier representing minor makes whose impact is less vital. The second tier would be simpler in structure but it would not be at a commercial disadvantage. Manufacturers have been contacted and seem willing to seriously consider investing in the proposed joint venture over which they would exercise management control as long as some method of remitting profits (or a portion of profits) can be agreed with the Central Bank. It is hoped that the new financial and economic changes now being considered will provide the impetus for such an agreement. Potential investment programs are now presented.

I. Issues, Prospects and Recommendations

86. Issues. The sector would benefit from general planning changes and specific restructuring at all levels of modal activity. It is characterized by the following constraints:

(a) Limited land-based modal operations due to the poor security situation, lack of infrastructure maintenance, reduced demand patterns and inadequate vehicular stock.

(b) Failure of centralized planning to recognize the importance of transportation and its needs, to adjust to market changes, modify tariffs, supply desired services and support existing operations. This results in costly passenger and cargo rates in real terms and an inefficient demand for modal services. In general, the supply of services is totally inadequate to meet the demand at official price levels and parallel pricing of maintenance and services is present in the road sub-sector, together with queuing and time delays in other modes.

(c) Inability to cope with the rapid urbanization noted in many provinces, especially those that are considered more secure. Freight shipments (notably food) are affected but the most chronic failure is the lack of urban passenger transit systems to meet the needs of the growing city populations.

(d) Foreign exchange limitations that complicate or prevent the purchase of equipment and spare parts for all transport and communications modes. Much of this is due to planning rules and National Bank procedures which combine to overrule the operational needs of managers and result in short service lives of road vehicles, railway engines and mechanical handling equipment of all types. These difficulties then contribute towards sustaining the present unreliable and inconvenient service schedules.

(e) Employment policies are inconsistent and ineffectual within the sector. Skilled staff are difficult to retain and state enterprises frequently required to maintain large numbers of untrained employees who are troublesome to motivate and manage. Training and educational schemes are not commonplace, and there is a dearth of technicians in all modes that affects productivity, service levels and preventative maintenance. Remuneration is poor and opportunities for auto-consumo limited so staff turnover, especially where skills are marketable, is high.

(f) Infrastructure maintenance is poor and costly in terms of its effect on modal output and profitability. It also has social opportunity costs given that labor intensive policies could be adopted to reduce operating costs while generating employment opportunities. Many land systems are in a quasi-abandoned state; airfields lack basic facilities, rail tracks and stations are damaged and inoperative, and the highway network is in a deteriorated condition and lacks any service facilities like fuel stations and food stops for drivers over much of its length. Ports require both physical works (quays) and equipment maintenance programs to improve efficiencies and preserve investments, especially for cabotage operations.

(g) The collapse of official price levels for many goods and services, and the attendant rise of the parallel market has caused distortions in the pricing of transport services. It is important that planning changes should avoid subsidies and allow modes to compete on equal terms. In this latter respect, the private sector needs to be stimulated and subsequently supported, and there is good potential for growth, particularly in highway and cabotage operations. MINTEC should be encouraged to avoid regulation and licensing as a means of controlling the sector and aim for a mixed competitive economy.

87. Prospects and Recommendations. In planning corrective action, the transport sector has limited capacity to absorb the related elements of large investment programs. Such limits are reflected, inter-alia, in inadequate local complementary services, lack of experience in managing large projects at Ministry and Provincial levels, and potential difficulties in meeting disbursement targets for locally-financed elements because of irregular supply of locally-manufactured materials. In these circumstances, a program focusing on short-term high impact projects and modest financing seems an appropriate form of investment, supported by policy changes at Government level. Large single projects should be evaluated separately once their consequences in terms of sectoral absorptive capacity are recognized.

88. MINTEC have proposed new transport plans reflecting Provincial, Regional and national/international needs and these should influence modal and inter-modal investments and project selection. In the short term it is desirable to reduce the national demand for air services, both cargo and passengers, by raising service levels in other modes, particularly highways and cabotage. In addition, all tariffs are grossly distorted and require urgent review. The following specific actions are recommended for the various modes.

89. Highways. Vehicle fleets should be increased and vehicle life extended through easier access to capital for new vehicles and spare parts, trained mechanics and improved maintenance facilities. In addition, stricter control of drivers and loads, and improved road conditions would contribute significantly to prolonging vehicle life. Highway infrastructure needs to be monitored on a regular basis to identify construction, rehabilitation and maintenance needs. This would require the creation of an effective highway maintenance organization in Angola, possibly in three-tier form to reflect a national-provincial-district structure. There should be an efficient private sector to complement State and company transport enterprises. Regulation should be very carefully evaluated, as excessive control has rarely had the desired effect in other countries and vehicle licenses should be freely available as long as applicants meet required operational standards. Tariffs should be determined by market forces and efficient operators should be allowed to run multi-vehicle fleets. In urban transport, bus fleets need expanding and their routes improved to reduce vehicle damage. The desirability of parastatal bus operations needs evaluation and the private sector comprising taxis, pick-ups and mini-buses should be allowed to grow. In planning terms, road investment is appealing because its flexibility permits regional impacts to be finely tuned. A variety of vehicle types, giving different levels of service at different prices will decide the appropriate demand and price levels without undue regulation. It also has attractive employment prospects, particularly in the areas of road construction and maintenance. As part of the program, consideration may also be given to determining a system of vehicle user charges to cover infrastructural investment and maintenance.

90. Cabotage. Regional development requires that goods and produce from the area are transported to major markets without delay and at low cost. Cabotage has an excellent potential for providing services over part of the regional transport link from the producer to consumer, though it present performance is dismal. MINTEC is proposing programs for both passenger and cargo cabotage investment, principally in the ship fleet which is presently old, unreliable and incapable of giving the desired level of service. Two new 320 passenger ships are operating between Luanda and Lobito but facilities at all ports need to be improved to allow coastal ships to be promptly berthed, unloaded and serviced. The existing arrangements represent a serious obstacle to efficient cabotage operations.

91. Railways. Investment requirements for Angola railway systems are considerable. There is a need to rehabilitate the permanent way, replace damaged bridges, renew rolling stock, purchase new engines, renovate signaling and communications, improve transshipment facilities, train adequate numbers of

technical staff and ensure a regular supply of spare parts for the entire operation. The analysis of the Lobito to Luau (Benguela) corridor should be treated separately under normal evaluation criteria to determine desirability and timing. Railway projects that promote short term sectoral impacts should be favored, such as improving rail transit in the port of Luanda, providing technical assistance to adequately maintain existing engines and rolling stock in all three systems and finally to plan sequential investments within selected corridors. Such corridors should include urban passenger traffic where appropriate.

92. Air. The evaluation of TAAG's long distance aircraft should be a separate project and only measures to improve domestic services should be considered in the proposed program. TAAG presently carries a large and costly eight-month inventory of spare parts because of difficulties in obtaining foreign exchange. Changes in Government financial policy, requiring little capital investment, are the most appropriate actions to remedy this problem. If ENANA airport safety and communications could be improved within the domestic system, TAAG could operate its aircraft over a longer daily period and so improve utilization. Due to tariff distortions and the fixed exchange rate, TAAG is subsidizing all its activities in real resource terms. A sequential adjustment to the tariff structure is urgently needed to allow TAAG to operate from a sound financial base.

93. Communications. The transport sector, in common with other commercial sectors, would benefit from improved public communications at all levels. Communications in general have failed to attract sufficient investment to match demand and to maintain standards of service, even though telephone subscribers have doubled to over 50,000 since 1975. Companies were nominally profitable in 1986 but tariffs do not reflect resource costs and the whole sub-sector needs reorganization in terms of tariffs, salaries, mail transport, maintenance, technical training and management control of staff and operating procedures. The mail system is essentially a low technology, personnel management operation while the telecommunications is characterized by high technology, substantial investments and good potential profitability. The reform of the mail service can be achieved by concerted Government action, with little help from external agencies. A number of projects in the area of telecommunications have been proposed by MINTEC and technical assistance and equipment could be provided where such investments contribute to the success of a transport project.

94. Human resources are a major issue in making all transport modes more efficient and productive. There is a lack of appropriate skills at virtually all levels of the modal employment hierarchy. A two-tier approach to the general problem is recommended in Annex IX, whereby basic educational programs in Angola provide the essential educational foundation for more skills-oriented training. The modes themselves would then be responsible for more specific training, possibly with the support of technical assistance. All modes would benefit from technical assistance to develop and train good managers, experienced technical staff and competent operators. Technical assistance should be targeted on critical areas. Equipment maintenance requires strengthening in all transport sectors and highway maintenance may

require technical assistance with labor-intensive methods used to the fullest extent possible. This can be achieved by adopting a regional/provincial focus and a pavement management system approach. Finally, training programs from unskilled operators upwards are highly desirable and should result in higher equipment utilization and modal productivity, to the benefit of the Angolan economy.

EDUCATION

A. Structure and Organization of the Educational System

1. The present educational system was established by Decree 26 of January 1977 and changed by Decree 40, of May 1980 which divided it into three levels: basic or primary education, secondary education and higher education. While the first two levels offer regular courses for students in the normal age range, vocational training and adult education are available also to older students.

2. Regular Education. Primary education is also divided into three levels, in addition to one year of preschool. The first level lasts four years and is compulsory. The second and third levels each last two years. School attendance should start at six years in preschool classes; the first level should be completed at age 10, the second level at age 12 and the third level at age 14. However, acceptable ages are up to 14 years old in the first level, 16 and 18 years old in the second and third levels. The purpose of primary education is to provide the knowledge required to obtain skills through on-the-job training or secondary education. Secondary education is open for students who have completed the third level and offers two alternatives: the pre-university, a two-year course leading to entrance in the university and secondary technical education, offering different specializations and having a duration of four years. The system does not track as the completion of a level or its equivalents opens the same alternatives. Thus, secondary technical education also provides access to higher education.

3. The 2-year duration of the pre-university course has proven insufficient to provide the students with the knowledge required for university entrance. As a result, it has been extended, on an experimental basis, to three years. Access to secondary education and higher education is determined by a system called "encaminhamento", which considers previous grades, vocational aspirations and the number of places available, in the selection of students. There are 14 pre-university schools. Of these, only three have their own facilities, located in Luanda, Uige and Malanje. Eight schools use facilities provided by the National Educational Institutes and three schools share them with secondary technical institutions. This, in part, reflects the fact that the pre-university courses conceived in 1978 are in a transition phase. Both curriculum and duration need to be reviewed in order that they can adequately fulfil their role of providing the knowledge required for admission to the university.

4. Secondary technical education is a four-year course and has two programs. The first program is a teacher-training course for primary education teachers at the National Institutes of Education, located in 14 provinces. Besides these institutes, there are, in Luanda, the National Institute of Physical Education and the Pedagogical Industrial Institute. The former provides training for physical education teachers and the latter trains teachers in industrial disciplines for secondary technical education. The second program offers specializations for technicians in areas such as agriculture, electricity, health, mechanics, fishing, and finances in the

secondary technical institutes. Only 12 of the institutes are functioning as two were recently closed. During the last two years, students have to gain practical experience by working as apprentices in jobs related to their specializations. Most students of secondary technical education are "working-students", i.e., are employees who are daily relieved of their duties for a number of hours in order to attend classes. For example, many teachers are also students at the National Institutes of Education in order to become certified teachers. The existence of working-students negatively affects learning.

5. The Agostinho Neto University, established in November 1976, is the sole institution of higher education and has three sites: Luanda, Huambo and Lubango. In Luanda, there are the Faculties of Law, Economics, Sciences, Engineering and Medicine. In Huambo, there are the Faculties of Agronomy and Medicine, as well as Economics and Law. In Lubango, there are courses in Economics and Law as well as in the Institute for Education Sciences. The purpose of this Institute is to provide teacher training for teachers of the National Institutes of Education. The Institute for Educational Sciences offers its courses also in Huambo and Luanda, although in these cities it does not have resident professors. These courses are correspondence courses and have many inadequacies. The faculties of Economics and Law at Huambo and Lubango do not have a sufficient number of teachers. As a result, many disciplines are not offered on a regular basis. To remedy this situation, professors from Luanda are sent at regular intervals to teach short-term, intensive courses.

6. Some faculties offer several specializations. All courses have two levels. The first level lasts three years and the second level two years, except for Medicine, which lasts six years. The teacher-training correspondence courses also last six years. Only the completion of the second level provides a diploma. Most students are "working-students" who receive full salaries. Students living in other cities receive free board and lodging. In Luanda, the University houses the National Center for Research; its policies are designed by the National Council for Research, a unit of MED having the rector as its president.

7. Adult Education and Professional Training. Students too old to be accepted by regular primary education have other options. Adult education is offered corresponding to levels I, II and III of primary education. In level I, it is a two-year program divided into four semesters, the first one corresponding to literacy. Levels II and III each have a two-year duration also divided into four semesters. Those completing level III have access to secondary education. Adult classes are given at night using the facilities of regular schools.

8. Literacy programs equivalent to the first semester of Adult Education are carried out by the National Center for Literacy. The Center conducts one-year programs using volunteer teachers and the program and manuals used are specifically designed for the students' needs. The resources for these programs and their execution are managed by the Party (MPLA-PT).

9. Provisional schools (concentrated in rural areas) offer a four-year course to children older than ten years and to dropouts. The first two years are spent learning basic skills and the last two years are dedicated to vocational skills such as agriculture, carpentry, masonry, shoe-making, printing, etc. Provisional schools are boarding schools and, as such, also cater to children and teenagers who have been abandoned or orphaned. Many provisional schools have had to be closed due to the war. At the moment, there are 13 provisional schools located in Bie (3), Namibe (2), Luanda, Benguela, Huila, Luanda-Norte, Malanje, Huambo, Kuango-Sul and Uige.

10. The centers for vocational training are in a state of flux, pending the reorganization that will occur according to legislation still being discussed. Up to now, these centers provide regular courses under the direct control of MED or offer courses for a firm's employees, financed by the Ministry that controls these firms. In the latter case, the role of MED is to provide manuals and exert some supervision. There are 45 Centers operated by MED and 73 within firms. The Centers controlled by MED offer two cycles. The first cycle, corresponding to level II of primary education, takes two years and the major difference in relation to regular primary education is its objective: to provide the student with a marketable skill. In other words, the Centers provide a terminal education and thus offer an opportunity for their students to acquire a skill that is in demand. The second cycle apparently has few students and offers courses equivalent to level III of primary education providing equal access to secondary education.

11. There are three main problems regarding the Centers. The first is the lack of coordination, supervision and control, that should be exercised by MED. As a result, many existing facilities are underused and the same specializations are taught with different procedures. The second problem results from the lack of knowledge about the need of qualified workers. There is a government questionnaire about the occupational structure of the existing labor force in a firm and its future manpower needs. However, many firms do not answer the questionnaire or do not answer that part regarding their manpower needs. Finally, there is the problem of financing the Centers. Recently, the government has made an effort to deal with these problems. The reform of MED has placed the responsibility for coordination of vocational training with the Vice-Minister for Vocational Training. New legislation establishing the National System for Vocational Training under the responsibility of the same VIce-Minister is being proposed. Thus, this system maintains the utilization under MED, which does not have the human and financial resources required for the job and is not familiar with the teaching procedures and curricula of professional training.

12. Ministry of Education: Objectives, Organization and Resources. The main objectives of educational policy are formulated through the MPLA-PT Congresses and resolutions, and through Government legislation. Important among the former are the First Congress of MPLA held in 1977 and the Second Congress. The first Congress set the nature and goals to be followed by the educational system, including nationalization and secularization of schools, compulsory basic education, free education, and cooperation between community and school. The First Extraordinary Congress of the Party (1980) reaffirmed

these policies and showed concern with the quality of education. The Second Congress went further in its concern, with the issues of quality and efficiency, recommending a diagnosis of the educational system. Recently, in its 20th meeting held in November 1987, the Party's Central Committee approved two documents containing the diagnosis and expressed its concerns for more effective actions pursuing the existing priorities.

13. All government responsibilities and resources related to education, with some exceptions, are centered in MED. This ministry has four administrative levels: central administration, provincial delegations, municipal delegations and communal units. The central administration coordinates the educational policies, sets the guidelines, allocates the resources, determines curricula changes, buys school materials, sets teacher wages, supervises schools, organizes teacher-training programs, etc. It has two Vice-Ministers, each responsible for Departments or Directorates (see Chart -). In addition, there are the supporting units and the hierarchical relationship with the provincial delegations.

14. Under the reorganization of MED, through the Decree 9/87, the responsibilities of the Vice-Ministers were changed. Previously, one Vice-Minister was responsible for primary education and the other for secondary technical education (including the pre-university course) and for the University Agostinho Neto. Now, the University refers directly to the Minister. One Vice-Minister handles all matters related to secondary technical education and vocational training and the other is responsible for general education, consisting mainly of primary education. The changes increased the number of the supporting units from five to nine. Many units, such as the Planning Unit, International Affairs, Legal Affairs, Budget Administration and Human Resources, exist in all Ministries. International Affairs deals mainly with the administration of the "cooperantes" contracts.

15. The Vice-Minister for General Education has under his authority the National Directorate for General Education, which comprises four Departments: Physical Education, Adult Education, Special Education and Extra-curricular Activities. The former organization does not differ significantly from the new one as the responsibilities of the Vice-Minister were maintained with one exception. The Vice-Minister for Technical and Vocational Education has three directorates under his authority: secondary technical education, vocational training and teacher training. A comparison with the previous organization reveals the following changes: university affairs are now handled directly by the Minister and the pre-university course is the responsibility of a Vice-Minister. The added responsibilities include teacher training and the coordination of vocational training. The advantages of reallocating the responsibility for this level of teacher training are not clear. The main purpose of the organizational change was to place the responsibility for coordination of vocational training, which is facing a major crisis, in MED. At the moment, regular education taxes the planning abilities of MED, which are very weak, and burdens the administration with unsolved problems and large inefficiencies. It is hard to understand how MED can deal with the additional problems of vocational training, the nature of which is quite different from the ones of regular education, with the same administrative resources.

16. A more promising direction of change would be toward decentralization of decision-making in favor of provincial and municipal delegations. Decentralization would result in shorter delays and a greater involvement of lower authorities. The scope for decentralization involves actions with regard to maintenance of schools and school supplies. An important measure in this respect was the decentralization of budget elaboration and implementation. The organization of the provincial delegations is similar to that of the Ministry of Education, with support units and executive departments, although their number is smaller. For example, the provincial delegation in Huila has three supporting units (Planning Unit, School Supervision and "Cooperantes" Affairs) and eight departments (General Education, Adult Education, Vocational Formation, Budget Administration, Physical Education, Human Resources, Extra-Curricular Activities and Public Relations). In addition, there is a Consultation Council, formed by the department's directors. Contacts between the provincial delegation and the municipal delegations and communal coordinations are severely hampered by difficult communications, large distances and poor roads. There is no reliable information network between the hierarchical levels, and the autonomy given to the school's directors is minimal. As a result, delays in decision-making affect the schools, drastically reducing the number of school days and causing more adverse teaching conditions.

17. Not all government resources for education are included in the budget of the Ministry of Education. Separate budgets exist for the Agostinho Neto University, the National Center for Literacy and the National Institutes for Languages and for Scholarships, as shown in Table IX.1. The allocation for the National Institute for Languages is very small. While the National Institute for Scholarships, which started in 1982, receives about 3% of the educational budgets, the National Center for Literacy is far more important, receiving in most years more than 10% of the government educational budget. The Center is part of the Department of Education, Culture and Sports, a unit of the Secretariat of Ideological Matters of the MPLA-PT. The Center promotes one-year literacy courses for agricultural workers, cooperative workers and employees. Those courses are equivalent to the first semester of the Course for Adult Education.

18. During the period 1980-87, education received an average of 12% of the government budget, with 10% being allocated to the Ministry and 2% to the other institutions, including the university. Even in nominal terms there are large fluctuations in budgeted educational expenditures. For example, in 1985 these expenditures were 12% below the 1980 level. Because of the cost of the increase in goods and services, the decline in real terms since 1983 is larger than the decrease of nominal expenditures. Cuts in budgeted expenditures reduced actual real expenditures even further. In the period 1980/82 (Table IX.2) sizable cuts were made both in total government expenditures and in educational expenditures; the National Center for Literacy and the National Institute for Languages were most affected.

Table IX.1 - GOVERNMENT BUDGET FOR EDUCATION - 1980/87
(Kz millions)

	1980	1981	1982	1983	1984	1985	1987
Ministry of Education	10.029	9.030	9.507	8.407	9.021	7.9	11
University Agostinho Neto	26	239	491	33	474	500	851
National Center for Literacy	1.33	1.125	1.071	858	950	762	600
National Institute for Languages	16	18	28	20	*	19	9
National Institute for Scholarships	-	-	140	81	*	377	384
	11.644	10.413	11.23	9.702		9.559	12.855

*Missing information

Table IX.2 - GOVERNMENT EXPENDITURES ON EDUCATION - 1980/82
(Kz millions)

	1980		1981		1982	
	Expenditures	Reduction (%)	Expenditures	Reduction (%)	Expenditures	Reduction (%)
Ministry of Education	7.883	21	7.929	12	8.097	15
University Agostinho Neto	235	12	236	2	358	27
National Center of Literacy	618	53	580	48	683	36
National Institute for Languages	6	63	8	54	18	38
National Institute for Scholarships	-	-		135	4	
Total Government Expenditures	76.920	17	91.639	16	72.138	29

19. The distributional impact of educational expenditures can be seen in regional terms by comparing the per-capita expenditures for education by the 18 provinces. For 1983, the central unit of MED absorbed 8.2% of MED expenditures. Expenditures in the provinces were an average Kz 916 per capita, varying from Kz 469 in Bie and Kz 715 in Luanda Norte, to Kz 3364 in Kuando Kubango and Kz 1784 in Benguela. The bulk of planned expenditures by the Ministry of Education is of a recurrent nature. Capital expenditures are, for most years, less than 1% of total expenditures. Personnel expenditures account for more than 80% of total expenditures. Expenditure on food is significant, which calls attention to the need to reevaluate the free room-and-board policy. The budget for the National Center for Literacy reveals that personnel expenditure is the most important single item, representing more than 80% of total expenditures and about 10% of the Ministry of Education personnel expenditures. This large share of resources employed in literacy programs for adults raises serious questions about its cost-effectiveness.

B. Primary Education

20. Enrollment in regular primary education in the period 1970/86 shows a rapid growth up to 1979, and a sharp decline thereafter. The number of students increased from 484,000 in 1970 to 671,000 in 1976, and 1,932,000 in 1979, declining subsequently to 1,047,000 in 1986. Enrollment growth since Independence reflects the priority education received from the new Government. However, the attempt to enforce compulsory education has suffered severe setbacks, which deserve some explanation. While data on number of classrooms, number and qualification of teachers and number of daily shifts is not available for this period, it is reasonable to assume that the increase in enrollment between 1976 and 1979 has overtaxed the capacity of the system in physical terms by increasing student/teacher ratio as well as increasing the number of schools operating with three or four daily shifts. Also, there is no evidence of an increase in qualified teachers in this period that would partially compensate for the loss of qualified teachers after independence. Thus, the threefold increase in enrollment must have been accomplished with a smaller number of qualified teachers.

21. School maintenance has probably suffered from a combination of intensive use and insufficient repairs. Similarly, school materials hardly kept pace with enrollment. Thus, enrollment expansion must have increased inefficiencies and would hardly be sustainable, even if other factors were kept in check. But during the early eighties, war problems and economic problems intensified, with damaging consequences for the educational system. War consequences were felt in many ways. Firstly, impairment of the transportation network disrupted distribution of school supplies in many areas. Secondly, the dislocated population overburdened facilities in urban or secure areas. Thirdly, they contributed to the decline in the number of teachers through the draft of young soldiers. Fourthly, production losses and the cost of the war effort reduced the resources available for peaceful activities.

22. The distortions in the economy and the centralized allocation system reduced local production of school and construction materials as well

as the distribution networks. As the import content of further education materials increased, their availability was affected by foreign exchange constraints, which also reduced the ability of the country to rely on foreigners ("cooperantes") to reduce the shortage of qualified teachers. Perhaps most damaging is the effect of distorted wages on teacher morale and supply. Since teachers do not receive payments in kind, many consider their income insufficient and leave their jobs.

23. The decrease in resources available for primary education is shown in Table IX.3. For three years there are figures for the number of schools, classrooms and teachers. The number of teachers declined 23.6% from 1981 to 1983, whereas the reduction in enrollment was less (12%). Those who left because of low wages were probably the most able and qualified. The decline in classrooms was larger (40%), forcing an increase in the number of shifts and in the ratio students/classroom.

Table IX.3 - PRIMARY EDUCATION - NUMBER OF TEACHERS, CLASSROOMS & SCHOOLS 1981/83

	1981	1982	1983	1983/81 %
Teachers	43.899	39.843	33.521	-23.6
Classrooms	17.921	16.742	10.670*	-40.4
Schools	7.097	6.612	6.120	-13.8

24. Gross enrollment rates for primary education and level I declined by 42%. The high figures for the gross enrollment rates for level I reflect the great number of over-aged students. For example, in 1981 almost half the students in level I were more than nine years old, as revealed by the comparison of gross and net enrollment rates. High dropout rates are also the main cause of net enrollment rates of less than 1% in levels II and III.

Table IX.4 - BASIC EDUCATION - ENROLLMENT RATES

	1980	1981	1982	1983	1984
Gross Enrollment Rate Basic Education (6-14 years)	75.7	69.2	62.8	55.1	43.7
Level I (6-9 years)	155.3	141.6	128.4	112.9	89.9
Net Enrollment Rate					
Level I (6-9 years)	-	72.4	69.4	-	-
Level II (10-11 years)	-	0.9	0.6	-	-
Level III (12-13 years)	-	0.1	0.1	-	-

Source: Etapa Diagnostica, MED, 1986.

25. The Censuses of 1983 and 1984 do not provide information on schooling level for those enrolled. However, they allow calculation of net enrollment rates for primary education and level I, on the assumption that students between 7 and 10 years old are in level I and that students between 7 and 14 years are in primary education. The results do not indicate major regional differences, as only Namibe has smaller enrollment rates, shown in the table below.

Table IX.5 - NET ENROLLMENT RATES - FOUR PROVINCES

	Luanda	Zaire	Cabinda	Namibe
Net Enrollment Rate				
Basic Education	94.4	83.5	80.5	70.8
Level I	83.3	81.2	77.3	68.1

Source: Censuses of 1983 and 1984.

26. There are indications that the deterioration in primary education has ceased. Enrollment figures show a small increase since 1984 and the number of teachers in 1985 increased to 35,221. Still, increasing access to primary education and improving its quality will require far more resources than those presently available. Adult education enrollment also shows a decline between 1980 and 1984 and a substantial increase in 1985 and 1986. This type of education will have to expand to accommodate the students who cannot attend regular primary education classes because of their age. The reduction in enrollment in regular primary education vastly increased the potential demand for adult education. The problems faced by primary education are illustrated by a study of demand for education in Luanda in 1986. Of the 221,400 students in the age group of 5-14 years old who tried to enroll, 31,200 did not find places in pre-school and first grade. Of the remainder 190,200, at least 71,200 were in the third shift or in classes with more than 40 students. If one considers that the third shift reduces the class hours/day of the other two shifts and that the high number of dropouts is partly a consequence of high repeat rates, the conclusion is that conditions for learning are extremely unfavorable. The study also mentions the need for an additional 780 teachers.

27. Internal Efficiency. Efficiency in primary education is low. One way to look at internal efficiency is to observe promotion, repeat and dropout rates (see Table IX.6). The promotion rates are higher for Level I than for Level II and III. Within Level I they are higher in 3rd and 4th grades; between Level II and III there is not a clear pattern, although on the average the promotion rates are higher in Level III. Taking the average value for 1980/84, promotion rates vary from 29.2% in grade 6 to 45.0% in grade 3 and retention rates (promotion plus repeat rates) vary from 63.4% in grade 8 to 74.4% in grade 3 class. In the period 1980/84, a clear trend is discernible. For Levels I and II, the promotion rate for each grade shows a steadfast

decline. The reduction of promotion rates in the Level I is always larger than 1/5. This evidence points to a severe deterioration in primary education in the early 1980s.

Table IX.6: PRIMARY EDUCATION, AVERAGE PROMOTION, REPEAT AND DROPOUT RATES, 1980-84

	Grades							
	1	2	3	4	5	6	7	8
Promotion	39.4	39.5	45.0	42.8	30.5	29.2	32.3	31.7
Repeat	33.8	34.7	29.4	31.1	35.5	35.9	31.4	31.7
Dropout	26.9	25.8	25.6	26.1	34.0	34.0	36.3	36.6

Source: Statistical Appendix, Table J.5.

For the Level I, a cohort study shows that of a 1000 students starting the 1st grade 604 are promoted to 2nd grade, 360 reach the 3rd grade, 326 attain the 4th grade, and only 142 students start Level II. The others became dropouts or had more than three consecutive repetitions. The average number of years it took to be promoted was: 1st grade - 1.46; 2nd grade - 1.85; 3rd grade - 2.12; and 4th grade - 2.43.

28. For each student who completes the Level I, the average number of years spent in school either by himself because of repetition or by dropouts is 7.03. Thus, wastage resulting from repetition and evasion increases the cost by 75%. The results are even worse for levels I and II. Of the 142 students which start Level II, only 60 eventually reach 7th grade, 23 go to Level III, 9 are promoted to 8th grade, and 4 graduate. Among the students which are promoted to the next grade, the average number of years it takes to be promoted continues the upward trend observed Level I. Thus, for 5th grade it is 2.60; for 6th grade it is 2.78; for 7th grade it is 2.89; and for 8th grade it is 3.25. For each student who starts the Level II and graduates from the Level III, the average number of years spent in school either because of repetition or because of dropouts is 40. In this case, wastage increases the cost tenfold.

C. Secondary Education

29. Secondary education has three major branches: secondary technical education, a four-year course offering several specializations; the National Institutes of Education, a teacher training course designed for primary education teachers; and the pre-university course, a two-year course leading to entrance into university.

30. Secondary Technical Education. Secondary technical education offers courses in agriculture (Huambo, Huila, and Uige), economics (Luanda and Huila), industry (Benguela, Luanda, and Huambo), health (Bie, Huambo, and Luanda), and other subjects (Fishing-Namibe, Petroleum - Kwanza Sul and

Journalism - Luanda). Economics offers the following specializations: administration, commerce, statistics, finance, and planning. Industry offers courses in construction, electricity, mechanics, chemistry, and politechnics. Enrollment in secondary technical education has grown every year since 1978, to 4646 in 1985, at an annual rate of growth of 23% (see Statistical Appendix, Table J.6). This continuous expansion of enrollment was achieved despite serious problems which affected drastically the quality of education. Students are mainly working students, i.e., they have a regular job which allows them to go to classes. There are three categories of teachers: full-time teachers, teachers having a main job outside the Institute, and students encharged with responsibilities (monitors). Full-time teachers are usually "cooperantes"; among nationals, those having an outside job constitute a majority because of a lack of incentives to be a full-time teacher. Thus in 1986, of 513 teachers, 37% were "cooperantes", 25% were part-time teachers, 16% were full-time teachers, 13.5% were monitors, and the remainder 8.5% were classified as "other". Because of language problems and cultural differences, the work of "cooperantes" is not very effective. These circumstances are aggravated by their many nationalities and different institutional and technical backgrounds. The burden of teaching falls mainly on part-time teachers and monitors.

31. Two other aspects which constrain learning relate to reading materials and equipment used. Reading materials are generally adapted from foreign sources and do not adequately cover the subjects nor are they produced in sufficient number for all students. Also, there generally is no library. Equipment is inherited from colonial times, is well maintained but insufficient, and modern imported equipment frequently does not function because of maintenance problems and a lack of imported parts. Thus, it is not surprising to find a high evasion rate in the first year (9th grade) and an average promotion rate of 48%. Aside from a generally low internal efficiency, Table J-7 in the Statistical Appendix reveals two facts. First, promotion rates in most cases are higher for the last grade. Second, the comparison of efficiency in 1983 and 1985, reveals an increase in efficiency in 1985. Low promotion rates are reflected in the modest number of graduates (see Statistical Appendix Table J.8).1/In Agriculture, the number of graduates fluctuates, with a maximum of 84 graduates per year. The Economics course shows a declining number of graduates, aggravating a serious bottleneck, that of middle administration echelons in government and in firms. Industry graduates are increasing at modest rates, far below the economy's requirements.

32. One positive change towards the improvement of efficiency would be to give the Institutes the authority to allocate their budgetary resources and so reduce the delay in the purchase of materials for class-rooms and laboratories. Another proposal, to allow the Institutes to sell goods and services and in this way have their own source of revenues, has not yet been considered by the Government.

1/ Additional information on agricultural education is provided in Annex VII.

33. National Institutes of Education. There are 14 National Institutes of Education with the responsibility for training teachers for primary education in four-year courses. Enrollment in these Institutes increased from 778 in 1978 to 3970 in 1985, at an annual rate of growth of 26% (see Statistical Appendix Table J.6). However, when one compares the number of graduates with actual needs, a wide gap is observed. From 1981 to 1985, the graduates were 1743 (1981-68; 1982-228; 1983-461; 1984-526; and 1985-460) or less than 5% of the stock of teachers. Thus the graduates of the Institutes are not enough even to compensate for normal attrition, let alone to replace those who left because of low wages. Since most students are teachers, the net addition of teachers is practically negligible. Efficiency, as measured by promotion rates, is not high. In 1985, the promotion rates were 9th grade- 56%; 10th grade- 72%; 11th grade- 66%; and 12th grade- 74%, with an average rate of 66%. A major learning problem is the low proportion of Angolan teachers. Thus, in 1986, 71 teachers (31%) were Angolans and 157 (69%) were "cooperantes". The predominance of foreigners poses serious problems already described with respect to technical secondary education. Moreover, this situation calls attention to the inability of the Institute for Educational Sciences to produce graduates to teach at the National Institutes of Education. The demand for these graduates is very high, not only to replace "cooperantes" but also to expand enrollment significantly in these Institutes.

34. Unless the institutional capacity to produce teachers both at undergraduate level and at secondary level is dramatically increased, primary education will have to continue to recruit unqualified teachers. These teachers have access to in-service training. In-service training is the responsibility of the National Department for In-service Training, which is part of the National Directorate for Teachers Training. It is divided into two stages. Stage one has the objective of giving education equivalent to Level II for those teachers who completed the 4th grade. Stage two is the equivalent of Level III and is given to those teachers who completed the 6th grade. Stage one was first applied in 1980 to teachers in 13 provinces. It is a correspondence course which uses radio, and its contents were developed within the National Department for In-service Training. The results were far from satisfactory, perhaps in part due to the large number of teachers enrolled (21,600). Also, the ability to send the materials in time and receive the homework was drastically affected by the war. Thus, a review carried out at the end of 1981 showed that of those starting (21,656), 6,614 became dropouts; of the remaining 15,042, 6,874 were advanced. Stage two suffered a 4-year delay because of lack of UNESCO support and is presently being implemented together with stage one. Although results are not known, one aspect deserving attention is the delay, caused by the mail service and the fact that teachers have little time to study after fulfilling their normal duties.

35. Pre-University Courses. Pre-university courses last two years and lead to entrance in the university. There is general agreement that two years are not adequate to provide the knowledge required in university courses. In a pilot experiment, the course was extended to three years in 1986, the options were limited to Social Sciences and "Exact Sciences", and the

attendance was limited to regular students. Enrollment increased from 1,382 in 1977 to 3,721 in 1985, at an annual rate of 13%. At the present, there are 14 schools, of which three have their own buildings, six share facilities with the National Institutes of Education and three are located in secondary technical education schools. Promotion rates were 57% for the 1st year and 48% for the 2nd year in 1986. As in other secondary schools, the teachers are predominantly "cooperantes" (48%), and part-time teachers (34%), followed by full-time teachers (15%) and other (3%). In this case, the relatively low number of teachers (134), makes it easier to substitute "cooperantes" and part-time teachers, provided that teacher wages became competitive.

D. Higher Education

36. Courses and Enrollment. The Agostinho Neto University, founded on November 26, 1976, offers undergraduate courses at three sites: Luanda, Huambo, and Lubango. Luanda has the largest campus with 70% of the students. The other students are in Huambo (10%), Lubango (7%), and in correspondence courses (13%). The facilities in Luanda are spread throughout the city and many buildings were adapted to serve as faculties. The problems of transportation aggravate the isolation among faculties and prevent better use of classrooms and other spaces.

37. Located in Luanda are the office of the President and its supporting units, the National Center for Research, and five faculties: Science, Law, Economics, Engineering, and Medicine. In Huambo, there are four faculties: Agriculture, Law, Economics, and Medicine. Located in Lubango are the Higher Institute of Educational Sciences, and the faculties of Law and Economics. The faculties of Law and Economics, both in Huambo and Lubango, function precariously because the number of resident teachers is far below the actual need. Because of this problem, teachers from Luanda are regularly sent to teach intensive courses. The Agostinho Neto University, part of the Ministry of Education, is under the direct supervision of its Minister.

38. One major problem is the great degree of divergence between the university and the needs of the society. Extension services, one of the main forms of interaction with society, are practically non-existent. The Center for National Research has not made any significant contribution to a better knowledge of the problems of the nation. The evidence is that the production of articles and books by teachers is minimal. Given these circumstances, the expected leadership is not provided by the university. The selection of the candidates for the university is done through a process called "encaminhamento". This process considers both grades in secondary education and the student aspirations. There is neither a clear description of how "encaminhamento" is carried out nor background information on the students who applied to the university and those who were selected.

39. Enrollment in the university has grown from 1,405 in 1975 to 5,732 in 1986, at an annual rate of 13.6%, even though it declined in 1976 and 1977 (see Table IX.8). Actually, only in 1982 did enrollment reach again the pre

-independence level. Most of the students also work, and the job assures them the possibility of attending classes. Students whose families live elsewhere have room and board provided by the university free of charge.

Table IX.7 - ENROLLMENT IN HIGHER EDUCATION - 1970/86

	No. of Students
1970	2,125
1971	2,435
1972	3,094
1975	1,405
1976	1,093
1977	871
1978	1,254
1979	1,918
1980	2,333
1981	2,798
1982	2,991
1983	3,441
1984	4,493
1985	5,034
1986	5,732

40. The number of students in the various faculties can be seen in Appendix Table J.9. Between 1984 and 1986, the increase in students was largest in Economics and Education, which also have the larger faculties. The great number of specializations in some faculties raises the question of the cost per student. Possibly, the alternative of studying abroad should be favored in some cases. Thus, for example, the Faculty of Sciences offers courses in the following areas: biology, physics, geophysics, geology, mathematics, and chemistry. This faculty has about 700 students and, like all other faculties with the exception of Medicine, the courses last five years. It may be the case that, given the quality of the course, its unit cost and low efficiency, some specializations should not be offered. Another similar situation is that of the Faculty of Engineering, which offers architecture, civil engineering, electrotechnics, mechanical engineering, mining, and chemical engineering. Of the remainder, Agriculture offers courses in agronomy and veterinary science, and Economics offers two specializations: planning and accounting.

41. Efficiency and Resources. Information on internal efficiency is not satisfactory and suggests that promotion rates vary in different faculties between 40% and 80%. One way to get an indicator of productivity is to relate the number of graduates in a given year to the number of new students five years before, only Medicine and correspondence courses last six years (Appendix Table J.10). The number of new students was estimated by taking 20% of the enrollment in the previous year plus the increase in enrollment. The indices of productivity obtained were 26% in 1984, 10% in 1983, and 23% in 1982, suggesting large inefficiencies. If the stock of graduates until 1984

(740) is related to enrollment up to 1980 (8,874), the indicator of productivity is 8%. The learning process is affected by many factors. Concerning the students, it was seen that most are part-time students and their previous schooling was not satisfactory. Another crucial factor is the inadequate supply of reading materials. Libraries do not have even enough textbooks, partly because of import restrictions on the acquisition of books. There are few bookshops and they have a poor selection of books. As a consequence, most of the readings consist of class notes distributed by professors or the translation of excerpts of foreign books.

42. Given the limited number of full-time Angolan professors, there is a widespread use of part-time teachers and of "monitores" or students with teaching responsibilities (Appendix Table J.11). In addition, as mentioned before, many courses do not have all the required teachers and hence the need to use teachers from Luanda to teach intensive courses. Finally, the most common used alternative--the "cooperantes"--have their efficiency impaired by language and cultural problems. Also, this solution is costly because their wages are partly paid in foreign exchange. In conclusion, the professors are inadequate in number and often in qualifications. There is a need of massive training abroad, coupled with attractive wages, to reduce significantly the proportion of part-time teachers and of "cooperantes". Most of the "cooperantes" are Cubans, Vietnamese, Italians, and Portuguese. The proportion of "cooperantes" was 42% in 1984, 47% in 1985, and 35% in 1986. Since part-time teachers have less contact hours with students and supposing these contact-hours are half of that of the full-time teachers, the proportion of the contact-hours by "cooperantes" is, respectively, 52%, 54%, and 43%. The decline in 1986 of the proportion of "cooperantes" reflects the foreign exchange crisis resulting from the decrease in oil prices.

43. Another question, related to the curricula, is the relevance of what is being learned. The curriculum for the economics course has been of particular concern to the Government. The Government's administration and the management of enterprises require, in the middle and higher echelons, people capable of utilizing the concepts and tools of economic analysis. However, the number of disciplines which offer such concepts is far from sufficient. Improving the curriculum, including a change in content to better reflect contemporary contributions, should improve decision-making and the prospects of successful economic reforms. Proposals now being discussed of changing the economics curricula at both secondary and university levels place more emphasis on disciplines such as statistics, economic theory and financial analysis and on better understanding the workings of a market economy, while reducing ideological training. These proposals have received considerable support from the government officials responsible for the implementation of SEF. Finally, laboratories and equipment in courses such as Agriculture, Engineering, and Medicine are in a poor state, pointing to the need for maintenance and the purchase of laboratory materials. In terms of research needs, the existing laboratories are greatly inadequate.

44. The Government's planned expenditures for the Agostinho Neto University have fluctuated in the past, even in nominal terms (Appendix Table J.12). Thus, these expenditures were smaller in 1983 and 1984 than in 1982.

The most important component, personnel expenditures, is responsible for between 51% and 67% of total expenditures. Outlays on equipment and other durable goods are very small, varying between 3% and 7% of total expenditures. Expenditure on food represents more than half of that on durable goods. The payment of "cooperantes" as a proportion of personnel expenditures is, in most years, in excess of 10% of personnel expenditures. The complete reliance on government sources of financing has two drawbacks: it restricts the funds available, which frequently suffer budget cuts, and it reduces the flexibility of spending. Since most students also work, part of their salaries could be used to pay for board and lodging, as well as for purchasing reading materials and, possibly, for a small tuition. Cost recovery could be extended to other areas, e.g., making the increase of extension services and the provision of consultant and research services to firms more viable. In this way, the degree of insulation of the university from society could be reduced.

45. Although the information on resources and enrollment is limited, it is possible to estimate recurrent unit costs for some courses. These costs were estimated using planned expenditures data. This overestimates actual costs because of budget cuts. The distribution of the general expenditures, i.e., those not appropriated to a course, were made proportionally to the number of students. The tentative results for 1984 are the following: the courses of Law and Economics in Huambo have a unit cost of 69,000 Kz, as compared to 73,400 Kz in Lubango. The unit cost for the Institute for Educational Sciences in Lubango is 88,300 Kz and for Medicine at Huambo is 95,100 Kz. Finally, the courses offered at Luanda (Engineering, Law, Economics, Sciences, and Medicine) have an average unit cost of 109,800 Kz, whereas the unit cost of the Agriculture course in Huambo is 300,700 Kz. The average unit cost for the university, considering all resources are spent only in teaching is 105,500 Kz.

E. Recommendations

46. A first recommendation deals with the issue of teacher training. It is evident that the negative effect of the massive exodus of the Portuguese continues in spite of the cooperation of foreign teachers and the efforts made to increase the number of qualified teachers. The first priority should be to train teachers, possibly abroad, to eliminate the need of correspondence courses and to replace most of the "cooperantes" at the Institute for Educational Sciences in Lubango. This measure, together with curriculum changes and provision of adequate reading materials should improve substantially the knowledge of the graduates of these institutions. At the secondary level, the National Institutes of Education would directly benefit from the availability of better teachers. Only when the existing Institutes have been strengthened through replacement of most "cooperantes" and improvement in facilities, should expansion be contemplated. The suggested approach places emphasis on quality and institution building and recognizes that there are no short-cuts to the time-consuming preparation of more qualified teachers. Measures with more immediate impact on primary education are changes in the curriculum to be set by the National Institute for

Educational Research and improvement of in-service training funded by international agencies. Finally, the issue of teachers' wages should receive careful attention as the solutions proposed are contingent on the ability of the educational system to retain its best teachers.

47. Reorganization of MED should have four goals. First, the recognition that the responsibility for vocational training should not be with MED. The nature of its problems differs from those of regular education, since its content and teaching methods are specific, and the demand of firms must be assessed to avoid external inefficiencies. Thus, the agency responsible for vocational training should not be part of MED, a tax on firms should finance its activities and the courses offered should reflect more closely manpower needs. A second goal is to place the responsibility of the National Center of Literacy with MED. The evidence is that the literacy programs are costly and ineffective. The resources of the Center should be used by regular education to help improve the very low efficiency. The third goal is to strengthen educational planning and management as well as improve the information system. At the moment, decision-making is hampered by poor information and a centralization of decisions. There is little awareness of the need for cost control and a large time-lag exists between decisions and implementation, which results in excessive delays. Thus, the fourth goal is to work further towards decentralizing decision-making, especially regarding the financial management of resources.

48. Reorganization will improve the use of available resources. However, there is a clear need for additional budget resources to increase the minimum level of capital expenditures to avoid further deterioration of school buildings, to replace needed equipment and teaching materials, and to improve teacher's wages. It is clear that school construction and maintenance should draw resources from the community, both local firms and parents, more intensively. This is the most viable way to expand enrollment in the near future. Cost recovery measures should start by imposing a fee for board and lodging. Food purchases are a large item in budget expenditure and it is not possible to justify, on equity grounds, their supply free of charge. Another potential source of revenues is permission for the schools, especially the secondary technical schools, to sell goods and services. The cash need of the schools could in this way be partially solved.

49. The lack of qualified management is a problem which negatively affects decision making and implementation both in the Government and in large firms. There is need for curricula reform in the economic courses, both in secondary technical schools and at the university. Also, the creation of administration courses should receive full support. For this purpose, better coordination of INORAD with the university is required. The best way to deal with the lack of Angolan teachers is to receive technical assistance from a reputable university for the training of teachers abroad, a program of visiting professors and the provision of text-books and other teaching materials. Of course, foreign aid to provide scholarships, books and equipment, and visiting professors is also crucial in other specializations.

50. Primary education can hardly keep pace with population growth. Until there is a substantial increase in efficiency, needed to restore the levels existing prior to the decline of the early 1980s, the priority should be on the quality of education. Improved maintenance of school buildings, better teachers and changes in the curriculum are the main steps to reduce the existing wastage to more acceptable levels. School construction should aim as much at the elimination of third and fourth shifts as at increasing the number of places. The cost of increasing quality can, to a large extent, be compensated by the reduction in the cost of inefficiency. The shift in resources that is required to produce these results is the main task in primary education. In other words, increasing the number of those students who complete four years of education should be viewed as more important than improving the odds of access to the first grade.

51. Secondary education has so far received relatively few students. Enrollment should expand as a larger number of students finish primary education. Before this happens, it will be necessary to deal with two issues. First, it is probably desirable to reduce the number of years of basic education to seven or six years and to increase in the same way the number of years in secondary education. Second, the role of general education should be enlarged vis-a-vis technical education, which is more costly and the graduates which do not enter the university should have access to training courses before entering the labor market.

52. The Agostinho Neto University has to increase the proportion of full-time Angolan professors, reducing both the number of part-time teachers and of "cooperantes". For this purpose, it is necessary to increase the relative wages of university teachers and the opportunities to study abroad. Considering the number of courses and specializations, the lack of teachers in some courses and the inadequate existing libraries and research facilities, available resources are spread too thinly. One possibility is to send students abroad instead of having them enrolled at the university. Another possibility is to increase the common core of the curricula. The university's buildings in Luanda are located in different sectors of the city and were built for other purposes. The existence of a campus should improve the use of the physical facilities, as well as teacher time, libraries and other resources. The first steps in this direction, i.e., selecting the land, and developing construction plans should be taken in the near future.

List of Tables

Page No.

A. KEY MACROECONOMIC INDICATORS

B. LABOR FORCE AND WAGES

C. GROSS DOMESTIC PRODUCT AND EXPENDITURE

D. GOVERNMENT FINANCE

E. BANKING AND BALANCE OF PAYMENTS

Page No.

Page No.

APPENDIX
Table A.2

ANGOLA

GOVERNMENT SECTOR MACROECONOMIC INDICATORS, 1982-87

	1982	1983	1984	1985	1986	1987
Current Receipts / GDP Ratio	0.304	0.316	0.386	0.389	0.363	0.290
Direct Taxes / GDP Ratio	0.154	0.176	0.216	0.232	0.182	0.169
Indirect Taxes / GDP Ratio	0.096	0.093	0.109	0.099	0.083	0.078
Others Receipts / GDP Ratio	0.054	0.048	0.060	0.059	0.098	0.043
Current Expenditures / GDP Ratio	0.326	0.331	0.361	0.402	0.387	0.344
Current Transfers / GDP Ratio	0.010	0.011	0.012	0.018	0.019	0.016
Interest / Current Receipts Ratio	0.000	0.000	0.000	0.000	0.000	0.000
Subsidies / GDP Ratio	0.052	0.048	0.049	0.070	0.031	0.025
Budgetary Savings / GDP Ratio	-0.022	-0.014	0.025	-0.013	-0.023	-0.054
Government Investment / GDP Ratio	0.015	0.009	0.017	0.011	0.024	0.016
Capital Transfers / GDP Ratio	0.092	0.045	0.048	0.035	0.030	0.033
Government Consumption / GDP Ratio	0.264	0.271	0.299	0.314	0.337	0.302

Source : Mission Estimates

APPENDIX
Table A.3

ANGOLA

FOREIGN AND MONETARY SECTORS MACROECONOMIC INDICATORS, 1982-87

	1982	1983	1984	1985	1986	1987
FOREIGN SECTOR						
Exports (Goods + NFS) / GDP Ratio	0.402	0.407	0.427	0.464	0.309	0.453
Exports Volume Growth Rate	-0.069	0.411	0.134	0.155	0.205	0.277
Nominal Exports Growth Rate	-0.122	0.119	0.116	0.101	-0.418	0.742
Imports (Goods + NFS) / GDP Ratio	0.487	0.399	0.441	0.409	0.371	0.335
Imports Volume Growth Rate		0.104	0.221	-0.087	-0.205	0.002
Nominal Imports Growth Rate	-0.133	-0.108	0.373	-0.101	-0.225	0.200
Resource Balance / GDP Ratio	-0.086	0.008	-0.014	0.056	-0.062	0.118
Net Factor Payments / GDP Ratio	-0.039	-0.041	-0.035	-0.039	-0.049	-0.057
Net Current Transfers / GDP Ratio	0.006	0.005	0.005	0.004	0.031	0.010
Current Account Balance / GDP Ratio	-0.119	-0.028	-0.044	0.021	-0.081	0.071
Stock of Foreign Reserves / Imports	0.067	0.098	0.109	0.125	0.106	0.139
Debt Service / Exports (Goods + NFS)	0.161	0.177	0.141	0.129	0.314	0.220
Debt Service / GDP Ratio	0.065	0.072	0.060	0.060	0.097	0.100
Stock of Long-Term Debt / Exports (G	1.146	1.113	1.072	1.045	1.747	1.255
Stock of Long-Term Debt / GDP Ratio	0.460	0.453	0.458	0.485	0.539	0.569
MONETARY SECTOR						
Stock of Private Credit / GDP Ratio	0.318	0.648	0.527	0.581	0.635	0.640
Stock of Loans to Government / GDP R	0.541	0.453	0.612	0.645	0.741	0.748
Stock of Money and Quasi-Money / GDP	0.714	0.836	0.890	1.010	1.124	1.136

Source : Mission Estimates

APPENDIX

Table B.1

ANGOLA

POPULATION, 1900-1986

YEAR	POPULATION (Thousand)
1900	2,716
1910	2,922
1920	3,131
1930	3,344
1940	3,738
1950	4,145
1960	4,840
1970	5,646
1975	6,520
1980	7,722
1981	7,918
1982	8,119
1983	8,326
1984	8,537
1985	8,754
1986	8,990

Source: Anuario Estatistico and Instituto Nactional de Estatistica.

APPENDIX

Table B.2

ANGOLA

URBAN AND RURAL POPULATIION 1970-1986

(thousands)

YEAR	URBAN	RURAL	URBAN AS % OF TOTAL
1970	789	4,857	14
1975	1,182	5,338	18
1980	1,781	5,941	23
1982	2,067	6,052	25
1984	2,385	6,142	28
1986	2,773	6,217	31

Source: Instituto Nactilonal.

APPENDIX

Table B.3

ANGOLA

ECONOMICALLY ACTIVE POPULATION BY ECONOMIC SECTOR FOR 1985

SECTORS	Number of Employed Workers	Percentage of Total
TOTAL	2109083	100.0
Productive Sector	1552912	73.6
Industry	237516	11.3
Construction	155298	7.4
Agriculture and Livestock	748094	35.5
Silviculture	8720	0.4
Transport	177566	8.4
Communications	12219	0.6
Commerce	186457	8.8
Others	27042	1.3
Non-Productive Sector	484956	23.0
Communal Services	47034	2.2
Education and Science	139655	6.6
Culture and Arts	24528	1.2
Health, Social Assist., Physical Culture, Sports and Tourism	103160	4.9
Finance and Insurance	19466	0.9
Administration	118872	5.6
Others	32241	1.5
Unemployed	71215	3.4

Source : Instituto Nacional de Estatistica - INE

APPENDIX

Table B.4

ANGOLA

NUMBER OF SALARIED WORKERS AFFILIATED TO THE UNTA BY TYPE OF EMPLOYER AND SEX, 1981-85

Type of Employer	1981	1982	1983	1984	1985
Total	606789	609477	621762	628860	665581
Government and State Enterprises	517544	515277	523389	528705	553881
Men	408935	404050	409602	413209	432416
Women	108609	111227	113787	115496	121465
Mixed Enterprises	28771	31662	32812	32802	34191
Men	27819	30510	31566	31529	32770
Women	952	1152	1246	1273	1421
Private Enterprises	60474	62538	65561	67353	77509
Men	52122	54575	57119	58447	66003
Women	8352	7963	8442	8906	11506

Source : Instituto Nacional de Estatistica - INE
Uniao Nacional dos Trabalhadores de Angola - UNTA

APPENDIX

Table B.5

ANGOLA

MONTHLY AVERAGE SALARIES OF UNTA AFFILIATES BY TYPE OF OCCUPATION, 1981-85

Type of Occupation	1981	1982	1983	1984	1985
Managers	16060	16500	16500	16500	16500
Technicians	14500	15500	18000	18000	18000
Employees	6500	6500	8000	8250	8500
Industrial Workers	5800	7000	8850	9500	9500
Agricultural Workers	4466	4466	5612	5761	5761
Average	7094	7692	9299	9640	9758
Average Growth Rate (%)		8.4	20.9	3.7	1.2

Source: Instituto Nacional de Estatistica - INE

APPENDIX

Table B.6

ANGOLA

NUMBER OF EMPLOYED WORKERS AND MONTHLY AVERAGE SALARY BY SECTOR UNDER BNA CONTROL IN 1986

Sector	Government		State Enterprises		Mixed Enterprises		Private Enterprises		Cooperatives		Others		Total	
	Number of Workers	Monthly Average Salary	Number of Workers	Monthly Average Salary	Number of Workers	Monthly Average Salary	Number of Workers	Monthly Average Salary	Number of Workers	Monthly Average Salary	Number of Workers	Monthly Average Salary	Number of Workers	Monthly Average Salary
Agriculture	3153	13251	57609	5039	105	13200	4283	9999	273	6648	2	15633	65425	5780
Commerce	1026	12419	15655	11002	125	15292	12095	11864	147	3518			29848	11419
Hotel	174	16608	5058	11332	18	1041	1820	11313	51	3067			7121	11371
Construction	5738	15906	18074	9955	445	11431	9676	4872					33933	9531
Transport	1075	13062	17615	12180	39	12153	8624	4841					28153	9991
Food	642	17139	10707	10090	137	16806	5429	5371	3	1568	4	12563	16922	8897
Metallurgy	114	16494	6045	9132			1304	8602					7543	9146
Education	36150	18593	6631	11243			88	10000					42869	17438
Wood	31	101935	1658	10467			763	7251					2452	11634
Credit and Insurance	593	16403	1090	6085			21	26490					1704	9927
Textile	519	15423	4667	9061	1369	9551	562	11129	97	1964			7214	9677
Graphic	968	13096	2063	7533			481	21902					3512	11255
Health	19417	12925	2000	10099			88	12923					21585	12653
Services	72931	17133	7351	13050	81	12403	4680	17315	129	32248	2215	10825	87387	16657
Fishery	628	30489	10592	9091	205	13384	1946	6813	257	9097			13628	9816
Electricity	306	20586	2170	16479	115	22570	331	8895	4	6904			2926	16277
Extractive	637	13634	2022	12542	233	435965	1034	11072					3926	37461
Manufacturing	6	968718	2305	12034			2351	9964					4662	12617
Defense														
Chemical	17	20010	5021	12870	46	10150	642	10220	2	5320	4	11130	5732	12569
Others	13736	7062	5673	12018	18	14986	3030	12791	180	4468	792	26673	23629	9630
Total	159661	15935	184086	9075	2936	45271	59328	9088	1143	8770	3017	14991	410171	12049
Corrected Total (a)	159624	13863	184086	9075	2703	10673	59328	9088	1143	8770	3017	14991	409901	11774

(a) Excludes wood and manufacturing in the Government Sector and extractive industry in the Mixed Enterprise Sector.

Source : Banco Nacional de Angola - BNA
Mission estimates

APPENDIX
Table B.7

ANGOLA

MONTHLY FAMILY BUDGET FOR 1980, 1985 and 1989

Product Items	Unit	Quantity (*)	Prices (Parallel Market) Luanda, 1989 (Kz)	Expenditures (Kz)	Prices (Official) 1980 (Kz)	Expenditures (Kz)	Prices (Official) 1985 (Kz)	Expenditures (Kz)
Rice	kg	15.0	1000.0	15000.0	21.0	315.0	35.0	525.0
Beans	kg	10.0	2000.0	20000.0	40.0	400.0	45.0	450.0
Pasta	kg	5.0	2000.0	10000.0	29.0	145.0	31.0	155.0
Cornmeal	kg	15.0	1200.0	18000.0	8.5	127.5	17.5	262.5
Fresh Fish	kg	20.0	1000.0	20000.0	28.0	560.0	30.0	600.0
Beef	kg	15.0	2000.0	30000.0	90.0	1350.0	90.0	1350.0
Chicken	kg	15.0	2500.0	37500.0	85.0	1275.0	110.0	1650.0
Sardines	kg	5.0	2400.0	12000.0	107.0	535.0	148.5	742.5
Soft Drink	l	20.0	4000.0	80000.0	27.0	540.0	40.0	800.0
Cigarettes	un	30.0	400.0	12000.0	20.0	600.0	40.0	1200.0
Soap	kg	5.0	2000.0	10000.0	28.0	140.0	37.0	185.0
Toilet Soap	kg	5.0	2000.0	10000.0	88.0	440.0	164.0	820.0
Beer	l	24.0	3030.0	72720.0	40.0	960.0	50.0	1200.0
Banana	kg	10.0	700.0	7000.0	7.0	70.0	13.5	135.0
Onion	kg	10.0	9000.0	90000.0	18.8	188.0	13.0	130.0
Edible Oil	l	20.0	1110.0	22200.0	42.0	840.0	65.0	1300.0
Margarine	kg	5.0	1000.0	5000.0	100.0	500.0	116.0	580.0
Instant Milk	kg	10.0	800.0	8000.0	90.0	900.0	90.0	900.0
Salt	kg	3.0	300.0	900.0	3.0	9.0	3.0	9.0
Garlic	kg	5.0	4000.0	20000.0	47.0	235.0	40.5	202.5
Wine	l	10.0	3500.0	35000.0	223.0	2230.0	355.5	3555.0
Coffee	kg	10.0	4000.0	40000.0	115.0	1150.0	295.0	2950.0
Bread	kg	30.0	2000.0	60000.0	17.0	510.0	17.0	510.0
Total Expenditures................................				635320.0	....	14625.5	....	20211.5

Memorandum Items:

Annual Average Official Price Increase in the Period 1980-85 (%)	7.6
Monthly Family Expenditures Ratio Between the Parallel and Official Markets in the Beginning of 1989..................................	23.5

Source: Planning Ministry and Mission Estimates
(*) For a typical family size of six persons

APPENDIX
Table C.1

ANGOLA

GDP BY SECTOR (SOURCES), 1985-86

(Kz millions at current offical prices)

	(%)	1985	(%)	1986	(%)	Average 1983-86
PRIMARY SECTOR	12.4	14310.6	10.4	16408.8	13.7	12.7
Agriculture and Livestock	10.4	11526.9	8.4	12679.6	10.6	10.5
Fisheries	2.0	2783.7	2.0	3729.2	3.1	2.3
SECUNDARY SECTOR (*)	44.2	64378.9	46.9	42597.9	35.5	41.5
Manufacturing and Mining	9.0	12616.4	9.2	13041.0	10.9	9.3
Petroleum	32.1	44601.1	32.5	23892.7	19.9	28.1
Construction	2.6	6131.4	4.5	4979.1	4.2	3.5
Electricity	0.6	1030.0	0.8	685.1	0.6	0.6
TERTIARY SECTOR	43.4	58519.8	42.7	60911.2	50.8	45.8
Commerce	10.8	14656.0	10.7	15022.4	12.5	11.8
Services	26.7	35949.4	26.2	37292.0	31.1	28.2
Transport and Communications	5.8	7914.4	5.8	8596.8	7.2	5.7
GDP at Factor Cost (*)	100.0	137209.3	100.0	119917.9	100.0	100.0
GDP at Market Price (*)		142993.3		130091.9		

Sources : Planning Ministry and Mission Estimates
(*) Mission Estimates : GDP at market price for the period 1983-86
GDP at factor cost for 1982
Value added by the secundary sector for 1982

Note : The estimates using the factor income approach are incomplete and therefore not comparable with the new estimates using the product approach. See Annex IV.

APPENDIX
Table C.2

ANGOLA

GDP BY SECTOR (PRODUCT APPROACH), 1982-87

	(%)	1985	(%)	1986	(%)	1987	(%)	Average 1982-87
PRIMARY SECTOR	21.3	32876.0	20.3	33112.0	19.5	28105.0	15.2	20.4
Agriculture and Forestry	20.4	31237.0	19.3	31392.0	18.4	26630.0	14.4	19.5
Fishing	0.8	1639.0	1.0	1720.0	1.0	1475.0	0.8	1.0
SECUNDARY SECTOR	43.8	76170.0	47.1	87877.0	51.6	105407.0	57.0	46.3
Oil	30.9	54300.0	33.6	66064.0	38.8	84179.0	45.5	33.2
Other Industry	9.6	13780.0	8.5	11467.0	6.7	14742.0	8.0	9.0
Oil Construction	0.2	600.0	0.4	4628.0	2.7	637.0	0.3	0.7
Other Construction	3.2	7490.0	4.6	5718.0	3.4	5849.0	3.2	3.4
TERTIARY SECTOR	34.9	52527.0	32.5	49227.0	28.9	51523.0	27.8	33.3
Commerce	8.9	11873.0	7.3	10542.0	6.2	11069.0	6.0	8.1
Services	22.3	33990.0	21.0	32479.0	19.1	34103.0	18.4	21.3
Transport and Communications	3.7	6664.0	4.1	6206.0	3.6	6351.0	3.4	3.9
GDP at Factor Cost	100.0	161573.0	100.0	170216.0	100.0	185035.0	100.0	100.0
GDP at Market Price	105.6	165583.2	102.5	176771.7	103.9	192085.2	103.8	104.1

Sources : Planning Ministry and Mission Estimates

APPENDIX
Table C.3

ANGOLA

PRODUCT ESTIMATES IN CURRENT AND REAL KWANZAS AND IN CURRENT DOLLARS, 1982-87

	1982	1983	1984	1985	1986	1987
			Millions of Kwanzas at 1980 Official Prices			
Industry	48122	56937	62859	68080	77531	98921
Oil	31745	41948	47937	54300	66064	84179
Other	16377	14989	14922	13780	11467	14742
Construction	4725	5158	5161	8090	10346	6486
Oil	606	353	270	600	4628	637
Self Construction	2806	2242	2443	1957	2843	3192
Other	1313	2563	2448	5533	2875	2657
Agriculture, Forestry and Fishing	34935	33206	32972	32876	33112	28105
Fishing	1760	1375	1316	1639	1720	1475
Forestry	341	399	576	570	412	59
State Agriculture	6980	5834	5595	4743	4921	3896
Peasant Agriculture Commercialized	1816	1209	991	1336	1226	974
Subsistence Agriculture	24038	24389	24494	24588	24833	21701
Transport and Communications	6620	6043	5811	6664	6206	6351
Commerce	15387	13882	13775	11873	10542	11069
Services	34572	34007	34554	33990	32479	34103
GDP at Factor Cost	144361	149233	155132	161573	170216	185035
Indirect Taxes	13779	13065	15765	13808	10439	10422
Subsidies	-7484	-6769	-7080	-9797	-3884	-3371
GDP at Market Prices	150656	155529	163817	165584	176771	192086
			US Dollars at Current Prices			
GDP at Market Prices	4508.5	4650.1	4986.1	5048.4	4555.4	5197.0
Net Income From Abroad	-151.2	-168.3	-147.3	-174.0	-84.5	-244.1
GNP	4357.2	4481.8	4838.8	4874.4	4470.9	4953.0
Population (millions)	8.119	8.326	8.537	8.754	8.990	9.215
GDP per capita (US$)	555	559	584	577	507	564
GNP per capita (US$)	537	538	567	557	497	537
Growth per capita GNP	-1.8	0.3	5.3	-1.8	-10.7	8.1
			Millions of Kwanzas at Current Official Prices			
GDP at factor cost	159592	167790	181578	190019	185734	210483
GDP at market price	166880	175634	193219	201803	195908	222256
GNP	161282	169276	187511	194847	192274	211818

Source : Planning Ministry and Mission Estimates
Note : GDP at factor cost estimated by Government using the product approach. See Annex IV.

APPENDIX
Table C.4

ANGOLA

GDP STRUCTURE AND GROWTH AT 1980 OFFICIAL PRICES, 1982-87

	1982	1983	1984	1985	1986	1987	Average 1980-87	Average 1982-87
	Percentage of GDP at 1980 Official Prices							
Industry	33.3	38.2	40.5	42.1	45.5	53.5	40.4	42.2
Oil	22.0	28.1	30.9	33.6	38.8	45.5	30.5	33.2
Other	11.3	10.0	9.6	8.5	6.7	8.0	9.9	9.0
Construction	3.3	3.5	3.3	5.0	6.1	3.5	4.3	4.1
Oil	0.4	0.2	0.2	0.4	2.7	0.3	0.6	0.7
Self Construction	1.9	1.5	1.6	1.2	1.7	1.7	1.5	1.6
Other	0.9	1.7	1.6	3.4	1.7	1.4	2.1	1.8
Agriculture, Forestry and Fishing	24.2	22.3	21.3	20.3	19.5	15.2	21.0	20.4
Fishing	1.2	0.9	0.8	1.0	1.0	0.8	1.0	1.0
Forestry	0.2	0.3	0.4	0.4	0.2	0.0	0.2	0.3
State Agriculture	4.8	3.9	3.6	2.9	2.9	2.1	3.7	3.4
Peasant Agriculture Commercialized	1.3	0.8	0.6	0.8	0.7	0.5	0.9	0.8
Subsistence Agriculture	16.7	16.3	15.8	15.2	14.6	11.7	15.2	15.1
Transport and Communications	4.6	4.0	3.7	4.1	3.6	3.4	3.9	3.9
Commerce	10.7	9.3	8.9	7.3	6.2	6.0	8.7	8.1
Services	23.9	22.8	22.3	21.0	19.1	18.4	21.7	21.3
GDP at Factor Cost	100.0	100.0	100.0	100.0	100.0	100.0	100.0	100.0
Indirect Taxes	9.5	8.8	10.2	8.5	6.1	5.6	8.5	8.1
Subsidies	-5.2	-4.5	-4.6	-6.1	-2.3	-1.8	-4.4	-4.1
GDP at Market Prices	104.4	104.2	105.6	102.5	103.9	103.8	104.0	104.1
	GDP Growth at 1980 Official Prices (%)						Average 1981-87	Average 1982-87
Growth Real GDP at Factor Cost (%)	-1.0	3.4	4.0	4.2	5.3	8.7	2.1	4.1
Growth Real GDP at Market Prices (%)	-1.0	3.2	5.3	1.1	6.8	8.7	2.1	4.0

Source: Planning Ministry and Mission Estimates

APPENDIX
Table C.5

ANGOLA

GDP BY TYPE OF EXPENDITURE, 1982-87

	Kz million at current official prices		Percentage of GDP					
	1986	1987	1982	1983	1984	1985	1986	1987
Consumption	163878.4	157457.0	91.4	83.1	84.4	75.1	83.7	70.8
Private	97893.4	90288.0	65.0	56.0	54.5	43.7	50.0	40.6
Government	65985.0	67169.0	26.4	27.1	29.9	31.4	33.7	30.2
Gross Domestic Investment	44213.7	38641.2	17.1	16.1	17.0	19.3	22.6	17.4
Private	39530.7	35050.2	15.7	15.2	15.3	18.2	20.2	15.8
Government	4683.0	3591.0	1.5	0.9	1.7	1.1	2.4	1.6
Total Domestic Expenditures	208092.1	196098.2	108.6	99.2	101.4	94.4	106.2	88.2
GDP	195908.3	222255.5	100.0	100.0	100.0	100.0	100.0	100.0
Resource Gap	12183.8	-26157.3	8.6	-0.8	1.4	-5.6	6.2	-11.8
Exports of Goods and NFS	60467.6	100696.8	40.2	40.7	42.7	46.4	30.9	45.3
Imports of Goods and NFS	72651.4	74539.5	48.7	39.9	44.1	40.9	37.1	33.5
Net Income From Abroad	-3633.9	-10437.8	-3.4	-3.6	-3.0	-3.4	-1.9	-4.7
Net Factor Services Payments	-9629.5	-12639.1	-3.9	-4.1	-3.5	-3.9	-4.9	-5.7
Net Current Transfers	5995.6	2201.3	0.6	0.5	0.5	0.4	3.1	1.0
GNP	192274.4	211817.8	96.6	96.4	97.0	96.6	98.1	95.3

Source : Mission Estimates

APPENDIX
TABLE D.1

ANGOLA

GOVERNMENT REVENUE, 1980 - 89

(Kz. billion)

	1980	1981	1982	1983	1984	1985	1986	1987	1988 (budget	1989 (budget)
TOTAL REVENUE	59 758	73 707	50 655	55 467	74 556	78 518	71 202	64 399	89 500	78 000
TAX REVENUE	51 580	2 704	41 583	47 148	62 930	66 143	51 750	54 658	63 100	64 686
Taxes on petroleum	33 917	45 185	21 046	26 672	42 267	41 667	30 070	35 803		41 500
Royalty	6 367	9 123	6 757	6 991	11 184	10 223	6 432	8 720		11 000
Tax on income			14 289	19 681	31 082	31 444	23 638			
- income tax	17 606	26 610	10 703	14 639	14 035	11 766	7 945	11 679		14 000
- transfers from Sonangol	1 630	1 052	101				9 010	2 869		3 500
- transaction tax	8 314	8 400	3 485	5 042	17 047	19 684	6 683	12 535		13 000
Non-Petroleum taxes	17 663	17 519	20 537	20 476	20 663	24 476	21 680	12 855		23 187
Taxes on income and property	10 090	10 672	11 440	11 188	10 768	14 897	11 969	10 314		9 020
- transfers from public enterprises (1)	7 864	8 331	9 199	8 481	8 032	9 750	7 247	4 916		
- corporate income tax (2)	1 406	1 949	2 028	2 283	2 023	4 076	3 331	3 681		6 957
- personal income tax	714	243	63	311	561	909	1 235	1 540		1 839
- other	106	149	150	113	152	162	156	176		224
Taxes on international trade	4 193	3 300	5 265	3 878	4 189	3 966	4 730	3 415		6 756
- import duties	2 337	1 915	3 210	2 528	2 700	2 533	3 150	2 225		4 961
- export duties	54	43	29	43	52	51	35	51		180
- other levies on imports	1 802	1 342	2 026	1 308	1 437	1 382	1 545	1 139		1 625
Taxes on domestic production and consumption	3 380	3 547	3 833	5 410	5 706	5 612	4 983	5 126		7 412
- beer	952	777	625	1 252	1 401	1 360	1 179	1 117		1 552
- petroleum products	473	264	214	1 216	559	871	1 021	808		1 000
- diamonds (royalty)			64	187	213	48	134	316		350
- other products	903	1 086	1 554	989	1 012	1 742	972	865		892
- stamp duty	964	1 353	1 316	1 696	2 439	1 503	1 528	1 924		3 500
- other taxes	88	67	60	70	82	88	149	96		118
NON-TAX REVENUE	8 178	11 003	9 072	8 318	11 626	12 375	19 452	9 741	26 400	13 393
of which : Rent from property	903	1 619	1 857	2 029	2 169	1 046	3 887	2 015		2 497
: Amortization of public enterprises	1 715	1 730	1 828	1 645	1 864	1 883	1 875	177	-	
: Dividends (3)	-	-	-	-	-	520	238	22	7 700	1 779

(1) Excluding Sonangol.
(2) Until 1989 not levied on profits of public enterprises.
(3) Includes transfers from public enterprises in 1989.

Source : Ministry of Finance.

APPENDIX

TABLE D. 2

ANGOLA

TRANSFER FROM PUBLIC ENTERPRISES, BY SECTOR, 1984 - 1986

(Kz million)

	1984	1985	1986
Industry (48) 1)	795	670	862
of which: Africa Textil	-	230	-
Vininorte	136	-	267
Agriculture (5)	145	1 319	980
of which: Frescangol	-	-	256
Cafangol	138	1 298	702
Fisheries (18)	837	1 501	1 227
of which: Edipesca (Luanda)	348	485	98
Edipesca (Namibe)	351	467	504
Expedicao Conjunta	-	229	349
Transport (46)	513	1 153	779
of which: EPTEL	61	161	213
Porto de Luanda	-	49	213
Construction (23)	101	250	49
Finance (4)	3 202	1 832	1 604
of which: BNA	2 098	955	850
National Lotteries	791	739	686
External Trade (7)	400	71	192
of which: Importang	327	-	-
Internal Trade (54)	1 073	2 105	1 347
of which: Egrosbal (Huambo)	-	28	214
Emprotel (Luanda)	-	546	-
TOTAL	7 067	8 902	7 042

1) The Figure in brackets indicates the number of enterprises that made transfers in 1986.

Source : Ministry of Finance.

APPENDIX
TABLE D.3

ANGOLA

SUBSIDIES TO PUBLIC ENTERPRISES, BY MINISTRY, 1980 - 89

(Kz million)

	1980	1981	1982	1983	1984	1985	1986	1987	1988 (budget)	1989 (budget)
Agriculture	3 922	4 379	3 366	3 430			1 816	1 961	1 250	1 280
Fisheries	309	433	326	168			196	76	-	-
Industry	1 122	907	1 185	1 638			1 429	1 374	1 450	1 500
Construction	-	2 052	2 052	1 848			905	685	400	1 000
Transport	718	565	640	310			232	263	-	250
Trade	390	236	166	84			143	-	-	-
Energy and Petroleum							262	208	300	400
Other	1 788	610	994	954			1 044	1 072	-	200
TOTAL	8 249	9 182	8 666	8 432	9 491	14 131	6 028	5 629	4 000	4 630

Source : Data provided by the Ministry of Finance.

APPENDIX

TABLE D.4

ANGOLA

ECONOMIC CLASSIFICATION OF GOVERNMENT EXPENDITURE, 1980 - 84

(Kz million)

	19d0	1981	1982	1983	1984
Recurrent Expenditure	58 769	57 472	54 386	58 056	69 735
Defence	16 821	18 505	18 257	23 295	31 943
Non-defence	41 948	38 967	36 129	34 761	37 792
of which :					
personnel	16 037	16 634	18 282	18 352	17 487
goods and services	2 606	2 457	2 069	1 694	2 800
subsidies	8 246	9 182	8 665	8 432	9 491
transfers	2 959	3 209	1 590	2 192	2 379
other expenditure	12 200	7 485	5 523	4 091	5 635
Capital Expenditure	18 151		17 752	9 522	12 567
	76 920	91 640	72 138	67 578	82 302

Source : Data provided by the Ministry of Finance.

ANGOLA

FUNCTIONAL CLASSIFICATION OF GOVERNMENT EXPENDITURE, 1980 - 87

	1980	1981	1982	1983	1984	1985	1986	1987 (budget)
Economic Services	28 486	45 719	28 697	20 077	24 449			21 114
Agriculture	7 350	7 838	5 337	4 875				3 388
Fisheries	1 030	1 046	1 195	476				568
Industry	4 752	3 345	2 599	2 672				1 980
Construction	6 055	9 760	7 198	4 898				4 242
Energy and Petroleum	964	2 493	232	206				4 146
Transport & Communication	2 082	8 138	4 684	2 120				1 239
Trade	2 614	1 294	789	1 089				451
Other services (1)	3 650	11 805	6 663	4 015				5 100
Social Services	13 738	13 886	15 073	14 838	16 754	18 780	21 475	21 964
Education	9 142	9 279	9 849	9 822	9 996			13 734
Health	3 377	3 327	3 848	3 618	4 637	5 286		6 000
Social Security and Welfare	1 219	1 280	1 376	1 399	2 121(2)			2 229
General Government Services	21 632	24 108	26 326	30 284	38 243			41 122
Administration	4 811	5 603	8 069	6 989	6 300(3)			9 022
Defence and Internal Security	16 821	18 505	18 257	23 295	31 943	34 306	32 629	32 000
Other Expenditure	13 066	7 927	2 040	2 379	2 857	4 063	7 619	9 200
TOTAL	76 922	91 640	72 136	65 578	82 302	90 488	86 205	93 400

1) includes some expenditure on administration
2) includes KW455 m. of unclassified expenditure
3) includes KW244 m. part of which is on economic services.

Source : Data provided by the Ministry of Finance.

APPENDIX
TABLE D.6

ANGOLA

GOVERNMENT-FINANCED INVESTMENT BY PUBLIC ENTERPRISES

(Kz million)

	1980	1981	1982	1983	1984	1985	1986	1987	1988 (budget)	1989 (budget)
Agriculture	2 790	2 760	1 164	714			877	501	1 000	1 000
Fisheries	615	510	718	174			245	100	300	500
Industry	3 521	2 337	1 283	918			519	365	300	-
Construction	5 270	6 736	4 581	2 557	N.A.	N.A.	1 947	1 950	2 500	2 700
Energy and Petroleum	902	2 401	62	8			619	1 228	3 300	3 300
Transport and Communication	1 130	7 382	3 789	1 573			264	206		
Trade	2 027	847	397	744			153	-	-	-
Other	1 862	11 195	5 669	2 787			3 061	3 057	5 100	5620
TOTAL	18 116	34 168	17 663	9 475			7 685	7 107	13 000	13 670

Source : Data provided by the Ministry of Fianance.

APPENDIX TABLE D.7

ANGOLA

SUMMARY OF GOVERNMENT FINANCE 1980-89

(Kz billion)

	1980	1981	1982	1983	1984	1985	1986	1987	1988 (budget)	1989 (budget)
Revenue	59.8	73.7	50.7	55.5	74.6	78.5	71.2	64.4	89.5	78.1
Taxes on petroleum	33.9	45.2	21.0	26.7	42.3	41.7	30.1	35.8		41.5
Other taxes	17.7	17.5	20.5	20.5	20.7	24.5	21.7	18.9		23.2
- on income & property	(10.1)	(10.7)	(11.4)	(11.2)	(10.8)	(14.9)	(12.0)	(10.3)		(9.0)
- on domestic goods and services	(3.4)	(3.5)	(3.8)	(5.4)	(5.7)	(5.6)	(5.0)	(5.1)		(7.4)
- on international trade	(4.2)	(3.3)	(5.3)	(3.9)	(4.2)	(4.0)	(4.7)	(3.4)		(6.8)
Non Tax Revenue	8.2	11.0	9.1	8.3	11.6	12.4	19.5	9.7	26.4	13.4
Total Expenditure	76.9	91.7	72.2	67.6	82.3	90.5	86.2	87.4	106.0	112.7
Recurrent expenditure	58.8	57.5	54.4	58.1	69.7	81.2	75.7	76.4	87.8	92.6
Capital expenditure	18.2	34.2	17.8	9.5	12.6	9.3	10.5	11.0	18.2	20.1
Overall budget deficit	17.2	17.9	21.5	12.1	7.7	12.0	15.0	23.0	16.5	34.6
Statistical discrepancy	-	-	-	-27.9	31.9	-9.2	7.3	-4.0	-	-
Financing	17.2	17.9	21.5	-15.6	39.7	2.8	22.3	19.0	16.5	34.6
Domestic : BNA (net)	16.8	17.9	21.5	-15.7	39.7	2.8	22.3	19.0	14.0	24.1
non-bank	-	-	-	-	-	-	-	-	-	5.0
External : loans	n/a	n/a	n/a	n/a	n/a	n/a	n/a	n/a	n/a	3.0
grants	0.4	-	-	0.1	-	-	-	-	-	2.5

Source : Ministry of Finance : Report on the Execution of the Budget.

APPENDIX
TABLE E.1

ANGOLA

BALANCE SHEET OF BANCO NACIONAL DE ANGOLA

(millions kwanzas)

	1983	1984	1985	1986	1987	1988
Assets:						
Foreign assets	8,317	9,539	16,174	8,322	11,473	11,259
Total domestic credit	188,624	215,444	242,973	265,179	301,584	349,363
Public sector credit	79,531	118,251	130,211	187,008	247,274	296,845
Other credits	109,093	97,193	112,762	78,171	54,310	52,518
Other assets (Net)	(15,501)	(14,333)	(2,929)	3,024	9,219	33,556
Total Assets	181,441	210,649	256,219	276,525	322,276	394,178
Liabilities:						
Notes in circulation	60,478	72,809	80,848	92,959	120,838	144,561
Total deposits	111,975	125,759	159,209	156,713	165,905	198,002
Government deposits	27,710	26,752	35,947	28,662	27,843	30,693
BPA deposits	15,305	22,570	30,021	38,291	45,907	55,026
Other deposits	68,952	76,423	93,234	89,752	92,144	112,279
Foreign currency liabilities	8,988	12,082	16,162	26,853	35,533	51,615
Total Liabilities	181,441	210,649	256,219	276,525	322,276	394,178

Source: BNA

ANGOLA

BALANCE SHEET OF THE BANCO POPULAR DE ANGOLA

(millions kwanzas)
(.. = not available)

	1982	1983	1984	1985	1986	1987	1988
Assets:							
Currency on hand	406	567	955	823	657	3,873	4,301
Deposits in BNA	10,040	15,305	22,571	30,021	38,291	45,907	57,707
Private Sector Credit	..	33	28	20	12	134	255
Net Other Assets	1,076	1,021	158	(209)	(762)	(1,043)	(1,681)
Total Assets	11,522	16,926	23,712	30,655	38,199	48,871	60,582
Liabilities:							
Demand Deposits	9,768	14,246	20,196	26,453	33,006	40,584	50,323
- Individual	9,560	13,561	18,762	24,691	29,927	35,934	NA
- Business	..	385	852	1,002	1,998	2,992	NA
- Organizations	208	301	582	760	1,081	1,659	NA
Time Deposits	1,754	2,680	3,516	4,203	5,193	8,287	10,259
- more than 180 days	612	841	780	813	806	667	NA
- more than 1 year	1,142	1,839	2,736	3,390	4,387	7,619	NA
Total Liabilities	11,522	16,926	23,712	30,655	38,199	48,871	60,582

Source: Banco Nacional de Angola

ANGOLA

APPENDIX
TABLE E. 3

MONEY SUPPLY DATA

(millions of kwanzas, end of period)

	1977	1983	1984	1985	1986	1987	1988
Currency outside banks	14,265	59,911	71,854	80,025	92,302	116,966	140,260
Demand deposits							
B.P.A.	NA	14,246	20,196	26,453	33,006	40,584	50,323
BNA less BPA and government deposits	NA	68,952	76,423	93,234	89,752	92,144	112,279
Time deposits							
BPA	NA	2,680	3,516	4,203	5,193	8,287	10,259
BNA	NA	8	14	8	8	11	4
Annual currency growth rate	NA	23.6%	19.9%	11.4%	15.3%	26.7%	19.9%
Money Stock (M1)	NA	143,109	168,473	199,711	215,060	249,693	302,862
Annual growth rate M1	NA	NA	17.7%	18.5%	7.7%	16.1%	21.3%
Quasi-Money (M2)	NA	145,796	172,003	203,922	220,261	257,991	313,125
Annual growth rate M2	NA	NA	18.0%	18.6%	8.0%	17.1%	21.4%

Source: BNA and mission estimates

APPENDIX
TABLE E. 4

ANGOLA

BALANCE OF PAYMENTS, 1980 - 1988

(millions US $)

	1980	1983	1984	1985	1986	1987	1988
Merchandise exports	1,883	1,822	2,033	2,238	1,303	2,269	2,466
Merchandise imports	1,368	1,147	1,575	1,415	1,097	1,316	1,385
Trade balance	514	675	458	823	206	953	1,081
Service & income exports	179	89	111	128	115	92	127
Interest & dividends	47	19	15	22	12	7	14
Transport	66	42	38	35	32	32	93
Insurance	43	18	18	67	41	33	18
Other	23	10	40	4	30	21	2
Service & income imports	604	920	811	864	828	729	1,767
Interest	23	41	23	44	81	91	371
Dividends	44	94	114	109	83	136	187
Transport	157	240	204	215	232	158	295
Insurance	39	49	64	62	33	20	70
Technical assistance	161	217	141	135	146	86	237
Foreign workers' salaries	26	75	50	63	72	75	64
Adminstr & exploration charges	45	126	108	144	133	107	489
Travel	11	21	33	34	13	15	15
Other	99	58	73	58	35	41	39
Balance on invisibles	(425)	(830)	(701)	(736)	(713)	(637)	(1,640)
Net unrequited transfers	21	23	26	20	139	51	32
Current account balance	110	(132)	(217)	107	(368)	368	(528)
Med & long-term capital balance	286	372	398	441	236	41	(221)
Inflows	475	781	765	845	785	716	948
Loans	432	349	456	431	368	354	499
Foreign investment	43	429	308	411	417	360	449
(In nonpetroleum sectors)	0	0	1	1	1	0	0
Other	0	3	7	4	0	1	0
Outflows	189	408	367	404	549	674	1,169
Principal repayments	183	293	277	260	360	427	843
Amort of petroleum investments	3	72	81	139	189	247	326
Other	3	43	9	6	0	0	0
Basic balance	396	240	181	549	(132)	409	(749)
Short-term capital flows & errors and omissions	(309)	(204)	(124)	(558)	(187)	(676)	384
Global balance	87	35	57	(10)	(319)	(267)	(365)
Financing:	(87)	(35)	(57)	10	319	267	365
Reserve variation (- increase)	(87)	(35)	(57)	(18)	78	(63)	(29)
Arrears variation (includ. resched)	0	0	0	27	218	(51)	45
Debt rescheduling	0	0	0	0	23	382	349
Memorandum:							
End Year Gross Reserves	309	182	240	257	179	242	272

Source: Angolan authorities and mission estimates

ANGOLA

MAJOR MERCHANDISE IMPORT EXPENDITURES

(millions U.S. $ and as percentage of total)

	1982	1983	1984	1985	1986
Total merchandise imports	1,286	1,147	1,575	1,415	1,097
	100.0%	100.0%	100.0%	100.0%	100.0%
Foods & beverages	306	334	460	387	246
	23.8%	29.1%	29.2%	27.3%	22.4%
Clothing & textiles	115	90	132	110	70
	8.9%	7.8%	8.4%	7.8%	6.4%
Instruments & optical goods	13	12	11	10	7
	1.0%	1.0%	0.7%	0.7%	0.6%
Paper, minerals, chemicals, & plastics	167	150	171	139	88
	13.0%	13.0%	10.8%	9.8%	8.1%
Cement, stone, & metals	151	105	253	205	131
	11.7%	9.1%	16.0%	14.5%	11.9%
Electrical & transport equipment	511	448	535	552	547
	39.7%	39.0%	33.9%	39.0%	49.9%
Other	25	9	14	11	7
	1.9%	0.8%	0.9%	0.8%	0.6%

Source: Ministry of Finance

ANGOLA

Major Export Earnings, 1980 - 1988
(.. = not available)

	1980	1981	1982	1983	1984	1985	1986	1987	1988
Crude Oil									
(Total - millions US $)	1,391	1,345	1,246	1,525	1,748	1,906	1,164	2,033	2,156
(thousand barrels)	40,705	37,792	39,265	54,852	64,165	73,419	92,151	116,356	154,000
(ave. price per bbl)	34.2	35.6	31.7	27.8	27.3	26.0	12.6	17.5	14.0
(percent of total)	73.9%	72.5%	76.5%	83.7%	86.0%	85.2%	89.4%	89.6%	87.4%
Refined Oil									
(Total - millions US$)	99	104	60	89	92	94	40	76	64
(thousand tons)	510	511	361	525	533	631	549	701	725
(ave. price per ton)	194.3	204.1	167.1	170.2	172.7	149.0	72.7	108.7	88.0
(percent of total)	5.3%	5.6%	3.7%	4.9%	4.5%	4.2%	3.1%	3.4%	2.6%
LPG									
(Total - millions US $)	..	..	..	32	32	34	22	24	23
(thousand barrels)	..	..	..	1,489	1,956	2,096	2,011	2,243	2,250
(ave. price per barrel)	..	..	..	21.5	16.3	16.4	10.7	10.6	10.0
(percent of total)	..	..	..	1.8%	1.6%	1.5%	1.7%	1.0%	0.9%
Diamonds									
(Total - millions US $)	228	181	190	101	65	74	8	101	176
(thousands carats)	1,459	1,408	1,259	1,002	953	744	175	871	1,046
(ave. price per carat)	156.6	128.3	150.6	100.5	68.1	100.0	46.7	116.2	168.0
(percent of total)	12.1%	9.7%	11.6%	5.5%	3.2%	3.3%	0.6%	4.5%	7.1%
Coffee									
(Total - millions US $)	164	97	95	71	81	55	53	35	37
(thousand tons)	47.2	44.6	41.0	26.6	22.8	18.7	18.6	16.0	16.0
(ave. price - US $ per ton)	3,468	2,183	2,309	2,667	3,572	2,936	2,851	2,151	2,300
(percent of total)	8.7%	5.3%	5.8%	3.9%	4.0%	2.4%	4.1%	1.5%	1.5%
Other	0	129	38	4	14	75	16	0	11
Total merchandise exports (millions US $)	1,883	1,856	1,629	1,822	2,033	2,238	1,303	2,269	2,466

Source: Ministry of Finance and mission estimates

APPENDIX
TABLE E. 6.1

ANGOLA

MAJOR EXPORT EARNINGS PROJECTIONS

	1988	Projections---> 1989	1990	1991	1992	1993
Crude Oil						
(Total - millions US $)	2,156	2,635	2,804	2,975	3,139	3,312
(thousand barrels)	154,000	155,000	155,775	156,554	157,337	158,123
(ave. price per bbl)	14.0	17.0	18.0	19.0	20.0	20.9
(percent of total)	87.4%	88.7%	88.1%	87.6%	87.0%	86.4%
Refined Oil						
(Total - millions US $)	64	82	83	86	92	97
(thousand tons)	725	747	720	720	727	734
(ave. price per ton)	88.0	110.0	115.0	120.0	126.0	132.3
(percent of total)	2.6%	2.8%	2.6%	2.5%	2.5%	2.5%
LPG						
(Total - millions US $)	23	24	25	27	29	31
(thousand barrels)	2,250	2,363	2,481	2,605	2,631	2,657
(ave. price per barrel)	10.0	10.0	10.0	10.5	11.0	11.6
(percent of total)	0.9%	0.8%	0.8%	0.8%	0.8%	0.8%
Diamonds						
(Total - millions US $)	176	200	240	275	314	359
(thousands carats)	1,046	1,000	1,200	1,320	1,452	1,597
(ave. price per carat)	168.0	200.0	200.0	208.0	216.3	225.0
(percent of total)	7.1%	6.7%	7.5%	8.1%	8.7%	9.4%
Coffee						
(Total - millions US $)	37	29	30	31	32	34
(thousand tons)	16	16	16	16	16	16
(ave. price - US $ per ton)	2,300	1,800	1,872	1,947	2,025	2,106
(percent of total)	1.5%	1.0%	0.9%	0.9%	0.9%	0.9%
Other	11	0	0	0	0	0
Total - millions US $	2,466	2,970	3,182	3,394	3,606	3,833

Source: Mission estimates

TABLE E. 7.1

ANGOLA

BALANCE OF PAYMENTS PROJECTIONS, 1989 - 93 (BASELINE CASE)

(millions of US $)

	1988	1989	1990	1991	1992	1993
Trade balance	1,081	1,191	1,276	1,361	1,446	1,537
Exports of goods	2,466	2,970	3,182	3,394	3,606	3,833
Imports of goods	1,385	1,779	1,906	2,033	2,160	2,296
Non-factor services (net)	(1,033)	(866)	(928)	(990)	(1,051)	(1,118)
Resource balance	48	325	348	371	395	419
Net factor income	(607)	(659)	(687)	(715)	(742)	(772)
Receipts	14	16	17	18	20	21
Payments	622	676	704	733	762	792
Balance on invisibles	(1,640)	(1,525)	(1,614)	(1,704)	(1,794)	(1,889)
Net unrequited transfers	32	33	35	36	38	40
Current account balance	(528)	(301)	(304)	(307)	(309)	(312)
Capital Account Balance	163	(46)	36	(158)	(73)	21
Med & L-t Loans (net)	(344)	(229)	(141)	(340)	(253)	(169)
Other	507	183	178	183	180	190
Overall Balance	(365)	(347)	(268)	(464)	(383)	(291)
Financing:	365	347	268	464	383	291
Reserve variation (- increase)	(29)	0	0	0	0	0
Arrears variation (includ. resched)	45	NA	NA	464	383	291
Debt rescheduling	349	NA	NA	0	0	0
Memorandum:						
End Year Gross Reserves	272	272	272	272	272	272

Source: Angolan authorities and mission estimates.

ANGOLA

BALANCE OF PAYMENTS PROJECTIONS, 1989 - 93 (Optimistic Case)

(millions US $)

		Projections--->				
	1988	1989	1990	1991	1992	1993
Trade balance	1,081	1,191	1,607	1,715	1,822	1,937
Exports of goods	2,466	2,970	3,818	4,073	4,327	4,600
Imports of goods	1,385	1,779	2,211	2,358	2,505	2,663
Non-factor services (net)	(1,033)	(866)	(1,070)	(1,141)	(1,212)	(1,289)
Resource balance	48	325	538	573	609	648
Net factor income	(607)	(659)	(743)	(761)	(778)	(798)
Receipts	14	16	21	22	23	25
Payments	622	676	764	783	802	823
Balance on invisibles	(1,640)	(1,525)	(1,813)	(1,902)	(1,991)	(2,087)
Net unrequited transfers	32	33	35	36	38	40
Current account balance	(528)	(301)	(171)	(151)	(131)	(110)
Capital Account Balance	163	(46)	258	36	90	153
Med & L-t Loans (net)	(344)	(229)	(13)	(222)	(147)	(75)
Other	507	183	270	259	237	228
Overall Balance	(365)	(347)	87	(115)	(41)	43
Financing:	365	347	(87)	115	41	(43)
Reserve variation (- increase)	(29)	0	0	0	0	0
Arrears variation (includ. resched)	45	NA	NA	115	41	(43)
Debt rescheduling	349	NA	NA	0	0	0
Memorandum:						
End Year Gross Reserves	272	272	272	272	272	272

Source: Angolan authorities and mission estimates.

APPENDIX
TABLE E. 7.3

ANGOLA

BALANCE OF PAYMENTS PROJECTIONS, 1989 - 93 (Pessimistic Case)

(millions of US $)

	1988	1989	1990	1991	1992	1993
Trade balance	1,081	1,102	944	1,007	1,070	1,138
Exports of goods	2,466	2,970	2,545	2,715	2,885	3,067
Imports of goods	1,385	1,868	1,601	1,708	1,815	1,929
Non-factor services (net)	(1,033)	(917)	(786)	(838)	(891)	(947)
Resource balance	48	185	159	169	180	191
Net factor income	(607)	(664)	(639)	(677)	(716)	(756)
Receipts	14	16	14	15	16	17
Payments	622	680	653	692	731	772
Balance on invisibles	(1,640)	(1,581)	(1,425)	(1,515)	(1,606)	(1,702)
Net unrequited transfers	32	33	35	36	38	40
Current account balance	(528)	(446)	(446)	(472)	(498)	(524)
Capital Account Balance	163	(46)	(185)	(351)	(237)	(110)
Med & L-t Loans (net)	(344)	(229)	(270)	(458)	(359)	(262)
Other	507	183	85	107	122	152
Overall Balance	(365)	(492)	(631)	(823)	(735)	(634)
Financing:	365	492	631	823	735	634
Reserve variation (- increase)	(29)	0	0	0	0	0
Arrears variation (includ. resched)	45	NA	NA	823	735	634
Debt rescheduling	349	NA	NA	0	0	0
Memorandum:						
End Year Gross Reserves	272	272	272	272	272	272

Source: Angolan authorities and mission estimates.

ANGOLA

STOCK OF EXTERNAL NON-MILITARY DEBT, 1982 - 88

(millions of US $)

(Source: BNA)	1982	1983	1984	1985	1986	1987	June 1988
Medium & L-T debt	2,075.3	2,106.4	2,282.7	2,449.4	2,456.5	2,956.[illegible]	3,210.2
Short-term debt	271.3	251.7	162.9	250.8	614.5	625.6	691.2
Total external debt	2,346.6	2,358.1	2,445.7	2,700.2	3,071.0	3,581.7	3,901.4
Debt/GDP	52.2%	50.9%	49.4%	53.7%	68.5%	70.1%	NA
Debt/exports of G & S	127.7%	123.4%	114.1%	114.1%	216.6%	151.7%	150.5%
Debt service/exports of G & S (1)	15.9%	17.5%	14.0%	12.8%	31.1%	21.9%	NA

Source: BNA and mission estimates

(1) Debt service includes only interest and principal payments actually made.

APPENDIX
TABLE E.9

PROJECTED DEBT SERVICE OBLIGATIONS ON MEDIUM AND LONG TERM DEBT (AS OF DEC. 1988)

(millions US $)

	1986	1987	1988	1989	1990	1991	1992	1994	1995	Other	Total
Western countries	13.2	51.2	196.1	387.9	331.8	368.5	308.1	139.6	101.9	280.5	2,433.0
Capital	9.8	39.4	152.2	264.9	228.0	285.1	249.2	115.2	85.3	251.3	1,895.4
Interest	3.3	11.8	43.9	123.0	103.8	83.5	58.9	24.4	16.6	29.2	537.6
Socialist countries	25.2	72.6	592.0	618.5	508.2	611.0	477.6	339.6	250.0	37.4	3,884.1
Capital	20.5	66.8	525.7	560.6	462.9	551.0	440.0	322.4	242.3	36.5	3,554.7
Interest	4.7	5.8	66.3	57.9	45.3	60.0	37.6	17.2	7.7	0.9	329.4
Official organizations	0.0	0.0	2.2	5.6	5.5	5.4	5.3	5.0	4.3	18.5	57.0
Capital	0.0	0.0	1.4	3.7	3.7	3.9	4.0	4.1	3.7	17.4	46.0
Interest	0.0	0.0	0.8	1.9	1.7	1.5	1.3	0.9	0.6	1.1	11.0
Combined total	38.4	123.8	790.3	1,012.0	845.5	985.0	791.0	484.2	356.2	336.5	6,374.1
Capital	30.4	106.2	679.2	829.2	694.7	840.0	693.2	441.8	331.4	305.2	5,496.1
Interest	8.0	17.6	111.1	182.8	150.8	144.9	97.9	42.5	24.9	31.2	878.0

Source: BNA

APPENDIX

Table F.1

ANGOLA

AGRICULTURAL PRODUCTION: PRESENT ESTIMATES AND EARLY 1970'S LEVELS

Products (tons, or as indicated)	71/72/73 Max. Production		86/87 Act.Production	
Cotton (Algodao)	86,015	(71)	307	(86)
Sugar Cane (Acucar)	80,000	(74)	14,000	(87)
Groundnuts (Amendoim)	26,936	(71)	1,688	(86)
Paddy Rice (Arroz)	57,604	(71)	772	(86)
Banana	75,000	(73)	24,000	(86)
Potatoes (Batata)	138,757	(71)	8,000	(87)
Sweet Potatoes (Batata-doce)	250,000	(73)	100,000	(87)
Cafe	240,000	(74)	13,500	(87)
Beans (Feijao)	65,500	(71)	2,452	(86)
Sunflower (Girassol)	21,008	(72)	120	(86)
Wood (Madeira)	553,664	(73)	64,000	(86)
Cassava (Mandioca)	1,134,262	(71)	250,000	(87)
Sorghum/Millet (Massambala/Massango)	74,000	(71)	20,000	(87)
Maize (Milho)	710,000	(71)	250,000	(87)
Palm Oil (Oleo de palma)	20,000	(73)	560	(86)
Sisal	47,920	(71)	238	(86)
Tobacco (Tabaco)	4,800	(73)	114	(86)
Wheat (Trigo)	22,500	(71)	210	(86)
Beet (Carne de bovino)	24,500	(73)	3,536	(86)
Cattle (Bois) (heads)	4,300,000	(73)	3,420,000	(87)
Goats (heads)	872,000	(71)	1,300,000	(87)
Swine (Suinos) (heads)	500,000	(73)	150,000	(87)

Source: As for Table 1. Refer to Chapters I and II and relevant Annexes

ANGOLA

APPENDIX

Table F. 2

AGRICULTURAL PRODUCTION TRENDS, 1955 - 73
(000 tons)

Product	55/59	65/68	71/73
Crops:			
Cotton (raw)	22.1	30.0	82.6
Bananas	N/A	N/A	98.7
Potatoes	N/A	N/A	100.5
Coffee	91.9	186.3	226.5
Beans	7.5	14.0	59.6
Sunflower	N/A	N/A	21.0
Groundnuts	15.0	N/A	26.0
Cassava	560.0	N/A	928.0
Corn	106.6	136.7	202.1
Sisal	47.1	59.0	53.6
Leaf Tobacco	2.9	5.0	4.0
Wheat	2.7	22.6	12.1
Rice	18.5	18.6	28.4

Source: Various Relatorios e Contas do Banco de Angola

Data is unreliable and referes mainly to marketed production.
Useful for general trends in production.

APPENDIX

Table F.3

ANGOLA

FARM LEVEL OFFICIAL PRICES
(Kwanzas per ton)

Product (tons)	1973	1980	1985
Cotton	7,901.3	40,000.0	
Groundnuts	4,674.4	27,500.0	50,000.0
Rice	2,297.4	13,500.0	
Sweet Potato	908.6	7,500.0	17,500.0
Potato	2,644.3	14,000.0	
Coffee Bean	11,741.6	67,000.0	
Onion	8,142.9	16,000.0	50,000.0
Coconut	1,710.2	17,000.0	
Cassava Flour	1,900.6	17,000.0	
Beans	3,632.1	23,500.0	35,000.0
Cassava dry	1,187.9	8,000.0	20,000.0
Sorghum and millet	1,000.0	10,000.0	
Maize	1,308.5	10,000.0	15,000.0
Palm Oil	5,563.3	38,500.0	100,000.0
Sunflower seeds	4,011.3	25,000.0	
Tobacco	6,008.6	70,000.0	
Livestock:			
Cattle	5,517.6	16,000.0	
Goats	5,897.0	15,000.0	150,000.0
Pork	8,025.4	19,000.0	150,000.0

Source: Ministry of Planning

Average prices of "campanhas de comercializacao no campo"

ANGOLA

SUPPLY OF AGRICULTURAL INPUTS

INPUT	Unit	1984 Imports	1984 Domestic	1985 Imports	1985 Domestic	1986 Imports	1986 Domestic
Tools							
Hoes	1	921,000	-	460,000	94,202	959,921	149,648
Knives	1	-	247,000	-	164,000	-	133,680
Other	1	469,004	482,000	25,616	954,239	100,000	
Fertilizers							
Simple	ton	-	-	10,800	-	10,550	-
Mixed	ton	8,250	-	12,000	-	20,000	-
Seeds							
Maize	ton	-	700	990	723	1,238	1,277
Beans	ton	-	399	965	554	203	302
Groundnuts	ton	-	33	500	55	100	17
Potato	ton	1,736	33	2,990	76	2,051	376
Vegetable	ton	42	-	2	-	59	1
Others	ton	-	503	214	300	3	253
Implements							
Plows	1	-	8200	-	-	-	3822
Sprayers	1	-	-	-	-	-	-
Motor Pumps	1	-	-	1997	-	1040	-
Grinders	1	-	-	-	-	116	-

Source: Relatorio Sobre a Actividade do Sector Agrario e 1986

APPENDIX

Table F.5

ANGOLA

AGRICULTURAL EXPORTS (IMPORTS)

('000 Tons)

Product	1962	1968	1979	1973	1980	1985	1986
Coffee	156.9	188.6	180.5	218.7	47.2	18.7	15.8 (a)
Cotton	5.7	11.0	23.6	23.3	-	-	-
Sisal	68.8	52.4	65.9	53.0	-	-	-
Bananas	2.0	14.8	36.0	77.0	-	-	-
Wood	51.2	135.7	129.4	182.0	1.2	24.9	-
Maize (b)	116.7	153.3	171.7	112.0	(142.7)	(79.6)	-
Tobacco	0.8	3.2	1.6	6.8	-	-	-
Beans	10.1	14.2	12.0	28.6	(31.6)	(59.2)	-
Sugar	36.5	13.7	11.3	9.7	(73.4)	(59.2)	-
Palm Oil	12.6	10.5	11.3	2.6	(1.2)	(0.7)	
Rice	2.5	2.0	1.2	4.5	(55.1)	(35.8)	

Source: Relatorio e Contas do Banco de Angola and Customs Data
(a) Does not include exports via VIGIMEX
(b) Total imports of cereals in 1988/87 were 152.5 thousand tons (Commercial imports plus food aid). See Table I.1

APPENDIX
Table F.6

ANGOLA

FOOD IMPORTS

(in US$ millions)

Products	1982	1983	1984	1985
Animal Products	37.2	43.8	40.9	36.1
Vegetable Products	90.9	72.0	103.3	76.1
Fats, Oils	27.6	31.5	33.5	39.9
Other (beverages)	63	80.0	65	63.1
Total	218.7	227.3	242.7	215.2

Source: Customs data - Incomplete and below actual levels

ANGOLA

APPENDIX

Table F.7

PROJECTED AGRICULTURAL PRODUCTION RESPONSE TO POLICY REFORMS (*)

Production (tons)	71/72/73	Present	Projected Output Year 01	Year 02	Year 03
Maize (**)	300,000	40,000	50,000	60,000	100,000
Cassava (**)	928,000	200,000	250,000	300,000	400,000
Beans	68,000	2,000	2,000	35,000	5,000
Sorghum/Millet (**)	N/A	2,000	5,000	10,000	10,000
Potatoes	100,500	5,000	10,000	15,000	25,000
Coffee	225,000	15,000	20,000	20,000	35,000
Cotton	80,200	2,000	4,000	6,000	8,000
Sugar	75,000	14,000	10,000	15,000	15,000
Tobacco	4,800	nil	50	400	800
Bananas (***)	10,000	25,000	25,000	30,000	35,000
Wood (***)	533,664	60,000	100,000	150,000	200,000
Cattle ('000)	5,408	3,420	3,600	3,800	4,000
Beef (tons)	24,500	3,500	3,700	4,500	6,000
Poultry ('000)	4,200	nil	4,200	4,500	5,000
Swine	361,000	540,000	570,000	600,000	630,000
Goats ('000)	872	1,300	1,400	1,500	1,600
Fisheries (****)(tons)	467,000	195,000	200,000	200,000	250,000

(*) Source: Mission Estimates; Relatorio e Contas do Banco de Angola; Relatorio Sobre Actividates do Sector Agrario em 1986

(**) Mainly for home consumption

(***) Export quantities

(****) Angolan share

APPENDIX

Table G.1

ANGOLA

OIL PRODUCTION AND RESERVES, 1986-90

(in 1,000 b/d)

Production by Area	Actual 1986	%	1987	Projected 1988	1989	1990	%
Cabinda	190	67.4	220	256	246	246	54.9
Block 3	50	17.7	85	113	128	136	30.4
Block 2	6	2.1	10	29	39	38	8.5
Onshore	36	12.8	36	36	32	28	6.3
Total	282	100	351	434	445	448	100.1
Reserves (in million bbl)	1,418	-	1,622	1,525	1,438	1,286	-
Reserves to Production Ratio (years)	13.7	-	12.6	9.6	8.8	7.8	-

Source: Sonangol, Ministry of Energy and Petroleum.

Table G.2

ANGOLA

PROJECTED CRUDE OIL EXPORTS, 1987-1991

	1987	1988	1989	1990	1991
Oil Production (million tons)	17.55	21.70	22.25	22.40	22.50
Exports (million tons)	16.05	20.02	20.75	20.90	21.00
International Price of Oil (US$/bbl)	17	18	18	19	19
Export Revenues (million US$)	1,992	2,631	2,727	2,899	2,913

Source: Sonangol and mission estimates.

ANGOLA

INVESTMENTS IN CRUDE OIL EXPLORATION AND DEVELOPMENT

(in US$ million)

	1980-1986			1987-1990 1/		
	Annual Total	Average	in %	Annual Total	Average	in %
Cabinda	816	117	30.0	815	203.7	39.7
Block 2	493	70	18.1	180	45.0	8.8
Block 3	879	126	32.2	770	192.5	37.6
Congo/Kwanza	242	34	8.9	80	20.0	3.9
Others	294	42	10.8	205	51.3	10.0
Total	2,724	389	100.0	2,050	512.5	100.0

1/ Projected
Source: Sonangol and mission estimates.

Table G.4

ANGOLA

PROJECTED PETROLEUM PRODUCTS CONSUMPTION

	1986	1987	1988	1990	1992	Average Annual Change 1/ 1980-86	1986-92
LPG	30,200	31,408	32,664	35,330	38,213	9.22%	4.01%
Gasoline	104,110	108,257	112,570	121,727	131,616	4.06%	3.99%
Kerosene	46,310	49,090	52,034	58,465	65,692	7.50%	6.03%
Jet Fuel	260,500	266,193	272,005	284,158	297,051	17.97%	2.21%
Gas Oil	344,770	357,874	371,481	400,284	431,346	4.58%	3.81%
Fuel Oil	119,200	122,984	126,896	135,120	143,912	-1.95%	3.19%
Asphalt	4,200	4,284	4,370	4,546	4,730	2.87%	2.00%
Total	909,340	940,090	972,020	1,039,630	1,112,560	6.63%	3.42%

1/ Least square estimates
Source: Sonangol

APPENDIX

Table G.5

ANGOLA

ELECTRICITY DEMAND FORECAST

	Energy GWh			Peak Demand (MW) 1/		
	Low	Medium	High	Low	Medium	High
1986	756	756	756	139	139	139
1987	771	771	771	142	142	142
1980	829	862	896	152	158	164
1995	1,140	1,351	1,602	208	247	293
2000	1,914	2,211	2,400	350	404	439

1/ Installed capacity in 1986: 431 MW; firm capacity in 1986: 324 MW
Source: Energy Sector Assessment Report

APPENDIX

Table H.1

ANGOLA

STRUCTURE OF INDUSTRY - 1984

Tutelage Ministry [or other institution]	# of Enterprises EEU	Priv	Mix	Coop	Tot	# of Likely Manufacturing Enterprises EEU	Priv	Mix	Coop	Tot	Likely Manufacturers as a % of all Enterprises
Industry	139	91	11	0	241	126	83	10	0	219	91%
Petroleum	2	10	0	0	12	0	3	0	0	3	25%
Energy	5	3	1	0	9	0	1	0	0	1	11%
Fisheries	21	15	1	0	37	9	7	1	0	17	46%
Construction	24	12	4	0	40	8	4	2	0	14	35%
Agriculture	65	14	0	0	79	15	2	0	0	17	22%
Transportation	64	21	1	0	86	0	0	0	0	0	0%
Internal Commerce	48	50	0	1	99	0	0	0	0	0	0%
External Commerce	9	18	0	0	27	0	0	0	0	0	0%
Education	3	1	0	0	4	2	1	0	0	3	75%
Culture	3	6	0	0	9	0	0	0	0	0	0%
Health	2	23	0	0	25	0	0	0	0	0	0%
Housing	1	1	0	0	2	1	0	0	0	1	50%
Coordination	1	0	0	0	1	0	0	0	0	0	0%
Finance	3	0	0	0	3	0	0	0	0	0	0%
Planning	0	1	0	0	1	0	0	0	0	0	0%
Labor	0	1	0	0	1	0	0	0	0	0	0%
Defense	1	0	0	0	1	0	0	0	0	0	0%
[Presidency]	1	0	0	0	1	1	0	0	0	1	100%
[MPLA]	9	0	0	0	9	1	1	1	1	4	44%
Totals	401	267	18	1	687	163	102	14	1	280	41%

Source: Mission Estimates based on data in:
Ministero da Industria
Registo Geral de Empresas
Luanda, Abril 1984

APPENDIX

Table H.2

ANGOLA

STRUCTURE OF EMPLOYMENT IN ENTERPRISES - 1984

Tutelage Ministry [or other institution]	Employment					Likely Manufacturing Employment					Likely Manuf. Employm. as a % of all Employment
	EEU	Private	Mixed	Coop.	Total	EEU	Private	Mixed	Coop.	Total	
Industry	52,184	9,719	23,050	0	84,953	48,911	9,470	3,496	0	61,877	73%
Petroleum	3,233	3,193	0	0	6,426	0	1,746	0	0	1,746	27%
Energy	2,473	201	602	0	3,276	0	96	0	0	96	3%
Fisheries	6,853	1,245	168	0	8,266	3,286	618	168	0	4,072	49%
Construction	12,053	2,070	2,001	0	16,094	2,999	1,449	1,666	0	6,114	38%
Agriculture	63,610	3,319	0	0	66,929	8,727	300	0	0	9,027	13%
Transportation	26,173	2,299	6,014	0	34,486	0	0	0	0	0	0%
Internal Commerce	19,990	3,827	0	350	24,167	0	0	0	0	0	0%
External Commerce	456	1,117	0	0	1,573	0	0	0	0	0	0%
Education	310	85	0	0	395	310	85	0	0	395	100%
Culture	228	259	0	0	487	0	0	0	0	0	0%
Health	157	258	0	0	415	0	0	0	0	0	0%
Housing	710	22	0	0	732	710	0	0	0	710	97%
Coordination	750	0	0	0	750	0	0	0	0	0	0%
Finance	712	0	0	0	712	0	0	0	0	0	0%
Planning	0	8	0	0	8	0	0	0	0	0	0%
Labor	0	75	0	0	75	0	0	0	0	0	0%
Defense	0	0	0	0	0	0	0	0	0	0	
[Presidency]	331	0	0	0	331	331	0	0	0	331	100%
[MPLA]	2,614	0	0	0	2,614	634	0	0	0	634	24%
Totals	192,807	27,697	31,835	350	252,689	65,908	13,764	5,330	0	85,002	34%
Max. for any one enterpr.:	9,060	1,571	19,554	350	19,554	9,060	1,571	1,025	0	9,060	
Min. for any one enterpr.:	4	1	35	350	1	14	11	60	0	11	
Standard Deviation	851	157	4,510	0	1,054	893	193	319	0	712	
Average	481	104	1,769	350	384	464	139	410	0	309	

Source: Mission estimates based on data in:
Registo Geral de Empresas; op.cit.

APPENDIX

Table H.3

ANGOLA

AVERAGE NUMBER OF EMPLOYEES IN COMPANIES W/OVER 500 EMPLOYEES DIFFERENTIATED BY PUBLIC AND PRIVATE

Ministry	UEEs	Private
Agriculture	1,537	550
Industry	1,627	659
Transportation	1,810	659
Internal Commerce	777	--
Average of all 87 1/	1,515	628

1/ There are 87 enterprises with more than 500 employees each under the combined tutelage of the Ministries of Agriculture, Industry, Transportation, and Internal Commerce.

Source: Mission estimates based on: Registo Geral, op.cit.

APPENDIX

Table H.4

ANGOLA

PRODUCTION OF THE MANUFACTURING INDUSTRY; COMPARISONS BETWEEN 1973 AND 1987 1/

Food Processing		Light Industry		Heavy Industry	
Products	87/73	Products	87/73	Products	87/73
	%		%		%
Beer	38.98	Cloth	32.93	Tires F/Vehicles	6.53
Soft Drinks	14.56	Covers	10.91	Inner Tubes F/Vehicles	0
Fermented Drinks	42.02	Cotton Threads	3.86	Buses	0
Liquors and other Spirits	18.61	Leather Shoes	43.42	Passenger Vehicles	0
Vinegar	36.01	Canvas Shoes	5.65	Bicycles	37.65
Sugar	18.96	Plastic Shoes	28.87	Motorcycles	89.75
Molasses	18.53	Processed Tobacco	57.10	Cisterns	0
Alcohol	19.67	Matches	9.52	Dry Batteries	5.78
Corn Meal	41.07	Plywood	54.55	Batteries	27.10
Wheat Flour	38.26	Vinyl	132.58	Acetilene	62.66
Fresh Yeast	0	Tarpaulins	1272.73	Oxygen	85.13
Spaghetti/Pasta	41.52	Soap	12.59	Electrodes	13.36
Biscuits and Cakes	29.37	Liquid Detergents	46.13	Steel Rods	9.41
Cooking Oil	31.04	Paints	16.45	Black Tube	0
Margarine	8.44	Glues	22.86	Zinc Sheets	0
Instant Coffee	0	Plastic Bottles	8.28	Machetes	65.65
Canned Meats	0	Sisal Bags/Burlap	41.51	Cardboard Boxes	0.45
Salt	3.87	Plastic bags	10.47	Conductor Cable Lines	11.01
Refined Salt	0	Sponge Cushions	23.06	Radio Recepters	129.62
				Paper	0
				Paper Paste	0
				Cutlery	23.91
				Metallic Capsules	0

1/ Comparison of physical output.

Note: 0% indicates that production had stopped by 1987. Products whose manufacture was started after 1973 are not included.

Source: Tables A2-1, A2-3 and A2-4 in Appendix 2.

APPENDIX

Table H.5

ANGOLA

PRODUCTION OF MANUFACTURING INDUSTRY - FOOD SECTOR; 1973 - 1987

PRODUCT	Unit	1973	--	1977	1978	1979	1980	1981	1982	1983	1984	1985	1986	1987	Average annual growthrate 77-87	87/77
Beer	hl	1,196,030		639,541	668,810	776,300	713,761	670,908	562,893	690,249	655,681	652,936	583,430	466,[illegible]70	-2.50%	73%
Soft Drinks	hl	492,520		284,720	248,550	234,220	263,125	276,491	181,816	124,383	99,382	110,200	71,310	71,720	-12.94%	35%
Juices and Concentrates 1/	tn							104	60							
Table Wine	hl							57,057	68,212	104,324	60,978	60,080	43,580	33,900		
Fermented Drinks	hl	136,200		31,770	28,638	61,163	94,533,	58,187	53,426	37,361	29,994	43,170	39,330	57,230	-0.39%	180%
Liquors and other Spirits	hl	75,220		21,050	37,687	23,465	11,202	28,838	23,787	20,825	20,763	14,444	16,440	14,000	-5.23%	67%
Whisky 2/	hl						861	1,619	1,474	73	171	410	70	30		
Vinegar	kl			224	178	26	352	134	58	350	419	483	490	350	16.03%	156%
Sugar	tn	972		38,071	36,089	31,843	25,271	19,905	27,768	22,405	20,236	17,416	20,287	15,342	-7.84%	40%
Molasses	tn	80,909		19,553	15,428	12,171	10,874	8,734	13,725	9,540	9,607	9,260	11,212	6,904	-6.56%	35%
Alcohol	kl	37,252		1,206	1,888	1,496	800	1,806	1,424	1,648	1,042	794	1,235	759	-4.86%	63%
Corn Meal	tn	3,859		24,969	32,489	60,085			33,627	35,868	29,524	49,471	42,025	24,252		97%
Wheat Flour	tn	59,050		39,107	52,607	47,581	51,212		41,502	35,919	27,628	47,167	25,085	31,730		81%
Fresh Yeast	tn	82,925		1,453	1,459	509	667	983	1,045	370	171		0	0		0%
Spaghetti/Pasta	tn	2,282		4,849	6,349	4,704	5,760	6,628	6,384	7,602	8,042	8,261	6,070	3,603	0.76%	74%
Biscuits and Cakes	tn	8,678		1,484	2,366	2,579	2,435	1,969	1,273	936	686	891	400	920	-13.54%	62%
Cooking Oil	kl	3,132		4,482	7,066	4,074	4,847	3,327	4,353	3,275	4,132	4,851	3,673	4,490	-2.18%	100%
Margarine	tn	14,464		984	2,443	2,351	1,519	898	1,122	535	563	260	245	237	-20.64%	24%
Instant Coffee	tn	2,809		0	16	6	4	15	26	12						
Canned Meats	tn	3,263		940	933	426	331	305	403							0%
Coffee	tn					1,424	1,305	1,268	1,189	976	439	386	105	170		
Canned Fruits and Vegetables	tn						2,599	1,675	1,212							
Pulps	tn						297	191								
Salt	tn	96,757				23,008	23,844	20,040	21,913			6,000	3,800	3,746		
Refined Salt	tn	8,126		3,723	4,014	4,477	3,953	3,135	2,369							0%

1/ Through 1980 included in canned fruits and vegetables; production halted since 1983.
2/ Whisky included in liquors and spirits through 1979.
Source: Ministry of Industry.

APPENDIX

Table H.5

Ext. 1

ANGOLA

PRODUCTION OF MANUFACTURING INDUSTRY - LIGHT INDUSTRY SECTOR; 1973 - 1987

PRODUCT	Unit	1973	--	1977	1978	1979	1980	1981	1982	1983	1984	1985	1986	1987	Average annual growthrate 77-87	87/77
Cloth	M2	17,975		3,890	8,408	11,532	18,546	18,619	17,081	15,739	7,530	11,814	13,894	5,919	2.03%	152%
Covers	000'	972		167	284	256	239	149	253	259	91	163	180	106	-5.36%	63%
Cotton Threads	tn	3,085		135	138	126	190	214	165	85	25	76	121	119	-6.72%	88%
Trousers	000'					810	877	739	811	517	642	784	606	372		
Skirts	000'					133	800	1,087	712	755	872	1,369	709	533		
Shirts	000'					1,926	1,873	2,726	2,506	2,175	2,132	1,782	1,369	588		
Linens/Sheets	M.J.								606	412	1,129	600	353	351		
Socks	M.P.									116	218	168	159	183		
Leather Shoes	M.P.	824			230	360	310	390	228	487	634	332	295	141		
Canvas Shoes	M.P.	1,008		268	369	286	206	159	215	135	91	131	84	57	-14.94%	21%
Plastic Shoes	M.P.	1,912		238	267	351	226	107	321	306	481	515	887	552	12.96%	232%
Processed Tobacco	tn	3,100		1,485	1,500	1,739	1,821	2,311	2,007	1,950	1,911	2,203	1,789	1,770	1.74%	112%
Matches	M.box	93,053		7,483	19,515	19,147	22,938	44,876	44,897	41,673	35,180	24,694	27,612	8,855	3.49%	118%
Plywood	M3	8,399		2,401	2,275	2,163	2,861	2,429	3,122	4,240	4,446	4,911	3,641	4,582	8.54%	191%
Vinyl	M2	264		173	429	493	345	186	655	324	46	294	124	350	-5.71%	202%
Tarpauline	M2	11		97	173	225	203	191	172	119	50	116	52	140	-7.21%	144%
Soap	tn	17,582			10,500	8,454	8,752	7,558	8,837	4,155	7,799	11,491	11,012	2,204		
Liquid Detergents	kl	310			702	592	1,309		125	745	536	532	801	143		
Paints	tn	8,449			2,636	3,904	4,072	4,483	3,563	2,239	3,302	2,814	1,969	1,390		
Glues	tn	455		259	341	513	498	476	395	557	743	276	274	104	-5.60%	40%
Painted Glass	tn						1,296	6,359	6,521	5,847	7,536	8,035	6,229	0		
Plastic Bottles	000'	13,326		827	1,585	1,426	1,054	1,201	460	869	1,375	884	1,356	1,103	-0.37%	133%
Plastic Crates	000'							282	82	89	35	29	23	0		
Sisal Bags/Burlap	000'	8,000		1,120	1,465	2,053	1,785	1,483	1,384	1,708	[illegible],344	1,780	2,777	3,321	-7.79%	297%
Plastic Bags	tn	2,672		1,286	2,854	2,796	3,186	3,224	2,733	1,461	[illegible],834	929	2,275	287	-11.64%	22%
Sponge Cushions	Yn	58,194			54,597	80,556	65,977	51,075	35,126	34,837	4[illegible],864	41,148	43,000	13,421		

Source: Ministry of Industry.

APPENDIX

Table H.5

Ext. 2

ANGOLA

PRODUCTION OF MANUFACTURING INDUSTRY - HEAVY INDUSTRY SECTOR; 1973 - 1987

PRODUCT	Unit	1973	--	1977	1978	1979	1980	1981	1982	1983	1984	1985	1986	1987	Average annual growthrate 77-87	87/77
Tires F/Vehicles	Un	191,000		50,543	73,042	108,651	87,086	72,750	55,250	54,882	34,815	47,707	31,714	12,480	-12.66%	25%
Inner Tubes F/Vehicles	Un	212,000		57,821	51,649	58,577	45,512	18,224	2,045	4,583	4,333	9,124	4,047			0%
Buses	Un	150		0	10	15	116	173	220	77	63	18	101	0		
Passenger Vehicles	Un	621		0	197	80	384	351	455	437	358	167	3	0		
Bicycles	Un	36,518		5,283	9,286	8,750	6,919	4,840	3,996	4,584	1,521	1,824	8,303	13,750	-3.09%	260%
Motorcycles	Un	6,128		1,232	2,007	3,980	6,308	7,606	2,718	1,297	1,697	1,391	5,975	5,500	4.00%	446%
Dumping Boxes	Un									54	69	38	13	70		
Street Towers	Un									32	9	136	0	0		
Semi-Towers	Un										0	10	11	0		
Agricultural Links	Un					18										
Cisterns	M3	100				8,991					53	77				
Disk Crates	Un							9	771	30	11	4	7	23		
Animal Ploughs	Un					1,616	1,915	1,847		273	0	0				
Dry Batteries	000'	4,329			3,522	4,741	3,153	2,931	2,808	155	1,214	1,076	657	250	-23.77%	6%
Batteries	Un	62,292		3,984	55,467	52,304	50,127	33,778	38,337	15,778	19,750	21,345	19,017	16,880	-10.23%	63%
Freezers	Un			26,596				5,744		3,746	3,092	2,804	4,946	6,346		
Acetilene	M3	238,000		82,456	102,346	116,080	126,560	125,408	116,713	127,130	121,362	126,122	154,805	149,133	4.46%	181%
Oxygen	M3	852,000		311,204	268,319	406,432	430,223	484,121	380,770	414,253	389,386	554,930	1,077,674	725,339	9.89	233%
Electrodes	tn	1,579			220	396	513	358	210	283	246	298	366	211		
Steel Rods	tn	26,572		3,560	2,465	4,134	3,595	2,654	1,670	2,328	1,832	4,099	6,600	2,500	0.61%	70%
Black Tube	tn	14,309		1,329	2,450	5,011	4,064	988	3,562	3,731	2,997	3,112	200			0%
Zinc Sheets	tn	12,009		1,924	2,626	5,258	3,970	3,817	3,137	2,584	3,596	3,882				0%
Machetes	000'	457		139	62	68	288	333	344		309	285	135	300		216%
Metal Containers	tn									1,424	361	1,206	866	390		
Cardboard Boxes	tn	22,882		2,319	4,124	3,360	2,655	3,341	2,896	1,406	1,000	1,455	1,615	102	-20.11%	4%
Conductor Cable Lines	tn	1,380		702	405	821	447	546	293	498	512	511	411	152	-7.01%	22%
Naval Const. and Rep.	H/h								710,878	550,000	663,164	942,657	1,095,000	1,240,000		
Radio Receptors	Un	25,821		3,338	50,661	70,945	72,774	90,055	86,598	38,828	36,989	33,831	21,427	33,468	3.39%	1003%
Televisions	Un	0		0	846	1,657	6,682	15,219	10,658	5,600	2,146	8,329	4,946	6,346		
Paper	tn	9,308			3,408	3,182	4,016	4,067								
Paper Paste	tn	32,436		0	0	141	1,757	1,793								
Barrels	Un							34,213								
Metal Buckets	Un							23,260								
Aluminum Dishes	tn									492	429	577	606	44		
Cutlery	000'	2,610		1,178	746	1,030	1,304	990		1,250	214	386	1,940	624		53%
Metallic Capsules	000'	574,000		218,298	221,488	214,276	261,820	102,164					0	0		0%
Rubber Products	tn									35	20	41	55	30		
Metallic Furniture	tn									510	720		215	160		

Source: Ministry of Industry

APPENDIX

Table H.6

ANGOLA

MAIN CHARACTERISTICS OF THE MANUFACTURING INDUSTRY IN 1974

(Values in US$ 000') 1/

	Numbers of Enterpr.	Employm.	Investm.	Value of Prod.
Food Processing	238	51,037	173,701	188,543
Beverages	65	4,141	54,449	73,819
Tobacco Industry	6	1,284	7,992	35,157
Textile Industry	316	43,327	152,874	97,402
Shoe Manufacture	466	21,862	21,575	4,449
Wood Industry (furniture)	528	13,171	186,890	4,331
Furnit. Manuf. (wo/metal)	88	2,439	3,898	n.a.
Paper Ind.	25	4,743	28,268	22,165
Typography	74	1,713	7,874	n.a.
Tannery	40	883	2,677	5,748
Rubber Ind.	58	2,307	13,976	14,961
Chemicals	125	4,898	37,913	58,307
Petroleum Derivatives Ind.	6	823	32,283	36,024
Non-metal Mineral Prod.	307	10,447	82,205	30,472
Basic Metallurgy Ind.	39	3,058	22,992	17,047
Metallic Prod. Manufact.	751	15,660	39,331	21,378
Non-elect. Constr. Mac.	116	2,543	8,031	6,339
Electric Constr. Mac.	172	3,510	12,795	16,024
Transport Constr. Mat.	336	9,355	29,331	17,717
Sundry Industry	90	3,049	20,827	2,598
Totals	3,846	200,250	939,882	652,480
Averages: (US$ for values)				
Per Company:		52	244,379	169,652
Per Worker:			4,694	3,258

1/ At an exchange rate of 25.4 Escudos per dollar.
Source: Ministry of Industry.

APPENDIX
TABLE H.7

ANGOLA

PUBLIC SECTOR INVESTMENTS IN THE MANUFACTURING INDUSTRY; 1980 - 1987

(Millions of Kwanzas)

Investment Category	1980 Food Proc.	1980 Light Ind.	1980 Heavy Ind.	1980 Mining	1981 Food Proc.	1981 Light Ind.	1981 Heavy Ind.	1981 Mining	1982 Food Proc.	1982 Light Ind.	1982 Heavy Ind.	1982 Mining
Civil Works	10	25	79			308	1,365	205	84	519	31	
Equipment	80	25	107		355	710	275	179	577	335	316	116
Technical Assistance	77	54	120		342	230	64	72			53	
Other 1/		54	23		4	80	17	12	39	184	9	
Totals by Sector	167	158	330	0	700	1,328	1,721	468	700	1,038	408	116
Yearly Totals				654				4,217				2,260

1/ Mainly for studies, financing costs and interest.
Source: Ministry of Industry.

ANGOLA

PUBLIC SECTOR INVESTMENTS IN THE MANUFACTURING INDUSTRY; 1980 - 1987 (Cont'd.)

(Millions of Kwanzas)

Investment Category	1983 Total	1984 Total	1985 Total	1981 Food Proc.	1981 Light Ind.	1981 Heavy Ind.	1981 Mining	1982 Food Proc.	1982 Light Ind.	1982 Heavy Ind.	1982 Mining
Civil Works		425,182	186,037	100	60	122		4	2		
Equipment	259,891	239,566	256,669	78	20	38	302				
Technical Assistance	431,908	7,000	20,583	31	110	26	16				
Other 1/				21	109	97	6				
Totals by Sector				229	304	283	324	4	2	0	0
Yearly Totals	1,064,295	671,748	463,289				1,140				6

1/ Mainly for studies, financing costs and interest.
Source: Ministry of Industry.

APPENDIX

Table I.1

ANGOLA

BUS PASSENGER DATA FOR MINTEC ENTERPRISES, 1984-1985

	1984	1985
Urban Fleet 1/	275	265
Non-urban Fleet 1/	367	359
Inter-provincial Fleet 1/	104	90
Total Existing Fleet	746	714
Passenger Traffic 2/:		
Urban	28,101	24,457
Provincial	6,161	4,863
Inter-provincial	902	479
Total Passengers	35,164	29,799

1/ Termed vehicles in existence, although most are non-operational.

2/ Units in thousands of passengers.

Source: Annuario Estatistico, MINTEC 1986.

APPENDIX

Table I.2

ANGOLA

ETP URBAN PASSENGER TRANSPORT IN LUANDA, 1985-1987

	1985	1986	1987
Bus Fleet (units)	155	155	118
Available Units	30	26	36
Active Units	22	17	15
Trips (number)	71,717	50,216	42,255
Route Kilometerage (thousand)	17,645	12,267	11,177
Passengers handled (thousand)	22,975	14,894	10,500
Receipts (thousand Kwz)	124,834	91,709	103,569

Source: ETP, MINTEC; 1987

APPENDIX
Table I.3

ANGOLA

VEHICLE OPERATING COSTS 1/, 1987

(Kz per 1000 vehicle-Km)

Component	Normal Operations 2/		MCurrent Operations 3/	
	Cost	(%)	Cost	(%)
Fuel and Lubricants	4,277	18	3,272	8
Tires	3,963	16	3,612	9
Maintenance:				
Parts	8,043	32	5,146	13
Labor	1,255	5	996	3
Depreciation	4,249	17	20,425	51
Interest	1,529	6	4,596	12
Crew	1,586	6	1,379	4
Total Costs, normal road maintenance 2/	24,902	100	39,425	100
Tonne/km cost 4/	0,778		2,464	
Total Costs, no road maintenance 5/	37,918		52,793	
Tonne/km cost 5/	1,185		3,300	

Notes:

1/ Financial costs (gross of tax), predicted for Volvo N10 6*4 22/24 tonne GVM vehicle from HDM III VOCs model. Cost inputs supplied by ETP Base Bungo depot, Luanda.

2/ Road; paved, 4 IRI, 1,5 positive grade, 1,5 negative grade, 50% uphill travel, 200 degrees/km curvature, default superelevation, zero altitude, one lane per travel direction.

3/ Road as 2 above.
Vehicle; 15,000 km per year, 120,000 km lifetime utilization, 5 years of life, 16 tonnes out but no return load.

4/ Normal operations: 32 tonnes per return trip, current operations; 16 tonnes per return trip.

5/ Predicted at 12 IRI roughness, with zero curvature.

Source: 1986 HDM III VOCs sub-model, ETP 1987 operating and cost data, Consultant's estimates of highway variables.

APPENDIX

Table I.4

ANGOLA

RAILWAY INCOME AND EXPENDITURE STATEMENTS FOR 1985 - 1986

	1985	1986
Luanda (CFL)		
Income	61,792	74,802
Expenditures	333,563	290,620
Balance	(272,770)	(215,818)
Benguela (CFB)		
Income	288,314	312,573
Expenditures	1,474,113	1,513,019
Balance	(1,185,799)	(1,200,446)
Mocamedes (CFM)		
Income	551,650	478,184
Expenditures	278,328	287,537
Balance	273,322	190,647
Total Deficit	(1,185,247)	(1,606,911)

Source: MINTEC, 1987.

APPENDIX

Table I.5

ANGOLA

TAAG CIVIL AIRCRAFT FLEET 1/ UTILIZATION DATA AT DEC. 1986

	Model	Year	Utilization 1986	Utilization Total	Landings 1986	Landings Total
Boeing	707-373C	63	1,743	64,623	880	16,203
	707-349C	65	2,117	65,988	760	15,863
	707-349C	67	1,971	64,110	468	14,384
	707-347C	68	1,770	54,932	425	16,066
	707-347C	68	2,139	51,748	330	18,074
	707-382C	69	2,459	56,672	559	16,778
	737-2M2C	76	1,663	14,141	1,528	15,888
	737-2M2	79	1,727	11,160	1,768	11,687
	737-2M2	82	1,765	7,811	1,884	8,430
	737-2M2	85	1,954	3,141	2,043	3,378
	737-2M2	85	1,931	2,889	1,811	2,799
Fokker	F27-600	69	1,709	23,043	1,526	21,015
	F27-600	69	1,285	22,457	1,158	22,776
	F27-600	71	1,601	18,847	1,205	17,996
	F27-600	77	851	4,050	689	2,961
	F27-600	82	1,399	5,737	1,238	4,924
Yak	Yak-40	77	934	5,700	906	6,640
	Yak-40	77	725	5,449	703	6,320

Notes:

1/ Excluding 10 light aircraft; Piper Aztec (3), Piper Navajo (2), Piper Cherokee (1), Piper Twin Comance (1), Islander (1), and Cessna Skyline (1). Also excludes 1 Lockheed L-100 and 1 Yak-40 not operational in 1986.

2/ Units in Hours.

Source: TAAG - Situacao Actual e Perspectivas, 1986.

APPENDIX

Table I.6

ANGOLA

ANGONAVE 1986 CARGO BY CATEGORY

(Tonnes 000')

Category		Tonnage	
Food:			
	Wheat Flour	35,400	
	Corn	29,300	
	Soya Oil	13,600	
	Malt	10,600	
	Powered Milk	7,200	
	Others	25,000	
	Sub-total		121,100
Alcoholic Drinks			7,050
Equipment and Vehicles 1/			6,800
Chemicals:			
	Fertilizer	23,100	
	Soap	5,260	
	Amonium Sulphate	3,514	
	Sub-total		31,874
Other Products			
	Wagons	3,973	
	Cement	2,910	
	Iron Plates	1,472	
	Others	20,153	
	Sub-total		28,508
Containers (2335 empty)			5,400
Overall Total			200,732

1/ Excluding military items.
Source: Angonave, 1987.

APPENDIX

Table I.7

ANGOLA

ENATEL TELEPHONE SYSTEMS, 1980 AND 1985

Exchanges	1980 Number	1980 Capacity	1980 Lines	1985 Number	1985 Capacity	1985 Lines
Automatic:						
Luanda	7	37,000	32,370	9	38,500	36,000
Interior	8	15,368	10,800	9	18,368	11,520
Manual	27	4,090	3,180	29	4,390	3,480
Automatic Index: 1/						
Local		93			93	
Inter-urban		5			25	

1/ Index based on number of automatic to manual calls.
Source: MINTEC, 1987

APPENDIX

Table J.1

ANGOLA

PER CAPITA EDUCATIONAL EXPENDITURES BY PROVINCES - 1983

(kwanza)

Province	Kwanza	Province	Kwanza
Angola	916	Kunene	974
Bengo	1,784	Luanda	717 *
Benguela	1,381	Lunda Norte	1,335
Bie	469	Lunda Sul	1,335
Cabinda	1,599	Melange	870
Huambo	752	Namibe	1,467
Huile	734	Moxico	764
Kuanda-Kubango	3,364	Vige	1,152
Kuanza Norte	1,326	Zaire	1,320
Kunaza Sul	844		

* Exclusive central administration expenditures.

APPENDIX
Table J.2

ANGOLA

MINISTRY OF EDUCATION - EXPENDITURE BY CATEGORIES - 1980/87

(Kw million)

	1979	1980	1981	1982	1983	1984	1985	1986	1987
Personnel Expenditures	9,325.1	7,211.9	7,265.8	8,232.7	7,628.2	7,840.7	7,651.9	8,764.4	10,055.5
Purchase of Goods	1,368.3	199.7	184.1	234.2	99.9	153.2	318.3	1,306.5	352.4
Durable Goods	1,192.2	30.0	21.4	113.6	39.0	56.2	168.8	1,227.4	283.8
Payment of Services	63.9	51.2	56.0	55.3	58.7	73.4	133.3	51.1	44.9
Other Payments	898.5	2,574.5	1,531.3	984.1	617.9	945.9	341.4	804.0	560.0
Food Purchases	254.1	700.0	600.0	597.0	400.0	600.0	162.0	296.5	261.3
Cooperantes Expenditure	510.9	0.0	0.0	46.2	50.0	74.4	92.7	379.7	152.5
Total	13,605.0	10,767.3	9,658.6	10,263.1	8,893.7	9,751.8	8,868.4	12,903.6	11,630.4

Source: Orcamento Geral do Estado

APPENDIX

Table J.3

ANGOLA

ENROLLMENT IN REGULAR PRIMARY EDUCATION, 1970-87

Years	Pre-School	I Level	II Level	III Level	I, II, III Levels
1970	2,567	440,985	29,263	13,911	484,159
1971	3,029	494,800	34,750	16,075	545,625
1972	3,464	517,421	40,024	18,324	575,769
1973	1,339	567,420	29,599	16,030	613,049
1976	361,446	592,450	70,933	8,025	671,408
1977	416,937	958,676	94,317	19,010	1,072,003
1978	746,328	142,839	113,884	24,663	281,386
1979	664500	1714817	176687	40272	1,931,776
1980	404,255	1,332,297	150,204	36,433	1,518,934
1981	342,316	1,258,858	111,191	21,025	1,391,074
1982	292,429	1,178,430	105,673	15,640	1,299,743
1983	254,736	1,065,025	132,284	27,971	1,225,280
1984	200,459	870,410	112,054	29,287	1,011,751
1985	227,054	970,698	130,749	34,745	1,136,192
1986	222,161	1,012,303	127,486	38,302	1,178,091
1987	200,352	1,033,502	108,878	31,707	1,174,087

Source: MED

APPENDIX

Table J.4

ANGOLA

ENROLLMENT IN ADULT EDUCATION, 1970-85

Years	I Level	II Level	III Level	Total
1980	165,497	56,680	12,757	234,934
1981	74,345	35,856	23,861	134,062
1982	62,420	50,055	32,077	134,552
1983	46,086	31,815	36,630	114,531
1984	40,968	30,303	36,587	107,858
1985	40,106	37,295	56,089	133,490
1986	107,426	51,766	27,811	187,003
1987	125,598	60,754	30,480	216,832

Source: MED

ANGOLA

PRIMARY EDUCATION: PROMOTION, REPEAT AND DROPOUT RATES - 1980-84

Years	Rates	Grades							
		10	20	30	40	50	60	70	80
1980	Promotion	45.4	46.7	53.2	51.0	32.4	35.6	32.1	30.5
	Repeat	30.9	30.6	24.9	25.7	24.1	24.0	23.7	25.7
	Dropout	23.7	23.7	21.9	23.3	43.5	40.4	44.2	43.8
1981	Promotion	41.9	42.1	49.0	42.1	31.2	28.9	34.4	36.4
	Repeat	31.7	33.0	29.5	34.4	28.7	32.0	28.3	23.2
	Dropout	26.4	24.4	21.5	23.5	40.1	39.1	37.3	40.4
1982	Promotion	37.8	37.3	44.2	42.2	30.0	29.2	36.5	31.8
	Repeat	23.6	35.1	29.8	32.0	28.2	31.5	28.8	30.7
	Dropout	28.6	27.5	26.0	25.8	41.8	39.3	34.7	37.5
1983	Promotion	36.6	36.2	39.5	41.0	30.0	27.1	34.3	34.9
	Repeat	39.9	39.6	32.8	35.8	55.5	54.5	49.6	52.0
	Dropout	23.5	24.2	27.6	25.2	14.5	18.4	16.1	13.1
1984	Promotion	35.1	35.1	39.0	37.6	28.9	25.2	24.4	24.9
	Repeat	32.7	35.1	29.8	29.6	40.8	37.5	26.4	21.0
	Dropout	32.2	29.8	31.2	32.8	30.3	37.3	49.2	59.0
1980/87	Average Promotion	39.4	39.5	45.0	42.8	30.5	29.2	32.3	31.7
	Repeat	33.8	34.7	29.4	31.1	35.5	35.9	31.4	31.7
	Average Dropout	26.9	25.8	25.6	26.1	34.0	34.0	36.3	36.6
1986	Promotion	42.4	39.9	40.4	45.1	22.7	18.6	22.9	20.3
	Repeat	30.3	33.1	27.6	28.5	24.6	21.9	16.5	15.2
	Dropout	72.8	73.0	68.0	73.6	47.3	40.5	39.4	35.5

Source: MED

APPENDIX

Table J.6

ANGOLA

ENROLLMENT IN SECONDARY SCHOOL COURSES - 1970-85

Years	Secondary Schools			Pre-University
	Technical	Teachers	Total	
1970	1,697	242	1,939	
1971	1,567	1,906		
1972	1,975	386	2,361	
1973	2,135	405	2,540	
1977				1382
1978	1,075	778	1,853	1912
1979	2,133	1,284	3,417	2043
1980	2,882	1,916	4,798	2299
1981	3,018	2,393	5,411	2722
1982	3,397	2,930	6,327	3713
1983	3,637	3,263	6,900	3424
1984	3,871	3,479	7,350	3195
1985	4,599	4,070	8,669	3721
1986	5,027	4,747	9,774	3776
1987	0	4,790	0	0

Source: MED

APPENDIX
Table J.7

ANGOLA

SECONDARY TECHNICAL SCHOOLS - PROMOTION AND EVASION RATES, 1983 AND 1985

		9th Class		10th Class		11th Class		12th Class		Total	
		Promotion Rates	Evasion Rates	Promotion Rates	Evasion Rates	Promotion Rates	Evasion Rates	Promotion Rates	Evasion Rates	Promotion Rates	Evasion Rates
Agriculture	1983	66.6	27.7	79.1	6.9	83.1	4.8	90.4	6.3	79.6	10.4
	1985	(71.3)	(14.4)	(78.0)	(10.2)	(70.2)	(17.5)	(84.7)	3.1	(76.7)	(10.6)
Economics	1983	47.6	2.4	45.7	14.5	28.9	9.9	90.0	10.0	41.7	17.9
	1985	(52.0)	(14.8)	(47.1)	(13.5)	(57.7)	(7.0)	(60.7)	(1.2)	(52.0)	(12.4)
Industrial	1983	35.7	30.5	36.8	24.5	42.6	15.2	48.4	11.3	38.2	24.5
	1985	(40.4)	(24.9)	(43.5)	(13.8)	(51.0)	(8.4)	(58.8)	(9.4)	(44.9)	(17.5)
Health	1983	67.6	16.2	89.7	2.1	67.8	0.0	95.0	0.0	75.4	7.2
	1985	(76.9)	(10.5)	(86.1)	(9.4)	(95.5)	(1.1)	(90.9)	(3.4)	(83.8)	(9.5)
Other	1983	46.1	14.2	40.3	2.2	75.7	8.1	60.0	0.0	51.6	6.7
	1985	(23.7)	(20.0)	(74.3)	(18.8)	(75.0)	(21.9)	(100.0)	0.0	(*)	(*)
Total	1983	44.6	25.6	49.4	15.0	47.9	9.4	66.0	7.7	48.3	17.6
	1985	(48.3)	(18.7)	(57.8)	(13.7)	(62.6)	(30.9)	(74.8)	(4.5)	(55.9)	(14.4)

Source: MED
(*) Missing Information

APPENDIX

Table J.8

ANGOLA

GRADUATES FROM TECHNICAL SECONDARY SCHOOLS - 1980/86

Type of Course	1980	1981	1982	1983	1984	1985	1986
Agriculture	0	10	34	57	61	83	29
Economics	139	119	83	89	13	51	64
Administration	23	29	14	15	0	0	0
Commerce	0	8	10	9	0	0	0
Statistics	0	0	7	9	13	0	0
Finance	55	44	30	38	0	0	0
Planning	61	38	22	14	0	0	0
Industry	0	53	69	60	81	94	104
Construction	0	7	4	11	13	0	0
Electricity	0	7	17	17	7	0	0
Mechanics	0	5	5	8	8	0	0
Chemistry	0	9	7	24	15	0	0
Politechnics	0	25	36	0	20	0	0
Other							
Health	0	0	42	20	75	80	88
Fishing	0	0	3	0	23	55	9
Petroleum	0	0	0	23	33	0	30
Journalism	0	0	0	0	8	0	
Total	139	182	231	249	294	363	324

Source: MED

APPENDIX

Table J.9

ANGOLA

ENROLLMENT IN HIGHER EDUCATION - 1984/87

	1984	1985	1986	1987
Faculty of Sciences	528	596	745	910
Agriculture	217	231	271	317
Law	636	662	741	546
Luanda	0	0	448	448
Lubango	0	0	22	21
Huambo	10	0	271	77
Economics	749	819	1047	1204
Luanda	622	662	784	855
Lubango	0	0	151	145
Huambo	127	157	112	204
Engineerings	760	795	874	999
Inst. of Educ. Sciences	921	1194	1276	984
Lubango	336	381	375	399
Correspondence Courses	585	813	901	585
Medicine	674	737	828	914
Luanda	553	617	673	676
	121	120	155	238
Total	4485	5034	5782	5874

Source: Universidade Agostinho Neto

APPENDIX
Table J.10

ANGOLA

HIGHER EDUCATION GRADUATES - 1975/84

	1975	1976	1977	1978	1979	1980	1981	1982	1983	1984	Total
Faculty of Sciences	0	0	0	0	0	0	3	6	6	27	42
Agriculture	0	3	8	0	0	0	0	5	7	14	37
Law	0	0	0	8	0	0	0	0	30	22	60
Economics	0	0	0	8	0	2	100	75	31	20	236
Engineerings	12	4	5	3	13	9	15	24	14	6	105
Inst. of Educ. Sciences	0	0	0	0	0	0	0	0	0	44	44
Medicine	7	30	14	10	6	36	21	21	40	45	230
Total	19	37	27	29	19	47	139	131	128	178	754

Source: Universidade Agostinho Neto

APPENDIX

Table J.11

ANGOLA

UNIVERSITY PROFESSORS BY TYPE AND NATIONALITY - 1984/87

	ANGOLANS			COOPERANTES *
	Full-time	Part-time	Monitors	
Faculty of Sciences				
1984	20	0	10	32
1985	19	1	17	36
1986	21	3	14	29
1987	22	4	19	40
Agriculture				
1984	6	11	18	22
1985	13	8	17	23
1986	20	10	17	13
1987	19	8	17	18
Economics				
1984	5	27	3	17
1985	5	32	0	20
1986	30	37	31	79
1987	7	38	29	50
Engineerings				
1984	26	25	13	70
1985	30	0	2	72
1986	30	37	31	79
1987	24	21	17	41
Inst. of Ed. Sciences				
1984	3	0	35	65
1985	17	0	16	59
1986	25	8	17	67
1987	39	9	28	5
Medicine				
1984	34	16	35	11
1985	43	0	26	34
1986	67	16	36	17
1987	55	101	64	4
Total				
1984	94	79	114	217
1985	127	41	78	244
1986	193	111	146	284
1987	166	181	174	158

Source: Universidade Agostinho Neto

(*) The proportion of part-time cooperantes was 1984 - 14% and 1986 - 6%.

APPENDIX

Table J.12

ANGOLA

UNIVERSITY - EXPENDITURES BY CATEGORIES, 1980/89

	1989	1980	1981	1982	1983	1984	1985	1986	1987
Personnel Expenditures	629.8	175.6	155.8	292.3	182.3	307.0	312.4	447.3	549.4
Purchases of Goods	128.5	54.7	41.9	89.0	72.0	72.4	92.5	110.7	125.0
Durable Goods	66.5	15.0	7.3	30.0	22.0	20.4	40.9	46.5	59.3
Payment of Services	19.1	11.1	11.3	16.5	14.0	14.5	16.8	15.5	16.1
Other Payments	173.0	26.4	30.5	93.4	67.5	79.9	94.5	133.3	161.0
Food Purchases	0.0	0.0	0.0	10.0	10.0	13.2	12.8	24.4	41.9
Cooperantes Expend.	84.6	0.0	10.0	49.7	30.8	33.3	52.2	74.0	74.0
Total	950.4	267.8	239.5	491.2	335.8	473.8	516.2	706.8	851.5

Source: Orcamento Geral do Estado

ANGOLA

NATIONAL CENTER FOR LITERACY - EXPENDITURES BY CATEGORIES, 1982/89

	1981	1982	1983	1984	1985	1986	1987	1989
Personnel Expenditures	658.5	727.3	729.0	821.7	683.5	676.8	520.6	595.0
Purchases of Goods	151.8	120.4	56.9	57.8	41.1	46.0	49.2	48.5
Durable Goods	39.0	26.5	15.2	15.2	18.6	18.8	20.7	21.1
Payment of Services	19.3	5.9	4.4	4.5	10.3	8.6	8.1	8.7
Other Payments	295.8	217.6	68.2	66.0	27.9	22.9	22.1	51.7
Total	1,125.3	1,071.2	858.5	950.0	762.8	754.3	600.0	703.8

Source: Orcamento Geral do Estado

Distributors of World Bank Publications

ARGENTINA
Carlos Hirsch, SRL
Galeria Guemes
Florida 165, 4th Floor-Ofc. 453/465
1333 Buenos Aires

AUSTRALIA, PAPUA NEW GUINEA, FIJI, SOLOMON ISLANDS, VANUATU, AND WESTERN SAMOA
D.A. Books & Journals
648 Whitehorse Road
Mitcham 3132
Victoria

AUSTRIA
Gerold and Co.
Graben 31
A-1011 Wien

BAHRAIN
Bahrain Research and Consultancy Associates Ltd.
P.O. Box 22103
Manama Town 317

BANGLADESH
Micro Industries Development Assistance Society (MIDAS)
House 5, Road 16
Dhanmondi R/Area
Dhaka 1209

Branch offices:
156, Nur Ahmed Sarak
Chittagong 4000

76, K.D.A. Avenue
Kulna

BELGIUM
Jean De Lannoy
Av. du Roi 202
1060 Brussels

BRAZIL
Publicacoes Tecnicas Internacionais Ltda.
Rua Peixoto Gomide, 209
01409 Sao Paulo, SP

CANADA
Le Diffuseur
C.P. 85, 1501B rue Ampère
Boucherville, Québec
J4B 5E6

CHINA
China Financial & Economic Publishing House
8, Da Fo Si Dong Jie
Beijing

COLOMBIA
Infoenlace Ltda.
Apartado Aereo 34270
Bogota D.E.

COTE D'IVOIRE
Centre d'Edition et de Diffusion Africaines (CEDA)
04 B.P. 541
Abidjan 04 Plateau

CYPRUS
MEMRB Information Services
P.O. Box 2098
Nicosia

DENMARK
SamfundsLitteratur
Rosenoerns Allé 11
DK-1970 Frederiksberg C

DOMINICAN REPUBLIC
Editora Taller, C. por A.
Restauración e Isabel la Católica 309
Apartado Postal 2190
Santo Domingo

EL SALVADOR
Fusades
Avenida Manuel Enrique Araujo #3530
Edificio SISA, ler. Piso
San Salvador

EGYPT, ARAB REPUBLIC OF
Al Ahram
Al Galaa Street
Cairo

The Middle East Observer
8 Chawarbi Street
Cairo

FINLAND
Akateeminen Kirjakauppa
P.O. Box 128
SF-00101
Helsinki 10

FRANCE
World Bank Publications
66, avenue d'Iéna
75116 Paris

GERMANY, FEDERAL REPUBLIC OF
UNO-Verlag
Poppelsdorfer Allee 55
D-5300 Bonn 1

GREECE
KEME
24, Ippodamou Street Platia Plastiras
Athens-11635

GUATEMALA
Librerias Piedra Santa
5a. Calle 7-55
Zona 1
Guatemala City

HONG KONG, MACAO
Asia 2000 Ltd.
6 Fl., 146 Prince Edward Road, W.
Kowloon
Hong Kong

HUNGARY
Kultura
P.O. Box 149
1389 Budapest 62

INDIA
Allied Publishers Private Ltd.
751 Mount Road
Madras - 600 002

Branch offices:
15 J.N. Heredia Marg
Ballard Estate
Bombay - 400 038

13/14 Asaf Ali Road
New Delhi - 110 002

17 Chittaranjan Avenue
Calcutta - 700 072

Jayadeva Hostel Building
5th Main Road Gandhinagar
Bangalore - 560 009

3-5-1129 Kachiguda Cross Road
Hyderabad - 500 027

Prarthana Flats, 2nd Floor
Near Thakore Baug, Navrangpura
Ahmedabad - 380 009

Patiala House
16-A Ashok Marg
Lucknow - 226 001

INDONESIA
Pt. Indira Limited
Jl. Sam Ratulangi 37
P.O. Box 181
Jakarta Pusat

ITALY
Licosa Commissionaria Sansoni SPA
Via Benedetto Fortini, 120/10
Casella Postale 552
50125 Florence

JAPAN
Eastern Book Service
37-3, Hongo 3-Chome, Bunkyo-ku 113
Tokyo

KENYA
Africa Book Service (E.A.) Ltd.
P.O. Box 45245
Nairobi

KOREA, REPUBLIC OF
Pan Korea Book Corporation
P.O. Box 101, Kwangwhamun
Seoul

KUWAIT
MEMRB Information Services
P.O. Box 5465

MALAYSIA
University of Malaya Cooperative Bookshop, Limited
P.O. Box 1127, Jalan Pantai Baru
Kuala Lumpur

MEXICO
INFOTEC
Apartado Postal 22-860
14060 Tlalpan, Mexico D.F.

MOROCCO
Société d'Etudes Marketing Marocaine
12 rue Mozart, Bd. d'Anfa
Casablanca

NETHERLANDS
InOr-Publikaties b.v.
P.O. Box 14
7240 BA Lochem

NEW ZEALAND
Hills Library and Information Service
Private Bag
New Market
Auckland

NIGERIA
University Press Limited
Three Crowns Building Jericho
Private Mail Bag 5095
Ibadan

NORWAY
Narvesen Information Center
Book Department
P.O. Box 6125 Etterstad
N-0602 Oslo 6

OMAN
MEMRB Information Services
P.O. Box 1613, Seeb Airport
Muscat

PAKISTAN
Mirza Book Agency
65, Shahrah-e-Quaid-e-Azam
P.O. Box No. 729
Lahore 3

PERU
Editorial Desarrollo SA
Apartado 3824
Lima

PHILIPPINES
National Book Store
701 Rizal Avenue
P.O. Box 1934
Metro Manila

International Book Center
Fifth Floor, Filipinas Life Building
Ayala Avenue, Makati
Metro Manila

POLAND
ORPAN
Palac Kultury i Nauki
00-901 Warszawa

PORTUGAL
Livraria Portugal
Rua Do Carmo 70-74
1200 Lisbon

SAUDI ARABIA, QATAR
Jarir Book Store
P.O. Box 3196
Riyadh 11471

MEMRB Information Services
Branch offices:
Al Alsa Street
Al Dahna Center
First Floor
P.O. Box 7188
Riyadh

Haji Abdullah Alireza Building
King Khaled Street
P.O. Box 3969
Damman

33, Mohammed Hassan Awad Street
P.O. Box 5978
Jeddah

SINGAPORE, TAIWAN, MYANMAR, BRUNEI
Information Publications Private, Ltd.
02-06 1st Fl., Pei-Fu Industrial Bldg.
24 New Industrial Road
Singapore 1953

SOUTH AFRICA, BOTSWANA
For single titles:
Oxford University Press Southern Africa
P.O. Box 1141
Cape Town 8000

For subscription orders:
International Subscription Service
P.O. Box 41095
Craighall
Johannesburg 2024

SPAIN
Mundi-Prensa Libros, S.A.
Castello 37
28001 Madrid

Librería Internacional AEDOS
Consell de Cent, 391
08009 Barcelona

SRI LANKA AND THE MALDIVES
Lake House Bookshop
P.O. Box 244
100, Sir Chittampalam A. Gardiner Mawatha
Colombo 2

SWEDEN
For single titles:
Fritzes Fackboksforetaget
Regeringsgatan 12, Box 16356
S-103 27 Stockholm

For subscription orders:
Wennergren-Williams AB
Box 30004
S-104 25 Stockholm

SWITZERLAND
For single titles:
Librairie Payot
6, rue Grenus
Case postale 381
CH 1211 Geneva 11

For subscription orders:
Librairie Payot
Service des Abonnements
Case postale 3312
CH 1002 Lausanne

TANZANIA
Oxford University Press
P.O. Box 5299
Dar es Salaam

THAILAND
Central Department Store
306 Silom Road
Bangkok

TRINIDAD & TOBAGO, ANTIGUA BARBUDA, BARBADOS, DOMINICA, GRENADA, GUYANA, JAMAICA, MONTSERRAT, ST. KITTS & NEVIS, ST. LUCIA, ST. VINCENT & GRENADINES
Systematics Studies Unit
#9 Watts Street
Curepe
Trinidad, West Indies

TURKEY
Haset Kitapevi, A.S.
Istiklal Caddesi No. 469
Beyoglu
Istanbul

UGANDA
Uganda Bookshop
P.O. Box 7145
Kampala

UNITED ARAB EMIRATES
MEMRB Gulf Co.
P.O. Box 6097
Sharjah

UNITED KINGDOM
Microinfo Ltd.
P.O. Box 3
Alton, Hampshire GU34 2PG
England

URUGUAY
Instituto Nacional del Libro
San Jose 1116
Montevideo

VENEZUELA
Libreria del Este
Aptdo. 60.337
Caracas 1060-A

YUGOSLAVIA
Jugoslovenska Knjiga
P.O. Box 36
Trg Republike
YU-11000 Belgrade